A NURSERY IN THE NINETIES

A Nursery in the Nineties

ELEANOR FARJEON

faber and faber

This edition first published in 2013
by Faber and Faber Ltd
Bloomsbury House, 74–77 Great Russell Street
London WC1B 3DA

Printed and bound by CPI Group (UK) Ltd, Croydon, CR0 4YY

A CIP record for this book is available from the British Library

ISBN 978-0-571-30038-9

We're
HARRY – NELLIE – JOE – AND – BERTIE

CONTENTS

ILLUSTRATIONS

The illustrations are to be found near the centre of the book

Foreword

"GOOD NIGHT, MY DARLING"

I PINE for my childhood, and the childhood of my brothers. But when feeling takes a flow-back into the past, thinly washing shores I cannot walk again, it is a childhood I never lived I long for most: the youth of my Mother, lovely Margaret Jefferson.

My Father left us ample accounts of himself; his own books contained much of his experience; he told and re-told stories of his early life of action and adventure, which he made vivid in narrative. His story is an easy one to remember and to recount; it is almost solid in my memory, where my Mother's talk of her American childhood floats like dandelion seed in an air it seems to me I once breathed, and cannot recapture. With my Father's past, for all its familiarity, I do not feel identified, yet with him I am identified more than with her. Since his death I have come to know how much I derive from him. More than half of me is drawn from his lavish source—his extra-vagances, impulses, imagination, demonstrativeness; also, his acceptance of life. I do not mean that he lived un-questioning things and people; but by instinct and experience he was a judge, not a critic, of character. His sympathies came first, he was hopeful, not sceptical, his impulse was towards, not away from.

My Mother, on the contrary, was reticent: gay and

gentle, delicate and fastidious, swiftly witty and irrepressibly humorous, she was still contained. She sparkled in the wine-glass—but my Father popped all over the place, unable to wait until the cork was drawn. He splashed you with his exuberance. His sense of humour was less fine than hers; jolly, not witty, manifested more in puns than in perceptions. His mood (when it wasn't irascible) was overflowingly generous; he blazed where Mother shone, was impetuous where she was moderate, capable of acting on impulses whose consequences, because of her finer judgment, she foresaw. She too could be spontaneous; in a party, her enchanting nonsense was almost inspired. She then displayed intimately gifts of impersonation which she had inherited from her father. Joseph Jefferson was famous for his smile; she had a smile as sweet, and an unmatchable quality of voice. She charmed with tones, gestures, glances; my Father maintained a lively mood of fun; both were animated; they were a delightful host-and-hostess.

I now know, by that inner identification with him which flowers for me with certainties, that he needed more of her than she could give. She loved with her affections, but his feelings went deeper. If he was angry, he exploded; but she, when displeased, was wounded, and withdrew herself. Towards the end of his life, it was hard not to resent the frequency of the explosions, but those boomerang-tempers came back to strike his heart. They did not mean that he cared little for us; he cared for us only too much. He would have died for us, and perhaps he did. If I know him better than I know her, it is, like him, to love her beyond himself. Perhaps that is why, more than for his past I hanker for hers, the veiled life of the beloved, of whom we both desired something she would not bestow.

She gave you only what she chose of herself. Lies hurt her, but she avoided self-revelation. It was not in her power to withhold her gay charm, and gentle humour, and dry wit; to the end she retained things that touched you like a note of music—the smile, the exquisite quality of voice. And this, after twelve years of wearying, incessant torment, that at last wore her out.

One of the cadences that stays in my ears for ever was the tone in which she said "Good night, my darling," when I was leaving her: an ethereal, silver tone, with her smile in it. The smile, the tone, were there like the reassurance to a child: "Don't think of me in pain, don't think of anything to-night but that you are my darling— and sleep well."

She lived through such years that she and we prayed for the end of them; and could speak of it together. "Oh Nellie! it's very difficult to die." Sometimes, not often this slipped from her with a small weary sigh. Whenever it did, I could take her hand and say, "I'll be so glad when you do." Then the ghost of that rare smile would come to acknowledge that lack of pretence was the last help we could give her—the one way left of sharing what she felt, and thought, and suppressed.

The Sunday before she died, when she had been so ill, and was so tired, that life scarcely flickered in her, I sat holding her hand, now and then whispering something into the silence that was falling between us. "You've been the sweetest Mother to us." She turned her head, and opened her heavy lids, and her eyes were quite dark in her white gentle face. The smile came: "I've had the sweetest children." And when I kissed her, before leaving her, suddenly the exquisite girlish voice, sweet, almost happy—"Good night, my darling." They were the last tones I heard from her. Next day she did not speak, though her eyes were on me as I fed her. On Wednesday when I left her at nine o'clock, I did not know if she was conscious. At midnight the nurse sent for me.

For the second time in our lives, Harry and I sat with her through the night, with death in waiting. Before she died in the morning, Joe and Bertie were with us. I had never been at a deathbed before. Her breath fluttered like butterflies through her trembling lips. The last went out, and they were still. In a few hours she lay looking lovelier and lovelier, younger and younger. During the next two days I was looking on a beauty I had always longed to see, and never expected to—the beauty of lovely Margaret Jefferson, the girl who became our mother. I don't think even in youth she had been quite so lovely as she was then.

The night before the funeral I lifted the handkerchief that covered her face, and was met by such a smile that I made it my last look. Joe was with us till the following day. I went to his room, where he was sitting by the fire. We sat for a little while without saying anything. Then he said, "I went in just now to say Good night to Mother, and at the door I felt I must turn back to look at her again. When I lifted the handkerchief, she smiled at me."

Good night, my darling.

BACKGROUND

ADVENTURE IN
THE FIFTIES
(*Our Father, B. L. Farjeon*)

A NOTE ON MY FATHER

One morning my Father came home from Billingsgate Market with 120 pairs of soles.

"But why did you buy them?" cried my Mother in dismay.

"They were so cheap!" explained my Father joyously.

FARJEONS

B ENJAMIN LEOPOLD FARJEON was born in 1838 of
Jewish parents. His mother, Dinah, was a native of
Deal; she had twenty-five sisters. Her parents' name was
Levy. His father Jacob had come from the East, and
romantic rumours clung about him in our nursery: as
that he had been the "Favourite Slave" of a Sultan, had
escaped, been shipwrecked, and marooned—when he
suffered an accident to his fourth toe which is transmitted
to his children as a malformation. (Did not Papa show us
his own twisted fourth toe as a proof of his father's ship-
wreck?) At all events, Jacob reached England eventually,
was an exceptional linguist, had a sweet tenor voice, and
brought up his children rigorously in the Jewish faith.
He had five that I know of: Israel, Esther, Benjamin,
Morris, and Solomon. One legend tries to establish the
Farjeons as a race of proud Spanish Jews; heraldic research has discovered Farjeons, complete with coat-of-
arms and motto, in the troubadour atmosphere of old
Provence; there was in the 1820's a charming French
artist called Farjeon, who looked like Alfred de Vigny,
and died young; there is still in France a Farjon who
makes crayons. But wherever and however these tribes
sprang out of the Family Tree, they were nothing to us
as children. We *did* know that in the Orient there were
relatives of an *Arabian Nights* flavour. One, Abraham
Fargeon, was very properly a merchant, who, in the

'Eighties, established touch with our Uncle Israel, long
settled as a jeweller in New York; the Merchant of Tunis
sent our uncle chests full of spices, essences, silks, and
gold-embroidered slippers. A pair of these I saw with my
own small eyes, when a son of Uncle Israel brought his
bride to England for a honeymoon; and the single instance was enough to set me gold-embroidering the
Eastern fabric of our family to my heart's content. Oh!
why had not the Merchant of Tunis—his descendants
had names like Haï and Halifa, his father was called
Scialon and his grandfather Schoua—why had he not
also established touch with Benjamin Farjeon in England, I wondered, as pretty newly-married Viney gave the
slippers to Mama, saying, "*You* can wear them, Aunt
Maggie, your foot is so tiny." Why did not chests of
merchandise arrive for us, too, from the Levant? Cedar
chests, packed to overflowing with rich, striped silks,
gauze veils sewn with pearls, flagons of attar-of-rose, and
chains of sequins? I tied a bright sash round my head,
lit a joss-stick (Santa Claus had put a packet in my stocking last Christmas), hung my Venetian beads around my
neck, and, reclining on a pile of cushions on my bed,
studied the Oriental Section of the Army-and-Navy Stores
Book. The Merchant of Tunis muttered *Open Sesame!*
Aladdin's Cavern glittered in my day-dreams. Should I
ever meet the Merchant face to face, become his favourite
great-niece or something, and be given gold and pearls
and purple silk and sandalwood—and a coffee-table inlaid
with mother-of-pearl, and a Benares brass tray, and an
Oriental gong, and—— ?

The joss-stick expired. No, I didn't suppose I'd ever
see the Merchant; any more than I had seen my Grandfather Jacob and my Grandma Dinah, who were dead;

or my Uncle Israel, so beloved, in New York, my Uncle
Sol in California; or my Uncle Morris—oh, but hush!
Uncle Morris was referred to with bated breath. He died
in Australia, and is impressed on my childish memory
by the ominous phrases "Wild Oats" and "Black
Sheep." It seemed my Uncle Morris shed no glory on
the name of Farjeon; though all I knew for certain of
him was that he frequented billiard saloons. For a long
time I thought billiards and damnation were synonymous.

But Aunt Esther, of course, I saw whenever she came
to the house. My father's only sister was a strangely
fascinating person, of mysterious airs, small education,
and unquenchable imagination. She used to relate, or
rather, to hint, at far weirder stories of Grandfather
Jacob's past than ever fell from Papa's lips, stories in
which mysterious black curtains and white waving hands
played vague and thrilling parts. *Sh-sh-ssh!* He had been
brought before "The Inquisition" (heaven knows where
or when!—if driven to it, Aunt Esther would have sworn
to Madrid in the days of Torquemada) . . . he had been
condemned to torture and stretched upon the rack . . .
the first twist was about to be made . . . suddenly I through
the "black velvet curtains" appeared the "white waving
hands," and "saved" him. And then? Aunt Esther was
never explicit, she was better than that, she was pregnant
with suggestion; her red mobile lips would break off
suddenly to sing snatches of song in a melodious voice;
her liquid brown eyes would swim with subtle smiles, she
would nod her head significantly, and the black silky
ringlets she always wore would shake about her face. She
was eight years older than Papa; she possessed an engraving of the "Keepsake" period, for which she said
she had sat to an artist as a girl. He must have seen the

rich possibilities of those lustrous brown eyes, those
lustrous black tresses. At the end of her life the black
had turned to pure white silk, but the ringlets were as
luxuriant, the imagination was as vivid, the smile of
mystery as potent as ever. Intc her tones and looks and
manner she imported a profound sense of conspiracy;
she implied to the uttermost "I could an if I would!"
—though what, we never quite fathomed. If we were
alone with her and, during some half-whispered, half-
sung recitation the door opened to admit a parent, she
would shake a meaning finger at her lips, and whisper,
"*Sh-sh-ssh! not a word!*" She was very poor. All our
old clothes and books and toys, every sort of junk that
Mother was allowed to clear out of the attic (nothing to
the junk left in it, after my Father's purchases in the sales-
rooms), went to Aunt Esther; there was nothing she
couldn't put to some use. She married young, bore three
children before she was twenty and fifteen afterwards,
and all who did not die she launched indomitably upon
the world, determined that they should be a little better
off than she had ever been. Her dark-eyed, jet-haired
daughters, Dinah and Carrie, came to the house; they
were musical, Dinah had a rich voice, and Carrie played
the violin. All Aunt Esther's children were older than any
of us; when Dinah married we saw less of her, and Aunt
Esther's sons were almost unknown to us. My Father did
what he could to help her; it is one of my most wistful
recollections that this remarkable soul had to be grateful
to us.

Such was the background of the Farjeon family. If I
seem to have stressed the *Arabian Nights* element, let me
add this only: a very few years ago, nearly thirty years
after my Father's death, a letter arrived from Alexandria,

asking for details of his parentage. For there was one of the tribe of Farjeon long ago who left the East for the West; and his descendants, if they could be traced, would be heir to the fortune of old Nessim Fargeon, just deceased. Now had the wanderer been our Grandfather Jacob, *Open Sesame!* we should have been heir to seventy-five thousand pounds.

The wanderer, however, was not our Grandfather Jacob.

PRINTER'S DEVIL

THE TALE of my Father's early life and emigration I heard him relate so often, that it took on a concrete shape. He was a born story-teller, and enjoyed his own narrative. To be honest, I am not perfectly certain that he was precise, if a high-light here or there enhanced the story. He wasn't above a little embellishment: witness his middle name of "Leopold," which sprang into being when he became an author. And then, his birthday—what lovelier month in all the year, than May? To May he transferred what Nature had ordained in December. But in their bones the tales he told were true. The following (supplemented from certain sources), is the narrative as it remains in my mind: perhaps a little dimmed by time, and my own forgetfulness.

Ben Farjeon, born a year after Victoria came to the throne, was brought up in poverty, almost without education. His home was in Whitechapel. The Jewish rites were observed with absolute strictness in his father's house; fire was not touched, or paper torn, on the Sabbath; at the Passover, poor as they were, everything used at table was new; and observances, of which I am obliged to speak in ignorance, were never violated. At least, they were not violated in the letter; but my Father, a quick, intelligent, and honourable boy, discovered that, when necessary, means *were* found by which the spirit of the Mosaic Law could be circumvented, while the letter was stuck to. I don't know what my Grandfather Jacob's business was; but if on the Sabbath a letter of importance should be opened—somehow Jacob Farjeon became acquainted with its contents. This was not good enough for Ben, whose fancy darted off at every angle, but whose honesty went straight from point to point. As soon as he could think for himself, he would not pretend that getting round a difficulty for a worldly reason was anything but a sham, or that a compromise was the Law.

Quite young, he got a job on *The Nonconformist*—a Christian journal! He began as a Printer's Devil (how the term fascinated me on Papa's lips), picking up everything else as he went along. His hours were eight to eight, with an hour off for lunch; his wages, about four shillings a week. For little Ben, the job was glamorous with the report that printers were allowed to wear swords in the streets by Act of Parliament! He rose early, as he must walk to his work; and before he left the house he made a cup of tea for his mother, whom he worshipped, and brought it to her in bed. On his way to the office, Ben had to pass a second-hand bookshop. Books were his passion, and he possessed none. In the shop-window one stood open, with two pages of reading exposed. One day Ben rose a few minutes earlier, so that he might read the pages, without being late at work, and, entranced, entered the world of Fouqué's *Undine*. The following day, he found the leaf had been turned; the next two pages were exposed, and he devoured them. The third day the same thing happened. While he was glued to the window, the old man who kept the shop came to the door.

"You're fond of books, my boy?"

"Yes, sir."

"Come inside whenever you like, and read what you please from the shelves."

The old man's bookshop became Ben's library; he spent the precious dinner-hour browsing, and with his first savings bought a book of legends by Musæus. (The German fairy-world was always dear to him.) It is still on our shelves, a little red cloth volume full of wood-cuts, "Ben Farjeon" scribbled childishly on the flyleaf. Whenever he could, he bought another book: *Faust, Peter Schlemihl, The Devil on Two Sticks,* Washington Irving's works, and Shelley's poems. Also, he had some teaching from a schoolmaster in the neighbourhood, one Mr. Hands, who, like the old bookseller, fed him with what he needed. Mr. Hands had never had a boy to teach like Ben, with his love of reading and his brilliant head for figures—for which he invented his own swift formulas. Ben became the schoolmaster's favourite pupil, as we were often told long afterwards by Mr. Hands' daughters, a perfect Cranfordian family of three: Miss Mary Ann, majestic and dominant; Miss Bessie, small and sprightly; Miss Susan, simple and sentimental. "*My* dear father," said Miss Susie, her prominent pale blue eyes filming with tears, "loved *your* dear father as his brightest scholar. And oh! how proud we all were of him, when he came back to England!"

Apart from such rudiments as Ben acquired from the kind schoolmaster, his education consisted of avid, in-discriminate reading. Meanwhile, in the *Nonconformist* printing-room, he was becoming expert with type and stick, a high-speed compositor in his early teens.

He had always liked writing; in his own words, as soon as he had "mastered the difficulties of the alphabet I began to spell out childish stories. But what finally determined me to be an author, was when I was about thirteen. I had devoured with my whole soul *The Caxtons,* reading it through twice and thrice. After that the house seemed all too small for me to breathe in. I rushed up to Hampstead Heath, and lay upon the grass for hours, thinking over and pondering over the wonderful novel. I even spoke my thoughts aloud, for I remember saying 'I should be content to die if I had written such a book!' Towards evening I strolled slowly home, vowing to my-self that I would lose no time, but commence a story that very night; and that is how I set about my idea of being an author."

The story has not survived. Of Ben's early efforts, two poetical fragments remain: the opening stanza of an Epic, and the final couplet of some cosmic composition, the nature of which cannot even be guessed from its conclusion:

> *For so it was, and so 'twill be*
> *While earth remains, or air, or sea.*

The Epic opens with a self-portrait:

A poet in his chamber sat with melancholy brow,
His book was spread before him, he took no heed I trow,
For though his eye was constant fixed, his thoughts were far away,
Tracing through dim futurity the bright and coming day,
The day when through his genius grand his name should mighty be,
When titled lords and jewelled dames to him should bend the knee.

So wrote the thirteen-year-old Printer's Devil, burningly, by candle-light, when he was supposed to be in bed; and his poor room gleamed with golden visions of a future in which, if duchesses in tiaras and dukes in coronets did not actually grovel as he passed, and if Ben himself did not swagger through London wearing a sword by Act of Parliament, he would at least correct his own galley-slips, instead of running about with those of other people

3

GOLD-RUSH

WHEN BEN FARJEON—with his unorthodox apti-
tude for figures; his reading opening up continual
new fields for him; his burning of midnight oil as he
explored them; and his expertness as a practical printer
—reached the age of sixteen, the breach between himself
and Jacob Farjeon came to a head. He could not swallow
entire his father's faith; much of it he revered, but he
was not *"from,"* in Jacob's eyes a thing unforgivable.
Rather than continue the violent scenes which grieved
his mother, he determined to leave home.

I dare say, urged by his adventurous spirit, he would
have left home in any case. The Australian gold-fever was
infecting Britain. Marvellous tales were on everybody's
tongue. Emigrants went out by every sailing-vessel,
hoping to return with pockets full of gold. Ben, too, would
emigrate; he, too, would find his fortune in the goldfields—"Don't cry, mother!" He would come home
some day to give her all she wanted. All she wanted was
her boy. All Ben wanted for himself was the adventure,
and the chance to drive his pen along with it. But even
the adventure would cost him his steerage-passage; and
he hadn't got it.

He had, however, an uncle, who was an atheist. He
was also, said my Father, from whom we heard the word
and its appalling meaning for the first time in our lives,
"one of the best men I ever knew." This uncle had once

said to him, "If ever you need fifty pounds for a particular purpose, Ben, come to me."

So to the atheist uncle the boy went, and the uncle, sympathising with the state of things at home, bought him a steerage passage to Melbourne, on *The Ocean Wave*, a sailing-ship that would take three months to do the voyage. And some time in 1854, when Ben was sixteen years old, he took leave of his sister Esther and her children, and said good-bye to his mother—a heart-breaking moment for both of them. Of course he would return to England one day! He did; but not to her.

Fourteen weeks in the close and crowded steerage! How to put the time to account? He would start a newspaper, a weekly paper of which he would be sole editor, contributor, and compositor. There should be leading articles, news items, poetry, jokes, a serial, and advertisements; and Ben would write them all. By the end of the week he had produced two hand-written copies of the first number of *The Ocean Record*; one was for the steerage, with the other he approached the captain.

"Have I your permission, sir, to bring out a newspaper during the voyage? Here's the first number; this copy is for the saloon."

The captain stared at the slight, bright, shabby boy, laughed, and agreed. When he had read the number, he sent to the steerage, and had Ben Farjeon transferred to the saloon for the rest of the voyage. A dozen numbers of *The Ocean Record* appeared from those palatial headquarters; steerage, saloon and crew were entertained; Ben travelled to Australia in luxury, and landed in Melbourne without a penny in his pocket.

The goldfields! That came next! To get to the goldfields! He could not, however, set out empty-handed, and his first step was to find a job of work. On a broiling day he started looking for one.

At noon he passed a brickyard, where brawny labourers sweltered as they toiled. "MEN WANTED! 12s. a Day!" said a sign. Ben stepped inside and asked to see the boss. The boss in turn asked him what he wanted.

"A job, sir. I see you want men."

The boss looked this "man" over with a grin, and told his foreman to take the boy outside and set him to mix mortar. It was manual labour of a sort Ben wasn't used to, but he went at it with a will, and soon was sweating with the best of them, a delicate, unmuscular, but eager figure among a band of giants. After an hour, when he paused to draw his arm across his streaming brow, he saw the boss standing by, still grinning as he watched him.

"You're not fit for this sort of thing, my boy."

Ruefully Ben agreed. Must he be turned away?

"Any good at figures?" asked the boss.

"Yes, sir."

"Come along in." The boss took him into his office, and sat him down to a mass of papers, dealing with complicated contracts. "See what you can make of these," he said. "Get out the estimates. I give you three hours."

An hour and a half later Ben reported. The boss said, "Got you beat, heh?" "No, sir, they're done." The boy laid the completed estimates before him. The boss looked through them, checked their accuracy, and offered the inadequate mortar-mixer a job in the office at a pound a day. Strong arms were plentiful in the Golden Land, good brains were rarer. Ben's uncanny arithmetic, the pride of Mr. Hands, was worth many a claim pegged out in Bendigo.

He held his job for a month, lived frugally, saved his

earnings, and as soon as he had enough to buy his kit and carry him through the Bush, went to his boss and bade him good-bye. The boss said, "What's the matter? Not satisfied with your job?"

"Quite, sir."

"Isn't the pay good enough?"

"Yes, sir. It's not that."

"What is it, then?"

"I want to get to the goldfields."

"Nonsense. You'll do far better here. Stay on."

"No," said Ben, "I must get to the goldfields."

"I'll double your wages," said the boss.

"I came out to go to the goldfields," was Ben's reply. Nothing could budge him. He didn't mind risks, he didn't want security, he wasn't specially keen on making his fortune. He wanted the fun, the adventure, the new start, the excitement of acting on his impulse—he'd throw up safety for *that,* at any moment. So, "Thank you, boss, good-bye!" The boss called him a fool, wrung his hand, and they parted.

My Father bought his blanket and his pannikin, and set out on foot through the Bush for the gold-rush of the moment, Ballarat, or Bendigo, or wherever it might be; and during the next year or two pursued the gold wherever it rushed next. Arriving at each new camp, he first pegged out his claim, and then—started a newspaper. His pet feature was *Salmagundi on the Goldfields,* taking a leaf from Washington Irving (an author who was to become curiously connected with his destiny).

A strange life for a boy, born and bred in the poor streets of London, with no experience and no physique, but with the spirit of a bantam-cock! Plunging into the rough, coarse, dangerous fellowship of the camps, and keeping

himself decent; liked by everybody, kow-towing to nobody; learning to trek, to ride, to shoot, to dig his claim
as often as was required to maintain his right; washing
gold, and finding little in his pan ("The Goldfields," to
us children, was represented by two lovely nuggets, dug
by Papa himself, one with white-and-black quartz setting
off the virgin gold, the other picked clean like a walnut);
learning to make damper, to smoke his cutty-pipe, to bluff
with a straight face at poker, to light a fire with three
sticks (he was a terror to our housemaids, demanding
their bundle of firewood per grate); and writing, writing,
writing wherever he went!

He had adventures, more than he related or than I remember; many were turned to account in his Australian
novels—*Grif, Silver Flagon,* and *The Sacred Nugget.* If
he had love-affairs, he didn't tell us those; but he respected women, stood up hotly for his opinions in any
company, kept his tongue clean, and drank moderately.

He saw hard times. Once, at hunger-point, in some big
city, he picked up a wallet with gold in it. He took it to
the police. They said if it was unclaimed in twelve days
it would be his. He lived for those twelve days on apples,
and returned to the police quarters; the purse had not
been claimed. His money-belt was full again. On to the
latest gold-rush!

In the Bush, a money-belt did not always spell security.
He once had occasion to travel with a large sum, not his
own, for delivery. He was still little more than a boy. His
way lay through the Bush. At nightfall he missed his
path. Being "bushed" was no joke; he was overjoyed
when, wandering, he saw the glow of a fire and heard
voices. A company of men was cooking the evening meal;
birds they had shot were rolled, unplucked, in clay, and

thrown into the flames—when they were roasted, the feathers came away in the clay. Ben hailed the men, told them he had thought himself lost, and asked if he might sleep among them till morning. They made a place for him, gave him meat and tea and damper, questioned him —his name? where from? where going?—till, tired and satisfied he lay down and slept. In the morning he woke and ate with them again, and was put upon his way; he reached his destination in safety, and delivered the money.

The end of that adventure came a few years later, when B. L. Farjeon was a leading citizen in Dunedin. An ugly murder-trial had taken place, and the prisoner been condemned. Ben had been in court. Before the execution he received a message; would he go to the prison and see the murderer? He went, as he supposed, to see a stranger. But the stranger said, "I knew you at once. You were the boy that slept in the Bush one night with me and my chums. You didn't know you'd fallen in with bushrangers. When you were asleep, my chums wanted to cut your throat for what you might happen to have on you. But I'd taken a fancy to you, and I said, 'A boy like that will have nothing worth cutting his throat for. Let him be.' They listened to me, and I saved your life. Will you do something for me?"

"If I can," said Ben.

"I come from the old country," said the man, "like you. I've got parents there in Kent. I write to them regularly; they don't know what I've become, and they mustn't know how I'm ending. But if they don't hear from me they'll fret themselves. Here's their address on this bit of paper. Their names are different to the name I go by. I want you to write and tell them that you've come across me, sick, and that I sent them messages before

I died. Then they won't worry, wondering what's happened to me. Promise to do this, because I saved your life that night."

Ben promised, and kept his word.

This was in Dunedin; for when he was twenty-three the gold-fever had carried him to New Zealand. In 1861 tales spread like wildfire of the gold discoveries in Tuapeka, fabulous tales which made the riches of Australia pallid. They swept the tide of diggers, rogues and adventurers once more across the sea. Inflamed like all the rest, Ben Farjeon found himself in Melbourne again. Six years ago he had been agog to land there, to-day he was just as agog to sail away. But every boat was crowded to sinking-point; passages could not be got for love or money. As if Ben could ever wait for the boat-after-next! He rushed to the shipping-office. Not a berth to be had. He rushed to the ship and argued with the captain for sleeping space on deck. Not one soul more! He rushed to the office of the *Melbourne Argus,* demanding the editor.

"What can I do for you?"

"I've got to get to Dunedin by the next boat."

"No chance of that, young man."

"There would be, if I went as your special reporter."

"Our special reporter?"

"Yes, sir. My name is Farjeon. I write." I see the bewildered editor's desk littered with Ben's goldfield publications. "They'll take anyone with an accredited position. Make me your special reporter for New Zealand—they'll have to get me across somehow, then, sir!"

"Impossible," said the editor.

Impossible? Poor fool! Didn't he see that Ben *must* get to Dunedin, and by the very next boat?

"Look here, sir! If I get over there and send you articles, will you print them?"

Perhaps the editor's eye had roamed those goldfield weeklies. "If your copy's suitable, Mr. Farjeon, we might publish it."

"Good!" cried Ben.

He knew his copy would be suitable; he rushed back to the quay; he darted on board and thrust himself on the captain. "New Zealand correspondent for the *Melbourne Argus*!" he cried; "you'll have to carry me somehow."

They carried him somehow; and Ben Farjeon landed in the city of Dunedin, when it was a town of wooden shacks in the making.

Among my Father's papers I found one account of an adventure in Australia when he was really bushed. He should have written his own Memoirs, but this is the only personal record I discovered. He spoke to us often of this, terrifying experience, and of the goodness of the woman who rescued him and bound and bathed his wounded feet. I think he saw in her, and in almost every kind and simple woman, all his life, the image of his mother. Before his narrative proceeds to New Zealand this seems a fitting place to let him speak for himself.

4

CHRISTMAS DAY IN THE BUSH

By B. L. Farjeon

ONE CHRISTMAS DAY in my life stands out in bold relief. I had been on the Australian goldfields for some eighteen months, unconsciously gathering experiences of which I have made occasional use in my literary career, when I received a letter from a friend on the Dunolly diggings, speaking in such glowing terms of the rich "finds" there, that I determined to visit it. I was but a lad at the time, and in those days there was no rest for the soles of my feet. A new "rush" drew me magnetically in its direction, and my eagerness to get to every fresh goldfield was not to be restrained. It was not the greed for gold that impelled me on, but the lad's thirst for adventure. So off I set, to see for myself whether my friend's accounts of the auriferous Tom Tiddler's ground were true.

The date, I remember, was the 20th of December, and a hot sun was blazing—over a hundred in the shade— when I commenced my tramp of ninety miles through the bush. Cobb's coach was running, but I could not afford six pounds for a seat in it, my worldly wealth not exceeding thirty shillings, more than sufficient for the expenses of the three days which I expected the distance would take me to walk. The low state of my funds gave me no concern; I was young, I was high-spirited and confident, and no fears of the future beset me.

On the first day I did my thirty miles, and that night
I slept in the bush beneath a glorious panoply of stars. I
was up with the sun, and at the end of the second day I
had completed, as nearly as I could reckon, sixty miles of
my tramp. I used the remains of my small bag of flour
in making a "damper," I found water to make my tea,
and I cooked on a bush fire the three chops I had obtained
at the last cattle station I had passed. I had made a hearty
meal at this station, and fortunately was not very hungry,
so one of the chops and about a quarter of the "damper"
sufficed for the last meal of the day. On this second night
I camped out again. On the third morning, as I did not
expect, before reaching Dunolly, to come to a place where
I could purchase a supply of food, I made a sparing
breakfast, and had still a chop, half the "damper," and
half a tin of tea, left when I resumed my tramp. At about
ten o'clock I met a gold-digger, who told me of a short
cut which would save me half-a-dozen miles. I was to
take a sheep track, and follow it through the woods. I
took that short cut, found the sheep track, and walked
on and on through a forest of gum trees, each so like the
others in shape, height, and dimensions, that the monotony of the road began to depress me. All at once I
stopped and looked around. I had lost the track. I turned
back, and endeavoured to take it up, without success.
Then I began to flounder, turned this way and that, and
so entirely lost my bearings. I fought against the uncomfortable feeling that stole upon me, and resolving upon a
certain direction, walked on, singing. But soon the stillness of the woods checked my voice, and I proceeded in
silence. I had not met a human being for at least four
hours, the sun shed its burning beams upon me, and I
was bathed in perspiration. I resisted the temptation to

finish the tea, and took only a few drops at a time, with occasional nibbles at the remains of my "damper." I had not yet learned to smoke, so the consolation of tobacco was denied me. As evening came on the sense of my dangerous position grew stronger. Each hundred yards I traversed was so like the hundreds of other yards I had trod that there was absolutely no landmark to guide me. I became more and more bewildered. Not a drop of water was in sight, not a sound of bird, beast, or human creature came to my ears. I was "bushed." However, I slept well, and on the fourth morning, the 23rd of December, I was up betimes. In which direction should I now proceed? Unable to determine which would be the right one I left it to chance, and walked a mile, stopped, walked on, turned back, cooyeyed and shouted in vain, stopped again, began to reflect, decided that I was going wrong, turned to the right, to the left, and at mid-day arrived at the spot on which I had slept the previous night. I recognised it by the dry leaves I had gathered for my bed and by three forked branches I had stuck in the ground.

What was now to be done? The last crumbs of my "damper" was eaten, and there was not a quarter of a pint of tea in my tin bottle. I was raging with thirst, and dared only put my hot tongue to the mouth of the bottle. However, it would never do to give up, and again I set forth. But the horrible monotony of the gum trees was maddening, and I closed my eyes a dozen times to shut out the view; and when I opened them did not know to which part of the woods I had been walking. Suddenly darkness fell upon me. It was night.

Well, I must sleep; it would make me strong; it would clear my brain. So I threw myself on the ground, and the mercy of forgetfulness was granted to me. But when I awoke in the morning I was seized with despair. Not a drop of tea remained in the bottle. I must have drank it in my sleep.

Now, indeed, I began to feel as if I were utterly lost. All the stories I had read of men being found dead in the bush rushed to my mind. Should I be among the number?

I had a pencil and a little book with some blank leaves in it in my pocket. I took it out, and commenced a letter to my dear Mother in the old country, in the dear old country I had left to make my fortune in the new world. To my Mother! To my dear, dear Mother! "God bless you, Mother! God bless you, dear!" I must have written these words a score of times, for I could not collect my thoughts. But I started up. I would not, would not die! There must be a way—there must, there must! Why should I bring to my sweet Mother in the dear old country the agony of reading that the boy she doted on was lost in the bush? There *must* be a road out of this dead eternal stillness. Yes, there was! The goldfield of Dunolly was not five hundred yards away. I saw it, saw the white tents of the diggers, saw the men at the windlasses, saw them stooping over the creek, with their tin gold-dishes, saw the picks at work, and the diggers signalling to each other. One was standing on the top of a great heap of pipeclay, beckoning me to come on. "I am coming—I am coming!" I cried, with joy. "It is all right, Mother!" My voice was hoarse, my parched lips were rubbing together convulsively. And then, as I walked towards the man on the pipeclay mound I began to sing, in a cracked dry undertone, "For Bonnie Annie Laurie!" But as I staggered on the man faded, the white tents, the miners at the windlasses, the fortunate ones swinging their gold-dishes round at the creek, all, all melted away! No objects met my sight except the horrible gum trees, this side of me, that side of me, all around me, thousands and thousands of them, staring down at me, and mocking me. Yes, mocking me! I saw their eyes, and the devilish glare in them; I saw their grinning faces. "Well, let me die," I mutely implored, "but show me first where I can get a drink of water. Then, kill me!" The awful silence answered me. No other answer. Only that. And the sun! The hot, blistering sun! How merciless—how cruel! "Dear Lord in Heaven!" I prayed. "Take the sun in, and send the rain! Deluge me with it, drown me in it—but send, oh, send it! Send the blessed rain!" With feeble steps I wandered on, and on, and on, and at length, spent and utterly, utterly worn out, covered my eyes with my arms, and slept.

For how long I do not know, but I awoke when the stars were shining. Gazing upwards I saw the trees bending down over me, and heard spiritual voices whispering that I would soon be dead. "Yes," I thought, "soon be dead—soon be dead!" Darkness fell upon me again, and when I again awoke it was broad day—Christmas Day! Lying there, too weak to rise, visions came to me of past Christmas Days in the old country. There was one of a shop in a narrow street in the east of London. A number of poor children were standing at the window, gazing rapturously at bundles of coloured Christmas candles, and piles of candied orange and lemon peel, and a broad expanse of raisins, decorated with bunches of holly and mistletoe. And there was a little old woman among them, a crazy, sweet-souled beggar woman, who gave the children coloured sweet-stuff out of a paper bag.

I knew her; she gave me some one Christmas, and my own dear Mother, when I told her, ran out and gave the old woman some pennies, with "A merry Christmas to you, my dear!" on her lips. So, with these visions before me, I lay at rest, and felt that I was dying. My strength was gone.

I heard the crack of a whip. It came from the driver of a haycart in Whitechapel. He was sitting on the hay, his jolly red face smiling, his lips moving as if he were singing. But I did not hear the song. Crack went his whip, and crack, crack, crack, again! He pulled up his horse, jumped down, and bent over me. "Poor little chap!" he said, and his voice was so soft and gentle that the tears ran down my cheeks. "Poor little chap! What are you lying here for? It's Christmas Day, my lad—Christmas Day! See—it's snowing! Dying of thirst, are you? Here, let me put some snow on your lips!"

He did—and he then lifted me in his kind arms, and I thought I died.

It was night again when I opened my eyes. But I was no longer in the forest of gum trees, I was in a room, with bright candles alight, and a woman and her daughter were standing by my side, putting sweet cooling stuff to my lips.

"Who are you?" I whispered. "Am I alive?"

"Yes, my dear," the elder woman said. "My man was out, looking for some strayed cattle, and he came upon you in the bush. Do you feel better, my dear?"

5

DUNEDIN: *Business*

"PAPA," I say, "don't forget 'Eh, Meester Fairr-john!'"

"Not so much of your sauce, miss!" says Papa, threatening me with his carving-knife.

He is in a beaming humour; launched over the Sunday supper-table on the relation of his adventures to new and already intimate friends, Tom Gallon the author, and his sister Nellie. They sit entranced, while Papa carves the York ham in slices like tissue-paper, and the big cold sirloin in slices rather thicker. (Thank goodness it was "rare" enough at dinner, and the kitchen has suffered no explosion to-day!) We children sit demurely pushing the mustard-pickles and the mixed-salad-bowl from one to another (why *does* Papa insist on more oil than vinegar?) We splash our helpings with extra vinegar from the big cruet, and, waiting for points in the story we know by heart, eye appraisingly (Nellie does, at least), the lemon cheese-cakes in the middle of the table. Fat Mary's lemon-curd was—*nymm*! Which of the tarts is the fullest, and can I manage to acquire it naturally? But there was also "Sho-Shay" (our short-cut for chocolate-shape) and whipped cream. Shall I have "Sho-Shay" instead? Or both, perhaps? Aha! here's Papa, Miss Gallon's plate re-loaded, landing at last in Dunedin. "Eh, Meester Fairr-john!" is becoming due. I shoot my reminder at him,

and he knows I'm cheeking. We laugh across the sirloin
at each other. The story goes on.

* * * *

In the year in which Ben Farjeon, aged twenty-three,
crossed from Australia to New Zealand, Joe Jefferson,
aged thirty-two, sailed from California to Australia. The
American actor's lungs were not sound; their chance lay
in the Australasian climate, and he left America with a
long tour in view. That spring he had lost his wife, and
he had four young children to think about; the eldest,
Charlie, a boy of ten or eleven, he kept with him. He
wanted his son's hand to hold, "and tightly too"; he
wanted the comfort of feeling "that there was someone
near who knew and felt an interest" in him. The three
younger children, Tiddie, Tommy, and Josie, must be
left behind in the care of Grandpa and Grandma Lockyer,
parents of his dead Margaret, whose name his pretty
Tiddie also bore. Before he left the States he had minia-
tures painted of the children he might never see again,
since only Charlie was old enough to travel. "Aunt Nell"
Symons, the mother of Joe's manager, would look after
him on the voyage; it was her lot, indeed, to look after
the Jeffersons for fifty years.

In September 1861, Joe Jefferson set sail for Sydney;
conquered that lovely city, steamed on to Melbourne,
played 164 nights in the Princess's Theatre (managed by
Fawcett Rowe), and later took the mining camps by storm.

Two years and more passed since Joe Jefferson had seen
his little girls. What did Tiddie and Josie look like now?
He hoped to receive new pictures of them in Dunedin, to
which he crossed in the spring of '64.

* * * *

Three years earlier, Ben Farjeon arrived in that "town of wooden shacks," agog to write articles for the *Melbourne Argus*. But he never staked out a claim in the Tuapeka goldfields; he staked it out in the office of the *Otago Daily Times*, the newspaper born of the Tuapeka rush.

This paper, now the leading daily in Dunedin, rose out of the goldfields as Venus rose out of the sea—with Ben Farjeon and Julius Vogel in attendance. Vogel, who had funds, was proprietor and editor; Farjeon, who had none, manager, sub-editor, contributor, and, frequently, compositor. On its Jubilee, in 1911, the *Times* claimed that it had never missed its daily issue except on holiday occasions; yet once it made this boast good by a hair's-breadth.

Dunedin had a practically all-Scotch population; her growth and business was in the hands of men whose views, religious and moral, were those of an Elder in Thrums. Every laxity was frowned on—and everything was a laxity. One Sunday, Ben Farjeon walked briskly along, whistling as he went. Hands of horror were thrown up. "Wheestling on the Sawbath, Meester Fairrjohn?" (I must reproduce, as best I can, my Father's notion of the Scots tongue; it sounded still worse than it looks.) For "wheestling on the Sawbath" Ben only escaped arrest because he was popular, in spite of his unregeneracy. But the Elders of Dunedin shook their heads at the bad young man, who went on whistling merrily on week-days; they also refused to advertise in his paper.

Among them was a man whose advertisements Ben wished to capture above all others; he owned the biggest business in Dunedin. Once he came in, the rest could not stay out; while he stayed out, they did not need to come in. Ben tackled him in person: why wouldn't Mr. Mac——

advertise in the *Otago Daily Times*? He gave his advertisements to the *Weekly Blank*.

"It's welcome tae them. Ye bring oot a Monday issue, Meester Fairrjohn."

"Of course we do. We are a daily paper."

"The Lairrd'll no prosper ye. Ye keep yer men wurrkin' on the Sawbath. I'll no gi'e ma advairrtisement tae a mon that wurrks on the Sawbath."

Mr. Mac—— was adamant, and Ben retired beaten; but a worse defeat appeared to be at hand. One Saturday fire broke out on the premises of the *Times*. A fire, in that tinder town, was a fatality. The young manager saw his offices destroyed, his plant reduced to so much molten lead.

It was instantly all over the town that the *Times* was doomed. While Ben stood gazing at the smouldering ruin, up came Mr. MacAdamant.

"Eh, Meester Fairrjohn, it's a judgment on ye!" he cried. "Ye canna bring oot yer Monday paper noo."

"Oh, can't I?" The bantam-cock sharpened his spurs.

"The Lairrd's against it, and ye canna dae 't."

"We'll see about that," said Ben. Mr. MacAdamant smiled grimly at this vain boast. "The *Otago Times* will be published on Monday as usual."

"If the *Times* is published as usual," scoffed Mr. MacAdamant, "it can hae ma advairrtisements."

"That's a promise?" cried Ben.

"I dinna break ma wurrd."

Not a moment to lose. Ben had his little band of compositors around him in a jiffy. They were only too well aware of what the calamity meant to them—yet here was the Manager, apparently undaunted.

"Will you stand by me?" he asked.

What did Mr. Farjeon mean?

"We're going to bring the *Times* out on Monday as usual."

What, with no office, and no fount or paper?

"We're going to break into the office of the *Weekly Blank* to-night, and set the *Times* up with their type and paper. Now then, will you stand by me in breaking the law?"

They would, to a man! That night, after dark, the little band of conspirators forced its way into the empty premises of the weekly paper, the paper that would not dream of working on the Sabbath. All through the night and day they stood at case, working with silent speed; the men from copy, but Ben himself direct from brain to type, composing his copy as he set it up.

Twenty years ago there were still connected with the *Otago Daily Times* men who recalled that when B. L. Farjeon wrote his first Australian novels, he frequently joined the compositors who were engaged in setting up his manuscript, and who recollected "the swift progress the author made owing to his not being under the necessity of referring to 'copy.'"

But the author never worked so swiftly as during those four-and-twenty hours, when, behind locked doors and shuttered windows, he beat the "Judgment from Heaven" by the skin of his teeth. They did it! By Sunday night Dunedin's Daily, thanks to Dunedin's Weekly, lay damp and ready for Monday morning's breakfast-tables. Then Ben Farjeon went off to the owners of the Weekly, who, with all the rest of Dunedin, liked, if they could not approve, of their rival's manager. When he stood before them, offering a hundred pounds for the use of their type to set his paper up, they refused.

"You'd better take it," smiled Ben Farjeon.

"Why?"

"Because the paper is set up already."

Unquenchable young man! They not only pocketed their hundred pounds, but promised him the use of their premises till his own were re-established. Dunedin read its *Times* on Monday morning; Mr. MacAdamant came round with his advertisement; the rest of the Scottish Colony followed suit.

And on its Jubilee, the *Otago Daily Times* was able to boast that, save on holidays, it had never missed an issue.

6

DUNEDIN: *Pleasure*

THE INCIDENT left no bad blood. Hot blood was my Father's native element; but never the bad variety. He was too generous to produce enmities, too honourable not to be respected, too magnetic not to be liked. He won both fame and affection in the city; Dunedin was growing proud of her young author—soon, he thought, he would begin to write his novels! First, a Christmas story "after" Dickens, his supreme god. Faithful to *The Caxtons* all his life, he never put anyone in a class with "Boz." He would dedicate his first book to his idol; meanwhile, he was supplying the theatre with plays, and had his finger in every social pie. He entertained the distinguished artists who sailed from all over the world to play their season with Dunedin's stock company. Ben knew them all: the tragic G. V. Brooke (whose *Othella* he held second to Salvini's); Charles Dillon (who borrowed £20 of him, and whose unredeemed I O U remains, its own sole asset, in my Mother's Autograph Album); Lola Montez ("Who was *she*, Papa?" "A very beautiful and fascinating dancer, my dear!"); some of the Broughs, I think, and Rose Edouin, sister to the funniest of men; George Fawcett Rowe, from the Princess's, Melbourne; and a certain young Mr. Roberts, not an actor, with whom, during his visit, Ben engaged in a match of twelve different games, an even pound laid on each. Eleven of the games Ben won—chess, draughts, backgammon, bezique,

whatever they might be; but the game of billiards went
to his adversary. Ben was no match with the cue for young
Mr. John Roberts.

And of all Dunedin's notable visitors the most lovable,
of all the one to whom the word "genius" in its purest
sense applied, Ben entertained, in 1864, Joe Jefferson from
the United States. The two men, not so very much
separated by years, must have been finds for each other.
Both were light-hearted and mercurial, both loved the
impulse and the fun of life, both were magnetic. Ben did
whatever he could to make pleasant this visit of Jefferson
and his boy Charlie; of the little ones left in America he
was shown pictures. "And this is Tid." Joe presses the
spring of the oval green-velvet case, and discloses the
miniature, painted three years ago—such a blue-eyed,
fair-skinned, golden-haired Tid, in blue gingham frock
and plain white scalloped jacket. Ben took a look; then
the green-velvet case shut her from sight again. Jefferson,
like many another friend, departed. The close of one more
chapter?

Later, Ben made at least one attempt to discover Joe's
whereabouts, and failed; no letters passed. The Jeffersons were shocking letter-writers, Joe's half-brother,
Charles Burke, and his friend, Edwin Booth—perhaps the
two best-loved men in his life—had both occasion to haul
him over the coals. "Friend and brother Joe-ferson"
(Booth opens), "we will *suppose* the letter written, sent,
and received—I mean, the one you've promised me so
long!"; while Burke, his other self, ends with a tender
elder-brotherly reproof: "A letter from you I look on as
a *friend*; think of that, Joe, and don't let me have to
remind you again."

Why, then, should Joe write letters to the young friend

he left behind him when he sailed from Dunedin? Yes, probably the close of another chapter.

* * * *

The permanent friends, however, were increasing; closest among them George Rowe, and Nicholas Chevalier the Swiss artist. Carrie, his wife, was a daughter of David Wilkie. These became Ben's good pals in walking and climbing; Nicholas carried his paints into the clouds, where Carrie followed him in knickerbockers ("Goodness, Papa! A *woman* in knickerbockers!" "And very sensible of her," Papa says.)

Better than many human friends, there was Kitty, Kitty was Papa's darling mare, who died. She died in the quicksands. When she plunged into them, she flung Papa, from her back, on to the safe part; and there he had to see his beauty struggle, and go under. (When Papa tells this story, Nellie retires and weeps.)

There were also Papa's friends among the Maoris. He speaks of the Maoris with great admiration, and never lets us mix them up with the Australian Aborigines. Among them was a certain Chief Wee-ta-ki, who was Papa's very great friend. One day, to show his love, Wee-ta-ki pulled from the ear of his favourite wife the square flat greenstone she was wearing, and gave it to Papa. Mrs. Wee-ta-ki uttered a piercing yell, but Papa made it up to her by giving her some port wine, which she liked better than anything else. The New Zealand greenstone is a lucky stone, and Papa always wore Mrs. Wee-ta-ki's ornament on his watch-chain.

Another time Wee-ta-ki saw Papa playing chess. Papa played all games with the head splendidly, especially cards, but he was very good at chess, too.

"What is that?" asked Wee-ta-ki.

"It is the game of chess," said Papa.

"Teach me!" said Wee-ta-ki.

Papa taught him the moves, and when he had learned them Wee-ta-ki said, "Play me chess!" And Papa played and beat him.

Wee-ta-ki went away for six months, and then came suddenly to Papa again.

"Play me chess!" he said.

And Papa played, and lost. They played more games, but Papa couldn't beat him; Wee-ta-ki had studied and studied chess for six months, and had made himself, said Papa, a master of the game. No Aboriginal could have done such a thing. The Maoris, Papa said, had the finest brains and the most splendid bodies of all the savage races in the world.

* * * *

And the *Otago Daily Times* became more successful, more powerful; Ben Farjeon was now partner with Julius Vogel. Dunedin increased in riches and importance; Ben bought land outside the city. Five of his plays had been produced in the theatres. And just before Christmas 1865 he started to write *Shadows on the Snow*—his first book, to be dedicated to Dickens. Eager as usual, he scarcely waited to write it; he stood again "at case" setting it up out of his brain. It was done, dedicated, inscribed! a letter was written—if Dickens liked it, would he, perhaps, re-print it in *All the Year Round*?

Whether he did or not, Ben Farjeon's position in Dunedin was established. He was likely to die in prosperity, one of the first citizens in Otago.

7

LETTERS FROM DINAH

HE HAD never ceased to write to his beloved Mother, sending her help whenever he was able. Now he could send it freely and regularly. No longer to England; life had changed its course for Dinah too, bearing her and Jacob over the water to Israel, in New York. Sol too was there, as yet unmarried; only black-haired Esther, with her increasing family, remained in London. What brought all this about I do not know. Perhaps hardships in England had led good Israel to suggest that he, married, and doing well in America, should provide a home for his parents.

My Father preserved only four of his Mother's letters, written on mourning-paper, after Jacob Farjeon's death. Three of the letters are addressed to Ben, and one, in Ben's care, to Morris—the hushed-up uncle who frequented billiard-saloons. So he and Ben *had* run across each other in the Antipodes; but no real light on Morris and his story is shed by these old letters, which I never saw till after my Mother's death.

New York, Nov. 20th 1863
67 Nassau St.

My Dearly Beloved Benjamin,

for the first time since the loss of your dear father rest his soull in peace I take up my pen to write to you you have I hope received the sad news in a letter which Bessie wrote to you for me your dear father apeared to be such a strong man I did not belive he was so near

his death the docter told us he could not recover but I
flatered myself good nursing & attention would again re-
store him to health but it was the will of the supreme &
all wise disposer of events to take him to a better world
we must console ourselves by the knowedledge of his being
a good man he said a day beffore he departed have you no
letter from Dear Ben we receved your Dear letter the day
after you may be sure I feell very lonely now but we must
not repine at the will of god if you can convay the sad news
to Morriss do so not that he will feell much at his loss but
he cant care much for a parent he has so neglected with
you my Beloved Son it must be a sweet consolation to
know that through your kindness I was enabled to get all
the nourishments and comforts he needed rest his soull
in peace the past seemes to me as a dream but I must not
dwell longer on this subject but pray the supreme all wise
being will take him to realms of blis where riches have no
power where good deeds and good acts alone availl for
your father was an upright man & now my darling Ben
God Bless & prosper you give my love to Soleman spiers
with dearest love your ever affectionate Mother Dinah
Farjeen.

To this letter (from which one gladly learns that the
old rupture between Ben and Jacob had been healed by
time and distance) a postscript is added in the hand of
Ben's second brother, Solomon, not yet married and
settled in California.

Dear Ben
                    I need not mention concerning the loss it
has pleased the Almighty to visit us with, as you were
apprized of it by dear Bessie and Israel. I seem scarcely
able to realize at times that it is so, for we all miss his
presence (*God rest his soul*) that it seems like a dream.
    Dear Mother will live I hope many many years, and
thank God I am with her to help cheer her path. Accept
my fondest love, Your affectionate brother
                                             Solomon

A week later, Dinah writes again:

Nov. 28 1863
~~185 West 20th St.~~
67 Nassau St.

My Beloved Benjamin
                    This day recived your dear letter with draft
for £15 for which my dear Son receive my thanks how
your dear letter has raised my drooping spirits I ~~will god~~
trust it will please god to spare me to see you once again I
am Boarding with Israell & Bessie but I have kept house so
long I like housekeeping for myself better I shall I think
soon make a change again perhaps not untill please god
you come home home with what pleasure that would thrill
through my heart Israell & Bessie are kind to me but they
have a young family & I like a quiet life god Bless the
children Sol also boards with them he earns no more
than pays his Board & cloaths himself I have not got your
papers yet shall get them tomorrow no letters from Morris
yet perhaps he was to late for the maill I sincerely trust
my dear Ben you are quite well wee are midling how proud
your Departed father would have been to have read your
letter and papers but it was not to be how is Sol spiers
my love to him I have not the least doubt you would do
well here Israell in the country I received the £10 for-
wareded from Uncle spiers from you no doubt you have
received my ~~answe~~ acknowdledgment of it good night god
Bless you 29th been to postoffice Papers not come yet as
soon as I can get them I shall have them noticed in the
papers everything here is as dear as in the war-time Butter
3s per lb I hope dear Ben you will soon come here I should
like to hear them performed I feell sure your play would
take here & oh how happy it will make me to have you
amongst us all again Bessie is out & now my Beloved son
I have no news to write sincerely trusting you are well
& that you will continue to prosper is the Prayer off your
every loving and affectionate Motner Dinah
                                                    Farjeen

god Bless

So might Miss Matty's mother have written to Peter
Jenkyn at a distance, the cherished son she longed to see
again before she died; like her, Dinah lacked punctua-
tion and spelled at random; like her, built her letters without architecture, running her longings for her son on to
the price of butter, blessing the noisy young children
swiftly after pining for the peace and quiet they destroyed,
reproaching and excusing the ever-remiss Morris in a
breath—indeed, her letters are all on one breath, and are
urged from first to last by her desire to bring her beloved
Benjamin to her side. She has not the least doubt that he
would do well in New York! She feels sure his plays
would "take" there! If he would only come.

Suppose he had! Would that short cut to the land of
Tiddie Jefferson have brought them together quicker, or
separated them for ever? If he had listened to Grandma
Dinah's pleas, thrown up everything and gone to her on
the spot (he so easily might!) he would have reached New
York two years before the return of Joseph Jefferson; and
perhaps at Dinah's death have hastened elsewhere, while
Tiddie was still no more than thirteen years old. Well
"it was not to be"; fate was arranging her moves in the
game twelve years in advance, and was not yet ready to
help him, when Ben tried, through his mother, to get in
touch with Mr. Jefferson again.

Decmbr 11*th* 1865
67 ~~Nausa~~ *Nassau street*

My Beloved Benjamin

we have receivded your papers and they do
indeed give a glowin description of your new Play not
more than it deserves I should like to see it performed
your Aunt Fany grandson was taken supper at an Hottle

& there met Mr Fawcet & Brought him home to see us
I was very pleased to see him as he had seen you so recently & he apeared quite as glad to see me Israell is not
at home I asked him for Mr Jeffersons adres but he is
not in new york so I gave him the newspaper inded I gave
him 2 papers & he will have it taken notice of in the papers
he says Mr Dillon is here & would have come with him
but his Wife is very ill & he could not leave her but promises to bring him to se me he sends his best respects to
you you must realy work very hard to manage your papers
& write Plays to I hope you will take care of your health
& not sit up late at night I hope you will soon make your
fortune & come to live in new York I have had your play
taken notice of in a newspaper here one of your aunt fany
sons was in London & spent mst of his time at Lee they
told him you sent papers but you never write to them if
you did they would be pleased to answere you please give
enclosed to Morris who I am pleased to say as wrote us
a letter Sol Bessie & children join me in Love to you God
Bles and prosper you with dearest love your ever affectionate Mother Dinah Farjeen.

I'm glad the last word of my hushed-up uncle is that
he wrote to his mother. But why did Morris never get
Dinah's reply? What kept it in Ben's budget undelivered?
Had he died? Or was he lost for ever among the billiard
saloons of the Antipodes?

My Dear Morris
                              I think you can imagin how happy your
letter has made me it appear verry hard to bring up your
children to the best of your Abilities & then to be forgoten
by them I am very pleased you have at last thought of
Us had your dear Father rest his soul in peice been spared
a little longer how glad he would have been dear Ben has
I suppose told you of it I assure you dear Morris I can
scarcely realise it I look round my room & find myself
very lonly but he is better & happier I sincerely pray

although your dear brother Benjamin made his last years very happy we were not in want of anything & it must be very pleasing to him to know he in his last moments ~~but that~~ I had some one to care for me now dear Moriss write often It will cheere me up it makes a Mother heart glad to know her absent children are well wich I sincerely trust you are I am midling I hope you will be more success-full in your futuer undertakens please God Mrs. Cohen who is siting here desires her love to you her son Josiah has been very fortunate since he has been here he is Schoollmaster at Pitsburg where he is much respected now studing for the law expects to pass the bar next month has given notice to leave the school is very good to his parents Isaac Lyons never sends or writes to his dear Mother over 80 years of age Brother Michiel is retired from Busines is liveing in the same House with her Brother Mr Marks in the haymarket Mrs Marks is no more has been dead sometime Michiel has never wrote me a letter since I have been in new York I had letters this week from england they are all thank god well Bessie & the children save the youngest a girll 2 years old the next a boy 3 years & the oldest Son 4 years they have lost 2 Boys since they have been here Israell in the country he works very hard for it takes a great deall of money to keep persons in stile in new york a lady thinks nothing of paying 100 dollars for a cloak and every thing must be changed every month & now dear Morris I must ~~now~~ conclud with dearest love your ever affectionate

Mother Dinah
Farjeen

Alas! Ben did not make his fortune soon enough to come to New York to see the beloved Mother; in readi-ness for that meeting he designed an exquisite shawl-brooch of almost virgin gold, dug by himself, a finely-wrought wreath of the New Zealand fern, the gold so pure that it was soft enough to bend. It was given in the end to a woman it was not made for. Grandma Dinah did not live to wear it.

There is one little scrap of paper with the four black-edged letters. The writing on it is hardly formed, the pitiful mis-spelled words trail off unfinished.

"Belov Ben I am a Little Bette God Bles You D Far——"

And across the corner a tiny note in a neat hand; that must be Israel's:

"Written by dear mother, Aug 10th 5 p.m."

These were her last words to her Benjamin. She must have died very soon after writing them.

About the same time Ben received a letter which completely changed the course of his life.

8

A LETTER
FROM CHARLES DICKENS

"I'M going back to England!"

The announcement from Ben Farjeon to his friends came like a bombshell. For a visit did he mean?

"No, for good! I'm going back to England to write. I've had a letter from Charles Dickens! He says I can write! I'm going back."

"What nonsense, Farjeon! You can write as well here as there."

No, he must go to England.

But the paper?

He would give it up.

But his career?

His career was in England. Dickens said he could write!

Think twice, Ben! Here in Dunedin you've everything before you! Friends, fame, success, property, fortune— all on the way Stay in Dunedin, and you can't *help* prospering. Go to England, where nobody knows you, and you must begin all over again.

What did that matter? What did fame, success, and fortune matter? Charles Dickens had acknowledged his Christmas story! Charles Dickens had found his dedication "acceptable." He might become a contributor to *All the Year Round*! He would throw up everything, and go back to England. Farjeon, you're a fool! But how often had that been said to him before; and when had it stopped him, on the spur of his moment?

It took a certain time to settle things. He couldn't leave the paper all at once; his property and affairs must be put in order. There were presentations, silver ink-stands, silver snuff-boxes, a gold card-case with his initials in diamonds; there were leave-takings, and, I dare say, heart-breakings; and B. L. Farjeon, barely thirty, returned to England, having compressed into little more than a dozen years a lifetime of experience—and of "copy."

* * * *

The "Dickens Letter" was a legend of our childhood. We knew how Papa's home-coming had happened. But curiously enough, the letter itself we never saw. It wasn't in Mama's wonderful autograph album, begun in America when she was Maggie Jefferson. The Charles Dillon I O U was there—why not the "Dickens Letter"? We never asked; I suppose we took it for granted that the letter was lost.

But after Papa's death it came to light. Among his multitude of papers we found the little oblong envelope, engraved C. D. on the flap, with a sixpenny stamp on the front, the London W.C. postmark, My 29 66, the "Private" in blue ink in the top corner, and the signature "Charles Dickens" at the bottom:

> B. L. Farjeon Esquire
> Times Office
> Dunedin
> Otago
> New Zealand.

The Dickens letter at last!

Mother and Harry and I read it together—

Gad's Hill Place,
Higham by Rochester, Kent
Tuesday TwentyNinth May, 1866

Dear Sir

     I am concerned to find that I have by an accident left your letter of last January's date unanswered.

Your dedication, as an interesting and acceptable mark of remembrance from the other side of the world, gave me great pleasure. And I read the little book with much satisfaction.

But I am bound to lay before you the consideration that I cannot on such evidence (especially when you describe yourself as having written "hurriedly"), form any reasonably reliable opinion of your power of writing an acceptable colonial story for All The Year Round. As to my reproducing this story, such a proceeding is as wide of the design and course of that journal as anything can possibly be.

If you write and offer for All The Year Round, any original communication, I will read it myself, very heartily desiring to accept it, if I can deem it suitable to those pages. Do not, I beg, suppose that I intend to discourage you when I say no more. I simply mean to be honest with you and to discharge a duty that I owe to you and to myself.

Accept my thanks And believe me Dear Sir

        Faithfully yours

          Charles Dickens

There was a moment's pause. Then,

"I don't call that so *very* encouraging," said Mother.

And suddenly we all began to laugh. How like Father! To throw up everything impetuously, everything he had done and made and become, to rush away from where he was to somewhere else, and begin all over again in a heat of excitement, because Charles Dickens had written him—this letter! This very kind and very moderate letter. Oh, how like Father!

PARADISE IN THE SIXTIES

(Our Mother, Margaret Jefferson)

A NOTE ON MY MOTHER

Extract from a letter from Mary Graham, née Mary Stout, written from Montclair, New Jersey, to Margaret Farjeon, née Margaret Jefferson, in London: August 1932.

"Your letter of April 18th with the pretty little picture—so like you and so sweet delighted me I never noticed before that Doad looked so much like you. I remember Eddie Stevenson (you will recall Eddie Mrs. Stevenson's youngest son), well, Eddie said you had eyes like wet violets fresh with dew. Josie too had lovely eyes gentle and expressive. I can close my eyes and see them now full of love and interest. All the boys admired you and the girls also for that matter—you were always so eager to do your share when we were working up some festivity—those were the good old days weren't they? Do you remember how you washed your hair with your Father's champagne and played croquet in the sun to keep your hair golden—that extravagance seemed to us like Cleopatra drinking pearls."

HARK! THE GUITAR!

IN THE EVENING, we went into the drawing-room to sing and dance with Mama. She sang Plantation Songs to the twangling notes of her guitar: "Git on de Boat, Chillun," and "Jerusalem, ma Happy Home!"—and snatches of old tunes, wistful and comic, "Mishy-ding-di-O," so haunting, "Paddy's the bhoy for me!" so rollicking, "Schneider how you vos," with its yodel, "The Cousins' Duet," so pretty and frivolous," The Cat Duet," which made us scream with laughter, and "Please give me a Penny, Sir," which reduced us to tears; and the exquisitely plaintive, tenderly romantic "Juanita." Songs and snatches sung by four generations of singing, dancing, acting, strolling Jeffersons.

Tiddie Jefferson had been taught to play the guitar in Paradise Valley, Pennsylvania. To that distant spot in that distant time the music-master arrived weekly from—was it Milford? staying all day, imparting music to the young Jeffersons, and partaking of their dinner. The holiday household, far from the conveniences of the stores, had routine meals through the week; the music-master's Thursday was boiled-beef-and-dumplings day. It was only at the end of the music-course that they discovered he could not abide the dish. How they found it out, I don't know; perhaps, on the last day of the lessons, he indulged himself by confessing his distaste; a thing the meek little sewing-woman, who also came to work by the

day, would never have permitted herself. But then, she
was a model of circumspection; when pressed by Aunt
Nell Symons to have a second helping, "Thank you,"
she invariably replied, "I have had a genteel sufficiency."

No doubt the music-lessons, like all Jeffersonian education, were taken lightly. My Mother played the guitar
with a sort of delicate, tentative thrumming, which was
not in any sense performance. She sits in her American
rocker by the hearth, her knees crossed under her long
skirts, one tiny foot tilting up the hem, the point of her
shoe (size 2) catching the firelight as the chair swings
slowly to and fro, her lap nursing the instrument whose
frets seem too far apart for her small fingers (her glove
is 5½). She leans her fair brown silken head over the keys
(never was hair so fine, except a baby's); she tries with
her thumb the thick strings that *thrum* like bumble-bees,
and the thin strings that *ping* like mosquitoes. A chord
trembles; a tune finds its way. It is all suggestive of something not quite begun, never quite finished; something
came before this, far back beyond her happy girlhood,
her music is the music of reminiscence, her instrument
is memory, she is not yet the wife of B. L. Farjeon, but
lovely Margaret Jefferson, who in America once sang and
played among her friends the Opera Bouffe of her time,
the tunes of the strolling Jeffersons, broken-Dutch songs
that came from Paradise Valley, darkie melodies heard
on an orange-island in Louisiana.

* * * *

Night on the Bayou Têche; the air is heavy with
magnolia scent; moonlight turns the gold-leaf of the live-
oaks grey as the moss that drapes them; a darkie in blue
cotton jean paddles the stream without splash or ripple;

a lantern gleams on a circle of black faces, a choir of
tuneful voices rises intensely in a simple song—

> *"Git on de boat, chillun!*
> *Git on de boat, chillun!*
> *Git on de boat, chillun,*
>   *An' we will sail away.*

> *"I tho't I saw ol' Massa,*
> *An' dis am w' at he say,*
> *Git on de boat, chillun,*
>   *An' we will sail away!*

> *"Git on de boat, chillun!*
> *Git on de boat, chillun!*
> *Git on de boat, chillun,*
>   *An' we will sail away."*

An emotional wail from a woman seized with ecstasy—

> *"Jee-ru-sa-lem!*
>   *Ma happy home!*
> *For I ain't got nuffin' at all to do,*
> *But shout Jee-ru-sa-lem!*
>   *Shout, Sinners!*
>   *Shout Jee-ru-sa-lem!"*

The negro parson strikes up with a vigorous hymn:

> *"Ma brudder came to* ma *house!*
>   Ah, my Lord!
> *I tho't he came to see me.*
>   *Shoutin' in de Jubilee!*
> *But when I came to fin' out,*
>   Ah, my Lord!
> *He only came to steal ma clo'es,*
>   *Shoutin' in de Jubilee!*

> *"De passon came to* ma *house!*
>   Ah, my Lord!
> *I tho't he came to see me,*
>   *Shoutin' in de Jubilee!*

But when I came to fin' out,
Ah, my Lord!
He only came to steal ma wife,
Skoutin' in de Jubilee!"

We scream with glee. "Yes," Mama laughs, "the Parson sang it too with all the rest."

The small slim fingers start a minstrel song from another source: "Please give me a penny, sir," born of Moore-and-Burgess.

"—A penny, please for bread!
For Oh, I am so hungry, sir,
And Mother dear is dead——"

"Don't sing that! don't sing that!" I plead. (Mother *dead*?)

"Who killed Cock Robin?
I, said the sparrow——"

Bertie sets up a howl. He can't bear it. This song is his quintessence of tragedy, and the teasing creature knows it. She makes a funny face, and changes quickly to the lively, larky, "Schneider how-you-vos?"

* * * *

Summer in Paradise Valley, wild and innocent, an unspoiled Eden, at the foot of Pocono Mountain. A ring of hemlock-crowned hills surrounds the valley, pebbly trout-streams tumble over rocks and run through meadows scattered with primitive farmhouses, unchanged since the old Dutch settlers built them for the families who live there now, and were born in Paradise. Here, far from anywhere by buggy-drive, the young Jeffersons spent long holidays; sweet-natured, jolly Charlie, pretty light-hearted Tid, Tom, the irrepressible scamp, always in mischief, little Josie, with her twinkling humour and her twisted spine (oh, that careless nurse, who dropped her in her infancy!). At any moment the child might have one of her "spasms." And here perhaps Joe Jefferson, a fine guitarist, picked up those songs he sang to the children, in the broken Dutch of the settlers, and Rip Van Winkle: "Schneider how you vos?" and "Mister Kaiser, do you vant to puy a dawg?"

> "As I took a glass of grog de udder day,
> At de Lager-Peer Zaloon across de vay,
>> A man he com in
>> Und he ask fer som gin,
> An' onto me did say:
> 'Mister Kaiser, don't you vant to puy a dawg?
> He'll make goot sausage-meat!
> He's chust as laight as any fairy,
> Und he's not so ferry hairy,
>> Und he's only got drei feet!
>> O! don't dat dawg look schveet!

(Guitar   (Tiddle-y-umti-umti-umti-
obligato)   tiddle-y-iddle-y-um!)

> Mit his schtompy tail und his only drei feet!'
>> (Ta-rum-ti-tum, ti-tum-ti-tum—TUM!)

> I tol' dat man gone vay mit his dawg!
> He said he vould ven he'd got his aiger-nogg;
>> Den he vent to de door,
>> Und he loudly did roar:
> 'Mister Kaiser! don't you vant to puy a Dawg?'"

Twaddle and doggerel! but it restored our gaiety in the fire-light, and in a queer way brought our American Grandfather very close. Mama was singing songs as he had sung them. And he had sung them as his Grandfather had sung, and he as his Father before him. Jeffer sons always sang.

Hark! the Guitar!

JEFFERSONS

A YOUNG YORKSHIRE YOKEL is singing comic songs, sending the tap-room into fits of laughter. It is 1745, the year of the Jacobite Rebellion. The north is rising for the young Pretender. One rides to Ripon with important news; some dispatch concerning the insurrection (can it be Culloden?) must be carried at once to London. Who'll carry it with the most speed? 'Twill take a good rider best part of a week. Nay, and he must be no chicken-heart, neither, who's to face those 220 miles of footpads, highwaymen, and hostile Papists! Ask young Tom Jefferson, then! he's your lad; always prime for a frolic, oh he's a dashing one, he's a wild one, Tom! the best saddle in these parts, and his father, the farmer, can give him the best of mounts. Ask Tom—he'll go, and glad to quit the attorney he's articled to. Articled? How old is he then? Fourteen or fifteen maybe. Nay, that's too young! Sir, Tom's your lad, believe me; that's him now singing over the way, he'll sing you a song as good as a play-actor!

So Thomas Jefferson, Yorkshire Farmer's Son, reluctant attorney, merry, handsome, intrepid, rides to London, delivers his dispatch, and drops into the tap-room of the White Hart Inn in Southwark. In the White Hart parlour a party of actors is feasting; to them, a laughing servant.

The host of the revellers asks what he's laughing at

"Oh, sir," says the servant, wiping the tears from his eyes, "there's a jolly young lad from the country keeping the tap-room in a roar with his stories and songs."

"Let's have the bumpkin in, and quiz him," says David Garrick.

But when young Thomas Jefferson joined the party, graceful and free and entirely at his ease, he so charmed his host and company with Yorkshire tunes and tales of north-country characters, that by the evening's end, "You shall keep no farm and carters, Tom," cries Garrick, "upon my word you shall go on the stage, and one day act with me! But you must go barnstorming first."

And so it was.

Thomas Jefferson stayed in the south; fell in love with Peg Woffington and foul of a magistrate, one Henry Fielding, over a prohibited performance of *The Fair Penitent;* toured the Home Counties; and met, at Rye, a tall and lovely lady called Miss May, and lost his heart to her. But she was a sea-officer's daughter; and the sea-officer frowned on an alliance with a play-actor. So Thomas carried a sad heart to Battle; and there received a letter from his lovely May, saying all was well. Her father had "investigated his character," and consented to the union provided Tom would enter into bond of five hundred pounds that *she* should not appear upon the stage. Anything, anything! post-haste to Rye, and the altar; and thence with his bride to Lewes—where the County, who knew the lady, desired Tom's manager to get up Richard Steele's *Funeral,* with Mrs. Tom in the part of Lady Charlotte. The Sea-Officer, appealed to, tore the bond in two. Was ever so amenable a Sea-Officer?

* * * *

Charming Miss May, "as virtuous as fair," her tune was not a long one, yet even its end was sweet out of the common. The lovely lady died of a fit of laughing.

But first she had won laurels as "a remarkably fine breeches figure" (when asked what characters she excelled in most, she innocently replied, "old men in comedy"); had been described by Tom Davies, in his *Life of Garrick,* as "the most complete figure, in beauty of countenance and symmetry of form I ever beheld . . . so unaffected and simple in her behaviour that she knew not her power of charming"; and had borne Thomas Jefferson two sons: one John, a missionary, was murdered in China, and one Joseph, an actor, emigrated to Boston for his passage money and seventeen dollars a week; reason, his sympathy with Republics, and his lack of it for stepmothers.

Thomas Jefferson remained in England to complete sixty years of stage-life, during which he realized his ambition of acting with Garrick, playing Buckingham to his Richard, Horatio and Claudio to his Hamlet, Sir Epicure Mammon to his Abel Drugger. At their last performance together of *The Alchemist,* when Thomas was soon to depart for a venture of his own in Plymouth, Garrick threw something after him from the dressing-room, crying, "Take that, my friend, and may it bring you as much good as it has brought me!" The object, passed on by Tom to his son Joseph, was Garrick's "Abel Drugger" wig.

In Plymouth Thomas Jefferson was first in a village, instead of second in Rome. With the artistic help of Benjamin Haydon's father in his productions, he was now playing, not Horatio, but Hamlet, and winning reputation as an actor and an incorrigible joker. He was the first to relish a good jest when the tables were turned on him. *Hamlet* was being played for his benefit night; a certain Tom Blanchard was the Guildenstern. When Hamlet called for "the recorders," Blanchard, who delighted in a joke, instead of a flute brought in a bassoon used in the orchestra. Jefferson, after composing his countenance, which the sight of the instrument had considerably discomposed, went on with the scene (which was described in Ryley's *Itinerant,* and made by Cruickshank the subject of an etching):

"H. Will you play upon this pipe?

"G. My lord, I cannot.

"H. I pray you.

"G. Believe me, I cannot.

"H. I do beseech you.

"G. Well, my lord, since you are so very pressing, I will do my best.

"Tom, who was a good musician, immediately struck up 'Lady Coventry's Minuet,' and went through the whole strain—which finished the scene; for Hamlet had not another word to say for himself."

Upon this note of Music, farewell, Tom Jefferson.

* * * *

The singing comes a little nearer now. Joseph Jefferson the First, having sung and acted his way from Covent Garden to the Boston Theatre, and from Federal Street to John Street in New York, presently becomes "the reigning favourite" in Philadelphia. . . . With his small light figure and his blue eyes full of laughter, he can, "although handsome, excite mirth by power of feature to as great a degree as any ugly-featured low comedian ever seen." He sings "John Bull's a Bumpkin" for the benefit of one M. de Blois; Sadi, Bombastes Furioso,

Mendoza in *The Duenna* are among his score of singing-parts. A true stroller, he grinds all grist in his mill: Pantomime, Opera, High Comedy, dancing, a little scene-painting when required—everything but Tragedy. The First Joseph Jefferson is a wonderful Squire Richard in *The Provoked Husband,* and a better Verges; he was "the best Polonius that ever trod the American stage," giving elegance and dignity to the character, combining the courtier and gentleman with the humorist; he plays Dogberry, and Gobbo, Mercutio, Jacques, and Roderigo; he triumphs in Scaramouch and Jeremy Diddler; he is almost a complete cast for *The School for Scandal,* Moses, Crabtree, Charles and Oliver Surface, Sir Peter, are all one—nay, all five, to an actor of his calibre; but in *Macbeth* he confines himself to the Witches.

He carries his wardrobe with him: its most precious content the Abel Drugger Wig of David Garrick, given him by Thomas Jefferson the actor—and next, the court-suit given him by Thomas Jefferson the President, as a mark of his admiration. They met, and believed they sprang from a common stock, but it was never proved. The strolling player understands that the connection is not one to be pressed on the President of the United States—although *this* Thomas Jefferson shines in one rôle only, while the son of *that* Thomas Jefferson shines in over two hundred.

"He played everything that was comic" (wrote John P. Kennedy), "and always made people laugh until the tears came in their eyes . . . I don't believe he ever saw the world doing anything else. Whomsoever he looked at laughed. Before he came through the side scenes, when he was about to enter, he would pronounce the first words of his part to herald his appearance, and instantly the whole audience set up a shout. It was only the sound of his voice. He had a patent right to shake the world's diaphragm which seemed to be infallible. When he acted, families all went together, old and young. Smiles were on every face; the town was happy."

Was he to be the high-water mark of the Jeffersons, this player who made towns happy, and drew tears of laughter from whole families? His son, Joseph the Second, was only mildly talented—but one was coming for whom towns were to close shops and proclaim holidays, whose performance was to be a national possession: the First Joseph Jefferson's grandson, Joseph the Third, who at the age of three sang "Jim Crow" on the stage, and could not keep his fingers off his grandfather's drawing-box.

"Joe, where's my paint?" was the grandfather's daily salutation.

"It's gone."

"Yes, sir, I know it's gone; but where? where?"

"Him lost."

"Yes, sir, I know it's lost and gone; but how and where?"

Little Joe looks up roguishly: "Him hook 'um!"

The idolatrous old gentleman prophesies that Joe will become a great artist—"let him destroy any amount of anything he chooses! he is the greatest boy in the world." (So grandfathers and grandmothers will often think; but this time it was something near the mark.) He carries the child to the window to watch the big raindrops pattering on pools of water in the street below; and the old gentleman tells his grandson that the drops are silver pieces, and presently he shall go down and pick them up. "Presently" all America became Joe's Tom Tiddler's

ground. One of his grandmothers was well-named
Fortune.

Euphemia Fortune and her sister Esther were daughters
to a Scotch widow who let lodgings to actors in New
York—amongst them Joseph Jefferson from London,
and William Warren from Bath. Euphemia and Joseph,
discovering they had been born on the same day in the
same year, made still more interesting discoveries. Esther
and William Warren followed suit; Warren-and-Jefferson
cousins were quickly born, and friendship stronger than
kinship united the families. There were at least six young
Warrens and eight young Jeffersons; among the Warrens,
William the Second, who was to become the idol of Boston,
among the Jeffersons, Joseph the Second and his sister
Elizabeth, whom Edwin Forrest was to hail as the finest
tragic actress on the stage: "the best Lady Macbeth we
have, and the only Pauline." Yet she was just a member
of the stock company, drawing thirty dollars a week. She
sang "like the beautiful Garcia," and would have become
a star could she have resisted domesticity, which she
sampled three times: first as Mrs. Chapman, next as
Mrs. Richardson, finally as Mrs. Fisher. Soon after her
nephew began to "Jump Jim Crow" in his childish pipe,
her father's rich baritone sang its last. The star of Joseph
Jefferson the First—he who had been reigning favourite
in Philadelphia, brought smiles to every face, and made
towns happy—had waned with age. The stone on his
grave in Harrisburg, commemorating his comic genius,
records that he died "in calamity and affliction," and
closes with Yorick's epitaph. Stroller's luck.

* * * *

What tune was Joseph Jefferson the Second's?

More than acting or singing, painting is his great passion. Among back-cloths and drop-scenes, little Joe still dabbles to his heart's content in colour. Joseph the Second is gentle, simple, humorous, "an inveterate quiz." To his father's company, while he was young, came one of the loveliest singers of her time, Cornelia Burke, accompanied by her devil-may-care Irish husband. When they perform Dibdin's *Cabinet* Joseph Jefferson the First plays Whimsiculo, his wife, Miss Fortune that was, Crudelia; Joseph Jefferson the Second is Manikin, dashing Tom Burke the Marquis de Grand Chateau; but Mrs. Burke is starred with Mr. Philipps (whose Benefit Night it is)—she as "Floretta," he as "Prince Orlando," unite in "The Bird Duett." Six weeks later her son, Charles Burke is born.

Young Mr. Jefferson, merely Manikin, envies Prince Orlando's shoes, since he may not wear those of Thomas Burke. But in three years' time the Irishman obliges by dying of *delirium tremens* in Baltimore. Cornelia Burke and her baby remain with the troupe; children-in-arms don't bother strolling players, they are all in the day's work, and Charles is already doing infantile parts when his father drinks his last. In one more year Cornelia Burke becomes Cornelia Jefferson, and in February 1829 gives birth to Joseph Jefferson the Third, who is to outshine them all. But he has done no more than smell the foot-lights, "Jump Jim Crow" with Rice the black comedian, and practise "Living Statues" before the looking-glass, when Joseph the First dies in affliction; and the impoverished Jeffersons take to the roads, and the rivers.

They suffer all the trials and tribulations so hard to live through and such larks to remember—and if a trial

had its funny side (as most of them had), be sure the
Jeffersons chuckled while they suffered. In Mexico, in
the war of '45, they turn camp followers, and give their
show in the American tents; and when Metamoras has
fallen by bombardment, act in the Spanish theatre in that
city. They play in farms and barns, for the price of their
board; they journey from town to town in oxcarts, and
in Tennessee are turned out on a forest road in a rain-
storm, when the driver learns that his wagon-hire depends
on the takings of their next performance; they act in
country-inn dining-rooms without a scrap of scenery,
creating illusion behind a row of tallow candles fixed to a
board on the floor—and act as sincerely, and as brilliantly,
as though it were Theatre Royal, Drury Lane. They
travel the frozen Mississippi in sleighs from Galena to
Dubuque—relieved when they leave behind a stretch of
ice that has cracked and slopped under the horse's feet.
Once, the passenger-sleigh comes safe across, but horror
to relate! the baggage-sleigh, with scenery, properties,
green curtain and drop, and all their private and professional wardrobe, breaks through the ice; the Mississippi
swallows all, to the Abel Drugger Wig. Cornelia weeps;
unworldly Joseph is in glee at their good luck, because
the sleigh has stuck upon a sand-bar. Wardrobe, scenery,
and properties are salved; the next performance waits
while the scenery dries. Great fun for Joseph Jefferson
the Third!—who, out of these years of larks and vicissi-
tudes, squeezes three months' schooling, and a lifetime
of education.

They never prosper. The gentle, humorous head of the
family goes bankrupt. A friend, come to condole, is told
by Cornelia that her husband has gone fishing; he is
found, sitting composedly in a shady nook on the bank

of the Schuylkill, humming a pleasant air, and sketching the ruins of a tumbledown mill on the opposite shore. To his friend's astonishment at this happy-go-lucky attitude to misfortune: "I have lost everything," smiles Jefferson, "and I am so poor now that I really cannot afford to let anything worry me." He lives only to the age of thirty-eight; enjoying life in a dreamy way, guileless as a child, never known to utter an unkind word, "his blameless nature as free from a thought or act of dishonour as the diamond is free from alloy."

In 1842 a last misfortune befalls him: a fire in the St. Charles Theatre in New Orleans destroys his theatrical wardrobe—and the Abel Drugger Wig. In the November of the same year, Joseph Jefferson the Second dies of yellow fever at Mobile. The theatre has to be closed for two nights, for the entire company consists of his family and connections—"and without the assistance of the chief mourners," said my Grandfather, "we could not make a performance."

Only a wooden grave-mark showed where he lay; Joe the Third, become the head of the Jeffersons, aged thirteen, was too poor to mark it in any other way. Twenty-five years afterwards he replaced it with a fitting monument, and brought the wooden grave-mark to be buried in the earth of his farmhouse in Hohokus, where eleven years later the dead man's great-grandson, Harry Farjeon, the first of our Nursery, was to be born.

* * * *

One more stroller laid to rest, and still they stroll. Charles Burke, young Joe's half-brother, seems like a father to him, There is "a strange and deep affection" between them. They are often separated; Joe may be

playing the burlesque of *Mazeppa* with Mrs. John Wood
in one city, while in another Charles, in a terrible version
of *Rip Van Winkle,* commands "the sympathy and awe
of his audience."

But in the Fall of 1849, at Chanfrau's New National
Theatre in New York, both Charles and Joe come together in a musical piece called *The Poor Soldier.* In the
company is "the young and talented actress" Margaret
Clements Lockyer. Her Somersetshire parents brought
her from Burnham to America when she was a child. She
has been but a year on the stage, is just seventeen, and
Joe's twenty-year-old heart begins to beat faster. After
The Poor Soldier comes *The Alarming Sacrifice*; in this,
to Joe's Bob Trickett, Miss Lockyer plays the part of
Susan Sweetapple—the very name is redolent of Somerset.

Cornelia's children are summoned by telegram to Philadelphia—and arrive only in time to bury their mother.
That day Charles and Joe walk the streets in misery, and
in the evening, not knowing where to go or what to do,
they turn into their natural home, the theatre. I heard
this tale when I was very small, and it coloured all my
notions of what was fitting on a day of mourning. Your
grief was in your heart—what mattered your body's
whereabouts? My grandfather must have told this tale
very vividly to his daughter, who made *her* daughter see
so vividly the two unhappy brothers, sitting side by side
through a theatrical performance on the day of their
mother's funeral. What if they were seen, known, and
criticized? They did what they felt like doing, and were
used to criticism. As for their sorrow, that was their own
affair.

The half-brothers separate, each going to his dressing-
room of the moment. In his, young Joe is humming "My

Pretty Jane" (but substitutes another name in thought). And, Easter over, in the month of May, he leads Miss Margaret Lockyer to the altar.

Charles hastens to delay the imprudent match. He reminds Joe how short a time he has known his bride; warns him that he is barely one-and-twenty, and Margaret but eighteen; is just a little jealous. There are almost "words" about it. But Joe is obstinate, or rather, is in love. He spends two months' salary on a lavender suit, issues a batch of expected invitations—and, on the appointed Sunday morning, sneaks with shy Margaret to another church. Only his sister Connie and his best man, Barney Williams, are in attendance. When Barney comments on the absence of audience at this morning performance, Joe, with a happy smile explains, "They would have been here, Barney, but I sent them to the wrong church."

"Susan Sweetapple" was seen little more on the stage; she soon became, not actor, but producer. Ten months after her marriage, Charles Burke Jefferson was born; and in 1853, to the tune of fire-crackers on the Fourth of July, Margaret Jane Jefferson made her entrance. She was known from the first as Tid.

When she was six she went to Paradise.

3

TIDDIE IN PARADISE

TIDDIE'S PAPA has taken them all to a lovely new place. It is called Paradise Valley. It is a farmhouse, with lots of funny old rooms, and a big piazza going all the way round, and the farmer and his wife they board with talk so funny, half Dutch, half American. There's a huge barn at the back, and a loft full of hay, and behind the barn there's a creek, where Papa has learned to fish for trout with flies; and now his hat is always hung round with pretty gleaming feathery flies, with hooks in. Tiddie runs in to kiss Papa good night, and flings her arms around his neck, and screams. There's a hook in her hand. Oh, Papa! take it out, quick! Tiddie is so terrified of pain. But it isn't the sort of hook he can take out quick.

"Stand still, Tiddie, be a brave girl," says Joe; he opens his knife, and Tiddie shuts her eyes. The poor little hand is cut, and the hook drawn out, as swiftly and as tenderly as possible; and her Papa sees that Tiddie is comforted somehow. Maybe he makes her laugh with a funny song; anyway, there's a quarter to buy candy with.

Other things besides trout are caught in the creek; about once a day Tommie is fished out of it. And he falls out of the hayloft, and sucks the eggs in the nests, and gets his fingers in the threshing-machine, and Papa's guns have to be kept out of his reach—for Joe goes hunting, too, with his big leather game-bag.

Papa has ponies. They come from Australia, but Tiddie doesn't know where Australia is, though she and Charlie have begun to go to school. Tiddie can write MOON already, and so can Charlie; and when Mama writes 'um a letter to Uncle Bill Warren, Tiddie and Charlie make their MOONS at the bottom of the letter. Then Mama writes "Tiddie's Moon" and "Charlie's Moon," so that Uncle Bill won't think Charlie made Tiddie's beautiful MOON.

"No, an' he won't think *you* made *my* Moon neither, Tid."

"Mama! tell Uncle Bill I can read now."

"Mama! tell 'um I can read better'n Tid."

"Mama! tell Uncle Bill I like my Teacher."

"An' tell 'um Teacher's very good to us, an' tell 'um I am a good boy but Teacher whips me nearly every day."

"Mama! tell Uncle Bill we got a Doe-Buck-Rabbit called Rip."

"Mama! tell 'um Teacher sends me out for a stick to whip all the children, and tell 'um to buy me a whip, an' tell 'um I wan't to see 'um, an' to bring the wagon what he promised me."

"Hark, children! Isn't that Papa's ponies?"

They run, and all the folk run out, to see the team sweep gaily round the hill, and up goes the cry: "Here comes Joe Jefferson!" Not only Charlie, Tiddie, and Tommie rush to greet him, but all the little Dutchies under Pocono. He can't break loose from the children! Why, after breakfast, when he goes on the piazza, there's always half a dozen or so squatting there, waiting for him to come out and tell them stories. And he sits in his old chair, with the fat little Dutchmen and Dutchwomen clustered all over him, and Charlie and Tiddie, too, and Tommie on his knee; and he tells them marvellous stories of fishing, and bear-hunting, and adventures when he was a little boy.

"Say, Mr. Jefferson! tell us 'bout when you sailed on a barge on de Ohio, wid a Palace for a sail!"

"Why, one time, when I was a boy, we were acting in places we had to go to by water, not by road, and the Cumberland River was too low for steamboats, so the company travelled in a barge, cabin, caboose, sleeping-bunks, and all. We shot duck and pigeon for dinner from the flatboat, and we lay off to fish, and at night I stood my watch like the rest of 'um. It was in the Fall, and every day the trees changed colour on the banks. When we came to a likely town we stopped, and gave the folk a play, whether we were expected or not. Where the Cumberland flows into the Ohio the river widens out, some stretches are five or six miles long, good for sailing, with a fair wind blowing down-stream. We had no sail, but we cut a hickory pole from the shore, and hoisted a bit of our scenery, with a wood painted on one side and a palace on the other. My! you should have seen the farmers with their wives and children run out of their log-cabins on the banks, to stare as we sailed by. And the passengers on the steamboats crowded the decks to look at us. For a bit of sport we changed the picture for them, and as a boat steamed past we'd first show 'um the wood scene, and then suddenly swing the sail around, and show 'um the gorgeous palace. Then our leading man and our low comedian got a couple of broadswords and fought a terrible fight on deck. I expect our barge was taken for a floating lunatic asylum."

"Papa," says Charlie, "tell us about when you-know-who got your taxes took off in Springfield."

"Why, one time, when we got to Springfield we found

everybody there having a bad fit of Religion; they'd no use at all for rogues and vagabonds like us. They didn't say poor strollers mustn't act, but they made such a heavy tax on acting that we couldn't afford to pay it. Everybody in Springfield seemed against us, and just as we were thinking of moving on, a young lawyer of the city came and called on us. In the name of fair play, he said, he'd speak for us before the council, and he didn't want any fee, whether he won or lost. Off he went to the council, and talked to 'um as no other man living could talk; he made 'um laugh, and he made 'um listen, and they just couldn't resist him. They took off the tax, and we gave our show, thanks to that young lawyer."

"You haven't said what his name is, Papa."

"His name was Abraham Lincoln."

"Now tell one about Gran'ma, Papa," said Tiddie.

And Joe tells about the lovely French girl, Mademoiselle Thomas, who lived in St. Domingo with the French gentleman, her father, who had a rich plantation there. And how there was a rising of the negroes; and how the faithful Alexandre, their slave, ran to warn his master and young mistress of their danger; and how they only escaped massacre by getting off in a small boat, just in time; and how they were tossed about on the open sea, and the boat seemed doomed; but, just in time again, they were seen by an American ship, which picked them up and put them down in Charlestown. And there, having escaped death from the negroes, and death from the ocean, it seemed they must now die of starvation. And one day, as M. Thomas, very sad, was wandering in the streets, he heard a voice say, "Bon jour, mon ami!" (That means, "Good day, old friend!") And there *was* an old friend, whom M. Thomas had known long years ago in

France. His name was Alexandre Placide, and he was manager of the theatre in Charlestown. He did gymnastics and rope-dancing in the theatre, and he had five children, all rope-dancers, too! Then he asked M. Thomas for *his* news. "I have one daughter, Cornelia, and no work to do." "Come to my theatre, then." "But I cannot dance on the ropes!" said poor old M. Thomas. "There are many other things to do in a theatre besides rope-dancing," laughed Alexandre Placide; "as for Cornelia, we'll teach her to sing and act."

"And that is how your Grandmother went on the stage, Tiddie," says Joe, "and one day met your Grandfather."

He gets up and stretches his legs; but the children pull him down. "Oh, Mister Jefferson, *please* tell us one 'bout de Red Men dressin' up."

So Joe sits down again, and tells how once in Florida, in the Seminole War, some Indians captured the wardrobe of a touring company that was playing in the American garrisons—and the Red Men dressed themselves up like Romans, Highlanders, and Shakespeare heroes, and galloped about in front of the fort the trembling actors had found refuge in.

"Were you there, Mr. Jefferson?"

"No, not that time." But Joe and his parents had acted in the war in Mexico while the cannon boomed. And he told how, when the American Army took the city of Matamoras, the band of soldiers trooped in with the band of actors bringing up the rear. And how when the war was over, and there was no army to act to, the actors opened a cake-and-coffee stall in the "Grand Spanish Gaming Saloon," which had whitewashed walls, and sand on the floor, and barrel-hoops covered with blue, white, and pink paper for chandeliers, and tubs of sand for the gamblers to spit in. And how they made a living selling hot coffee, flat pies, pyramids of sandwiches, and sticky dark Mexican cakes, in which you couldn't tell the currants from the flies. And how Metta was a beautiful Spanish-Mexican girl who smoked cigarettes, and had a skin like a pale cigar, and sparkling eyes and pearly teeth, and was as graceful as a deer—but couldn't speak a word of English, or Joe of Spanish. But this didn't prevent her from teaching Joe to play the guitar and sing this song. (*Hark! the Guitar!*) "And now *Vamoose!* as we used to cry in the Grand Spanish Gaming Saloon at three o'clock in the morning. And that, children, means be off with you!" Oh, Mr. Jefferson! oh, Papa! just *one* more story. Very well, just this one more.

"Once upon a time there was a Giant! And he had *Three Heads*!! And he lived in a BRASS CASTLE!!! Now —*Vamoose!*"

They *Vamoose,* with candy-money all round, a dime apiece, maybe; off they run, the happiest children on earth. It was such fun with Mr. Jefferson! It was stories that made you laugh, that made you shiver; it was "Living Statues," when you marched round to a tune, and stood still like a statue when the music stopped; it was money to this one, money to that one, all the time. Sometimes, for fun, when Joe saw a lot of boys together, Why, he'd just put his hand in his pocket and throw a whole fistful of silver, to see 'um scramble; then stand looking on, shaking with laughter.

And Gosh! his kites! Mr. Jefferson made better kites 'n anybody's you ever see, as tall as *he* was, 'n taller; why, they had to be carried out to the lot in a wagon!

"My, my! ef you'd seed Joe in the lot this afternoon!

He fetched out a kite 'bout six-an'-a-half foot high. Up Joe sent it, and then he axed Hans Vedder to get a holt of it fer a minute, an' jest as Hans got a holt o' the rope a gust o' wind come along—way went the kite, an' roun' the lot went Hans, hangin' on to the rope-end an' yellin' Help, while Joe stood laffin' till the tears ran down his cheeks!"

Now it was ball games and cricket Joe got up for the young fellows; and in the Fall, when the harvest was done, he had the great barn cleared behind the farmhouse, and the floor waxed; and invited everybody from ten miles round to come and dance. The fame of "Jefferson's Ball" dwelt in Paradise Valley when Joe dwelt there no more. From Buckhill Falls and Swiftwater, from farms beyond Cranberry Creek and Rattlesnake, from Seven Pines, Cresco Heights, and the Devil's Hole—from far and near the families drove in their buggies, or picked their way on foot. It was as good as a Circus Night, to Tiddie, to Charlie, to everybody! By ten o'clock three or four hundred dancers thronged the barn, and Joe, giving his arm to the prettiest girl among them, led the first dance. Then he devoted himself to looking after his guests. The dance was followed by refreshments; the refreshments by more dancing. At two in the morning the ball began to break up. "Good night an' thank you, Mr. Jefferson!" "Oh, Mr. Jefferson, such a lovely party!" "My! Joe, I hain't enjiyed myself so much in years!" "Good night, Mr. Jefferson!" "Good night, Joe!" The settlers go home, and talk for decades to come of the good time they had at Jefferson's Ball. "We hain't had no such times since Joe left," twenty years after sighed an ancient settler.

And on hot summer nights, fishing and hunting over,

Joe brought his guitar out to the piazza, and sat on in the dusk among the fireflies, and played and sang soft, dreamy Spanish airs. Sweetly he played, and Tiddie stole out to listen: to listen and think how *she* would like to play like Papa, singing "Juanita" in the dark, and many an air he learned in Mexico, of Metta wild as a deer, with skin like a pale cigar.

Hark! the Guitar!

* * * *

Summer closes. The lovely time in Paradise must end —must, because in November little Josie is to be born, Tiddie's one sister, to whom she will become almost a mother. Back to the New York home in 97 East Twelfth Street they journey; and on November the 10th Josephine Duff Jefferson enters a world that is to be so full of pain, and yet so full of salt and sweetness for her.

But Joe's health carries them back to Paradise again next year; again the ponies and the kite-flying, the singing and dancing, the game-bag and the trout-rod. Sometimes it rains, even in Paradise. The long dull day doesn't invite you to hunt, or, for once, to fish. Joe takes to the barn with a book, climbs to the loft, and lying on the hay reads the letters of Washington Irving. My, my! here is his own name! Irving once actually saw him play in *The Road to Ruin,* and thinks it worth mentioning that he resembled Joseph the Second "in look, gesture, size, and make." Joseph the Third is thrilled to realize that, when he was an obscure young actor (he has long ceased to be that, his "Asa Trenchard" is famous, he has made his name, but has yet to discover some part he can make his own) he was seen and praised by Washington Irving. Irving, with whose character of

Rip Van Winkle, beloved, vanished Charles Burke once commanded "the sympathy and awe of his audience" in an ill-made play. Gosh! here it was! why not? (Joe sits up with hay in his hair.) Burke's old play was a bad play, but still—why not?

"Where's Papa?" ask Charlie and Tiddie. Suddenly he has disappeared for days, and there's nobody on the piazza to tell them stories.

"Gone to the city, he will be back soon," says Mama.

But it takes Joe five or six days to find what he wants among the secondhand theatrical wardrobe-stores, and the wig-makers: old leather and mildewed red cloth, and a long tangled wig and beard, such as would grow grey on a sleeping man in twenty years.

"Oh, look at Papa!" cried the children, a week later. Joe has returned with his booty, and three old dramatized versions of the story; even before he thinks about the new play for himself, he is in character, standing at the looking-glass in a washed-out blue shirt, shabby red Dutch bloomers, stained and ragged leather jacket, gaiters and game-bag, and worn, torn, shapeless hat. All that summer the children heard Papa talking to himself, in the funny broken tongue of Paradise, as he rehearsed the part arranged from the dead material. The rafters of the old Dutch Farm in Pennsylvania were the first to hear Joe Jefferson say, "Are we soon forgot when we are gone?" How he spoke those words for forty years in the theatres of the world there are many who remember; and yet he did not—would not—speak them as Charles Burke spoke them. Of that one speech he said, "It is possible I might speak it as he did, but——" And left the reason untold, an open secret. The tones of Charles Burke's voice were too sacred to Joe's memory to be echoed upon any stage by him. Yet I think no audience wept, even for Charles Burke, as it wept for Joe Jefferson; and when Joe Jefferson died, a nation wept.

The play was a poor thing still, in 1860; but the part was there, and, leaving Paradise, he carried it to Washington in the Fall. "Susan Sweetapple" lived just long enough to see Joe, "saturated" with the part of Rip, stir his first audience.

* * * *

That long spell of rest in Paradise, if it helped Joe's health, did not secure it. Suddenly, in March 1861, Margaret died. The New York home broke up. Joe Jefferson's lungs are in a delicate state. If he does not travel for years in another climate, his four children must perhaps lose a father as well as a mother.

4

FIVE YEARS

TIDDIE'S PAPA has gone away, she won't see him for a long time now. And Charlie's gone, too; Papa has taken her playmate with him. And Mama's gone. First there was a new President, then Mama died. The new President's name is Abraham Lincoln, and he is the one who made the people laugh way back in Springfield, and take the tax off Gran'pa and Gran'ma Jefferson.

Before Mama died was Valentine's Day. Charlie and Tiddie saw a Valentine in the store-window, and it was about a Lady Teacher; it was not a very pretty picture, but it was so funny. They would like to buy it for Teacher, and put it under her door for a surprise. Only it cost ten cents, and Charlie and Tiddie had not even five cents. Should they ask Papa? No, Mama. If you ask Papa for a dollar, he gives you the dollar; but if you ask him for a dime, he says, "A dime! what *can* you want with a dime? I hope you ain't goin' to grow up mean!" Mama gave them the dime, and Charlie and Tiddie bought the funny Valentine and pushed it under the door and ran away. Next day in class, before lessons, Teacher held up her hand and said in a very grave voice: "I have something I am very sorry to tell you all. Yesterday some little girl or boy put this under my door." She held up the Valentine with the picture of the funny Lady Teacher on it, and Charlie and Tiddie sat as still as mice. Teacher went on: "It was a very unkind thing to do, to send me this ugly vulgar picture, and I want whoever did it to confess and beg my pardon." Nobody spoke. Charlie and Tiddie dared not look at each other. Their Valentine Surprise had gone wrong, and they did not understand why they must beg Teacher's pardon. They sat stiller than ever, and Teacher never knew. This remained Charlie's and Tiddie's secret. How lucky Mama had not asked them what the dime was for! It was only a month ago.

Papa's letters come from California. That's where he and Charlie are now. It's a long way off, but they're going longer off still. A letter says they're going to Australia, where Papa's ponies in Paradise came from. Before he goes he wants Tiddie's picture painted; she wore her blue frock and her white jacket to be painted in.

1862

Tommie goes to school with Tiddie now. Grandma and Grandpa Lockyer look after them, and Baby Josie. The war is on. You are not just American any more, you are North or South. Tiddie is North, of course. The war doesn't make much difference, you still go to Paradise.

In Paradise Tiddie and Tommie roll coloured Easter eggs. In Paradise Tommie sucks "all the nasty juice" out of Baby Josie's orange for her, and Josie thinks he's such a nice kind brother till she gets her orange back, and then she cries. Tiddie runs and hits Tommie for being such a mean thing to little Josie, with her bad back that makes her have suck awful "spasms." When one is coming, someone puts something quick between Josie's teeth, or she'll bite her tongue. In Paradise Tommie'll get drowned in the creek one of these days, "and serve him right!" cries Tiddie.

Papa's and Charlie's letters come from Australia now.

1863

Tiddie is ten. The war's still going on. Butter is very dear, and you have credit tickets printed by the grocer's store, instead of money. The battles are far away, but you hear more talk about them now, and there are more soldiers, and more people look sad.

At Christmas, when Papa and Charlie have been away two years and a half, Charlie writes her this letter from Australia.

> *Warren Cottage*
> *Decb. 23rd* 1863

My dear Sister

            I just wright you a few lines to tell you how Papa and I where pleased with your letter Dear maggie you dont know how we want to get back to see the family I suppose tomy is as wiled as ever we have a grait many curious things to show you when we get back papa is liked by every body in the colonys. We want your likenessess as quick as posible

> I remain your
> aff brother
> C. Jefferson

PS dear Josey Papa and I send our best love to you all

1864

It's next year when Tiddie reads that letter from Australia, with its true Jefferson spelling (they all spell like that, all their lives; but Tiddie differs from most of them in being, all her life, a constant letter-writer). The "likenessess" will be sent to Papa in New Zealand, where he's going in April to act in a town called Dunedin. His letters come from there now, and not from Warren

Cottage in Australia. Most likely, when she read the "Warren," Tiddie thought "How funny!"—she'd tell Uncle Bill.

Some time or other Grandma Lockyer dies, and apple-cheeked Grandpa Lockyer goes on looking after them alone. And perhaps it is about now, because Grandma is gone, that her Papa writes from New Zealand for Tiddie to go to a Convent School. He knows the teaching is good, but more than that, he knows the Nuns are kind. So Tiddie becomes a pupil at the Convent of the Sacred Heart. Not that she's a Roman Catholic, she isn't anything exactly (although she kneels down and says her prayers every night, to be on the safe side), but she likes the Convent, for the Nuns are lovely, and she has lots of friends there, especially the Duffs. Maggie Duff becomes her greatest friend (except Katie Holland). There are just one or two girls who, like Tiddie, are not Catholics, and before they leave the Convent they mostly are. But not Tiddie; Grandpa Lockyer sees to that. He has insisted that she is to be allowed to eat meat on Fridays (for which she has something called "a Dispensation" which confers a certain distinction on her); also, that she must come home to him every week-end—during which he takes her firmly to Church on Sunday, tells Tid to listen to the Protestant preacher, and putting his bandanna over his face, begins to snore.

The girls in the Convent School are divided into four Corps; each has a different coloured ribbon to wear. There are nice festivals and rites, but painful ones, too. There's a day in the year when you mustn't open your lips; and if you do (or commit some other little sin) you must stick a pin in a fat red heart like a pincushion. It is the Heart of Jesus you are wounding as you stick in the pin

of your small sin. Some girls faint or scream as they do it.
It is Tiddie's terror that she may one day have to. But
she's a good girl, and she never does. And when you have
your bath, you must put on a long coarse white sheet
that ties round your throat, and undress under it; you
must even wash underneath the sheet in the bath, and
never take it off. So on the whole, dearly though she
loves the Nuns, and though Maggie Duff *is* her very best
friend (except Katie Holland) Tiddie Jefferson does not
wish to become a Catholic.

Only once does she wish it. The little Maynards,
daughters of the great New York confectioners, are
among the Catholic boarders. One of them has a birthday,
and a wonderful birthday-feast is sent from the New York
store—such cake, such candy, such ice-cream as make
one's mouth water. All the girls know about it, and look
forward to the treat. Suddenly the word goes round:
"Only Catholics are invited to the Maynards' Birthday-
Party!" Most of the school files in to the sumptuous
feast; the two or three little Protestants stay outside,
protesting! If Tiddie could change her religion, for one
afternoon, she would.

1865

The war is over. Mama has been dead four years.
Papa and Charlie gone, almost as long. They are on their
way to London now, in April—and before they get there
Tiddie, like everybody, is aghast, because John Wilkes
Booth has shot Abraham Lincoln dead! Why, she *knows*
John Wilkes Booth, she has his picture in her Photograph
Album, by the side of Edwin Booth's, Papa's best friend.
Why, it was in *her* friend Annie Ford's father's theatre
in Washington it happened; and beautiful Laura Keene,

with whom Papa first acted it, was playing *Our American Cousin.* If Papa had not been on his way to England, he might have been Asa Trenchard on the stage, when Mr. Booth jumped from the President's box. Soon she hears that all the actors and actresses are arrested till things have been found out about the dreadful deed. The houses of the friends of the Booths are watched. If Papa had been here, he too—— For the first time since he left she was glad of his absence. Perhaps Joe Jefferson, shocked in far-away England, also thanked God that he was clear of a shadow of complicity in the plot which destroyed the man he most honoured by the hand of a friend.

1866

"Oh, *Papa! Charlie!*"

"Tiddie! Josie! Tom!"

They're home again—how well! how happy! how changed! how *little* changed!

The happy Jefferson life begins anew.

Papa has left friends, and love, and fame behind him, all the world over. In England Mr. Boucicault helped him to re-write the play of *Rip Van Winkle,* and London took him to her heart with it. Now, three weeks after he lands, and five years since he has been seen in America, Joe Jefferson offers himself to New York in the new "Rip." Willie Winter, the first American critic of his time, says: "The fame of its beauty ran over the land like fire along the prairies."

From Frederic Whyte's "Actors of the Century"

The new Rip was in truth an immense, an unparalleled success. Jefferson's performance in it was recognized at

once, as it is still universally regarded by all who saw it
as quite marvellous. We who saw it not must be content
to picture it by the light of the descriptions by those who
did. I have read none so vivid as that which appeared in
1867 in *The Atlantic Monthly,* in an article entitled
"Among the Comedians":

"From the moment of Rip's entrance upon the scene,"
it begins, "the audience has assurance that a worthy
descendant of the noblest of the old players is before
them. He leans lightly against a table, his disengaged
hand holding his gun. Standing there, he is in himself
the incarnation of the lazy, good-humoured, dissipated,
good-for-nothing Dutchman that Irving drew. . . . The
kindly, simple, *insouciant* face, ruddy, smiling, lighted
by the tender, humourous blue eyes, which look down
upon his dress, elaborately copied bit by bit from the
etchings of Darley; the lounging, careless grace of the
figure; the low musical voice, whose utterances are 'far
above singing'; the sweet rippling laughter—all combine to produce an effect which is rare in its simplicity
and excellence, and altogether satisfying."

The scene, however, in which the real greatness of the
player was shown is the last scene of the first act:

"It is marvellously beautiful in its human tenderness
and dignity. Here the debauched good-for-nothing, who
has squandered life, friends, and fortune, is driven from
his home with a scorn pitiless as the storm-filled night
without. The scene undoubtedly owes much to the art
of the dramatist, who has combined the broadest humour
in the beginning with the deepest pathos at the close.
Here there is 'room and verge enough' for the amplest
display of the comedian's power. And the opportunities
are nobly used. His utterance of the memorable words,
'Would you drive me out like a dog?' is an unsurpassed
expression of power and genius. His sitting with his face

turned from the audience during his dame's tirade, his stunned, dazed look as he rises, his blind groping from his chair to the table, are actions conceived in the very noblest spirit of art. In a moment the lazy drunkard, stung into a new existence by the taunt of his vixenish wife, throws off the shell which has encased his better self and rises to the full stature of his manhood—a man sorely stricken, but every inch a man. All tokens of his debauchery are gone; vanished all traces of the old careless indolence and humour. His tones, vibrating with the passion that consumes him, are clear, and low and sweet—full of doubt that he has heard aright the words of banishment—full of an awful pain, and pity, and dismay. And so, with one parting farewell to his child, full of a nameless agony, he goes out into the storm and the darkness."

Then comes the contrast between the young Rip and the old:

"The versatility of Mr. Jefferson's powers is finely shown in the scene of Rip's awakening from his sleep in the Catskills and in those scenes which immediately follow. Here he has thrown off his youth, his hair is whitened, his voice is broken to a childish tremor, his very limbs are shrunken, tottering, palsied. This maundering, almost imbecile old man, out of whose talk come dimly rays of the old quaint humour, would excite only ridicule and laughter in the hands of an artist less gifted than Mr. Jefferson; but his griefs, his old affections, so rise up through the tones of that marvellous voice, his loneliness and homelessness so plead for him, that old Lear, beaten by the winds, deserted and houseless, is not more wrapped about with honour than poor old Rip, wandering through the streets of his native village."

5

GOOD-BYE TO PARADISE

In the fall of '67 Joe Jefferson writes, from Boston, a family letter beginning "My dear Children" —to tell them he is to have the happiness of marrying immediately his second cousin, Sarah Warren, Uncle Bill Warren's niece. Next year, in the Dutch Farm under Pocono, they'll have their young stepmother "Toney" with them. That summer is their last in Paradise.

Once more they all run wild among the natives, who are overjoyed because their friend Joe has brought back the good times. Toney, herself only in her twenties, enters their life, and girl and boy friends come and go on the farm. Greatly daring, Maggie Duff and Maggie Jefferson face public opinion one day by going barefoot. But after all it isn't very comfortable, there are stones in the brooks, and what the tough-soled natives can walk on unscathed are plough-shares to the two Maggies' tender feet. They put on their shoes and stockings and go fishing, riding, and practising duets. They play the Overture to *Zampa* on the piano, and sing to the guitar. They are cosseted and petted by Aunt Nell Symons, who keeps them in fits of laughter with her "last." A bereaved gentleman calls to invite Joe Jefferson to his wife's funeral. The children fly away to stifle their giggles at Aunt Nell's effusive, "Oh, I'm *so* sorry, Mr. Jefferson's away—if he'd been here he'd have been *delighted* to come!" At cards, Joe will have nobody except Aunt Nell for partner—she screams with delight if she sees but a Jack in her hand, revokes so often, and trumps so many of her partner's aces, that it keeps him in a state of constant mirth. No Jefferson *can* take games seriously, or life; in mistakes and mishaps they discover lively jokes.

Maggie is given a young mare to ride; Topsy, black and spirited. But she is never a confident horse-woman; and even if she were, Tospy is a shade *too* spirited. So, having made a gift of the mare to his daughter, Joe offers to buy her back, for a hundred dollars.

"I won't have it all at once, Father," says Maggie. "I'll ask for some when I want it."

Topsy keeps her in pocket-money for two or three years.

"Father, can I have ten dollars Topsy-money?" "Father, I'd like twenty-five dollars Topsy-money, please." Joe reckons that Topsy costs him Five Hundred in the end; but he laughs and forks out—as he would, if no Topsy at all stood as security. Any child still could demand five or ten dollars any time, and no questions asked; but let them go to him for a quarter, or fifty cents, and it was still: "What *do* you want a quarter for? Don't grow up mean, whatever you do!"

And Tom's next scrape is always in the offing: will he be brought home with his finger-tips sliced off in the threshing-machine? or will he climb in the back of a travelling wagon, and be carried unseen for miles, lost for a day and a night, and having scared them all out of their wits, be brought home dirty, ravenous, and unrepentant? or will the irate store-keeper come to Mr. Jefferson, demanding vengeance, because he has found a whole basketful of new laid-eggs sucked dry?

"Tom! go into the barn and wait till I come."

But Tom instead goes in search of Josie.

"Dode!"

"What is it, Tom?"

"Father's told me to go and wait in the barn."

"Oh, Tom!"

"He's goin' to whip me again. Beg me off, Dode."

Josie, adoring the brother who sucked "all the nasty juice" out of her oranges, would limp as quick as she could to Joe's room. "Papa, don't whip Tom, he's sorry, *please* don't whip him!" And Joe Jefferson, who hated whipping anybody anyhow (but really Tom's pranks *demanded* correction!) would look on little Josie's scared white face—and knew that his bad boy had got the whip-hand of him again. He could refuse this ambassador nothing; he spent his life trying to spare her pain, to compensate her for the pain she couldn't be spared. If he whipped Tom, Josie would have another "spasm" in the night. (Maggie kept a spoon in her pocket now, ready to slip between the child's teeth at the first alarm.) Back to the barn went Josie with the reprieve: the bad boy got off scotfree again, as usual; and Joe, humming "Schneider," went back to inventing a new and cunning fly—not sorry to be spared tanning Tom's trousers.

Tom didn't always get off quite scotfree; sometimes his pranks and gibes and naughtinesses wrought even gentle Maggie to a frenzy; and she would cry to the young Stepmother, as wrathful as herself: "Hold him down for me, Toney, while I *hit* him!" And Tom, wriggling in Toney's clutches, would jeer at the futile blows of those little hands.

* * * *

One last strange memory of Paradise. From here Joe

Jefferson tries to touch the other world. America is swept by a wave of Spiritualism; among the genuine seekers and enquirers, charlatans spring up like mushrooms, and Joe is caught in the stream. He wonders if he can reach the spirit of Margaret Lockyer. He attends seances in strange rooms, with mediums to whom he is sure he is unknown—and is amazed at the results. (As if all Amercia did not know Joe Jefferson!) He goes to spirit-photographers, and is photographed with pale shapes behind his chair. Tiddie, scared to death, is photographed too—oh, is that ghost behind her *really* her mother? Every new outlet offered Joe he tries; and whether, among the fakers, he ever finds truth, no one can say. But certain it is the charlatans flock round him; they boast in their papers that Jefferson plays "Rip" under spiritualistic influence; and a wonderful Medium is brought out to Paradise Valley, to stay for several weeks. Because the rooms are full to overflowing she has a bed put for her in Tiddie's room. During the nights she may at any moment become possessed by one of her two Spirit-Controls, who are known as "Tilly" and "The Indian Doctor." Tilly is mischievous, the Indian Doctor terrifying. When his gruff voice comes booming through the dark, Tiddie, a girl of fifteen, cowers under the sheets; while he issues to her commands largely concerned with additional comforts for the Medium.

* * * *

That is why Nellie's Mama can't go into a dark room by herself, you know, and never goes to bed without a nightlight.

6

INTERVAL

THEY go no more to Paradise.

Joe Jefferson has found another farmhouse in another valley, not now in Pennsylvania, but New Jersey. A lovely estate in Hohokus is for sale, in the little valley of the Saddle River; the old house has large low-ceilinged rooms, and is surrounded by hundreds of rolling acres of forest and hill, level fields, and trout-streams. In front of the house Joe plants a screen of evergreen—off the stage he retires from the public gaze. To the right of the farm the plain leads to a forest; to the left, a shaded "English" lane borders a stream, damned for a trout-reserve twenty feet below. Cows pasture in the meadows where it drains; there is a farm-barn, just as in Paradise, stacked with hay, stalks, farm-tools, and painting-tools. Guardian of all, home, cattle, and human beings, is Schneider the Scotch Sheepdog, brought back by "Rip" from England, in a sailing-vessel. Fresh milk being one of Joe's necessities, he also brought in that ship a she-ass that had foaled—and unable to bear to part mother and son, he included the foal. The little donkey was fat by the journey's end, and if Joe was any fatter it was not due to ass's milk.

Even more lovely than Paradise or Hohokus, is the orange island Joe has bought on the Bayou Têche. Here Toney's first baby, Joe, is taken when in danger of pneumonia—little Joe who adores the sister he calls

"Maggie-May." When Toney, in a moment of impatience wants to spank him, he runs to her as Tom once ran to Josie. "Save me, Maggie-May!" "You shan't spank him!" cries Maggie. "He's *my* child!" cries Toney. "I don't care if he is! you can hit Tom as much as you like, but you shan't hit Joe!"

The Orange Island saves little Joe's life. And here, whenever he lays off from acting, big Joe can paint, fish, shoot to his heart's content. They summer on the farm in New Jersey, and winter on the plantation in Louisiana, where mocking-birds and red cardinals sing like feathered angels, and blue- and red-shirted darkies sing like black ones:

> *"Git on de boat, chillun,*
> *An' we will sail away . . ."*

7

PRETTY MISS JEFFERSON

I T IS THE DAWN of the Seventies. She has put up her hair, with a gold-brown plait like a coronal, and mysteries of "switches" and "waterfalls" behind. She has achieved her dream of having her ears pierced, and Joe has given her the prettiest earrings in New York, long delicate drops of blue enamel and fine gold, that swing when she turns her head—and the heads of others. She so fears pain that she could *never* have had it done but for this queer new gas the dentist gives; she was fearful of that too, when her tooth must come out, and begged to be let off in the waiting-room. Time after time she said to the other victims, "You can have *my* turn!" till Joe said she must go in or go home; but if she would let the dentist take her tooth out, she could have her ears pierced at the same time, feeling nothing, and he promised her "the prettiest earrings in New York." So she was brave, went in, and had the gas; and now she swings fascinating pendants when she dances. Tiddie has turned into Miss Jefferson.

How do these things happen? How does one slide gradually from simple childhood, where everybody calls you by your baby nickname, into the years when new friends call you first "Miss Jefferson," and soon after, "Maggie"?—and Tiddie, the dear old name, comes now and then to the tongue of the family only (*"Tid!"* cries Charlie, when he and she meet in their fifties, after a separation of thirty years). Even the familiar friends slip into the "Maggie" you have become to the new ones; it is to Maggie, not Tiddie, Eddie Stevenson says, "Your eyes are like wet violets, fresh with dew." It is on "Miss Jefferson" Mr. Beebe (whose name rhymes with Hebe) gazes foolishly from afar, while she floats, in crinoline and blue illusion, round the room in the arms of Jim Duff, Gus Stout, or Ned Holland—she never will be Maggie to Mr. Beebe. Dearly would he love to call her name, like the rest of the happy crowd with whom she dances in the parlor, and plays croquet on the lawn; but he dare only stand in corners, and gaze at the gold-brown head gleaming in the gas-light and the sun. Poor Mr. Beebe! is it *his* fault if his eyes are snared by that bright head, those swinging pendants of blue enamel and gold? and is it *her* fault if she swings them to his undoing? After all, she has paid for the pretty things. It's really very hard on Mr. Beebe.

Naughty Josie calls him her "Mr. Guppy"; and indeed, Maggie thinks this beau of hers *is* like Mr. Guppy, and wishes he wouldn't stare at her so foolishly, because it is so difficult not to laugh at him, especially when Josie exchanges a sly glance with her. Now if he were a little more like Sydney Carton——! Everyone knows that Charles Dickens is her idol. She is teased about him; he is her favourite author. Mr. Clarke Davis, quite a good author too, sending her a present of his own books, writes:

"I am sorry these stories are not as beautiful as those of Mr. Dickens, but there is only one Dickens, you know, just as there is only one Mr. Jefferson."

When her idol dies, and she weeps for Boz, dear Uncle Bill Warren writes to her from Boston:

"What a sad shock to all the civilized world, the death of Charles Dickens has been. I never spoke with him but for half an hour, and yet, I feel as if I had lost some dear and daily friend.

"Fechter came here on Saturday, and among the letters, waiting for him on the hall-table, was one that struck me, as in Dickens' hand, and so it proved. The Frenchman cried like a child on reading it. It was written in London May 27th, in the office of his paper, "All the Year Round," and was full of life and hope, and the future, and yet in thirteen short days after, all that was mortal of that mighty genius had passed away from earth. Dickens spoke of the sudden death of Mark Lemon, and of his intended endeavour, through the interest of Mr. Gladstone, to obtain a pension for the family. He pointed unconsciously to the cause of his trouble in saying he should be glad to return to Gadshill and quiet, as he had been dining and receiving courtesies of entertainment since January."

She pastes sad newspaper clippings in her scrapbook: "It is understood that the Queen will confer upon Mrs. Dickens, with reversion to the eldest son, a peerage."

(In London, B. L. Farjeon, mourning *his* idol, whom he has met at last, writes to the eldest son, who has become his friend, and is not destined to succeed to a peerage.)

* * * *

Still, you *do* dry your eyes, when you're eighteen. You *do* enjoy going to Boston to stay at Miss Fisher's in Bulfinch Place with Uncle Bill (who is really a first-cousin-once-removed), and being present at those famous suppers you've heard Father tell about—those suppers after the play in Miss Fisher's kitchen, when all the actors lodging with her come back from the theatre, bringing with them the visiting Star of the season: fascinating Charles

Fechter, or John McCullough, or Mr. Couldock: while Uncle Bill at the table-head, hidden behind a scarlet mountain of lobsters, piles the passing plates, until his dignified grey head emerges above the dwindling red hill. You *do* enjoy having that courteous old gentleman give you his arm, as ceremoniously as though you were quite grown up, while everyone on the street turns to look at the actor Boston is proudest of, taking the air with Joseph Jefferson's daughter.

You *do* enjoy having Mr. Willie Winter stop writing articles for the *New York Tribune,* to compose for your new Autograph Album such pretty lines as these:

> *Her young face is good and fair,*
> *Lily-white and rosy-red,*
> *And the brown and silken hair*
> *Hovers mistlike round her head.*
>
> *And her voice is soft and low,*
> *Clear as music, and as sweet;*
> *Hearing it you hardly know*
> *Where the sound and silence meet.*
>
> *Pretty lips, as rubies bright,*
> *Scarcely hide the tiny pearls:*
> *Little wandering stars of light*
> *Love to nestle in her curls.*
>
> *All her ways are winning ways,*
> *Full of tenderness and grace;*
> *And a witching sweetness plays*
> *Fondly o'er her gentle face.*
>
> *True and pure her soul within—*
> *Breathing a celestial air!*
> *Evil and the shame of sin*
> *Could not dwell one moment there.*

And you *do* enjoy conspiring with the Fords, the Stouts, and the Duffs, to give a "Surprise Party" to Katie Holland, who is your dearest friend.

* * * *

She sits in the window, tuning her guitar, listening for sleigh-bells. The streets are crisp with snow, the night glitters with stars. Waiting, she tries over the accompaniment to an old Irish song, sung by her Father, but where it came from she has never asked: perhaps from Father's father, Joseph the Second, or *his* father, Joseph the First, or *his* father, Tom, the Yorkshire Farmer's son, this haunting Irish ditty:

> "As Oi was goin' down Georgias way
> Oi met wid a ship a-goin' out to say.
> Och ship, dear ship, stand by for awhile,
> An' give me some intilligince av Felix my dear chile,
> Misky-ding-di-O,
> ding-di-O,
> Ding-di-ding-a-ding-a-ding-di-O."

There are the bells. The sleigh draws up in the street. A snowball rattles the window-pane. She throws up the sash.

"Maggie!"

"Jim?"

"Sure!" Jim Duff, also his sister May (not yet Mrs. Augustin Daly), also his sister Maggie (not yet a Mother-Superior). "Ready, Tid?"

"All ready, cakes and candy. You got the sandwiches?"

"Right here; the Stouts are bringing lemonade, and the freezer. Josie coming?"

Little Josie pokes her head under Tiddie's arm. "Think I'm going to be left out of the party?"

"Good!" Josie has so often to be left out of the party. "Wrap up to your eyes, girls, or the frost'll bite your noses off." Maggie rubs her sharp Jefferson nose with snow from the window-sill, and starts to pull down the sash. "Bring your guitar!" cries Jim.

"And 'The Cousins,'" calls Maggie Duff. "The Cousins" is the Maggies' latest duet, a regular performance.

Down she flies, muffled to the ears, followed by eager Josie; under the buffalo robes, quick! and off they go, over the snow, under the stars, silver laughter ringing, silver strings jangling, silver bells tinkling.

"Katie! Katie! Hullo, Katie!"

"Tiddie! May! Jim! Josie! Maggie! My, what a crowd!"

"It's a Surprise Party, Katie."

"*Well!* isn't that dandy! Joe—Ned—come along down and help. Here's the Duffs and the Jeffersons, with more cake than they can carry! My! there's another sleigh coming, *piled* with people. Hello, Gus! hello, Mary! Oh, Maggie—Mr. Beebe is in the parlor."

"Now, Tiddie," whispers Josie demurely, "you're sure of your beau for the evening."

"You mean thing!" Maggie tosses her head. Mr. Beebe indeed!

Clear the decks for dancing, Joe and Ned! Jim Stout and Jim Duff, bring in the freezer between you—careful, don't shake it! Why, Maggie, a Five-Pound box of Maynard's? (Which of your beaux sent you *that,* I wonder?) Open the piano, somebody! Let's dance!

"I'll play!" Maggie Jefferson runs to the piano.

The boys protest. The lightest-footed waltzer, the prettiest partner, play? Later, perhaps: but the first waltz, no! Maggie Duff good-humouredly pushes her off the stool, into Joe Holland's arms. "Go ahead, Joe!" She swims into the Introduction of *Manhattan Waltzes*.

Away they sail. (Mr. Beebe, turning music at the piano, gazes mournfully after Miss Jefferson, who is whispering—what?—in her handsome partner's ear.)

"Maggie Duff and I have a new duet. We'll try it after supper."

"Did you bring your guitar?"

"It's somewhere around."

"Sing 'Juanita'——"

Supper over: ice-cream, cake, candy, and lemonade; the two Maggies stand up and give the company

"THE COUSINS"

"It was, after all" (sings Miss Jefferson frivolously),
"A most exquisite ball!
The music, the dancing, the lights were divine!
I could dance day and night
In a dream of delight
If partners were all like that last one of mine!"

(Oh, Mr. Beebe!)

Maggie Duff statuesquely brings up her heavy guns:

"How now, my giddy cousin!
I do not wish to hurt,
But really, if you ask me, dear,
I fear you are a flirt——"

(Don't you, Mr. Beebe?)

The frivolous minx, accused of I-know-not-what concerning "a gentleman with dark moustache," retorts:

"Of course, your usual lecture, coz,
Or it would not be you!"

She divulges that she also has seen what she has seen—
"Ahem! you understand?" Incriminating details
follow.

The mature cousin falters, is brought to bay, owns up;
one is as bad as the other; and they end by confessing,
each to each, in a burst of ecstatic confidence that

> "It was, after all,
> A most exquisite ball!
> The music, the dancing, the lights were divine!"—

and by dwelling on the dream of delight in which they
could dance for ever were all partners only like "that
last one of mine."

The singers throw themselves into their parts; Maggie
Duff's majesty, Maggie Jefferson's frivolity, delight and
enchant. After this, every gentleman in the room hopes
to qualify as the ideal "Last Partner" of the pretty
girl and the handsome one. Jim Stout bears off Maggie
Duff; Mr. "Guppy" Beebe hovers timorously, but too
late—Eddie Stevenson has captured the girl whose
nature, as well as her hair, is washed in champagne.

("*Maggie! your eyes are like violets wet with dew.*")

And then, when youth has danced itself tired, after
more lemonade, more candy, more innocent flirtation:
pretty Miss Jefferson tunes her guitar, and sits in the
Yankee firelight, singing in her sweet soprano:

> "Nita! Juanita!
> Ask thy soul if we should part"—

as twenty years later she will sing it, in English firelight,
to B. L. Farjeon's children.

Alas for Mr. Beebe!

* * * *

And on Katie's birthday, in 1874, they all get together
to repeat *The Doctor of Alcantara* in the spacious parlors
of the Holland residence in New York City. Katie is now
a favourite at the Union Square Theatre. It's four or
five years since her name was printed on one of Mr.
Augustin Daly's pink satin programmes, and even her
home-affairs win notice in the Press now. They have
done the thing before, but this time they are doing it in
style; the rear parlor has been transformed into a miniature theatre, with drop curtain and footlights complete;
and, if one may trust the programme, no expense has
been considered in the matter of the performers. "The
caste," remarks a discreet reporter, "comprised the
names of many celebrated professionals."

It did indeed! Lucrezia is sung by the famous "Kel-
logg" (looking and sounding very like Clara Fisher);
"Pauline Lucca" stars as the Doctor's Daughter (but
her rich chestnut tresses resemble singularly Katie's
matchless hair); Carlos, her lover, is taken by the great
Tenor "Theodore Wachtel" (whose nose, for the
evening, has miraculously taken on the Jefferson cast,
and whose eyes are like wet violets). "Santley" and
"Christine Nilsson" figure in minor parts, "Mario"
is a mere name in the chorus, the pianist is "Anton
Rubenstine" (*sic!*); while action and dialogue are super-
vised by the great Dion Boucicault (hardly to be distinguished from Ned Holland). It isn't the first time Maggie
has played the lover to sweet Katie. There was that lark
in Ford's New Opera House in Baltimore, when Miss
Maggie Jefferson, "the beautiful and charming Lyric
Artiste," played "Bertie Ray" in *Verita* —can it be the slip
of a thing prides herself on being "a fine breeches figure,"
like her great-great-grandmama, the lovely Miss May,

who died of laughing? Once before the Gala Birthday Night, this same Don Carlos has courted this same Isabella. The girls, while dressing for the parts, recall their comic *critiques*.

"As the *sentimental lover,* Miss J——, you were *simply immense!*" laughs Katie.

"As the *innocent sweetheart,* Miss Holland," rejoins Maggie, "you held, as it were, *the mirror up to nature.*"

"Give me that hand-glass," says the innocent sweet-heart, "and let *me* see *my* back-hair."

The "simply immense" lover, who weighs about 90 pounds, relinquishes the hand-glass, quoting one of Katie's first *critiques,* pasted in Maggie's higgledy-piggledy Scrapbook: "The toilette of the charming young soubrette, who has created quite a furore, was, like herself, perfection!"

The charming young soubrette adds a few hairpins; those heavy chestnut locks must not come down during the love-duet.

After the performance Don Carlos, Isabella, Lucrezia, and the rest of the merry creatures, mingle with their audience, an assemblage of the leading citizens of Brooklyn and New York. They convoy the brilliant company to the dining-room, where a sumptuous collation is served, and Katie's health is drunk in sparkling wine. The evening swings along with games and dancing, enjoyed by old and young; Katie is showered with presents and floral tributes; she is the queen of the ball to-night, and all men want to partner her; but ever and anon Don Carlos filches his sweetheart from their arms, and waltzes with her, laughing like champagne.

At a late hour the guests begin to leave, and as they bid her clever brother, her amiable mother, and her sweet

self good night—"or rather, good morning"—they express themselves as greatly indebted for a most enjoyable
time, and wish that the lady's bright young life may never
be clouded by a single shadow....

"Good night, Isabella! Good night, Katie!"

"Good morning, Carlos! Good morning, Maggie
dear!"

"Many, many happy returns of the day! Good night,
my darling!"

* * * *

Not many more returns of the day for sweet Katie
Holland. Next year, when Maggie is being carried to
England at last with Joe, she waves light-hearted fare-
wells to her dearest friend. She'll be home in a year or
so, back in the old paradise of Jefferson's family life,
which is unimaginable without Katie Holland.

But another family life lies in wait for Maggie across
the water; and Katie goes to another Paradise.

ROMANCE IN
THE SEVENTIES

"BLADE-O'-GRASS"

O NE DAY, IN 1872, Joe Jefferson came into the parlor at Hohokus, and found Maggie absorbed in a paper-covered book.

"A good story?" he asked.

"A lovely story."

"What is it called?"

"Blade-o'-Grass."

"Who is the author?"

"Such a curious name—Farjeon."

"Farjeon!" It *was* a curious name, once-met to be remembered, and not very likely to be met with again. "I wonder," said my Grandfather, "if that can be my young friend in Dunedin?"

Maggie hardly heard him, immersed in the Christmas-story which reminded her more of her dead idol, Dickens, than anything she had read since. She did not know that the English papers were already speaking of B. L. Farjeon as "a preacher of the brotherhood of rich and poor, more powerful, graphic, and tender than any since Dickens," and saying that "Mr. Farjeon's writings— especially his Christmas Tales—are to our thinking the most perfect stories in our language." She did not know that of *Blade-o'-Grass* itself they were proclaiming that it could only be compared to the *Christmas Carol,* that it was "a great national social lesson," that "for pure pathos and sympathy" B. L. Farjeon had hardly a rival; "a satire as grim, as suggestive, and as applicable to

the days we live in as those written by Swift were to his,"
cries one; "Such a story should ring through English
Ears from land's end to land's end," cries another.
She does not know that young Ben Farjeon is on the
rising tide of his fame and popularity in England; she
only knows that she has discovered an author, who has
become her favourite since Dickens is no more, who
writes in Dickens' vein, and whom she hopes—if Joe
ever goes to England again—she may yet meet, since
the meeting with Dickens has been denied her. She
pictures her father's "young friend in Dunedin" (but
that was a long time ago, when she was a little girl)
as a venerable gentleman with white hair, whom it is
quite safe to have for a favourite author. It is not Ben
Farjeon's name that causes Mr. Beebe to sigh in secret.
Whose then? Eddie Stevenson's? Willie Boucicault's?
One of the Holland boys? (That's what Mama never
tells us. "Mama, did you use to be a flirt?" Out peeps
the charming smile: "Perhaps I was.")

                              * * * *

Luckier than Maggie Jefferson, Ben Farjeon had met
his idol before it was too late. In *Famous People I Have
Met* Mrs. George Augustus Sala gives an account of
the first meeting between the two authors. "Charles
Dickens was in his box at a theatre one night, and was
speaking in terms of admiration of the story (*Grif*) to
Andrew Halliday, when the latter, glancing down into
the stalls, exclaimed, 'Why, there *is* Farjeon just below
us.' A few minutes later Mr. Farjeon was being introduced
to Dickens by Andrew Halliday. But the acquaintance
thus begun was not one of long duration, for Charles
Dickens died soon after that evening"—and Ben's
ambition to submit and see published "an original

communication" to *All the Year Round* was never achieved. It might have been, had he not begun his conquest of the "Titled Lords and Jewelled Dames" of Britain by re-writing his most famous Australian story *Grif,* a tale that launched him on a tide of popularity, and brought from Belgrave Mansions a letter signed "G. Grey":

"I have delayed thanking you for the copy of 'Grif' in a new form, in the hope that I might have found time to go and see you, but as I have not been able to do so, I must no longer put off writing to you. I am very much obliged to you for sending me your book, which I shall value alike for the sake of the giver, and for its own great merits, and I hope most sincerely that you will at once take that place in the literary world in this country, to which your abilities entitle you. I am not quite certain how long I shall remain in England, but if I stay here, I hope we may meet often."

Aha! the Titled Lords are coming to heel. Ben has only to strike while the iron is hot.

To his horror, when *Grif* was in demand at the Libraries, and Tinsley Brothers were clamouring for his next, an unforeseen calamity befell him; for the first and only time in his life he had not an idea in his head! He, so prolific, so suggestible, who saw a story in everything, whose pen could not keep pace with his invention, who left behind him twenty unfinished novels, a dozen starts of plays, and endless jottings of stories and ideas, stared into an empty mind, and wondered if it would ever bring forth again. In a state of desperation, he wandered about the poor familiar streets of Stepney and Whitechapel, and halted before a shop where birds were sold, A large cage, labelled "The Happy Family," had caught his attention; it contained an assortment of bullfinches, linnets, tits, canaries, and blackbirds. From this chance birdseed grew Dan, the crippled bird-lover, with a boy for a friend as strong as he was weak, who could pursue the adventure of which the cripple only dreamed. Ben hastened back to Buckingham Street, and wrote the opening chapter of *Joshua Marvel*. The half-domestic, half-adventurous romance doubled his fame, and he never again was troubled with lack of ideas; his fancy plied him with more than he could use.

By the time this book was published, Charles Dickens had ceased to consider original contributions from any-body. His bequest to the young author was the friend-ship of his sons and daughters; there was liking between Ben and them, and between him and Charles Dickens the younger there was love. This dear and unsuccessful writer happening to be connected with the firm of Tinsley Brothers, Ben saw himself published by one Charles Dickens, at least, though he was the one who said, "My father killed me when he christened me; there could not be two Charles Dickens."

Well, Boz was dead, but Christmas Stories were not. In October 1871 Ben saw through the press *Blade-o'-Grass,* a tale of twin baby girls, born in a slum. The mother dies at their birth; a childless couple, who adopt from time to time the poorest of children, receive one child without suspecting the existence of the other. The story traces the lives of the two girls, to one of whom life has given fair, to the other foul, conditions. My Father's innate socialism speaks strongly in this work; he never forgot what dire poverty may do to mar, and a decent start in life to make, character. *Blade-o'-Grass* completed what the first two novels had begun.

Early in November Charles Dickens Junior wrote from the office of *Tinsley's Magazine*:

"Blade o' Grass is not selling that is in the ordinary meaning of the term the book is actually flying away and out of the first 20000 I don't think I shall have any copies left by Wednesday next. In fact I have serious thoughts of ordering the printers to go to press with a second Edition to-morrow or Monday. . . . Let me embrace you, no not me, but let someone else try a lovely Candian girl you will find them awfully nice at heart. . . . I am sure the parents will only consent to your having one and dont try more."

(C. D. Junior may have been hanged quite as much by bad grammar as by a good name!)

Ben did not take these lovely Candian (!) girls, so "awfully nice at heart," to his; indeed, the only hint of romance-before-marriage concerned one Miss Marks, in Liverpool.

(This shameful secret was, I find, a skeleton in my brother Harry's cupboard. He hushed up from the rest of us that Papa might have married somebody else. I am sure he thought it was "wrong" for Papa ever to have been in love before he married Mama—and if Papa WAS *engaged to Miss Marks of Liverpool, he oughtn't to have "jilted" her, for to be a "jilt" was still worse than being "a flirt." But whether Papa really was a jilt—or was parted from Miss Marks because she was a Jewess and he wasn't "from" —or whether he was only paying her attentions, and wasn't really engaged to her at all—neither we nor Leon M. Lion can say for certain. All* HE *knows is that his mother would sometimes speak of the fascinating young Mr. Farjeon she might have married, and did not. All* WE *knew was suppressed by Harry—in deference to whom I relegate this episode in Papa's life to Italics, and bury it between parentheses.)*

Meanwhile, two copies of *Blade-a'-Grass* went "flying away" to America to some purpose. One fell into the hands of a youthful Mrs. Smith, who had lately lost her child; she and her husband there and then resolved that if ever fortune came their way they would do something to give a chance to babies like *Blade-o'-Grass*. The other copy was read by Maggie Jefferson, to the undoing of lovely Candian girls for ever.

BOHEMIA

BEN had taken chambers in No. 12, Buckingham Street, in the heart of the Bohemia of the Seventies. Old London could no more submerge him than could young Dunedin. He went everywhere, knew everybody, did everything. He was *persona grata* in all the publishing houses; on his enthusiastic recommendation, Tinsley published a manuscript sent in by a new writer, a pastoral novel, *Under the Greenwood Tree*; he was behind all the scenes on all the First Nights; at other people's children's parties, he romped with little boys and flirted with little girls; he was genial, clubbable, eager to serve a friend, and had an infectious brand of enthusiasm. His bachelor establishment could always conjure oysters and a steak out of the bars and chop-houses of the Strand. Friends dropped in freely at 12, Buckingham Street, or, as H. J. Byron put it—

> *"I will drop in or rather hop up to you between*
> *one and two on Monday."*

And while the author of *Our Boys* hopped up to that top-floor-but-one, down the old bannisters *slid* R. H. Horne, the Farthing-Epic poet, to whom Ben had sent *Grif* on publication. "Being yr first move with a London publisher," (writes the excellent, but disgruntled, author of *Orion*) "I may have something to say in friendly advise. Tinsley's is a good house. As to the 'critics' the

contents of a book, are in too many cases, a very minor consideration. . . . Failing to-day—you out, or I not coming
—I shall hope to call to-morrow." The old man called and
continued to call, spry as a young one in mind and body.
He never forgave the critics in contempt of whom he had
published his own *Orion* at a farthing; and he never
left Ben Farjeon's chambers decorously, but letting out
a whoop slid down the bannisters like any schoolboy.

Ben never knows who may next turn up to make him
throw down his pen, or on what impulse of his own he
may interrupt himself; for what spree with Johnny
Toole and Henry Irving, what lark with Lal Brough,
Charles Wyndham, or Willie Edouin; what punning
matches with Byron over dinner, where H. J., having
to propose a toast for the Ladies, rises, says muzzily,
"*It's swimmin'* in my head—*it's Women!*" and sits
down amid laughter at the briefest toast on record.

At a moment's notice he and George Rowe dart off
to walk in Switzerland, with which he has fallen in love;
he prefers the dizziest heights, with thunder and lightning
obbligato. Sometimes the Chevaliers are his fellow-
climbers, for Nicholas is now settled in London, under
the patronage of the Duke of Edinburgh; the Swiss
artist paints Royal Wedding Groups, Australasian
landscapes, and disdains Burlington House. They return
from the mountains, the Chevaliers to Porchester Terrace
and old Dame Wilkie, Ben to Buckingham Street, where
the pot-luck days recommence. George Rowe, the best
Micawber on the stage, has flitted from the Strand to
Broadway, but scores of others remain to flock in and out
to supper or breakfast. James Albery, the brilliant author
of *Two Roses,* in which young Irving made his first marked
hit, Burnand and Planché, with whom Ben discusses

dramatic collaborations, James Mortimer of the *London Figaro,* the dazzling young critic Clement Scott, the gentle old one E. L. Blanchard (whose forebear played the bassoon and the buffoon with Thomas Jefferson); George Honey, the inimitable Eccles—unless, having imitated old Eccles only too faithfully, he sends a messy scrawl—"Excuse these blots and stains. McKay and I were at the *'frols* last Night—everything very shaky to-day!"—and David James, John Hare and Herman Vezin, Besant and G. S. Sala, and those handsome young romantics, Bill Terriss and Henry Neville: no matter who, it's "Stay to supper, my boys!" and old Mrs, Chizlett is despatched to the chop-house for chumps, to White's for natives.

It is in the Seventies that B. L. Farjeon reaches the crest of his fame; that, in return for free boxes in the Strand, free consultations in Harley Street, free passes on the London-and-South-Eastern, free books from brother-authors, he scatters broadcast each new novel published, and for that purpose insists, in every contract, that he shall be given at least ninety copies gratis! The publishers, prepared to cede the usual dozen, stare, protest, groan—and give in. A few years more, and Edward Prince of Wales will be telling Ben, "The Princess's favourite is *In a Silver Sea,* but mine is *Great Porter Square."* (How's that, you Titled Lords and Jewelled Dames?)

Yes, after all, that kind and moderate letter of Charles Dickens, sent to the young Ben Farjeon in Dunedin, had borne full fruit. The impulse "to come back to England to write" had justified itself. He was still only thirty-seven, black-haired, bright-eyed, revelling in life, a bachelor, when, in March, 1875, the most delightful of those New Zealand friendships was recalled to him in an unexpected letter from America.

HER FAVOURITE AUTHOR

Orange Island
Feb 27th 1875

My dear Farjeon

You will doubtless be surprised when you receive this.

I hope that you have not quite forgotten me for I have often thought of you since we parted and your increasing fame has not only given me great pleasure but I have always felt proud to think that I knew and admired you long before you had made your great reputation.

My wife and daughters delight in all that you have written and our fireside is often made happy by listening to your charming and useful work.

Mr. William Winter, who is spending some time here with us, and I have been lately talking of you, he seems much delighted with all you have done and I know looks forward with the hope of some day meeting you, he is going to put a few lines in this note.

When I visit England which I shall do next summer I hope to bring him with me, for nothing would give me greater pleasure than to see you together in this hope I am

Ever yours
J. Jefferson.

Below the flowing Jefferson signature, the dramatic critic of the *New York Tribune,* appends a note in his tiny ornamental script. Their mutual friend, George Rowe, has forged this last link in the long chain from Melbourne to Dunedin, Dunedin to London, London to New York.

To Willie Winter in America he has brought from England an inscribed copy of Ben Farjeon's novel, *Jessie Trim*. It goes with Willie Winter to Louisiana; and in the evenings, when she is not listening to the darkies singing on the Bayou Têche, Maggie delights in hearing her favourite author read aloud. A letter is on its way, telling him so. Now surely when they all go to England in the summer, she will meet the dear old gentleman, and make him write something in her Autograph Album—if only he does not disappoint her, like Dickens, by dying first.

A little longer only in America; once back from Orange Island in Hohokus, there's so much to do, so many lists to write out (Josie always makes fun of the "lists of things" her methodical sister makes for every occasion); so many frocks to prepare, so many good-byes to be said, so many children to keep an eye on—for the party is to include not only Father, Toney, Aunt Nell, and herself, but Tom and Josie, and her two small half-brothers, Joe and Harry. Not Charlie, this time: Louisiana has thrown her spell about him, and he is devoting himself to planting orange-trees, and to picking orange-blossom; which a certain tender, dark-eyed Lauretta Vultee has consented to wear for him.

Time flies; they are actually in London at last! While Father arranges his season in the Fall with Mr. Chatterton, at the Princess's, the children visit that Mecca of visitors to London, Madame Tussaud's. On leaving the Napoleon Room, where they have sat for a moment in the travelling-carriage, Tom whispers furtively, "Here, Maggie, quick! hide this!" and thrusts at her a scrap of the carriage-lining. "Oh, *Tom!*" Maggie looks at him terrified, but thrilled; and when they reach home, having escaped arrest and penal servitude, she puts the illicit

treasure in an envelope, and sticks it in the precious
Autograph Album.

* * * *

29, *Hyde Park Place*
Wednesday

My dear Farjeon

I am living at the above address. My family
are with me and we will all be delighted to see you.
Won't you come and take a family dinner with us on
Sunday?

We are vulgar enough to dine at 3, and if you can
bring yourself down to the level of that hour, and
don't mind children (who don't mind anybody) do come.
Or if you have time to drop in any time between this
and Sunday I am nearly always at home.

Yours as of old
J Jefferson.

And on some summer Sunday in 1875 Ben Farjeon
makes his way to Hyde Park Place, to shake the hand he
last shook in Dunedin, and to meet Joe Jefferson's
children. Has he in mind the face of a little fair-haired
eight-year-old Tid, in a blue gingham dress and white
scalloped jacket, as he stands on the doorstep?

He is warmly welcomed, and soon at home with everybody. Shyness is as alien to Ben as to the Jeffersons. With
Joe there is no ice to break; Joe's young wife has all the
American friendliness, and Aunt Nell tickles Ben's
humour from the start. The daughters are charming,
too, lively and sweet, and the elder, Margaret, one of the
prettiest girls he has ever seen; they all express their
pleasure in his works—and Margaret is too gentle to let
him suspect the shock she gets at her first sight of him.
She sees not one grey hair in her favourite author's head;

only curly black locks, bright brown twinkling eyes, and such a mercurial manner that it is difficult to imagine Mr. Farjeon fifteen years older than herself. "I was very disappointed in you," she will tell him one day.

But Ben is not at all disappointed in Miss Margaret; as for the children, Joe, the seven-year-old is a shy, endearing child, and Harry, the younger boy, friendly and confiding. He has the face of an angel under a whitey-gold poll.

Somebody asks him, "What have you been doing?"

He answers casually, "Just been out killin' some lions."

"I should like to see them," says Ben.

"They're a long way off," says Harry, standing by his knee and looking at him with his heavenly eyes.

"Well, let's go and find them."

"You couldn't find 'um."

"Why not?"

"I buried 'um."

"We'll dig them up."

"I buried 'um too deep," says Harry earnestly.

"Some people call that lying," says Joe Jefferson aside to Ben. "*I* call it imagination."

Ben knows something about that type of imagination himself.

When he leaves, Maggie finds she has forgotten to foist her precious Album on him, and as they are on the eve of a summer in France, she must now wait till November.

Paris is heavenly! The Jeffersons overflow a flat near the Arc de Triomphe, and Joe engages a plump, flamboyant, over-dressed Madame Chose to teach them all French in three months, himself included. But his French is awful! At the end of the first month he abdicates in favour of his children. Tom proves the best at it, and

in shops, hotels, and places of entertainment, they have
to rely on that unreliable youth. At a smart restaurant,
when finger-bowls decorated with lemon-slices are
brought, he raises his to his lips and summons the waiter:
"Garcon! encore de sucre!" The children giggle; it's
no use telling Tom to behave, nothing will ever make
him.

The theatres! the Bois! the Champs Elysées! the
Tuileries! the pictures from which Joe cannot tear himself—except when he goes out all day painting himself,
spending hours in the little villages round Paris, painting
poplars and streams, châteaux and tumble-down cottages.
He learns to love above all the Barbizon painters. When
the patronne assures him he paints like Corot, he swears
she is the perfect landlady; and perhaps she is, for she
has arranged her apartment, crammed with bric-à-brac,
with a view to damage and damages—already broken
objects fall at a touch, expensive "pieces" vibrate on
shaky brackets, and the French cook ramps in with
various obsolete utensils routed out from heaven knows
where, which Madame Vert must be compensated for!
But nothing clouds the enjoyment of the Jeffersons. When
Joe pays through the nose, they take it out in laughter,
led by himself. Before they leave France, Maggie has
added to her Album a pencilled head of Christ by Gustave
Doré.

And now, in Tavistock Square, they wait anxiously for
the opening night at the Princess's. It is ten years since
Joe Jefferson took London by storm. Since then his Rip
has matured and perfected itself; he has re-written
Boucicault's version, and made important changes. What
will London think of it, and of him?

A still deeper anxiety clouds the opening night. The

little lion-slayer is lying ill, white-headed Harry, whose angelic face wins everybody. Only a short time before his illness he leaned out of a carriage he was driving in with his sister, to kiss his hand to a ruffianly-looking crossing-sweeper. "Whoever is that, Harry?" Maggie asked. "He's my great friend," the child sweetly replied. He has not waved to his friend for some days now, when the elder Jeffersons sit in their box on the night of November 1st, enduring the laughable farce (*Brother Bill and Me*) with which the performance begins at seven o'clock. At eight o'clock *Rip Van Winkle* takes the stage—and Maggie hears how an English audience can laugh and weep. And the critics? They keep her scissors and pastebrush very busy.

"The mere sight of the bright and lovable face and the mere sound of the chirp of musical laughter are enough to produce in the audience a delight strangely compounded of amusement and tenderness, and as strangely manifested in laughter and tears," says the critic of the *Athenæum*.

In the *Academy,* Frederick Wedmore writes: "In Rip a character, a career—one might almost say a life itself—is put before the spectator. On the stage of our day nothing quite so complete has been seen; nothing giving one the sense of quite so easy and unlaboured a mastery. The pathos is very gentle: the humour has something of Charles Lamb in it. . . . The voice is capable of what would be called an almost womanly tenderness, by those who have never observed that the tenderness of a man—as here to children—may be even a profounder thing. . . . And if his humour is as mild as Lamb's, his pathos is as gentle as Hans Christian Andersen's. There is the delicate suggestion—for those who can seize it—the suggestion and nothing more. When Rip goes out from the home from which his wife has at last banished him—goes out, pointing to the child in answer to his wife's reproach that he has no part in this house, 'you say I have no part in this house'—the pathos is of a simple and suggested kind, comparable only to Hans Andersen's *Story of a Mother*. And as there is nothing in literature like the one, there is little on the stage like the other."

While young Clement Scott cries out, in a long article in *Concordia*: "The effect of Mr. Jefferson's acting is almost indescribable. People go about saying it is marvellous, but they cannot tell why it is. 'What is there in this man,' they helplessly ask, 'which persuades me he is so entirely right, and so thoroughly different from the conventional acting to which I have been accustomed?' I answer, my dear sir, this is the rare art that conceals art. This is nature brought to as much perfection in its way as the actor is able to achieve. . .. Those who have not seen Mr. Jefferson can form no idea of the value of repose and the simplicity of sentiment as an important art-study. When Rip sits on the table chatting with his friends; when he emphasises his conversation with a look here and a pause there; when he chats with the children and enters into the fun of their baby enjoyment; when he discusses their lilliputian matrimonial contest, apparently with all the gravity in the world; when he listens to his enemy's villainy as betrayed by the lisping lips of his little friends—we have here innumerable instances of the actor's repose. Nothing is hurried, nothing is flurried; every look and each hesitation has its proper value. It is all so studied that it looks like nature; but it is art. The same value is gained when we notice the simplicity of the actor's pathos. It is never worked up. It comes like a rush of blood to the heart and is gone again. No pumping up of tears, no hard struggles for effect. The sentiment arrives somehow, like the dew on the grass, and fades away softly as we watch it. It is not exaggeration to say, that for picturesqueness, for truth, for expression, and for the sublimity of tenderness, the departure of Rip into the storm is perfect. It startles one with its truth, and wrings the heart with its beauty."

Such are the notices, and dozens more like them, that Maggie will paste into her Scrapbook during the coming weeks. But they must lie a little; for though Joe Jefferson will not cheat his audience (have not four generations of Jeffersons learned to act above their private tragedies?), on the fifth of November he comes to the theatre leaving at home a child he has more surely parted from than Rip from his little Meenie. The ruffianly crossing-sweeper has lost his friend; the lions are safe now.

Toney buries her baby; she must not weep too much, for in April there will be another. But little Joe is lonely, and Maggie-May, busy with balls and dressmakers and riding-school, isn't always there to play with him. However, Mr. Farjeon has some little nieces, and the Jeffersons welcome his suggestion that black-haired Dinah and Carrie should come daily to play with Joe.

They are beginning to see a good deal of B. L. Farjeon. He is a constant visitor in Tavistock Square; and Maggie at last invites him to put something in her Autograph Album. He takes it away with him, leaving her to wonder what he will write. Something personal to herself, like Mr. Winter, who composed those pretty lines? Well, no; Mr. Farjeon doesn't know her well enough for that. Perhaps he will put in something from *Blade-O'-Grass*.

The silly man puts in a poem headed "Translation from the German"—three long-lined verses about

Lilliput, source ungiven; written in Ben's beautiful clear script, and dated "London, 11th Decr. 1875," it makes a good-looking page.

No doubt Miss Jefferson, having read it through, thanks him prettily, and reads it a second time when he has gone. Goodness knows, it's impersonal enough! She would have preferred something by himself to any translation.

But "Translation from the German" looks very well on the Album-leaf. And how should Miss Jefferson know that German is a language her favourite author can neither speak, read, nor write? I rather suspect that as be traced those words, Ben Farjeon had gone out to kill some lions.

4

"MY DEAR MISS JEFFERSON"

IN 1876, things germinate. There has been some teasing tussle about the Boat Race. He writes to her on the eve, heading his letter with a pen-and-ink picture of the straining crews:

"Cambridge wins! No—Oxford wins! No—Cambridge! Oxford! Oxford! Cambridge! The boats are mixed. I don't know which is which.

———

Thursday eg.

My dear Miss Jefferson—

It did slip my memory, about the box for "Gascon." Here is one, for to-morrow evg. If you go, I dare say I should manage to pop in for an hour. I write in great haste. Kindest regards to all. Faithfully yrs

B. L. Farjeon.

No doubt Mr. Farjeon managed to pop in.

They meet at theatres, dinners, the houses of friends; particularly at Finchley, where Fred Burgess (Moore's own Burgess) entertains generously at "The Hall." Both Ben and Maggie, who have a reciprocated affection for his wife, are often all-night guests, when a big affair is afoot. At one grand-scale evening fête, when the house was filled with guests, and a stream of broughams and hansoms brought all professional London out to Finchley, into the ballroom, quacking foolishly, strutted a Brobdingnagian Goose. The plumed head and red beak topped the face of little Mr. Alias the costumier. The surprise of the dancers was nothing to the embarrassment of the bird, when he realized that this was *not* a fancy dress ball. In vain Mrs. Burgess assured Mr. Alias that it did not matter in the very least—a red-faced goose took the next hansom back to town, pursued by shouts of laughter. The only melancholy figure in these lavish parties was the host's. Late in the night, or early in the morning, Burgess would be found sunk in a chair in the conservatory, gazing gloomily at the revellers through the azaleas. "Look at 'em! look at 'em enjoying themselves!" he muttered. "None of 'em consider what it costs me! Champagne flowing like water! and nobody even drinks a glass with me."

Perhaps Maggie's only regret on such occasions is that Mr. Farjeon dances so badly, and doesn't know it. Still, when he has written his name upon her programme, she can always suggest sitting out the polka on the stairs, or, while the waltz is playing, strolling in the fairy-lamp-lit grounds. Mr. Farjeon is *not* an ideal partner on the parquet; but then, when he proposes riding with her, neither is Miss Jefferson in Rotten Row. She never *has* been confident, since Topsy.

Joe offers her proper riding-lessons, to bring the horsemanship learned in Paradise up to the elegant level of Hyde Park Dianas. So to a riding-school she goes in a fine habit; mounts her horse nervously and is put through her paces, among a bevy of young Englishwomen. Before her course of lessons is complete, the riding-master announces one day that they will jump. Maggie has never jumped in her life, and when a five-barred gate is set up on the sawdust, her heart sinks to the bottom of her riding-boots. One after another the English girls ride forward, and clear the gate with more or less success.

"Now, Miss Jefferson!"

Miss Jefferson longs to refuse the dreadful ordeal; in physical bravery she is sadly deficient. But in moral courage she is never wanting; and before those English girls she will not flinch. She sets her teeth, canters to the gate, rises, clears it, and lands successfully. Then she slips from the saddle, goes to the dressing-room, takes off her habit—and never rides again. Topsy, the spirited mare, is avenged at last.

* * * *

In April the new baby had been born at Bedford House, and in June was carried to Stratford-on-Avon, to be christened William Winter at the font in Shakespeare's church. The Theatrical Season was over, and a long holiday near Edinburgh had been planned, before Joe tried Rip on Scotch and Irish audiences. It was good-bye to London friends for several months.

Canaan Lodge was a big old rambling mansion at Morningside, standing in seven acres of walled ground; oak-tree shaded lawns, ivy-shrouded windows, and twenty old rooms, dark with antique furniture. The sunny Jeffersons loved it, if it *was* a little damp with time.

Maggie kept up a correspondence with Mrs. Burgess. A hint in a letter gave her some concern; she may have instigated, if she could not write, the resulting invitation to her author:

Canaan Lodge
Canaan Lane
Edinburg

My dear Farjeon

We hear from Finchley that you have not been very well. Now you had better start for us at once, the change of air will do you good. Bring your printing

press by all means come and do as you like. All join in
love. . . Telegraph when you start and we will meet you
at the station

As ever thine

J. Jefferson.

Ben telegraphed, was met, and spent some happy weeks
falling deep and deeper in love. Whatever Maggie's feelings were, the family behaved discreetly. I think there
wasn't much doubt in anyone's mind; but love-affairs, in
the seventies, grew to conclusions where now they leap
at them. No proposal of marriage took place to thrill that
summer romance in Morningside. The greatest thrill
Canaan Lodge provided was of another kind.

One night Ben, in his room, heard a knock on the door.
He opened it to Tom, white as a ghost, hair literally on
end, teeth chattering.

"M-Mr. Farjeon!"

"What's the matter, Tom?"

"Oh, M-Mr. Farjeon, come with me to Father! We've
found something awful!"

Up jumps Ben, prepared at least to tackle thugs and
cut-throats. "What have you found?"

"A c-c-coffin!"

It was true. Tom led Ben to a room where Joe Jefferson
was contemplating a little brand-new coffin, about two
feet in, length, placed on the table. Tom had made the
horrid discovery on the top shelf of a big dark cupboard
in Toney's room. Toney was ill, and Joe, seeing Tom's
fright, had hushed him up until the invalid slept; then
he quietly removed the upsetting object.

Canaan Lodge had been rented from a not-very-young
maiden lady. The three men held a debate behind locked
doors over the coffin. Did it conceal a scandal and a

crime? Should they inform the authorities, or act themselves? One thing was clear; the girls must not be alarmed.

Between them, they decided to make the gruesome discovery before acquainting the Coroner, and Tom was sent for a screw-driver. The three conspirators raised the coffin-lid reluctantly, and looked with startled eyes upon the little form—of the elderly maiden lady's dead pet parrot.

Their yells brought the girls running, and one more standing joke was added to the Jefferson repertory.

Ben left Morningside; Joe proceeded in due course to Ireland; but the girls returned to London in the autumn, where Asia Clarke, the tragic sister of Edwin and John Wilkes Booth, kept them under her eye. Her daughter, Dolly, was one of Maggie's chief new friends.

Asia looked after their clothes, chaperoned their dances, helped Maggie choose a lovely toilet for a fancy-dress ball —a "Boulogne Fisher-Girl," in white silk with a broad blue satin stripe, and thick silk stockings in rings of blue and white. A greater pity than ever that Ben—that Mr. Farjeon can't dance! In the ballroom, where Maggie and Willie Mathews waltz in the "American style," they are the admiration, and talk of all beholders; chaperons and chaperoned do not consider it quite *comme-il-faut* for them to dance so frequently together. Is Mr. Mathews paying Miss Jefferson attentions? No, not at all, they are merely ideal partners—and in the ballroom prefer each other openly. What *does* it matter what people say and think?

Out of the ballroom-she has her private preference.

5

"MY DEAREST MAGGIE"

JOE IS HOME FROM IRELAND. The Jeffersons re-unite in Mayo Lodge, Belsize Avenue.

Everybody is waiting. Everybody *knows*.

Into the Scrapbook, begun in Hohokus, Maggie now pastes, not only her father's notices, but laudatory notices of B. L. Farjeon; also the wrapper of his this-year's Christmas Book, *Shadows on the Snow,* re-written since the Christmas, eleven years ago, when he set it up "hurriedly" in the compositors' room of the *Otago Daily Times,* and dedicated it to their common idol, Dickens.

New Year, 1877, dawns; and *will* the stupid fellow never speak?

He does—but not to her. Circumspectly, in the ac-credited good old style, he addresses himself to Joe. As if Joe expected it of him! As if Maggie couldn't answer for herself! As if, whatever she answered, Joe wouldn't endorse! But no; Ben must go to her father, tell him he loves his Tid, and ask formal permission to propose to her. If Jefferson consents, he'll do it next day. Mr. Jeffer-son not only consents, but is delighted, though the pros-pect of leaving Maggie in England is a sad one; but there is no one he would rather leave her with than "his young friend from Dunedin." The young friend is getting horribly nervous. He begs one more favour. Will Joe prepare Maggie for the proposal?

Yes, Joe will do that too; and no doubt Maggie is

prepared with as much gentle teasing as her sensitive nature can sustain. Teased she must be, they are Jeffersons; and teasing she can take, she is one, too; but fond as she is of Ben, she is rather annoyed with him for making her feel so *foolish* next day, as all the family get out of the way, and she sits waiting in the parlour for what is coming.

The door-bell! he's in the hall! he's at the door! Oh dear! The door opens. In walks B. L. Farjeon with—a teapot.

It might have been flowers, or candy, or even, however prematurely, a ring. But a teapot! He shouldn't have tickled the Jefferson sense of humour at such a moment. It's all she can do not to laugh; it's more than she can do not to blush. He gets out his proposal; she gets out her acceptance. In a burst of joy he rushes off—and presents the teapot to Aunt Nell.

Not even *her* teapot!

* * * *

Miss Jefferson and Mr. Farjeon are engaged.

* * * *

Monday night
January 22nd 77

My dearest Maggie—

It seems to me that I do nothing but think of you, and as the best things are (said to be) wrapped in small parcels (proverb), I select the smallest sheet of paper I can find—(it is, as usual, very late with me)—to make you acquainted with the sad state of affairs. *Your* small parcel from the butter shop came safely to hand, and I hope I shall never receive any harder "pats" from you. I had a splendid letter from MacDonough this afternoon, from Rome, in reply to mine; he expresses himself as "overjoyed" at the news, and appears for a long time to have had hopes (and doubts) that it would be so. It is really most mysterious. I wrote to Tom this evening. I have had a busy day—(there are already in this short note

tea capital I's, and this last makes eleven—and enough
pairs of parentheses to set up a parenthesis shop)—and
have written just half as much of my story as I intended.
Must try to do a little tomorrow morning, before I come
to the Hall. Half-a-dozen persons have remarked to me
to-day that they have not seen much of me lately, and
I replied to them that I was "very much engaged." The
exact truth. Till tomorrow, with fond love,

Yours affectionately,
Ben L. Farjeon.

He designs her ring for her himself, and will not tell
her what it is to be. One day he slips on her finger two
turquoise hearts, surrounded by a diamond true-love-
knot. Nobody ever had so sweet a ring to precede the
one that she will wear this summer.

They are to be married in June. For their honeymoon
he will take Maggie to his beloved Switzerland, and show
her the lakes and mountains he adores. They will stay in
Paris on the way. And afterwards? Where are they going
to live? She has hopes of America; and Ben himself must
have had an idea that he might not settle down to married
life in England, for he does not take advantage of an
invitation, very much after his own heart, that was made
to him in 1877 by Lal Brough.

Committee Room
Vaudeville Theatre

Dear Farjeon,

I have been requested by a Committee
consisting of the gentlemen whose names are given below
to communicate to you the institution of a new club of
a social character for members of the dramatic, literary
artistic and liberal professions. By establishing the club
on a modest and unpretending basis, there will be no
temptation to open the door to any but approved candidates—— The subscription for the present year (for the

first hundred members) will be 3 guineas and the entrance 3 guineas. The management of the Club will be vested in the Committee so that joining members will incur no liability beyond their entrance fee and subscription——— I shall be very glad to have an early reply from you on the subject so that I may inform the Committee whether you are disposed to accept their invitation to become one of the original members.

Yours ever

Lal Brough.

COMMITTEE.

H. NEVILLE	C. WYNDHAM	H. J. BYRON
J. L. TOOLE	E. G. CUTHBERT	J. HARE
T. THORN	C. HARCOURT	H. VEZIN
D. JAMES	A. J. FLAXMAN	J. L. FILDES
H. T. PIKE	H. IRVING	AND
L. WINGFIELD	J. HOLLINGSHEAD	L. BROUGH

That Ben would have failed to become one of the original members of such a club, among such a group of friends, would have been, in normal times, unthinkable. But the time was not normal; he was courting, and preparing for a new life, perhaps for a new land; so on July 23rd, 1877, the Green Room Club was formed without Ben who, two and a half years later, was to become one of its most devoted members, and, from 1881, begin a service of twenty-one years on its committee. He explains to Lal that he is on the eve of his honeymoon and his departure from England, and begins clearing out his bachelor chambers, tearing up papers and MSS, writing new MSS for the publishers, pursuing all the lives of London at once, social, domestic, professional, in the highest spirits; pausing on March the First to take part in a Benefit Morning Performance at Drury Lane for Mr. Compton, whom illness will prevent from acting again. Ben is on the executive, helping to arrange a marvellous programme; it includes an act of *Money*, with Marie

Wilton, Ellen Terry, and Madge Robertson in the ladies' parts, Hare, Henry Neville, David James, Kendal, Bancroft, and William Farren supporting them; Mr. Henry Irving recites "The Uncle"; Joe Jefferson plays Mr. Golightly in *Lend me Five Shillings;* Mr. Phelps appears as Sir Pertinax Macsycophant; H. J. Byron, Charles Mathews, Buxton, and Johnny Toole lark through *The Critic,* with Miss Ellen Farren as Tilburina, and Willie Edouin as a Sentinel; in *Trial by Jury,* the new Dramatic Cantata, every remaining London actor or actress with a name throngs the court, where George Honey sits on the woolsack. Arthur Sullivan directs the orchestra; Mr. Clarkson is, of course, the Perruquier; and you can get into the gallery for a bob.

As Maggie claps her hands over the last delicious item, does she consider the costumes of bride and bridesmaids? Her fancy is for thick white corded silk, lovely lace, and orange blossom: blue for her bridesmaids—it is her favourite colour—their dresses to be made in Bond Street, and paid for by Father (it never occurs to Maggie that you *can* invite a girl to be your bridesmaid, and not provide her outfit, from hat to shoes). The wedding-breakfast will come, of course, from Gunter's. Only three months more—oh, she must begin making lists of things at once!

* * * *

April 17th 77
From the Palace of Buckingham

My darling Maggie—
I have had another clearing out to day of another drawer, and have found two poetical (?) pieces written between the ages of 12 and 14. One is a very ambitious attempt, entitled "Midnight Musings," denoting that even at that age, now some—never mind how

many years ago—I must have been in the habit of musing
by midnight. There are some dreadful lines in it (as
regards construction, disregard of feet, and perhaps confusion of metaphor), but I perceive some small merit in
it, my child, and I am not altogether disposed to burn it,
as you did *your* romance, by which you might have won
fame and renown. However, there is plenty of time before
you, thank heaven, and I foresee the time when we shall
be trying to cut each other out, and when publishers will
sue to Thee, and bend their proud and calculating Knees
before Thy Shrine. Two writing-tables will be required—
one for Thee and one for me. The second poetical Composition has no title, but from its tenor I must have intended to call it "The Dying Poet"—cheerful and
appropriate. I discovered also a very large sheet of paper
with two lines written on it, evidently intended as the com-
mencement of a poem on a sacred subject. They are as
follows:

> "Give me a woman in whom are combined
> Moderate Graces of beauty and mind."—

I suppose I could not get any further. Finish it for me.
I found, also, my written Introduction to "Blade-o'-
Grass." You might like to keep it, so I enclose it. . . . By
the way, how would a series of sketches do, written in
America upon American themes, as they occur to me,
after the style of Sketches by Boz?

I enclose a few stamps—Jamaica, New Zealand, and
Australia.

Your Constant Lover
Ben.

Here at last is "something from *Blade-'o-Grass*" in
her Favourite Author's exquisite tiny hand; a foolscap
sheet-and-a-half (with over a thousand words to the sheet,
clear as copper-plate). They do not go into the Autograph
Album, but are kept in the envelope as they were sent her
by her Constant Lover; and in the letter itself—did she
or he place those few flattened lilac blossoms, that time
would transform into pale pink stars? He asks her advice

about his work—how wonderful! (He is to ask it always, accept it, and act on it, or reject it—and act on it!) He speaks of writing articles in America—yes, it is settled now that, after the long honeymoon, they will return with Joe and Toney to Hohokus. His brothers are in New York. It must be her secret longing that in America will be their home.

It's getting nearer and nearer. Wedding-presents begin to arrive. Father's generosity is overwhelming. American friends write their congratulations. Little Joe rushes out by himself, and comes in bearing with great pride the loveliest thing in London that he could find for Maggie-May—a huge ivory cameo, chosen by himself, and paid for with his own shillings and sixpences. He looks at her eagerly, to see if Maggie-May loves it. How Maggie-May hugs him! But he has another surprise for her and Ben, he has written a story for them, all by himself, on a sheet of bluey foolscap, with many scratchings-out. What more appropriate wedding-gift to an author than another author's first-fruits? The lovers read the story together, suppressing their feelings under the author's shy, proud eye.

The young wanderers

~~The duel~~

They were born in India with out farther or mother. after they were ten years old they got away from India and escaped away to ~~America~~ America the war began at 1829 they went to the backwoods of America and ~~bil~~ built a log house, and as they walked ~~thr~~ on the ~~lon lonn~~ lonely path they slep on the soft green grass and the little stars and the ~~bright brite~~ bright ~~mon mon~~ moon shining ~~over~~ over then they thought of their perents, in ~~they~~ the morning when they awoke they found a man ~~lying by~~ lying dead they felt in his pockets and found a purse containing *gold* and *silver* they tooket and ~~and~~ went back to their

lonely cabin, and the girl made the beds ~~we~~ they got to bed at ten oclock they got up in the morning at nine they went to the city to by food *Henry was token ill* he ~~dide d dy~~ dide 1856 they other too went back to India they got married, and now I bring my story to ~~a close~~ an end
                    ~~I give it~~
                 I give this story to
             Maggie and Ben with love

It outlasted most of their wedding-gifts.

The date is fixed now. June the Sixth. If only Charlie could be there that day! But he is on the Bayou Têche, so far away in distance and in time; it is two years since Maggie heard the darkies singing in the Orange Grove:

> *"Git on de boat, chillun',*
> *An' we will sail away."*

She has sailed away, the child, from orange-grove to orange-blossom. Eighteen days before the wedding, Lauretta Jefferson, who was Lauretta Vultee, writes to her from the memory-haunted plantation:

May 19th 1877
Orange Island

My dear Maggie

I suppose by the time this reaches you, the wedding will be over, how I wish I could have been near you to have assisted you as you did me on my wedding day. I shall never forget your kindness, but as it is I can only send my best wishes to you and Mr. Farjeon. God bless you both, from yr. loving sister

Lauretta.

And Josie, that other, still more loving sister, that sister between whom and Maggie there is a tie beyond the common tie of sisters, will add her own significant touch to the occasion that perhaps will separate them for life. On the morning of the day when Ben will put his gold ring on Maggie's left hand, Josie will put on Tid's left wrist a silver bangle: a thick, plain, tube-like bangle, a circle, but for two knobs that don't quite meet. As Josie slips it over the little hand, she will "wish" the bangle on; and they will get a silversmith to fix it so that it can never, never come off again; and Maggie must promise to wear it as long as she lives. She promises.

(And so she did, for more than half a century, when the silver bangle turned black as ebony, and its wearer, nearly worn out, was told she must wear it no more. During twelve years that bangle had marked her pain: bright on the days she was better, black on the days she suffered most; then it grew black for ever, and was thought a danger. She told her daughter to send—once more—for a silversmith; she thought it must be forced off, as it had been forced on; and while she waited she was almost sick with a strange nervousness. But when the silversmith came he only seemed to touch the two knobs, and the bangle was in her hands instead of on her wrist. She uttered a light sigh of surprise, and fingered it with a lovely wondering smile; then she gave her sister's gift to her daughter's hands, saying: "Burn it, Nellie. Don't let anybody else touch it." That same week, she removed the gold wedding-ring from her finger and gave it to her eldest son. Ben had been dead for thirty, Josie for several years; a fortnight after the removal of the bangle, Tiddie died too.)

* * * *

The envelope is postmarked "London W C Ju 6 77"
The little note inside is unaddressed and undated.

My darling Wife—
                    The cathedral bells have just struck 12, and it is the 6th of June. May it be the harbinger of many happy years!   Ever yours, Ben.

MARRIAGE IN
THE EIGHTIES

I

HONEYMOON

"IF YOU HAD TOLD ME THAT BEFORE," she cried, "I'd never have married you!"

What was it Ben had confessed to his bride on their honeymoon? Somewhere—under the trees of the Champs Elysées, or lingering on the lovely Lake of Lucerne—he had owned to her that his Mother was one of twenty-six sisters! And Esther, his sister, had a family of eighteen! She looks at her husband in comical dismay. Oh, these prolific Farjeons! What is she in for?

Ah well! The size of her Nursery doesn't shadow her for long. She's a young bride; it's summer; Paris is so gay—and Ben is gayer. He runs out every morning to buy her roses and peaches from the Madeleine; they see in a shop an exquisite painted cup, and he has an idea! they'll buy a cup and saucer at each stopping-place, and she shall bring home a honeymoon tea-set with her. When she lifts a cup to her lips, she will sip, not merely tea, but memories of Paris, Vevey, Interlaken, and Lucerne. Sip tea, indeed! Not she; the horrid stuff! She tasted it once, and never will again. She will drink only chocolate from the silver cup from Paris, painted with birds, or the flowered and turquoise cup they found in Montreux.

Letters from Joe; he sends a card of introduction to Daubigny—will they ask his advice about lessons for Josie?—and "Uncle Bill's present to Maggie is very beautiful, just like him" (oh, what can it be? Father *might* have said!) "G. F. R., the champion butterfly, fluttered into my dressing-room last evening fresh from France. He lighted only for a moment, gave me a patronizing nod, spread his wings, and sailed away into the cool shade of the more genial Strand." Joe's business is good, and he expresses his "delight in the continued health and happiness of Ben and Maggie." They have actually "continued" to be happy now for ten full days of married life!

She has her twenty-sixth birthday in Vevey. Oh, Switzerland! Lovely Lake Leman, lovelier Lucerne! Sweet Vevey, Chamonix, mysterious Chillon! the winged boats, the sunsets on the water, the yodelling peasants, the purchases of carved things—chalets, nut-crackers, exquisite whitewood chamois hard as ivory, and ivory chamois delicate as lace, the corals, the mosaics, the coloured photographs, framed in Alpine flowers and edelweiss—Ben never stops buying! gifts for her, for the family, for friends, for occasions that may one day arise! And *oh,* the mountains! If only Ben wouldn't go up them! if only she needn't!

Ben, unaware that heights to Maggie are worse than five-barred gates, is only eager to show her everything in his enchanted land. From Lucerne they must mount to see the sun rise on the Rigi, where he once beheld "the most beautiful death" imaginable. A very old man came overnight with his two sons. At dawn, the horn summoned all travellers to the mountain-top; there the old man stood waiting between the young ones. The glory of the sun broke through the mists, mountain and sky turned gold, the old man's face was bathed in light and wonder—"Oh!" he breathed—and was dead, in his sons' arms.

Up the Rigi they go—the funicular sparing Maggie most of her qualms. She sees the sun rise—wonders—and survives. But at Interlaken Ben is equally enthusiastic about the wonderful climb up the Gemmi Pass. Maggie says nervously she cannot climb. Oh, that's all right! for ladies, there are always mules and guides; but Ben will go afoot.

They start, with two nice guides, Maggie on her mule, Ben singing beside her. Presently the path narrows, and he darts ahead, still singing. Oh horror! as they mount ever higher and higher, as the blessed valleys fall behind, and the world becomes all space and precipice, as the hours creep by, and the end, like Ben himself, is out of sight—as all she sees is a wall of rock on one hand and a fall of rock on the other—as each sharp bend of the pass swings wall and fall from right to left—sense, nerve, and power desert her. When they are half way up, she stops the mule. "I can't go on."

The guides recognize the symptoms.

"*Bien*, Madame. We will go back."

"I can't go back."

"Madame must go back or forward."

Madame refuses to do either.

The guides commune.

What's this they are proposing? One will remain with her—while the other goes down to the valley and returns with a straight-jacket! "If you do that, I'll throw myself over! "That is exactly what they are afraid of.

Ben reappears. "What's happened to you all?" His hands are full of flowers; he balances with apparent indifference on the edge of the path. Her hands and feet turn to ice-water. She can hardly chatter out an explanation.

The guides tell monsieur what the matter is. "The only way is the straight-jacket for Madame."

"I won't be put into a straight-jacket!" cries Maggie.

"All right, darling." Ben reassures her. Just listen quietly; this is what they'll do. Maggie shall open her parasol shutting out the precipice; one guide shall walk just in front of the mule, shutting out the turning-points; one guide behind, keeping her quite steady; and Ben himself will walk beside her all the rest of the way. But he'll be half over the edge! Pooh! Edges are nothing to him.

So they progress, crawlingly, for hours, it seems, Ben talking, joking, singing, doing anything he can to divert his trembling bride's attention from the chasms below them. She asks one question: "How shall we get back?" She sees the rest of her married life passed on the summit of the Gemmi. Ben tells her there is another way down, not a pass, but a gradual descent. After this, Maggie shuts her lips, looks into her parasol, and endures to the top. It did not kill her love of Switzerland; but Ben submitted her to no more mountains.

The month runs on; they end July in Paris, where Willie Winter writes that he hopes to join them for three days before he "bolts away" from his friends in London, where he has had "merry hours with the boys at the clubs," and has met "some of the kindest spirits in the world—there has been no end of dinners, no end of good feeling and mirth . . . I have met Henry Irving, and found him very cordial, bright, and interesting." He will always cherish Ben's friendship, he knows "you and Maggie must be very happy, and I think of you, and have all along so thought of you, with the tenderest goodwill and sympathy."

The honeymoon wanes; they return to the city of "the

kindest spirits in the world," rejoin Joe Jefferson in Belsize Avenue, and see his last performance at the Haymarket (Musical Director, one E. M. Lutgen); in October, they will all sail home together.

But first Ben must finish clearing out his chambers in Buckingham Street, which keeps him in London transacting various business, while Maggie stays in Finchley, at The Hall. The first excuse since they were married for an exchange of letters.

Tuesday Evg.

My darling Wife—

I couldn't for the life of me make out for a moment or two what was the matter with my shirt last night—then I unpinned your note. It was like kissing me Good Night. Your sixpence was put in the box, and I went to sleep. Your second note came this morning, and just now your lines written in the train. Perhaps you would like to know how I have passed the day. It has been a busy one. Breakfast was over *before* 10 o'clock. Then to the Club—and the tailors—and Tinsley's—and into the city about some bothering business. Back again into Chambers,—and thence to Wardour Street to buy the chairs for your papa. I told him I should make a commission out of them—something off the price he was going to pay—and I did so. The box benefits by it. Then I went into *every shop in Wardour Street* to find the Venetian Pitcher for Mr. Clarke Davies. Tell Toney this. At length I came to the shop—of course the last one—where they remembered it. It was sold, however. I walked home, and a minute afterwards Mr. Manchester popped in. We had a chat, and when he was gone I commenced my next chapter, and having written about forty lines, sat down to scribble this letter to my dear Girl. When this is finished I shall post it, and go to the little French place for dinner—and return home to work—to finish the Side I hope—Now, my dear, if you want to stop another day, do so; I am used to getting along by myself you know, and though I miss you, I shall be glad to know that you are enjoying yourself and giving pleasure to others. My love to all and every one. For ever yours, my dear wife,

Ben.

While they are preparing bag and baggage, friends call to say farewell; among them, one of the oldest in years, and dearest in affection, the dramatic critic of the *Daily Telegraph,* the writer of Old Drury's pantomimes. Gentle Edward Blanchard is, besides, an enthusiastic astronomer. On that October evening, when he takes his leave of them, he is presented with Maggie's Album, and writes an impromptu fitting to the moment:

EUROPEAN AND AMERICAN GRAND JUNCTION
TRAINS OF THOUGHT ACROSS THE ATLANTIC
EVERY HOUR

No wonder in this railway Age,
   Of which we are always hearing,
To find across an Album page
   Fresh lines are still appearing.
Consider mine a Pleasure Line—
   Description brief but graphic—
Projected with a great incline
   To open Friendship's traffic.
To keep a Station clear for us,
   Be Memory's special function,
And out of sight the Terminus
   To Heart and Hand's "Grand Junction."

He subscribes his name in his clear, but already slightly shaky hand, and dates it

"In the Twilight"
of
Monday October 15th
1877

No doubt as he hands back the book they all wonder whether those "Trains of Thought Across the Atlantic" will be their main lines of communication henceforth. Ben, after many years, will embrace his brother Israel in the city his Mother died in—New York, where Dinah Farjeon had not "the least doubt" her beloved Benjamin would do well. It was a hope which Maggie must have carried across the Atlantic with her. Along with that hope she carried yet another.

Ned Blanchard is saying: "If you are still in New Jersey in the Spring, remember to look out for a most interesting event. The Transit of Mercury occurs on the Sixth of May."

FAREWELL, AMERICA

S HE IS NOT yet so bashful of her condition as to avoid company. She does not hide herself entirely in the low-ceilinged farm-rooms of Hohokus; she emerges sometimes through the evergreen screen to meet in New York Ben's brother Israel, whom she quickly loves; and Bessie, his wife, and some of the young family that made their Grandma write to Uncle Ben in Dunedin: "I like a quiet life, God bless the children." In December she accompanies Ben to Philadelphia, by invitation of Clarke Davis, where they attend a breakfast party to J. S. Clarke; in the evening Ben goes to a Club Reception. If only American hospitality, and American publishers, and family ties that hold them on both sides, will induce him to settle in New York or New Jersey!

After Christmas, Joe goes South as usual, to Charlie and Lauretta in Louisiana. Maggie remains quietly in Hohokus, with Josie, Grandpa Lockyer, and Ben, who travels frequently to New York on business—attempts to arrange for plays, lectures, publications. She begins to realize that when work is not fixed up, her favourite author is worried by his responsibilities. No plans of a home in America are made, while she sits sewing in Hohokus with Josie, "making lists" of things the baby will need; and, when unsuspecting friends drop in, retiring in confusion if they are male and single. One day Mrs. Farjeon is caught by two young men who were Miss

Jefferson's admirers. Before she can escape, they are in the parlor. Maggie, much flustered, snatches a song-sheet from a pile of music, and holds it upright in her lap during the visit. She sees that Josie is in fits of laughter, and when the visitors depart, rounds on her sister. "What were you laughing at?" Josie points to the song, and Maggie finds that the shield she has presented to the young men's eyes, flaunts the title: "In Mother's Nest."

One wintry day she goes driving with Grandpa Lockyer, who is especially tender of his Tid; on the return, she alights too soon from the high buggy, the horse shies, and she slips. Grandpa Lockyer catches her in his arms, and bears her into the house, blaming himself; for a day or so the Nursery is endangered—but, delicate though her condition is, she weathers the fright she has given them all.

She has still seen nothing of Charlie, who writes to her when Joe leaves the Plantation.

> *Orange Island*
> *March 20th* 1878
Dear Maggie,
> Just 27 years old today, how the time passes on, and how old I will look to you when you see me; which I hope will be soon as you don't know how much I want to kiss your dear face.
> I think Papa improved in health when he was here, as he seemed in such good spirits and was so good to all of us, and in fact was more like a young man than a man of 50—How Tom has improved boath in looks and manners; why he is the Gentleman of the family. He came up to see me for a week and I went down to New Orleans with him and was pleased to see that he was loved by his company and in fact everyone. I saw him *"play act"* out on the *Theatre* & he is a stunner he has got it in him, the blood of the Jeffersons will tell no matter when, or in what capacity they are engaged.

Dear Maggie I am now pushing my men to their utmost, as in the case of the place paying I stop here & if it does not I will then return to play acting—but there is no fear this year of it's not paying as I have everything in my favour.

Give my kind love to Ben and tell him he owes me one. All send love and kisses.

God Bless you all your loving Brother   Charlie.

Was this the orange-season in which Charlie, after deducting expenses, received from St. Louis, for a large shipment of fruit, three two-cent postage stamps? In time he will be obliged to combine Theatrical Management with orange-growing, but he always prefers that fragrant existence to the smell of naphtha, and leaves Tom to carry on the "play-acting out on the Theatre" (some childish phrase of his and Tid's of old?) While Tom has improved in looks, it doesn't appear that Charlie has in spelling.

How she would love to run down to the Plantation, be kissed by Charlie, kiss Lauretta's babies, and hear the singing on the Bayou Têche!

A day or so later Uncle Bill Warren writes from Boston to thank her for her "pretty present of the old tobacco-box and the nutcrackers from Interlacken. . . . After the usual supper in the old Kitchen, and the consequent chat, I find it is 1.30 A.M. on reaching my room to scribble this, though I am not on the stairs very long, for practice makes perfect, and I have been climbing up here for many years before you were born. Some people live on 5th Avenue, and others on 4th floors."

How she would love to sup again in Bulfinch Place in the grand old kitchen, with Uncle Bill at the table-head concealed by his scarlet mountain; and, while he served lobsters liberally, see it sink slowly "as if it were going through the stage in pantomime, revealing as it descended the fine face of the genius at the feast." What jests! what laughter! what flowing of wine and ale! in Miss Fisher's Kitchen in the city where, as in London, one met "the kindest spirits in the world." Perhaps, as she sits and sews, she wonders whether in Boston, more quiet, more "English" than most, her restless author might find a congenial life.

But two days later a letter from New York shows Ben more unsettled than ever.

March 28th, 1878

My darling Wife—

. . . I have felt very strange all to-day, and coming home (a mis-applied word in this instance) now at 10 o'clock after hearing Mr. de Cordova lecture, the feeling is intensified. I shall not repine, however, for I look forward to the time when we shall be in a proper home of our own. . . . The enclosed from Maggie Mitchell explains itself. I replied, saying the time wd suit me; but this evening a special messenger brought me a line from Mr. Puddock, asking me to make the appointment for Friday instead of Thursday. So it remains.

I received a letter also from Mr. Clark Bell. He does not explain his business, but wishes to see me. It seems he called on Sunday, a few minutes after we left, and asked that a message and his card should be given to me. Of course I received neither. It is this sort of thing that makes me nervous—it is impossible for me to continue to live in this way. He made an appointment with me for last night—which I could not keep, as I was at Hohokus.

Mr. Habberton knocked at my door at 1 o'clock, and he and Dampier stopped with me, chatting, until past three. He tells me he has received, in royalties, over 10,000 dollars from his publishers for 'Helen's Babies.' It sounds almost incredible to me. He wants me to come and see him one day next week, and I have half promised.

I am in hopes of receiving good news from you to-morrow. Good night, my darling. God bless you. With fond and unchanging love believe me Ever yours,

Ben.

April is here. They say the first baby sometimes comes before his time. Maggie is feeling ill, and hopes she won't be kept waiting. Perhaps before April's out—? But April passes, May dawns. May? What were those words, spoken seven months ago in the London twilight? "If you are still in New Jersey on the Sixth of May, remember to look out for a most interesting event——"

On May the Sixth Harry Farjeon was born, during the Transit of Mercury.

* * * *

Greatly excited, "We'll call him Mercury!" cries Ben.

"We'll do nothing of the kind!" cries Maggie, clasping the funny mite she is too ill to nurse.

It's a near thing; but she wins her way when she says she wants him to be called Harry, after the unforgotten little lion-slayer.

Teasing Josie goes about saying, "Maggie has started making lists of her children!"

* * * *

They will return to England. She knew they must. Ben couldn't really settle anywhere else. As soon as she's better they'll sail. But she doesn't get better quickly, the fragile creature, who weighed 96 pounds on her wedding-day—one of whose lungs, like Joseph Jefferson's, is suspect.

Ben rushes about New York, buying and buying! Big

furniture—a walnut suite—the bedstead is six-foot wide!
Tallboy and dressing-table to match. An American rocker
for Maggie. Then two more. Vast orders of fine silver-
plate, from Israel—three or four dozen of every table
implement, except, by some mercy, soup-ladles—he must
be spending hundreds of pounds, thousands of dollars!
They'll want a mansion in London to house them all.

But they must see June out before they sail. Little
Joe has his name printed ("Joseph Jefferson Jr.") in real
print on the programme of the "Valley School Hohokus"
entertainment, on June 28th. Maggie-May *must* be there
to hear him recite "Cupid and the Roses." His first star
piece of "play-acting." Think of it! Joseph Jefferson the
Fourth!

And they must see Maggie's birthday out, as well; her
25th, on the Glorious Fourth of July. How time flies! A
year ago she was a bride of a month in Vevey—now she's
a married woman of a year's standing, with a baby.

Independence Day celebrations come and go. Berths
are taken for later in the month, on "S.S. *Italy*." They
will be home in August. She must not think of Hohokus
as home any more.

Farewell America.

3

"No. 12"

SHE is so ill on the ship. She cries when she tries to bath the baby. A motherly Stewardess looks after her and Harry. Partings lie heavy on her. It is not, for her, a happy voyage home.

In England, with nowhere immediate to go, she and her baby are welcomed by the hospitable Burgesses. She remains for some time in Finchley, while Ben rakes London for a suitable place to live in.

She makes a tiny velvet suit for Harry, braids it with gold, and concocts a little peaked hat which makes the miserable mite look like a monkey on a hurdy-gurdy. For the moment she is only filling in time.

One day Ben turns up jubilant. "What do you think? I've taken a place to live in!" She envisages some pleasant green-shaded house in Belsize Avenue. Where is it?

"My old Chambers in Buckingham Street!" Maggie stares in dismay. "I found I was able to take them on, with the top storey added. There'll be plenty of room for us all on the two floors."

Yes—perhaps. But those inconvenient quarters, with all those stairs, and stale town air for Harry, and no real nursery apart from their living-rooms—and Ben so nervy always when at work. *Chambers!* No garden. It isn't like home, at all.

But there's no help for it. She sheds and wipes some

tears; and, bitterly disappointed, sets about arranging her first establishment.

The enormous furniture from New York is got up somehow. There is no wardrobe; so Ben calls in a working carpenter, and in a fit of enthusiasm has all sorts of things made on the premises. A tall two-divisional wardrobe is contrived in yellow wood, with four sunk panels. The working carpenter stands back, head on one side.

"Shall I paint them for you, sir? They'd look nice with a gold ground, with birds on."

By Jove! what luck to have found an artist as well as a carpenter! By all means go ahead. An astonishing quartette of panels is produced, very gold backgrounds, very bright blue birds, perched upon flowery twigs, as good as Christmas cards. Ben is delighted. (Maggie soon discovers his mixture of good and bad taste; in words he can stand nothing that is trash—but when it comes to colour, it's a toss-up.) Other big objects are crowded into the rooms—there is Ben's double-length writing-table; there is the pair of enormous Chinese vases which Esther gave them for a wedding-present—and which, in fact, Ben bought for her to give them, knowing she was too poor to afford a gift. There were the three American rocking-chairs. Maggie began house-keeping in that excess of "things" of which she was never to be free while Ben had money in his pocket, and catalogues came through the letter-box. Books—toys—curios—pictures —china—food—flowers—stationery—gloves—wherever there were wholesale markets of *anything*, Ben would bid in lots, would bid in *lots* of lots, "because they were so cheap!" It was not always easy to find gloves for Maggie's little hands. What a chance, then, when a wholesale draper's was sold up, to buy in

96 pairs, size 5½! Black and white and fawn and green
and pink gloves, long evening gloves and wrist-length,
kid and suède gloves! What a chance, when a wholesale stationers' was sold up, to lay in reams of typing
and carbon paper in packets by the gross! Paper of
all sizes and colours; and pens and pencils, india-
rubbers, note-books, copy-books, india-rubber rings and
clips—enough to fit out a small retail shop, and all of
them so useful to a writer. "Why did you do it?" she
cries. "They were so cheap!" And pictures! Paintings
and lithographs (some of them ghastly), engravings and
etchings (some of them quite good!), two or three dozen
framed watercolours, rather effective and extremely ugly,
by a French caricaturist; four or five dozen Bartolozzi
prints. And books—But no, one can't begin to think
about the books. A room "out," in 17 Buckingham St.,
took some of the overflow.

To help her, she had old Mrs. Chizlett, who used to
do for Ben as a bachelor; and of course there must be a
nurse for Harry. Julia was found.

* * * *

It was no easy start for delicate, undomesticated Maggie.
She hated housekeeping; she disliked food; the tiny
hands that played on the guitar attempted nothing more
solid than Oyster Soup and Floating Island. But she had,
besides sweet temper, so much good sense; and Ben,
besides impulses, so many sympathies; and both of them
were loved by so many jolly, clever, fascinating people,
who streamed up and down the staircase of Buckingham
Street—that, in spite of the muddle, the illness, and the
attempts to keep things quiet when Ben was writing, life
was a strangely gay and exciting affair. Once more it was

"Mrs. Chizlett! Mr. and Mrs. Barnes and Mr. and Mrs. Mortimer to supper—run out for four more chops!"—or, as the Edouins and the Huys appeared: "Seven dozen oysters, Mrs. Chizlett!"—then several dozen more! "G. F. R. the Champion Butterfly" turns up, with a bunch of the boys at his heels. No. 12 Buckingham Street was a house of call for the whole Strand.

Or else they went up other people's staircases.

"Maggie in wonderful form to-night, sang and played, was very gay and witty, enchanted everybody as usual," ran an entry in one of Ben's note-books. There were homely evenings at the Nicholas-Chevaliers', parties full of good talk at the Blanchards', and livelier gatherings when brilliant, devil-may-care "Georgie" Drew and her husband, the attractive Maurice Barrymore, happened to be in London. Georgie, whose wonderful Mother had acted with Maggie's wonderful Father; Georgie who had been one of Maggie's school-friends *not* debarred from the little Maynards' candy and ice-cream in the old Convent days; Georgie who defied conventions, and clung to her religion. Early one Sunday morning, leaving the house, she met Maurice on the door-step—coming home. "Hello, Georgie! where are you going to?" "I'm going to Mass," she flashed, "you can go to Hell!" The Barrymore's own parties ended after the milk. Ben never allowed Maggie to see them out; things got rather more larky than he cared about in the small hours, and Maggie's health justified early departure—at three a.m. or so. "How late did the party go on, Georgie?" asked Maggie, one following day. "Oh," Georgie yawned, "some of 'em went away about seven o'clock, and the rest stayed all night!" When she was acting in London, they frequented each other's homes; but a cable might haul Georgie away in a jiffy. Maggie saw one arrive from an important manager, offering an engagement: "State Terms." Georgie cabled twice her usual salary. "Terms Impossible," cabled the manager. "Oh," cabled Georgie Barrymore.

Or if it wasn't parties, it was theatres; they were guests at all the First Nights her health allowed, and at the behind-the-scenes receptions afterwards. ("Was it all right, Mrs. Farjeon?" asks Henry Irving, as they shake hands; "what does *he* think about it?" Ben's opinion was one of those first sought.)

Or there were private theatricals at the Laboucheres; or wildly-foolish garden-parties at Toole's, where tomatoes grew on all the rose-bushes, and the vines drooped with bunches of turnips and carrots—the host had expended hours on turning his garden into a bower of nonsense. When Toole heard a new arrival engaged in a point of difference with his cabby, he rushed out and dragged in both guest and Jehu. He conducted the bewildered cabman round the garden, loaded him with cucumbers off the gooseberry bushes and onions off the cherry-trees, and toasted him in champagne. The guests hilariously followed suit. The cabby was given a glass of fizz and a fistful of silver; then Johnny led him away amid howls of laughter. "Don't take any notice of 'em," whispered Toole; "they're none of 'em in their right minds! To tell you the truth, this is a lunatic asylum!" "That's all right, Mr. Toole," said the grinning cabby, and drove off, leaving his host gibbering at the gate.

And when Maggie's health demanded a respite from entertaining and being entertained, there were always the Burgesses at Finchley to go to.

* * *

She depended greatly on letters from America, and kept in faithful touch with friends and family. No birthday remained unmarked by Maggie in England, no letter long unanswered. Joe Jefferson, that bad correspondent, became a good one for his daughter's sake. She replied to him, and to all others, promptly, in the least expressive letters ever written—brief strings of facts, undescriptive, undemonstrative, but never-failing. She kept a small *Walker's Dictionary* in her Davenport, to help her with the spelling. Breaths of home were brought her by every American company that acted in London; while with her countrymen, resident in London, she could still share something of a life that was past.

Asia Booth: Mrs. John Sleeper Clarke: Edwin's sister, unmentionable John Wilkes' sister: the mother of Dolly, Maggie's prettiest bridesmaid: is dying. She has known Maggie from a little girl; Ben of all later friends is the most trusted. She sends for him. She has something important to confide to him. He goes to her at once.

Her secret is a Memoir she has written of her brother—the brother she loved, the brother the world execrated. After the shocking act, Edwin commanded every sign of John Wilkes to be expunged from the family records; every portrait destroyed, every letter, every mention of his name. It must not even be spoken. Asia's husband felt as Edwin did. But Asia adored the fanatic; she shrank from what he had done, but not from him; she understood that dark and fatalistic strain in his nature which, she averred, had been played on by others who remained unimplicated; and she had written an account of John Wilkes which, though it might not be publishable for years (since any tender word of him must long be rejected), she hoped might see the light one day, and give his name a less hated place in history. Only—if Clarke or Edwin, if either husband or brother, should discover it, they would destroy that Memoir as soon as she was dead. She gave it into B. L. Farjeon's hands, to do anything he pleased with except destroy it. Ben carried away from her death-bed a small thick leather book, fastened with a lock, and none of her family knew of its existence.

Asia died. Another link with Maggie's American girl-hood snapped—but left in her keeping a link with American history.

4

LITTLE CHARLIE

HER SECOND ORDEAL IS BEFORE HER, and her health is precarious; that treacherous lung is giving the doctors and Ben intense anxiety. The next baby will not be born in the sweet country air of Hohokus, with Aunt Nell and her genius for nursing, to see that nothing goes wrong. High up above the traffic of the Strand and the Thames she will be born—for Maggie hopes that this time it will be a daughter.

Mrs. Whittaker, a little thin wizened midwife, is engaged to attend to her; and Mrs. Chizlett (who tells tea-leaf fortunes in the old blue willow-pattern cup and saucer she herself has added to Maggie's honeymoon tea-set), will, as usual, attend to Ben.

On March the twentieth, 1880, "Little Charlie Farjeon" is born. So Maggie writes him down in the small squat *Shakespeare Birthday Book* where all loved birthdays are recorded and remembered. (Better not delay recording this one.)

In April, Joe Jefferson writes from Scranton, Pa.:

"Your welcome letter announcing that Maggie had passed safely through her trouble gave us all great pleasure. It seems strange to me to think of Maggie as a Mother tho' I saw her first boy. She of all my children was so timid of pain, and scenes of distress, in others that I wonder at her braving her own shock with fortitude. I have known her to count the days approaching some appointed time for execution of a criminal, and when the hour arrived a gloom would settle on her that was quite distressing to see. Give her and the children a kiss for me and my love, God bless them."

She has come safely through; but not the baby. He lived for sixteen months, with an affected lung. During the whole of his life, he had to have the pus drawn off from it; and lay, said Mama and Papa, without a murmur, white and heavenly, in his cradle. He never seemed quite mortal from the first. Mama was ill, too; and soon was dismayed to realize that not a year would elapse between the coming of her second child and her third.

"I was disgusted with you for being so quick," she laughed, years afterwards to the third child. "The only thing that saved your face was that you were a girl."

Little Charlie was not eleven months old when the girl, a Sunday-child, arrived on February 13th, 1881. One day later, and she would have been called Valentine; as it was, she was named for Aunt Nell Symons. She was registered, not "Ellen," but "Eleanor," and during her childhood never called anything but Nellie, Nelly, or Nell. Almost as soon as she appeared in the flesh, she appeared in print.

From the *London Figaro*
"I have received from Mr. B. L. Farjeon, the popular novelist, an invitation couched in the following terms:—

COMPLIMENTARY
The presence of Count and Countess
ALMAVIVA is invited at the
UNDRESS REHEARSAL
of an entirely new and original uproar, entitled
OUR DAUGHTER,
By Mr. B. L. Farjeon.
Music by Miss Nelly Farjeon.

Dramatis Personæ.

MOTHER. . . . . Mrs. B. L. Farjeon

(Her third and *last* appearance in that character.†)

DAUGHTER (with familiar cries). . . .

Miss Nelly Farjeon

(Her first appearance in public).

*

ROSINA and myself have great pleasure in accepting Mr. Farjeon's invitation, though I am not particularly fond of music, myself. I congratulate Mr Farjeon upon the completion of his new work, in which, I understand, he has had the valuable co-operation of the charming and amiable lady who bears his name.

*

† *Never prophesy unless you know.*

———————

The daughter played her part so ardently, and in early life uttered her "Familiar Cries" so incessantly, that a year later Ben risked a further prophecy, this time in verse:

> "*Imperious Babe! that yet can scarcely speak,*
> *Doth rival Chanticleer in piercing shriek.*
> *May not those lungs which now such yells emit*
> *One day enthral a world with sense and wit?*"

* * * *

I have said I was registered as Eleanor, but I was never christened; none of us were. Mama, in spite of her nightly prayers "to be on the safe side," had no religious conviction; Papa was a devout believer without a creed. Though he was never seen in Synagogue, he remained a Jew by instinct, as well as by race; the Jews were proud of and claimed him, and in their organs condemned his marriage to one who was not a Jewess. But though this debarred him from giving his children his race, he gave them the rich inheritance of his blood. Their "Christian" mother taught them her artless prayers; he told them tales from the Old Testament; and that was all their home-religion amounted to.

Well might Mr. B. L. Farjeon's latest work be described as "a New and Original Uproar." Harry was a good child, Charlie a heavenly one; Nellie was a passionate little screamer, a really "bad" baby, though she sat laughing and crowing on little Charlie's cot, the day he died.

Let me tell out the last of that wistful life. He died in the summer after I was born. My Father wrote, in his memory, *A Christmas Angel,*

To
MARGARET
My Beloved Wife
I Dedicate This Story,
The Inspiration of which sprang from the
Deepest sorrow of our life.

The story, illustrated by Gordon Browne (the son of Dickens' *Phiz*), was a very tender, very touching imagining of what little Charlie's life might have been, had he lived to be a young man. It opens with his death: "In the grey light of morning we lost a little child." It speaks of my Mother's thought of the time when death would re-unite her with Charlie, of the flowers gathered for him by three-years-old Harry, who had been sent to Finchley "so that he might be out of the way of death"; and tells how my Mother slept at last, from fatigue, with her "girl-baby" in her arms. That intimate tale was one which, written above all for Maggie's comfort, was scarcely to be sold, or seen, soon after publication.

Fifty-two years after Charlie's death, thirty years after my Father's, and less than a month before my Mother's, which she and we were waiting and praying for (not Grandfather, or anyone, could have foreseen the fortitude with which she, "so timid of pain," had endured her twelve-years' agony), an accident led me to go through a Hampstead street I never have occasion to pass through. In the window of a second-hand bookshop I saw a book I had long been looking for. While the shop-keeper took it out of the window I examined his shelves. To my surprise, I saw there a copy of *A Christmas Angel*. I took it down, opened it, and a note from my Father fell out into my hands, fresh as the day it was written, in the year of the publication of the tale. I carried it home to my Mother; she looked at it, and at that half-a-century-old, fresh letter of my Father's, with her unforgettable smile. Once during the following week I heard her murmur, "I am so glad about that book." This was the real end of Little Charlie's tale.

5

"FAIRHAVEN"

T HE NURSERY has sunk back again to two. She cossets and plays with her children; she makes a minute Swiss dress for Nellie, and has her taken in it when she is little older than Harry was, in his velvet monkey-suit. Nellie looks-just as mournful as Harry did. She stands Nellie on the table, holds her by the out-stretched finger-tips, and says, "Be a fairy!"

"Ta-ra!" chants Nellie, before she can speak, and sticks one bare foot as high as she can in the air. She *will* not keep shoes on those doll-sized feet of hers. "Let me tiss her peet! Let me tiss her peet!" cries little Lionel Barrymore, brought by Georgie to see Áunt Maggie; and fiercely grabs the shoeless baby's toes.

Still before she can speak, Mama sings with her the Turkey-and-Lamb Duet from *La Mascotte*.

"Glou-glou-glou!" sings Mama.

"*Baa!*" from Nellie, in perfect tune, a fifth below the last note.

"Glou-glou-glou!"

"*Baa!*" (a third below).

"Glou-glou-glou-glou-glou-glou!   Glou-glou-glou——"

"BAA!" On Mama's own note; she never misses the right note to complete the phrase, and is always in per-fect tune. Old Mr. de Cordova hears this performance, and exclaims, "Shut that child's mouth! Don't let her sing another note before she's sixteen! She'll be a second Patti!"

* * * *

Next year the Nursery will be three again.

No more children must be born in Buckingham Street. A little house, a garden, a new nurse, she is determined on. Harry had been too much confined upstairs with Julia. They thought that all was well. Whenever he climbed downstairs to them, he came down singing *The Old Arm-Chair:*

> "*How vey tittered! how vey roared!*"

his quavering little voice chanted all the way.

"How happy the child sounds!" smiled Ben and Maggie; and when the happy child ran in crying, "I-do-love-Julia-I-do!" they smiled again.

One night when Julia was out, and Mama was giving Harry his bath, she noticed his little skinny arm was black and blue.

"Why, Harry, what's this?"

The child looked at her with his dark solemn eyes. "Julia did it."

Mama feels sick. "When did she do it, Harry?"

"When I come downstairs. Julia says sing-ve-ol'-Armchair an' pinches me *ee-eee!*" The little features are suddenly contorted.

"Harry," asks Mama," who tells you to say I-do-love-Julia?"

"Julia does," says Harry.

Julia has also told him—it is Harry's earliest recollection—that there is a tiger under his bed at night.

What happens to Julia when she comes in, I can guess.

Knowing Mama, I am certain she never touches Harry again; knowing Papa, I wonder she lives to be sent packing next day.

* * * *

They too will go packing from 12 Buckingham Street. A little house is found in Adelaide Road—No. 13, at the Chalk Farm end of things. They call it "Fairhaven," the name of the house in *Golden Grain.* (In this sequel to *Blade-o'-Grass* figures a wonderful home in the country for neglected children—and young Mrs. Frank Smith, in America, absorbs the sequel as once she absorbed *Blade-o'-Grass.*) In "Fairhaven" Joe Jefferson Farjeon is born, on June the fourth, 1883.

Fanny Dodd, dear rosy, buxom little Fanny, some-times helped by her young sister Janey, takes charge of Harry, Nellie, and Joe; a wonderful improvement upon Julia. She has a sense of fun which endears her at once to Maggie; mistress and maid become so confidential, so closely attached, that Mama always said she never *had* a maid with whom she shared things as she did with Fanny, or whom she loved so much. Fanny was a main-stay in all the difficulties of her early married life, more like a youthful sister than a servant; only one other was to equal her in Maggie's heart, but that was in the last four years of her life, when Bertha, like a second daughter, was to be her mainstay through more painful difficulties. She enjoyed, first and last, the gift of both girls to bubble into laughter over anything funny. But Fanny could be properly firm when necessary.

One day she caught Nellie by the baby's cradle con-tentedly sucking Joe's bottle for him, as selflessly as Tom had once sucked Josie's oranges. Fanny took to watching through the clear stars in the ground-glass panes of the breakfast-room door, and discovered that Nellie made a practice of sparing her little brother his labours. One morning the kind sister found Joe's lovely bottle full of warm sweet milk lying on a chair near the cradle, well out of the baby's reach, well within hers. A moment later she had dropped the bottle and crawled under the table, where she sat cramming her tiny fists in her mouth, squeezing tears of silent agony out of her eyes. Fanny came in, said nothing, removed the bottle, and washed a trace of cayenne pepper from the rubber teat. "I wasn't going to let you drink Joe's milk," she told "little Nelly" fifty years after.

Well, anyhow, I could chew my rabbit's cabbage-leaves. I liked taking the fresh green leaves to the hutch every morning, and feeling the pull of the rabbit's teeth as I held it through the bars; I liked chewing secretly the juicy stem myself; I liked the smell of the hutch. Mine was a dun-coloured lop-eared rabbit, Harry's a white one. They were among the ravishing changes in life brought about by the removal from the Strand.

The friends who used to tumble up and down the staircase at all hours of the day and night, now come instead—but less confusingly—to the little house near Chalk Farm, with a garden which Ben begins to stock with roses and chickens, in the intervals of clearing his old Chambers of all the lumber he can bring himself to part with.

6

MY FATHER'S DIARY
A fragment: 1884

1st January. Attended meeting of Green Room Committee—business as to new premises. Chop at the Club. Bancroft, Fernandez, Righton, and others there. Chat with Charles Dickens about version of "Old Curiosity Shop" for Lotta. . . . Paid subscription to Green Room. . . . . Prepared Magic lantern for Children's party tomorrow. Bed 1.30.

   Dr. Saul called to see Maggie.

2nd January. The Children's Party a great success, though some of the little ones could not come. There were quite enough, however, little people and big—Aunt Louie —little Marie Barnes—Aunt Ellen—Minnie and her wonderfully fat baby—Lily and Minnie Mortimer—Mr. and Mrs. Warren Edwards and Elsie—and our own family circle, comprised the party. The Magic Lantern was a triumph, the most popular feature being the Story of Cock Robin. Then the Xmas tree was stripped, and the youngsters went home rejoicing. Mrs. Huy stopped till the last—and when she went, Maggie and I had another long chat. I stopped up till 3 in the morning, getting my magic lantern slides in order and finishing up the Xmas tree, carrying it out of the house, so Harry and Nelly should not see it when they came down in the morning. Our Xmas and New Year time has been very enjoyable.

3rd January. Letter from Jim Duff, about obtaining Gilbert and Sullivan's new piece and also "Falka" for America,—am afraid I can't manage it, as J. D. makes no definite offer. Shall go to-morrow to see D'Oyley Carte and Farnie. . . . Very tired after party. . . . Returned magic lantern slides I borrowed (or rather that Warren Edwards borrowed for me) of Mr. Kemp, at Sharland's Thavies Inn. Gave Mr. Kemp a copy of my "Little Make-Believe" in acknowledgment of the compliment.

4th January. Dr. Saul called, and lanced Joe's gums. Says that Maggie is a little better. Called to see D'Oyley Carte and Farnie—they were not in.

Invitation from Mrs. E. L. Blanchard to a dance next Friday. Do not think Maggie will be able to go.

Wrote to D'Oyley Carte and Alexander Henderson with reference to "Princess Ida" and "Falka" for Jim Duff.

Wrote to Tillotson (post-card) about not receiving proofs.

5th January. Wrote to Jim Duff on his business. Sent cheque for rent £16. 5. o—Also cheque for rooms in Buckingham St. £5. 4. o—Also cheque for Poor Rate etc. £5. 3. 6.

Received reply from D'Oyley Carte, saying that all arrangements for America are already made for Gilbert's new Comic Opera, "Princess Ida."

Recd letter from F. W. Robinson (in reply to one of mine congratulating him upon the First No. of "Home Chimes"), and asking me to give him a short sketch or story for the paper. Shall do so.

Gave the children half-an-hour with the musical

box. Harry is delighted with the new book I bought for him. He is going to be passionately fond of reading.

7th January. Posted the 23rd weekly instalment of my "Sacred Nugget"—nearly 7000 words. Went to Drury Lane Pantomime, and afterwards, at midnight, was present at the cutting of the Baddeley Cake on the stage. Between two and three hundred persons invited—saw a great many friends, and did not get home till late in the morning.

8th January. A busy day at the rooms 17 Buckingham Street, preparing to clear away superfluous books and pictures. Warren Edwards greatly assisted me, and purchased between £9 and £10 worth of pictures and ornaments. Received tickets for Opera Comique, and gave them to Warren Edwards, Major Elliott, and Esther. Tickets also for Lotta's first night here (next Saturday) in Little Nell and the Marchioness.

9th January. Wrote a number of letters—accepted invitation to dine with "Aunt Ellen" and "Uncle Joe" on Sunday next. Posted letter to J. C. Duff with reference to "Princess Ida" and "Falka." Went to Buckingham Street rooms, and "cleared up" for two or three hours. Bought some flowers.

11th January. Dr. Saul called in my absence. Said that Maggie was not well enough to go to the first night of Lotta's "Little Nell" and "Marchioness." Wrote to Major Elliott, inviting him to accompany me.—Worked at the rooms, clearing up. Gave Miss Elliott a copy of Shakspeare. A pleasant hour with the children. Received letter from Henderson with reference to "Falka," the

American right of which is sold. Wrote to Jim Duff to that effect—which closes the business upon which he communicated with me.—Warren Edwards came to the rooms in Buckingham Street, and we hung up some pictures for sale.

12th January. Went to the Opera Comique to see the Younger Charles Dickens's version of "The Old Curiosity Shop." Although very well received, I do not think Lotta will be a success in the dual parts. Utterly out of place for the Marchioness to sing a medley of operatic songs and dance a variety of dances. C. D. however very pleased. I should not be, in his place.—Received letter (to Maggie) from Mary Anderson, with 3 portraits of her. She is very lovely. Recd. also more New Year's Cards from America. —Am not at all well. Want change. Have not had it now for four years and feel the need of it. Should be grateful if I could afford, after my "Sacred Nugget" is finished (which it will be in about a dozen days) to take a three or four weeks trip. Would do me a power of good.—Received invitation for Edgar Bruce's new theatre, the Prince's.

13th January. Dined at the Daffarns. Maggie's first day out for some weeks past. A very pleasant party. Mr. and Mrs. Huy were there. Home before 12.—on our way to Daffarns, called to see Jack Barnes and wife.—While we were out the Mortimers called.

14th January. Hard at work on my "Sacred Nugget." Wrote and sent off somewhat over 6000 words. Next week, thank God, I shall finish the story. Went to bed late in the morning, very tired.—More and more do I feel the need of change.

15*th January.* Two or three hours in the Buckingham
St. rooms. Warren Edwards there, with some friends.
Sold a few oddments, and brought home some pictures.
Went to Army and Navy Stores, and got a few hyacinth
and tulip bulbs.—Letter from Mary Anderson, with her
Box for to-morrow night. Maggie very anxious to go. Of
course she must go, and I don't think it will do any harm.
Sent telegram to Chevaliers inviting them. Telegram in
reply, accepting. As the Box is very large, and will hold
half-a-dozen comfortably, wrote to Warren Edwards,
inviting him and Queenie. During the evening Mortimer
called and stopped some time.

16*th January.* Warren Edwards telegraphed, and is
delighted. Wanted his sister-in-law to be of the party,
but unfortunately there was no room. Later in the day,
however, the Chevaliers telegraphed again, saying that a
friend of theirs was dying, and that they could not join
us. Then sent to Warren Edwards, inviting his sister-in-
law.—Committee Meeting of Green Room Club about
new premises. Settled to take them, and sub-committee
appointed to make necessary alterations.—A very enjoyable night at the Lyceum. Mary Anderson played charmingly, and paid us great attention, sending refreshments
into our box and half-a-dozen messages, from time to
time, during progress of the play, "Pygmalion and
Galatea." After the performance went behind the scenes,
and had a chat with her.—From the Lyceum Maggie
drove to Mrs. Huy's, and stopped there for me, while I
visited Edgar Bruce's new theatre "The Prince's."
Private View—"everybody" there—animated scene.—
Went to Mrs. Huy's, and brought Maggie home, none
the worse for her outing. Warren Edwards and Queenie

wonderfully delighted at the whole entertainment. Introduced them to Mary Anderson. Said the most enjoyable evening they had ever spent. It is a great pleasure to be able to give pleasure to one's friends.

18th January. Maggie not going to a ball to which we were invited. Walked in and out of town. An hour or two with the children—they are very sweet, Harry especially. Mortimer called.

19th January. Went to Billingsgate, and bought some fish. Bank book in a low state. Israel's bill not paid— nor as yet the *Kansas Times.* Read to Harry, who, when he goes to bed, takes his book with him, holding it very close. He will be passionately fond of reading—will need wise guidance.

20th January. Worked on the last instalment of "The Sacred Nugget." The Mortimers called in the afternoon —also in the evening, bringing with them Robt. Lyons. Righton also came, and we had a jolly party. They did not go away till past two.

21st January. Worked hard at "The Sacred Nugget," and finished it, feeling much relieved that the work is completed. Sent it off to Tillotson, with a request for the balance of payment, a bill for £150.

28th Jany. During the past weeks have been busy in "clearing up" and getting my loose Mss. together. Put most of my books in order. Corrected the last proofs of "Sacred Nugget," and received bill from Tillotson for £150.—The Mortimers have called three times. On Sunday Esther dined with us. Barnes and his wife called, and we accepted an invitation to dine with them on Sunday next. Mrs. David Anderson and her son called—and in the evening Major Elliott. Sent books to Mrs. Ward and Mr. Isitt—and cheques for subscription to Savage Club and Whitefriar's Club.—Also letter to Mr. Mowbray, announcing my intention not to continue a member of the Junior Garrick Club.—On Friday went to Billingsgate, and bought fish which lasted us for three days.—Great gale yesterday and Saturday.—blew our fences down, and destroyed them.—Did some "potting."—Generally busy.

29th Jany. Attended meeting of Green Room Committee, at which much business was transacted with respect to new premises.

4th Feby. On Wednesday spent evening with Mrs. Huy —went to Opera Comique and got box for Thursday night—the three of us went, and after the performance had chat with Lotta in her dressing room. Lotta's "Nell" as weak as it well could be—her "Marchioness" an exceedingly clever piece of *caricature*. Mortimer called three times during the week. On Sunday (today) dined with Barnes; Willie Edouin there—both Mrs. B. and Mrs. E. ill, and absent from dinner. After dinner a game of "pile-up," a very amusing game. Won a few shillings. Commenced a kind of farcical comedy with Toole in view for the principal character—a barber—thus endeavouring to carry out an idea I have had for some time.

11th Feby. During the past week done very little work. Went to Toole's Theatre (taking Warren Edwards and his wife with us) and had a hearty laugh at the burlesque on "Fedora." E. D. Ward, as Bancroft, was admirable. Had some correspondence with Tinsley concerning 3-vol. novel, "House of White Shadows." Original terms, as arranged, were 4/– a copy royalty. In answer to a letter of mine saying copy was ready, and specifying terms, numbers of copies to be sold at that royalty, etc., he wanted the first 100 copies without royalty. I distinctly refused, insisted upon the original terms being adhered to, and gave him the option of throwing up the book. This he did not care to do—therefore he will publish the novel upon original terms. Have gone through the copy of "H. of W. S." again, for the purpose of shortening it a bit, and it is now ready for the printer. Have not much hopes of it. Willie Edouin called to-day. Mortimer was here four times during the week.

7

PLEASURES AND CARES

THEY WERE CLEAR at last of Buckingham Street. Not clear, of course, of "things." But "Fairhaven" began in comparative good order; the tall three-winged glass-doored book-case filled a wall of the dining-room from floor to ceiling; other shelves everywhere took the best of the books. The passage and staircase walls teemed with pictures. For the remainder, and the surplus ornaments and furniture, Ben once more hired a cheap back room near by, at a florin a week, and into it was crowded all that he could not or would not get rid of to friends and dealers. His sister Esther came in for a barrow-load of things. The big furniture was got somehow into "Fairhaven." When it came to removing the painted yellow wardrobe, made on the premises, it would not go through the door, so it was sawn in half from top to bottom, and the two sides never consented to lock securely afterwards. The bulky writing-table Ben did try to dispose of, and a dealer came, turned up his nose at it, and offered half a crown——

"Out you go!" shouted the ruffled bantam-cock.

"What?" said the dealer; prepared to rise, by sixpences, too late.

"*Out you go!*" Red in the face, Ben flung open the door and pointed down the stairs; and at his gesture, the dealer cluttered down them. A moment more, and he would have found himself at the bottom quicker than

R. H. Horne had slid the banisters. So the too-large table was installed in "Fairhaven" in the study allotted to Ben—who began, as he always did, to write anywhere else but there. He could not keep away from his wife and children. He pursued them from room to room, and wrote on their tables; meals were laid on any space left over by his pens, paper, ink-pot, books, piles of exquisitely hand-written "sides" (his name for any sheet of MS.), masses of neat typescript, and the first Remington typewriter seen in England, with its uniform block letters, and neither double keyboard nor shift key for capitals.

His work, always a "nervy" matter, was not made less so now by the responsibilities of a house with rates, a very delicate wife, three small children, and a modest "staff." He wrote prolifically, but erratically, sometimes, if the children had upset him, or visitors created sudden diversions, he would not start his "copy" for next week's instalment (due in the morning) till Maggie had gone to bed about midnight. At four o'clock she heard him run to the post. The copy was always in time, and exact to the amount required within ten or twenty words. He knew precisely how many words went to a "side"; how many "sides" to an instalment; and by instinct produced his material to the week's requirements. His books were still very successful; but he had never managed his business very well, and had exceptional bad luck. His huge success, the famous sensational novel *Great Porter Square* (the Prince of Wales's "favourite") would have brought him a fortune on the three-volume edition—but Tinsley, not anticipating results, had distributed the type after the first printing for the libraries. The edition, like *Blade-o'- Grass,* literally flew away; enormous demands rushed in —and there was nothing to meet them with. To re-set

the three volumes was unthinkable, and Ben was the loser
by untold royalties. Besides this, Tinsley's affairs got into
confusion; and the failure left Ben with claims which
he might have pressed, and did not. In lieu of them,
he took over mountainous packets of unbound sheets of
all his publications (they cumbered that dusty back-room
"out" from floor to ceiling, and took Maggie and the
children nearly a week to destroy, before being sold as
waste-paper after his death); also hundreds of small
packets of leaden plates, which paved the floors of wine-
cellars, to be sweated over by astonished moving-men in
every migration of the Farjeons in South Hampstead.

Ben had always hankered to write plays; he loved the
theatre, and thought he had the making of a dramatist in
him. But despite those five successes in Dunedin, he had
no theatre-sense; he saw his scenarios as he saw the plots
of his novels, and wrote acts that ran to page after page
of dialogue. Maggie dreaded the evenings when he would
read aloud to her the dramatization of some novel he
loved, laughing at his own humour, wiping his eyes at
his own sentiment—and waiting for an enthusiasm she
was unable to pretend. One venture in the seventies at
the Olympic (*Bread-and-Cheese-and-Kisses*), with Fanny
Josephs for the star, had failed. Although he objected to
Lotta's performances in Dickens, he sent her his *Little
Make-Believe,* anxious to turn it into a play for her. She
expressed interest, but nothing came of it.

Collaborations with well-known writers, enthusiastically
mooted on both sides, invariably fell through. In 1885,
he and Clement Scott think of dramatizing *Great Porter
Square* for Mrs. Bancroft, who considered it would make
"a most interesting play and you could do it. Mrs. Holdfast is a most charming person for afternoon tea! . . . I

could not leave the book." Grace Holdfast was an effective character—adventuress and murderess, winsome on top, and deadly underneath. But Mrs. Bancroft never played the part. "An idea!" wrote C. S. next; "the wicked woman in 'Great Porter Square' is made for Mrs. Bernard Beere. She is exactly the woman in every phase of her character. As soft as a sucking dove, and as fierce as they are made. She is the modern Lady Macbeth. Mrs B. is going on tour in the autumn with a good company. Why not let her take the play for a 'trial trip'? If it goes well we will go at once to Haymarket or Prince's."

Mrs. B., for whatever reason, did not take *Great Porter Square* on a trial trip.

Next, C. S., after interviewing Miss Florence West, asks Farjeon to find in his archives a tale with "a striking plot. I want a vigorous dramatic scheme in which the heroine is a good woman, something quite as sensational as *Great Porter Square,* with a heroine who will be loved for herself and her noble deeds."

Apparently she wasn't forthcoming. The collaboration lapsed, but not the friendship.

A few years later, and it is F. C. Burnand who writes from the Whitefriars:

My dear Farjeon

Everything is "making for you". I should suggest your being at the head of the Detective Department with Wilkie Collins for nominal chief and assisted by Miss Braddon. . . . By the way why not a melodrama in collaboration and scatter Sims and Pettit? I am game for it if you are. Speak up!

Of course Ben's game. When isn't he? Once more he sees fortune in the box-office ahead, and Maggie, ever sceptical, holds her tongue. Ben and Burnand arrange to hold preliminary discussions at the Café Royal, since smoking over dinner is taboo at the Garrick, and their cigars are essential to both when ideas are on the move. Ben's body, too, was usually on the move, when he was working out a plot or a character—up and down, up and down, he paced the carpet, cigar in mouth, puffing, thinking, talking rapidly.

The two writers met, and laid out their scheme, against the time when they would be free to tackle it. But Burnand's next letter was written on black-edged paper, after a lapse of months—

> "That a pure innocent soul after some suffering here, borne patiently, should have gone home to God is what we cannot mourn."

Another four months, another note on mourning-paper, promising

> "I will draw you a model of a *scenario*."

Another collaboration that came to nothing.

Ben bobs up from disappointments like a cork on the sea. He redoubles his efforts, always with optimism. But anxieties increase, he is under constant pressure. At some point, I don't know when, Joe Jefferson comes to the rescue with three hundred pounds a year, paid quarterly to Maggie. She hands every penny of it over to Ben; beyond her Housekeeping Allowance, she has nothing regular for herself, but out of Housekeeping contrives small hoards in little boxes, and Ben aids and abets her, going out to buy big joints or barrels of oysters, or all the fruit and vegetables for Saturday and Sunday—so that she can put extra into her little boxes. He adores playing any sort of game with his family.

* * * *

From America comes other news—another baby for Toney and Father! Frank Jefferson, younger than most of his own nephews and nieces, known from the first to all as "Uncle Boll."

About the same time, Charlie's fourth girl is born. Shortly before, wistful Lauretta Vultee had written the last letter Maggie will receive from her:

Dear Maggie,
                    Yours just received I thank you for the card that was the only remembrance of the day I had. I was all alone, children had gone to a picnic in town. Charlie had left for Chicago on thursday. I did not get even any dinner, as I let the Girl go to a picnic. It was the saddest day I ever had, even without the boy, but I am looking every day my time will be out by the fourteenth sure. I feel so badly at Charlies going and just think I am not to see him for five months, I was pleased you had received the photographs also that the children liked the book. I wish you many happy returns of your birthday, you will excuse my not write any more I have got the blues so badly I can't. With much love and kisses for the children I hope Harry is improving. God bless you all From your loving sister Lauretta.

Who will look after Charlie's four young daughters? Oranges failing, he tours in management—sometimes with his father, sometimes in queer ventures of his own (he discovers a Hercules called Eugene Sandow, whom he presents in some preposterous melodrama). Lauretta dead, who will take care of Margaret, Josephine, Sally, and Baby Lauretta? Josie, who never would let herself think of marriage—it wouldn't be fair to the men that wanted her—becomes the guardian angel of Charlie's girls.

But not all tidings from America are sad; in 1886 dear Uncle Bill, on a visit to Hohokus, sends Maggie tit-bits of news from "the dear place with which you are always so closely associated." Charlie's charming little girl, Josephine, is there, "enjoying herself as often in male attire as in skirts, for Willie's suits are most becoming to her. Old Couldock, the actor, has passed a day there—idle, with no work in prospect, good actor as he is. . . . The song-and-dance men in the Burlesques seem to be in ascendant now; and very clever some of them are too, and deservedly very popular too; but they have nearly revolutionised theatrical business in this country." She learns from Uncle Bill that Bar Harbour, on the coast of Maine, is the last freak of the fashionable world just now; that her father has just finished two large landscapes, and is busy writing his "biography," which promises to be a most entertaining book. And when Joe Jefferson opens next month in Denver, "little Joe, as tall as a bean-pole, enters the family profession. . . . Were I not quite so ancient," ends Uncle Bill, "I know nothing that would afford me more pleasure than to see you, in the midst of your family; but at my time, I can't indulge in freaks, one's own home is the best place for us old 'uns. . . . Kiss the three little ones."

* * * *

For some years now her nursery has stuck at three. She carries them to Cobham, where E. L. Blanchard told them of sweet old-fashioned Rose Cottage, kept by equally old-fashioned Mrs. Shearman, and her pleasant family of girls; there Nellie and Harry get their first taste of country life, hear cuckoos, behold seas of bluebells, smell carpenter's shavings, and are driven to Rochester, to feed the castle pigeons from their hands. When the tame pigeons sit on Nellie's lap she is filled with ecstasy. But a woody country is not good for Maggie from the moment the weather becomes chilly and damp. There was a time when that right lung of hers had been a matter for specialists in the house; and she lay in bed suspecting the verdict they were giving to Ben outside: "She cannot live." Ben re-entered the sick-room so triumphantly, and for weeks kept the air about her so joyous, that it never occurred to her to question the lie he acted, when she asked—or did not ask—"What did they say?" He could not have laughed and smiled if she were dying; he could not have hummed about the passages—and what was in his heart as he smiled, and in his eyes as he hummed, she was not to know. She recovered, to live on one lung for nearly fifty years; she always said it was Ben who pulled her through.

A year after the sentence of death was passed, Maggie at some big reception came face to face with the specialist who had pronounced it. He stared at her as though she were the ghost she ought to have been. "Good God, Mrs. Farjeon, what are you doing here? You have no business to be alive at all!" That was Ben's reward.

But after that he wrapped her in cotton wool; he was terrified of open windows, tops of buses, nights out when there was the least suspicion of fog, east wind, or rain; respirators, mufflers, galoshes, were her wear; and his fears for her descended on the nursery, with the filling of which his anxieties increased.

* * * *

Things would have been more prosperous, of course, if he had not been so absurdly lavish in his buyings; so open-handed whenever hospitality or charity demanded it. He was a fierce defender of the "Indiscriminate Charity," which was beginning to be inveighed against by the Societies. A hungry child was to him a child who needed food instantly, a shivering woman a woman who must be warmed. The sorrow and the sordidness of poverty were acute to him. He hated drunkenness in men, and far more in women (the streets then teemed with squalid sights at nightfall), he hated cheating and hypocrisy; but he never forgot that poverty loses itself in liquor, and is forced, by necessity, to cheat and sham.

As for hospitality—his own nature was here reinforced by his racial joy in entertaining gloriously. His Christmas parties, beginning with eight children and nine grown-ups, swelled with years to phenomenal proportions. The Christmas-trees grew and grew, till twenty or thirty feet had to be lopped off before they could be stood upright in the drawing-room, and it took him two weeks to dress them in secret before the 25th. From each party half a hundred children bore off boxfuls of toys and treasures to last the year round. Not only were the trees laden with thousands of entrancing little gifts and curios, purchased wholesale from January to January, collected in France and Switzerland whenever he spent a week in foreign lands: Venetian beads in strings by the dozen, French scent-bottles and exquisite little dolls, chalets and chamois, pencil-cases, compasses, silver chains, toy watches, purses, sweetmeats in all manner of forms, trinkets, lovely glass birds and baskets, gay fanciful trifles too numerous to recall or to record: but round the tree, for half the space of the room, were piled such stacks of

books and boxes of toys as the branches would not bear—
boxes of soldiers, farms, tea-sets, bricks, doll's furniture;
Noah's Arks, kaleidoscopes, telescopes, microscopes;
libraries suited to babes of two or three and school-
children of twelve or fourteen; and dolls! glorious dolls,
some bought ready-dressed in Paris or Interlaken, bevies
of others dressed through the year by Mama and her
friends—Aunt Louie Huy, Aunty Lou Williams, Aunty
Fan Moore (lovely Aunt Mary Albery's kind sister)—
those dolls, in ravishing bits of stuff from Mama's boxes,
were bound all round the enormous tub, and, in skirts
stiffened with buckram, stood out in radiant ranks on the
oilcloth laid down on the carpet the day the tree, dropping its needles, arrived. Once these vanguards represented a wedding-party, with a bride in white satin, lace,
and orange-blossom, attended by twelve bridesmaids, in
pink and blue; their hats were made by Aunt Marie
Barnes, who had a genius for millinery. "Little Marie,"
her one child, with Lily and Minnie Mortimer, May,
Daisy and little Lal Edouin, Irving, Bronnie and Wyndham Albery, and the two friends we called "Nina" and
"Adrian," were my earliest constant playmates, after
Harry.

8

HARRY AND NELLIE

HARRY AND NELLIE ARE INSEPARABLE. She follows his lead in everything, what he does she must do, as it is with him it must be with her, because without him she is not. If Harry has a thing Nellie lacks, she weeps and wails: "I want a different same!"

"Don't cry, Mrs. Cook!" says Papa jollily. He generally sees that she has a "Different Same." Whenever she cries he twits her, "Don't cry, Mrs. Cook!" and it acts like a charm. She does not know, and has never known, who Mrs. Cook was; but she didn't like Mrs. Cook who cried, and wished not to be like her. Papa's and Mama's other name for her, when she does not cry, is "Tippety Witchet!" "Now then, Tippety Witchet!" "Come along, Tippety Witchet!" This she likes. Funny little elfin Tippety Witchet is not a bit like commonplace Mrs. Cook.

Once she is found roaring by Bronson Howard, the American playwright, who married Mr. Charles Wyndham's sister. He stoops over her and asks her, "What's the matter, Nellie?" She pauses to fetch her breath, sobs out, "My brother's clo'es won't fit me!" and roars again.

"What *does* the child mean?" asks the bewildered visitor.

"She heard a clown say it in a circus," explains Mama, "when he was asked why he was crying."

For a long time, when Nellie cried without knowing

why (always the case with those terrible storms that racked tiny body and soul), she gave this reason, if she must give any. Perhaps it had nothing to do with her attachment to Harry; perhaps "my brother" had everything to do with her adoption of this cause for tears and temper. For if ever sister longed for identity with her brother, Nellie did. And if she could not wear Harry's clothes, at least she could wear his wishes and his thoughts. She knew what he wanted her to be and do as soon as he did, and before it was said. She understood his meanings that were obscure to everybody else. Once when they were little, Harry not more than five, she about three, they were left alone at a children's party at Aunt Mary Albery's. It was the first time they had been "out" without a nurse or parent in attendance. Aunt Mary brought them home from the party herself.

"Were they good?" asked Maggie.

"As good as gold," said Aunt Mary. "And they stood up and sang us such a *sweet* little duet!"

"But they don't know any duets," said Maggie, astonished. "What did they sing?"

"Something about birds and butterflies," said Aunt Mary.

When Mary left, Maggie went in to the children. "What was the song you and Nellie sang at the party, Harry?"

"I don't know," said Harry. "They asked us to sing and we made it up as we went along."

And nobody, apparently, suspected! Harry, whose invention was abnormal and instantaneous, had no hesitation in obliging the company, and extemporizing a tune with words to it—and Nellie had no hesitation in obliging with him. She was able to follow his lead almost unconsciously. This incident is the first indication on record of something that I have always believed influenced my development more radically than anything else in my life. Known to us under the secret name of TAR, it claims a later chapter to itself.

* * * *

The power to produce words and ideas at a moment's notice was easily accounted for by Papa; music came, I think, from the Jeffersons. I always liked singing better than speaking; I could not take a railway journey without settling in a corner seat, if I was lucky, turning my face into the cushions to shut out everything, and sing and hum endlessly, songs that I knew and songs that I made up. The noise of the train going on above my voice acted as a sort of insulator for me, enabling me to cut myself off in consciousness from everything about me. It surprised me when, at the end of a journey to Sydenham, to visit Uncle-Nicholas-and-Aunt-Carrie-Chevalier, an elderly lady and gentleman on the opposite side of the carriage leaned forward as I climbed down off the seat, and said with very nice smiles, "Thank you, my dear." Why had they thanked me? We didn't know each other, did we?

"I expect they thanked you for singing," said Mama.

But music was really Harry's province, not mine. The first time he was told the names of the piano-notes, he went away, and scribbled with his pencil. He brought the result to Mama: "Mama, I've written a waltz. Will you play it to me?" On a scrap of paper out of his copybook, without stave or bars, crotchets or quavers, time or key-signature, he had written his "Waltz" in the letters of the Alphabet, and what he had written was an actual tune.

Music affected us deeply; and when allied to such words of pathos as "Please give me a penny, sir, A penny, please, for bread!" or "Little Darling, come and kiss me, Kiss me once before I go!", wrung one's heart-strings with insupportable grief. Then there were strains so beautiful that to hear them was to weep. (For instance, the "Miserere" from *Trovatore*.) I discovered a still different motive for tears the first time Mama played a certain dance-piece.

"What is that one, Mama?"

"Weber's Last Waltz," she said.

My eyes swam instantly. Not because the music was so very very sweet (I don't remember if I even liked it), not because it had words to it so very very sad (it had none at all), but because it was Weber's *last* Waltz. Then Mr. Weber died. Poor Mr. Weber. I did not know who he was, but I wept because he died, because everybody died....

I came in from the garden. "What's that green in your mouth!" said a sharp voice.

"Grass."

"You naughty girl!" said the nurse of the moment. "Don't you know grass is poisonous?"

My heart stood still. One day, like Mr. Weber, I must die. Was this the day? In case I should not live overnight, I sat down on the spot and made my will. There wasn't much to leave; my greatest treasure, the tiny gold ring with the garnet, a Christmas present from Uncle Israel in America, I left to Papa "if it fits him."

* * * *

In summer, 1885, Harry appeared to be on the verge of serious illness. He was always so skinny that Maggie's medical friends told her, "People who didn't know you, Mrs. Farjeon, would think you starved your children!" When she saw Harry screwing his eyes and jerking, she hurried him off to Dr. Eustace Smith, the dear, queer, faddy children's specialist in Queen Anne Street. He helped her with her children all her life, and, like the rest of their doctor-friends, refused her guinea. "Dear-dear-dear! I *wish* you wouldn't do that!" he fussed, the first time she brought out the diffident envelope. She must put it away and bring the children to Dr. Smith whenever she liked; she must do this for them and that for them— "But mind, Mrs. Farjeon! you'll have to fight your Family Doctor about it!" She did; delicate Margaret Jefferson hid surprising firmness under her gentleness. When the three boys had whooping-cough, Eustace Smith asked: "Do you want them to be over it in six weeks, or have it all the summer?" Maggie chose the six weeks. "Then not one breath of air—keep all the windows closed, don't let them go out, and when they pass through the passage from the night nursery to the day nursery, cover them from head to foot in shawls." They were over it in six weeks. When we had our frightful sore throats and colds on the chest, "Don't wash 'em, don't wash 'em, let 'em be *dirty*," said Dr. Smith fretfully. When our appetites were in question, "Cheese? certainly, if it is cut as thin as a wafer!" and "Don't make them eat rice-pudding if they don't like the nasty stuff!" "I expect you don't like it yourself," said Maggie demurely. "I detest it," said Dr. Smith, turning pink—and smiled rather charmingly like a shamefaced small boy.

Now, after examining Harry, he said, "Take him to Margate to-morrow, if you don't want him to have St. Vitus's Dance."

Maggie fled back to "Fairhaven," and set about preparations to take the child away by the earliest train in the morning. There was a mysterious Mr. Forbes, who passed us in and out of Kent First-Class. Ben rushes to see Mr. Forbes—there, *that's* settled! What can he do next? To Maggie's relief Ben has an evening appointment, and presently leaves her to her swift, methodical arrangements with Fanny Dodd, who will stay at home, to look after Mr. Farjeon, Joe, and Nellie. She looks up trains, makes lists, finishes packing; and, without waiting for Ben to come back from the club, goes to bed, in preparation for her early rising. She knows Ben won't be late; he never is.

At six she wakes, to find he hasn't come home. Worried to death she gets up and dresses herself. She must leave for Victoria Station before long, and what, oh what has happened to her husband? She runs downstairs to Fanny, up and busy.

"Have you seen anything of Mr. Farjeon, Fanny?"

"No, ma'am."

"He hasn't been home all night."

"Why," exclaims Fanny, "there's the Master now!"

They run to the door. A cab has pulled up at the gate, and *what* a cab to see of a summer morning! The roof is heaped with masses of red roses; the cab door is swinging open, Ben is tumbling out, among more masses of roses; red roses spill in the gutter, his arms overflow with them, he stays on the kerb presenting bouquets of red roses to the grinning cabby, then staggers up the path to the front-door, strewing red roses round him as he comes. On reaching Maggie, he flings the rest of his armful all over her, and gaily cries, "I'm-coming-with-you-to-Margate!"

"You're not," says Maggie firmly. "You're going to bed."

What had happened? For once he had stayed convivially at the Green Room. He had won at poker. Dawn was breaking when he left Bedford Street, and the market-carts were rattling into Covent Garden. Following in their wake, Ben found himself one of a crowd of greengrocers and florists to whom a barrow-load of red roses was being auctioned. Such quantities of red roses! irresistible! He outbid all other buyers, hailed a four-wheeler, loaded it inside and outside with his purchase, and drove home gloriously, like some Cæsar after a feast.

"It was the only time, in all our married life," said Mama, "I ever saw Papa tipsy."

9

MARGATE HOLIDAY

S O THEY BEGAN to spend their holidays in Margate instead of Cobham. The strong sea air is breath of life to Mama, but Nellie is troubled with perpetual headaches, nobody thinks of asking why. In Margate there are enchanting annual charms. There are pink stones in the breakwater that goes down from Royal Crescent to the Sands. On the Sands there's "The Canadian," where Papa buys boxes of chocolate dominoes. On the Green in front of Royal Crescent they play their first cricket; and in No. 6 Royal Crescent are Fat Miss Albon and Thin Miss Albon, and Tiny, their first dog, shiny-black like the horsehair sofa. The day they arrive there is a big bunch of all-sorts-of-coloured flowers specially for Nellie on the dining-room table (if they are the first floor) or the drawing-room table (if they are the second). Both floors have the delight of balconies. And there are the niggers every year—Uncle Bones, who is "Harry's," and "Spider" who is "Nellie's." "Kiss me, little girl," said Spider, and Nellie did, and Mama was so disgusted, and made a face. On the hot cliff-walk to Westgate there are flowers to pick! butter-and-eggs, moon-daisies, poppies and pimpernels. Pimpernels are magic flowers, poppies are poison-flowers, you mustn't pick them. Behind Royal Crescent is a long rock shrubbery, one year full of marigolds. It is open to the road, it never occurs to Nellie that the marigolds are not for picking too. She

runs in with her heart full of joy and her hands of marigolds.

"Why, Nellie, dear!" says Mama. "Those flowers
belong to the old man at the end."

Nellie stares with horror. She is a thief. Mama gives
her some money to give the old man, and tell him it was
a mistake. Nellie reluctantly steals forth and gives the old
man the money, but never says why. She is too ashamed.

The other way than Westgate is Ramsgate; a horrid
place, compared with Margate. But Button and Bronnie
and Bay are there, and Button is Nellie's sweetheart.

There's Pegwell Bay; they drive there to see Mr.
Toole, who gives them a pot of bloater paste with a
picture on the lid. And that drive, or another drive,
there is a tea-gardens in a place with Spring in its name.
There's swings in die gardens, and you may eat all the
fruit you can, but take none away. There's bright screaming birds in the gardens; and Papa hangs cherry earrings
on Nellie's ears. There's fairy-lamps in the gardens.
Tea-gardens are like Fairy-land.

There's "The Club," where are pink-and-white ices,
the best in the world.

There's Sanger's Circus, and Mrs. Perkin's Bathing-
Machines, and Alf.

Lord George Sanger and his two little girls! they ride
in the procession on cream ponies. They are like fairies
and princesses. One of them is "Harry's," other
"Nellie's"—Nellie thinks about them at night, and the
lovely girl on the horse who jumps through paper hoops;
and the Clown who cries, and when he is asked why,
blubbers, "My brother's clothes won't fit me!" One
night, suddenly, all strange and wonderful, Nellie's
"thinking" *comes true* as she lies in bed. She can say

it no other way; she was not just thinking about these beautiful things, but in her thinking they were suddenly *there,* moving and riding and flying through paper hoops, and the music of the band and the lights were there, as real as in the daylight. She lies in ecstasy under the spell; will it come again on other nights? Will it be in her power to make it come? It is! it is!—and she waits for the nights when she will lie awake and make her thinking come true.

But bathing is not one of Margate's delights. Every day it teems with terrors for her. The sea is so big, so deep, so cold, so easy to be lost in. She and the sea do not love each other. But Harry bathes fearless, and what Harry does she wants to do too. If he has anything, Nellie wants "a different same." So every day she says bravely to Mama, "I *will* go in the sea to-day." Every day Mama undresses her and puts on her bathing-dress; and every day Nellie screams with fright, upon the steps of the machine where the green water slops, hiding the lowest ones. Below the step where she can still see her feet through the green water, Nellie shrieks and clings to Mama, gasping to be taken out. And Mama takes her out at once.

"Why don't you make the child go in?" asks Aunt Marie Barnes impatiently.

"I'll *never* make her do what she's afraid of," says Mama.

"Then don't undress her when she says she'll go in," says Aunt Marie, "unless she promises she really means it."

Nellie *did* mean it, really and truly she did, every day when she said bravely, "I'll go in the sea," she *meant* to go in like Harry, and splash about with him and the children in the Ladies' part of the Margate sea; afar, she can see from the steps the Gentlemen's part, where Papa is, and she really did mean to tell him afterwards, when

he takes them to buy buns at "The Canadian," that she
had bathed like Harry. But the narrow half-door of the
machine swings open, and all the sea stretches on for
ever and ever, and it is deep, and she is tiny and frightened
—"Mama! Mama! I won't! don't let me go in!" She
grasps the rough thick rope that swings by the steps, she
clings fiercely to Mama's rough serge bathing-dress;
and Mama puts her safe inside the machine, and she is
dressed again, with chattering teeth and subsiding sobs.
She loves Mama for not bearing her screaming, like little
Marie Barnes, into the terrifying moving water.

One day she goes down two steps before she screams!
One day, she is standing on the sand under the sea—
and the sea does not come over her head and swallow her!
It is lovely, lovely. Mama and Harry take her hands, and
they play "Ring-a-ring-a-rosy!" And Mama wets her
hair, because of the sun, and Nellie, keeping very near
to the steps, and the rope, and never leaving go of Mama's
hand, looks far far away to the specks of gentlemen, one of
which is Papa. Another day, and she is plunging through
the water by Mama, and Papa is swimming to meet them;
for there is a halfway-line between the Ladies' and
Gentlemen's seas, where it is not wrong for families to
meet each other. Oh, it is *lovely*. Nellie is not afraid of
the sea any more, she bathes every day like Harry; but
why will they try to make her swim? Take both feet off
the sand? Oh, no, never! Mama lays her on her back on
the water, and puts her hands under her, and says,
"Make yourself stiff." One day Mama says, "You floated
by yourself; I wasn't touching you." Nellie is very proud
that she can float; she isn't afraid of lying on her back
and getting stiff. But there is still the ride out in the
shaky crowded cart, and when you reach the machines,

and walk along their ledges to find an empty one, there are chasms between the ledges, filled with green water, waiting. She feels sick, jumping across the chasms—but here they are at Number Eight at last, the "Family Machine" all in one piece. It is the coveted machine, where all can be together as they undress, and dry themselves, and dress again. (Only why does Mama say, "Turn your backs, dear," while she is drying herself?) There is a lovely sip of port wine out of Mama's silver flask, and two Marie Biscuits, so much nicer than Milk ones (Milk Biscuits are Harry's, Marie Biscuits Nellie's). There is the run on the Sands to get warm again, and the bun at "The Canadian," and Nellie and Mama always feel "splendid" after the bathing, but Harry and Papa always are shivery. Harry is blue, "like a little drowned rat," said Mama. Yet Harry is brave in the water, he is good at bathing, and Nellie still is rather bad at it. Except for floating.

Alf. He is brown and has silver rings in his ears. He laughs, and everybody likes him. Nellie adores him. He is Hers. She likes being near him on the bumpy drive out to the machines and back again. One year another one drove them out, not Alf. What had he done? Something. Harry and Nellie never were told what. Something not good. They grieved, and loved Alf still. Next year he is back. It is all right again.

The Hall by the Sea! You have to go through it to get to the Margate Zoo, beloved by Harry and Nellie. As you walk through, people are singing in the hall, in fancy dresses. Papa won't let you stop and listen or look. He hurries you through. It is something else not good. It is worse than that, it is Bad. You get to the Zoo part, and are safe again.

The Harbour is a part you don't go to much. It is a strange place, full of muddy, fishy smells, and ropes, and masts of ships; the seaweed smell is strong and stale, and it all seems part of a world you don't understand, and shrink from a little. Mama is afraid you'll tumble in, so you are glad not to go into that strange messy part of Margate; and yet it haunts you.

There's pink shrimps for tea; even at Ramsgate, so near, they have not such good shrimps; and there's lovely seaweed, branches of the sort you can pop, and broad smooth shiny ribbons that disappoint you so when they are dry. There's the green sort, like smooth slippery hair on round rocks, you slide dangerously when you step on them. Being caught by the tide on the rock is the most alarming of all.

The Jetty! There are Mites in Cheese through the Microscope, and there's the Camera Obscura. Papa says, "I'll blow my nose," and Mama takes you inside where it is all dark, and you stare on the queer pale round table, and see the pier and what you have left on it outside. And there, coming towards you, is Papa, blowing his nose like he said he would; and he smiles and waves his hand at you, and walks off the table. When you go out, Papa takes you to the Glass-blower, who blows your name in frosty letters on little glasses, "NELLIE" and "HARRY," surrounded by spots and curls. How you hope, before you go off the Jetty, it will be the day when Papa will buy you Margate's greatest treasure—something with shells on from the shop on the Jetty! A box, with a looking glass in the lid of it; or a red pin-cushion, stuck round with lovely shells. Or will this be the day you stop to look at the Performing Fleas?—strange little things that Nellie can never enjoy, she feels too sorry for them.

Or will Papa take you to the fearful parts below, where limpets cling, and the ironwork ways are dim and perilous? Once you went out in a row-boat, and were sick. You and Mama, who was sick too, were landed somewhere that wasn't Margate, and bought a lemon, and sucked it, and got a train back to 6 Royal Crescent. I *think* Uncle Charlie Vandenhoff was there.

But most wonderful night of all is Regatta Night; you do not see much of the Regatta, but at night from the pier, and afterwards from the Crescent balcony, you see the sky-rockets run hissing up the dark blue, and break and fall—and again you do not know what to do about your ecstasy. In bed you make skyrockets drop golden showers and coloured stars around the little princesses, leaping from their cream ponies through paper hoops.

The day you go home is scarcely to be borne. You say good-bye to Tiny and to Thin Miss Albon and Fat Miss Albon, who gives you a pot of red currant jelly that is your very own, not Mama's, or even Harry's. And the station, the waiting on the piles of luggage, the terror of the train rushing in and hurting your ears, the tunnel-smells that make you feel so sick, so that you *always* get back home with one of your headaches—and worst heart-break of all, the white-faced ragged man who suddenly is running behind the cab, clutching his chest and gasping, while there are still miles and miles for him to run before you get there. When there is not too much luggage, sometimes Papa stops the cab, and makes the man sit somewhere. But not always. Nellie used to pray the man would not spring up out of nowhere till they were nearly home; in case he was there, she tried not to look and see— but she always did look, and he always was. Poor man, poor man, poor man.

10

"196"

BEFORE a baby was born, they always moved. Little No. 13 wouldn't run to four children. Among the tall houses at the other end of Adelaide Road, No. 196 was vacant. In 1886, Ben, Maggie, Harry, Nellie and Joe, with Fanny Dodd and some unremembered cook, moved into it. No livestock travelled with us towards Swiss Cottage. The chickens were sold, because Maggie refused to eat what she had fed. Perhaps the rabbits had died—I can't remember.

A new house was an excitement; one thought possessed us. Would the garden be plain, or windy-walky? Plain gardens you could see from wall to wall; windy-walky ones (like a lovely dim paradise I remember of the Edouins', who had cannon-balls or pineapples on their stone gate-posts), had paths and bushes, places to hide in, and different ways to run, so that escaping from each other in excitement, you might suddenly be met by your pursuer. There were rosebushes in windy-walky gardens, summer-houses, and currant and gooseberry bushes. Windy-walky gardens were mazes of leaves and flowers.

The garden at 196 was *rather* windy-walky. True, it was almost visible from wall to wall; but it was divided into promising plots and compartments. A path ran all round, with flowers-border next the wall. At the far end (and it seemed very far) was a greenhouse. The upper third of the long garden was a grass lawn, on which grew trees, slender young plum-trees that never came into full bearing, a glorious white-heart cherry-tree, and such an apple-tree as one only knows in childhood. Childhood's *own* apples taste like no others, ever. They set, once and for all, the true apple-taste. For some the true apple-taste is Pearmain, for others Quarrenden; what ours was I don't know. It was a large green tart and juicy apple— just not too tart to bite, luscious! delicious! The tree had all those shapes which no other tree can offer. An apple-tree plays your game with you, and invents others. It is hard to talk about at least one tree in childhood as though it were not a person. Our apple-tree was. It stood at the yonder end of the fruit-tree plot; the cherry-tree at the hither end, the slim little plum-trees up the sides between. The cherry-tree oozed small rich pickings of gum. When apple-tree and cherry were in leaf, that plot became shaded, you could no longer see clear to the end of the wall, and a certain effect of windy-walkiness was achieved, in essence if not in fact.

The middle third of the garden was a broad gravel plateau. The long garden seat stood there, under the cherry-boughs, flanked by two chairs to match. Every couple of years the green paint grew bright and smelly again on the wooden slats and curved iron arms of the seats. The edge of the gravel plateau nearer the house was adorned with stucco pots, re-dressed each summer with marguerites and geraniums.

The remaining third of the garden, nearest the house, was devoted to a three-sided flower bed—a "horse-shoe," angled instead of curved at the corners. The open side of this section was next the house, the gravelled interior making a smaller more immediate playground than the bigger belt beyond. The three-sided bed was

devoted to roses, especially to Papa's favourite Gloire de
Dijon. As there is one apple, perhaps there is also one
rose of childhood. The Gloire de Dijon was ours.

Yes, it was a great step-up in gardens; you could run
different ways, in and out, among the gravel-paths and
belts; you might, in a chase, be penned in the rose-bed
playground (woe betide you if you then trod on the rose-
bed!) you could play touchwood on the fruit-tree plot,
uttering in a crisis the magic cry of "*feynits!*" which
rendered you immune; the greenhouse gave you a sense
of "difference"—the air loaded with the scent of cherry-
pie and musk, was fascinatingly oppressive. In the far
corner, standing on a chair, you could scramble over
the wall into 194, by means of your neighbour's heaps of
sooty rockery. That side lived a family called Leveaux.
The other side, a family called Lutgen (nieces and
nephews of the Musical Director of Grandfather's last
season at the Haymarket). The Leveaux had a superb
pear-tree in their garden, against our wall; its great
boughs dropped hard little unripe pears upon our path.
We learned, with secret triumph, that we had "rights"
in neighbour's trespassing trees. What they shed was
"ours." The pears puckered our mouths. *Our* only
garden-wall tree was a willow. It broke the flat border-
beds on the Lutgens' side, and the long slim leaves had
rosy-pink lumps on them, small fleshy lumps that re-
pelled and fascinated me. I investigated them at my
peril—and shuddered. The willow added a romantic
touch to our garden, and shed no windfalls on that of the
Lutgens'. Further up the borders, parallel to the fruit-
plot, Papa planted currant and gooseberry bushes.

Cricket was played in various parts of the garden.
Sometimes we set the stumps up in the grass near the

apple-tree; sometimes they were driven into the middle belt of gravel. After rain, when we were told "not to go on the grass," we played in the gravel-square near the house, where cricket was a risky business. If you batted with your back to the rose-trees, you imperilled the windows; if you batted with your back to the house, you endangered the roses. The garden increased the scope both of our pleasures and of our sins. Bits of it were given us for our own; we each had a short length in the border-beds; the mustard-and-cress that spelled our names in them could be *eaten*. Harry adventured in radishes as well.

And *in*side 196, there were two big nurseries at the top of the house, one to sleep and one to play in. And an exciting stair on our own top-floor to creep up, into two hot, musty, fusty, dusty attics, crammed with trunks and things. You never knew *what* discoveries you might make there, and if anybody called up the stair "What are you doing?" there was always the legitimate excuse of the "Dressing-up Trunk" to fall back on. Into this Mama threw anything we might delight in wearing. Such as a pair of thick ringed blue-and-white-silk stockings, and a blue-and-white-striped satin "body" I knew as The Boolong Fisher-Girl. Such as a lovely corded-silk cream-coloured dress with elbow sleeves and lace, and a big lace veil. For years I dressed-up in Mama's wedding-dress, till the yellowing glacé lining split, the corded silk "went," and the laces dropped to rags.

And in the attic, squeezed in the darkest channel between the trunks, in the thickest of the cobwebs and the dust, you could crouch and cry, when you were most unhappy, till somebody came to find you.

* * * *

Where *were* we all on the morning of March the Fifth, in the year of Queen Victoria's Jubilee? I cannot remember being sent away. But Mrs. Whittaker was among us again; Ben suddenly dashed out to fetch the doctor—and had barely banged the door when Maggie flung herself upon the bed and cried, "Quick, Mrs. Whittaker! the baby's coming!"

"Oh-dear-oh-dear!" cried Mrs. Whittaker. "I'm going to have diarrhœa! What *shall* I do?"

"*Have* it," said Maggie, "and I'll have the baby."

Bertie had done the trick in three quarters of an hour. The Nursery was full.

FOREGROUND

A NURSERY IN
THE NINETIES

PAPA

WHATEVER happens, he mustn't be kept waiting.

He plays games with us. There are two special
Sunday Games: "ONE-TWO-THREE-FOUR" and "Sunday
Books." "ONE-TWO-THREE-FOUR" is our pocket-money.
He takes the table-cloth off the dining-room table, and
spins a penny, calling "ONE!" We watch it till it falls, and
then it is Bertie's. There are three more pennies to be
spun in Round One, for Joe, Nellie, and Harry as they fall.
Bertie's part in the game is over. Round Two begins.
In this there are only three pennies, for Joe, Nellie, and
Harry in turn. Out goes Joe. In "THREE!" two pennies
are spun, for Nellie and Harry. In "FOUR!" a single
penny spins, and that is Harry's. We have played this
game with Papa for infinite Sundays, when one year
a startling change occurs. Instead of Pennies, Papa spins
Sixpences! A year or two later, he surprises us again—
he plays "ONE-TWO-THREE-FOUR!" with Shillings. We
all have Post-Office Bankbooks; it is left to us to save
what portion of our pocket-money we please, and we
have the habit of *trying* to reserve a shilling, or a sixpence, or a penny or two each week. Then there is the
Christmas money from America. In December Grandpa
sends Nellie a cheque to divide with the boys, and there
is always Two-Pòunds-Ten-Shillings apiece! We spend
about a pound of this freely, and the rest goes to the
Post-Office. One year, Grandpa surprises us as Papa did;
he sends Nellie a cheque for Twenty Pounds to divide.

Such wealth is worth the difficulty of the letter beginning,
"Dear Grandpa, Thank you very much."

The "Sunday-Books" Game began when I was about
ten. We all had book-shelves, mine were crammed with
fairy-tales and "The Greeks." Now Papa started giving
to each of us a new book every Sunday after dinner.
My first one was called *In Memoriam,* and it was bound
in Real Morocco, with gold edges and a red silk ribbon
marker. When the books had been given, Papa sometimes
read bits out of mine with me. He told me about Lord
Tennyson, and his great friend Arthur Hallam, and picked
out some of his favourite verses; then I went away to
read the rest for myself, and of course it was beautiful.
I already knew Longfellow; now I knew Tennyson,
and liked him even better. But in Poetry, there was nobody
like Shakespeare. Papa was always enlarging the boundaries of the world of Poetry for me; so were Papa's
friends. For instance, at Christmas, 1891, Mr. Clement
Scott sent his own book of poems, and wrote in it "To
the Youngest Treble in the choir of Sweet Singers from
an old Bass." I liked his writing that, although I did not
find myself reading very many of the poems. The *Gems
from Sir Philip Sidney,* which Mr. Lestocq gave me,
I read from cover to cover, and put under my pillow at
night; and it was the same with *Elizabethan Love-Lyrics,*
which he sent next. When I was thirteen, there was Keats
and Shelley; that birthday, Papa read me *La Belle Dame*
and *The Nightingale,* then *The Cloud* and *The Skylark.* Papa
liked Shelley best; in spite of this, I liked Keats best. I
pounced on the *Ode to Psyche* and *Hyperion* (especially
Hyperion). We agreed, however, that after Shakespeare
these two were the *best* poets. Papa never told me I must
read anything (but when he had read me a bit out of a

new author or poet, he had wound up the watch and it went of itself.) He never told me, either, that I *mustn't* read anything; only when he found me once in the dusty little bookroom, reading *The Tragic Comedians,* he said, "I think you'll like that better, Nell, when you're a bit older." So I put it down, for there was plenty else to read; Papa had eight thousand books in the tall glass bookcase in the dining-room, and the small crowded bookroom, where they filled the shelves and over-flowed in heaps on the floor. And there was always some particular book in my own room which Papa had put there—all the lovely German romances by Reuter, Marlitt, Ebers, and Auerbach, *The Caxtons* and all the other Lyttons; above all the inexhaustible delights of Dumas.

Papa read aloud to us every night he was at home. Dickens and Stockton, *The Silver Skates, Vice Versa* and *Monte Cristo*—but that one he had to stop. The night Dantes was escaping from Château d'If I screamed in bed. Fanny Bagge snorted and said, "The idea of your Papa reading you such stuff at bedtime!" She fetched Mama and Papa; they sat on my bed, and Papa promised me that Dantes escaped and no harm came to him. Next night he started reading something "humorous," and Harry went on by himself with *Monte Cristo.* (Three years later Dumas captured me utterly, yet it was thirty before I tackled *Monte Cristo* again.) Papa read aloud very dramatically. When he was Quilp, he cried "Aquiline, you hag!" with a horrible jeering snarl, and tapped his nose. "What's aquiline?" I asked; "like your nose Papa?" "Much more like Mama's," said Papa.

* * * *

Sometimes he read us his own books, and sometimes we read them to ourselves, admiringly, uncritically.

But a new book had its penalties. In Papa's day, everybody did everything for everybody for nothing. The
actors sent boxes for every new production, and were
hurt if you didn't ask to come. The physicians threw
open Harley Street to us, and after sounding Mama's
lungs (always our source of fear), old Richard
Quain would answer her question with, "My fee?
A Thousand Guineas, my dear—or nothing!" Then he
patted her hand and said, "That's all right; I make my
money out av rich ould ladies wid nothing the matther wid
'um." Sir Anderson Critchett saw the whole bevy of us
twice a year, for love. And authors sent all their friends
all their books. So courtesies were bestowed and repaid
in kind, warmly and lavishly. Papa demanded eight dozen
free copies of his novels—and got them! Unluckily,
the eight dozen came uncut, and Papa had seen other
authors' Presentation Copies lying, obviously unread,
on his friends' occasional tables. We were set to cutting
his novels interminably, before, autographed with due
sentiments, they were packed and posted to doctors,
actors, musicians, artists, and writers. I did not realize,
as I sat by the hour slicing the sections with his tortoise-
shell paper-knife, lacquered with gold fans (trying not to
slip, or to cut too fluffily—otherwise, skyrockets!), that I was
paying the small tedious price of uncountable delights from
Irving, Augustin Daly, and Augustus Harris, of untold
benefits from Critchett, Lennox Brown, and dear old
Eustace Smith. And even while you cut, Papa walked up and
down, round and round, smoking cigar after cigar while his
thoughts prepared a future eight dozen for your little bored
fingers. Papa couldn't write without a cigar in his mouth,
though so much smoking wasn't good for him.

* * * *

But nothing else you did with Papa bored you. Treats, like tempers, occurred on the spur of the moment. Suddenly he wanted you to go with him to "the City." The City began with the Bank in Bishopsgate Street (how interminably those grown-ups stand at the counter, writing and chatting, before they come away with their little bag of gold), then anything might follow. A visit to a warehouse, to buy vast stores of toys for Christmas-to-come; a walk through Petticoat-Lane, close-pressed to Papa's side among the booths and the strange smells and the queer chatter; lunch at Sweetings, with endless delicious sandwiches and oysters; a stop to drink at a city water-fountain (no water ever tasted so exciting as from the cold metal cup Mama wouldn't have dreamed of letting you touch!); or your dusty boots were blacked by a red-coated shoe-black, and the final polish tickled your toes through the thin glacé kid. And always parcels of all sorts were brought home, food for the larder, presents for Mama, some trifles for the boys and for yourself, and new-minted golden pennies, for next Sunday's "ONE-TWO-THREE-FOUR!" And how often, on that visit to the City, the brown pennies came out for poor people in the gutters, for ragged children pressing their noses against bun-shop-windows, for old women hesitating over their purchase of fried fish. "Why didn't you have a big piece, mother?" "Ain't rich enough, guv'ner." "Here you are, mother! go and enjoy yourself." "God love you my dear!"

* * * *

Of course, in the shops you never knew whether it was to be fun or a flare-up. The least impudence, the least endeavour to oblige Papa to take pins instead of his farthing-change, the least short-weight-on-purpose—

phew! But it was always jokes and kind words for the tired shop-girls, who forgot their poor feet in the pleasure of serving the merry gentleman. On tops of buses (with perilous journeys up the corkscrew stair, and careful descents backwards), there was jovial conversation with the driver; but cabs were another matter. Two times out of three, the "Growlers" meant a fuss about the fare. I seem to remember fewer fusses with the Hansom-Cabbies—perhaps their liberal jingle suggested its silver equivalent to the gay gents brought so dashingly to their doors. Inside the house, fusses with maid-servants punctuated the days. A scandalous dinner sent Papa flying to the basement.

"You're no gentleman!" hiccoughed one offender.

"You're no cook!" retorted Papa, and left the field triumphant.

The triumph took a little tarnish when, after the departure of the delinquent, discoveries were made. Papa kept a small, but perfect, cellar, but that cook's palate wasn't for the dry; two or three dozen opened bottles of various vintages had been tried and poured away, and those part-full had been improved with sugar.

What I prayed for, on such occasions, was that Papa might not swear.

* * * *

Swearing was terrible! It came very near the Devil and Damnation. "Bad language" (with ladies present) was not the common currency of a gentleman's speech in those days, and Papa was exceptionally moderate with his epithets. So "bad language" on Papa's tongue was twice alarming. There were, as I knew it, three degrees in Swearing: "Confounded!" "Infernal!" and "Damn!" "Confounded" was not, although swearing, inexcusable;

"a confounded shame!" might be the expression of honour-able indignation. "Infernal" was much worse, smacking of Hell—but you might still call a thing "an infernal shame" and remain on the side of the angels. But "Damn!"—no, "damn" should not pass anybody's lips; it wasn't a syllable, it was an electric shock. When Papa, in a temper, did say "Damn!" it really, for a moment, shook life's foundations. Of course, the seldomer he said it, the worse it was, for Papa really disapproved of "Bad Language." His dislike of it had such an in-fluence that in the Green Room Club (where he was held in great affection), when he came into the Card Room, Mr. Fred Terry stopped anathematising his luck with "I beg your pardon, Ben! I didn't see you were there."

* * * *

I always showed him everything I wrote. I wanted him to see it, of course, but I could not bear showing it, or being there while he read it. When I had pushed it under his door and run away, I had a stomach-ache till he came and told me if he liked it. He never kept me waiting. Even if he was writing his own stories, he stopped at once to look at my last poem, and came straight to the Nursery to talk it over with me. He taught me how to correct proofs and to be particular in the clearness of my "copy" for the printers, long before I had any printers to con-sider. I almost always agreed with his "corrections" in the work itself. But once we had a tussle about a word. I had been reading some antique romances, and liked the queer language they were written in; therefore, in my own *Alan-à-Dale* I wrote:

> *"O gentle is my own true-love,*
> *And like a flower is she,*
> *But they have riven her me from*
> *A rich man's wife to be."*

Papa scratched out the "me" and put it after the "from."

"I don't mean that," I said, "I mean 'mefrom'."

"Why?" asked Papa.

"Because it's an *old* way of saying it."

Then Papa became very emphatic about "from me" being better than "mefrom" because it was more natural, and he did not want me to write affectedly. He wasn't anywhere near a temper, but he was so much in earnest that I had to do what he said, though I still thought, in my heart of hearts, I was right to say "mefrom" in *that* poem, anyhow. I changed the word reluctantly, and minded very much. When Papa had gone out I changed it back, and never let him see it.

* * * *

When I was ill, he was constantly popping in and out of the room, with little surprises. He had a magnetic hand, and sat by my bed, stroking away my headache. Then he walked about the room, up and down, up and down, sometimes talking, but quite often not, until he halted, looked at me with a smile, nodded, and went out. Once he stopped walking to stare at a picture over my bed, as though he had never seen it before, although it had hung there for at least two years.

"What's that?"

"It's Ascanius," I said, with some surprise.

"Nonsense," said Papa, "it's no more Ascanius than I am. It's not worth keeping."

My great friend Nina had given me the picture on one of my birthdays; the coloured head of a little boy in a fur tunic, with a shoulder bare, and the name below it. Enough for me that it called itself *my* Aeneas's son.

I didn't want Papa to persuade me to remove it. I pointed to a great big picture in a heavy gold frame, one of the enormous things Papa had bought at a sale, for which room had to be found somewhere. "It's just as much Ascanius," I said, "as that is Rebecca."

"You ought to know the difference between a good picture and a bad one," said Papa. He tried to point out to me how the tall dark olive-skinned girl, in the rich striped dress, with the water-jar, *was* Rebecca, and my little boy was *not* Ascanius. I couldn't see that one was one more than the other was the other; you only had the artist's word for it, anyhow. I felt myself growing sulky with my wish to protect my own. Papa stopped talking suddenly. I saw that he wasn't going to insist any more, and I could keep my Ascanius, but when he came and said, "Let me stroke your headache away, Nell," I said, "I don't like my head touched." Papa looked puzzled and sorry; "I thought you did," he said, and went out quietly. Next time he came in, he probably brought me some fruit, a new volume of *St. Nicholas,* or a box of paper-flowers that I could amuse myself by making.

One rather bad illness occurred when I was busy on a story for a prize, offered by a publisher. I completed my longest effort, nearly 20,000 words, in bed; it was called *The Tricks of Pepita,* and was laid in Spain, because I had just been reading *The Corregidor's Hat.* I sent it down to Papa, and lay back on my pillows, awaiting the awful moment when we must face each other about it. He came in rapidly, and walked round and round the room. "I have hopes of you, Nell! I have hopes of you!" he exclaimed.

"Do you like it, Papa?"

"It is the best thing you've written," said Papa. He stopped by my bed. "I think you are going to make a writer." Then he took my hand and looked at me, smiling anxiously. "I don't think it will win the prize, my dear. Will you be very disappointed if it doesn't?"

"No, I shan't mind much," I said. This was true in itself, and doubly true, since Papa was pleased with the tale. His good opinion was better than any prize to me. But he could not believe I would not be upset if the tale came back; he watched every post, and one evening called me into his study, put his arm round me, and said, "Try not to mind, dear—you haven't won the prize."

"But *really* Papa, I don't mind!"

He looked at me with relief; the tears rushed into his eyes and his face beamed as he kissed me. His own disappointment for me, his fear that I would be unhappy and discouraged, had been overwhelming. But I had told the truth. I wanted to write: I cared next-to-nothing for results, and *The Tricks of Pepita* had already served its turn—Papa thought I would make a writer one day.

* * * *

How jolly he was! how sudden! how like a sky-rocket, followed by coloured stars! how like the thunderstorms he loved to watch, while Mama ran and shut herself up in a cupboard. I had most of the fears possible to a child, but Papa (who once, in Australia, had been blinded for days by a flash,) made me lose my fear of storms—except when *he* was the thunder-and-lightning. Oh, this exciting, excitable, unself-seeking, unreasonable, honourable, generous, *irritable* father of ours!

His was certainly the most dominant mood in the house, though in the Nursery Harry's ran it close. Harry dominated with a Spartan sense of justice, exercised as rigorously on himself as on us. Papa's powerful effect was not stabilised for us by a sense of justice. His irritations put him in the wrong, his tempers lacked judgment. While they lasted there was no appeal against them; but he suffered from them even more than we did, and was hurt because he had hurt us. He wanted to be close to us, and too often made us slip out of his way. When the explosion, which was past his control, was exhausted, he would spend himself in creating compensations. Towards the end of his life, as illness and worries, unallowed for by us, told more on him, his nerves were at the mercy of the most unreasonable trifles. If a door banged, if he called you, and you did not answer *at once,* the whole house was in for it. No explanation was valid, once the nerve-storm rose; I remember being in the lavatory when called for, and the natural reason came too late to spare us both his anger. He had called me several times, and got no answer—I *"should* have answered," it appeared, and I remember feeling aggrieved in my sense of delicacy by the mere suggestion. In those days an inconvenient modesty was inculcated with regard to lavatories; you hesitated to enter one if an observer was in the passage, and found difficulty even in rising and leaving the room for a normal purpose, when "company" was present.

To stave off these frightening moments, things had to be "kept from" Papa, such things as small breakages, forgetfulnesses, a dozen of the minor mistakes we all make every day. There was, perhaps still is, nearly always one member of a household who claimed chief right to be angered or offended by accidents impersonal in themselves, one member from whom such things *had* to be kept. Decidedly, we kept things from Papa that were certain to upset him, though discovery and the fact of concealment might upset him still more. We ran that risk. How could we not, when any moment an outbreak might be caused by Mama's failure to lay out his studs for the evening, to pack the blotting-paper when going for a holiday, to send the carving-knife to the butcher to be ground? To a child, the resulting storm was wildly unjust, and much to be dreaded, at any cost avoided; and we did not realize *how* painful was the illness he suffered from, how pressing the family budget, and that his outbreaks, due to deeper causes, seized on any triviality for their excuse. In the thirty years since his death I have grown certain, through self-knowledge, of my Father's unsatisfied needs. I loved him dearly, but while he lived I did not understand him, and when he stormed I winced with misery. I loved my Mother more; I loved her with a fullness that went unsatisfied. Because in my blood I am more his child than hers, I know that he did, too.

Not to speak of Papa's irritable and oppressive moods would give a one-sided picture of him, but they were not the most vital things he meant to my childhood, or has contributed to the whole of my life; and to speak of them does not mean that I did not love him profoundly. The fears have now to be deliberately recalled, they exist only in the recollection of my mind; in the memory of my heart, love of him is as warm as when he lived, with the fear destroyed for ever.

It was not omnipresent. Papa's thunder ended in a rainbow; if he was lightning, he was also sunshine; and as both, he crackled and sparkled in our Nursery.

MAMA

I CAN NOT bear her to go out of the house.

* * * *

The house is not the same when she isn't in it. Especially at night. If she goes out before I go to bed I have the lovely pleasure of being in her bedroom while she dresses. She has one evening dress at a time, always most beautiful. For two or three years it is a pale-blue-green French silk, like the sea, with beautiful bits embroidered on ivory cloth; then it is a salmony-silk brocaded with bunches of lemon-coloured flowers; then a white silk diapered with silvery garlands. When she wears this, Papa comes and smiles behind her in the looking-glass and says, "Mama looks as though she ought to be put on top of the Christmas-tree, doesn't she?" I nod. We both feel the same about her. I bury my face in her large soft Maltese Lace head-scarf; it smells of sandalwood and still more of Mama. Her dresses are high in the neck, because of her one lung, but her sleeves are elbow-sleeves, and on the bed are her long pale biscuit-suède gloves, and one of her very fine lace handkerchiefs, and the diamond crescent Papa gave her once (he told it me as a tremendous secret first), and the solitaire diamond earrings that Uncle Bill Warren gave her for a wedding-present; and her rings. I play with them. There is the engagement ring with the two blue hearts and the diamond knot—*that* is the very prettiest ring in the world;

and there is the chased ring with the diamond in a claw, that was Mama's mama's; and there is the plain thick gold ring, with three little diamonds bedded in the gold, which Mama calls "Katie's Ring." There is the grey corded silk evening cloak, lined with pale pink quilted satin, and the long mother-of-pearl fan, of lace and painted gauze, and the tiny, slender gold-beaded suède slippers—now she is taking off her bedroom shoes and wants the evening slippers. I hand them to her.

"Where are you going, Mama?"

"To the Opera."

"What is an Opera?"

"It is like a play, only the actors sing things, instead of saying them." Suddenly Mama flourishes her arm and sings dramatically, "Give me a chair!" I laugh, and Papa laughs, and I give her a chair; she sits and lifts her foot, and the frills and flounces of her silk petticoat and her lace one are like foam under the silver-white silk dress. On the bed, too, are her respirator and galoshes. The time for her to go is very soon.

"Mama, will you be back late?"

"Look under your pillow when I'm gone," says Mama to comfort me.

"And can I get into your Tuck?"

"Yes," smiles Mama, "you can get into my Tuck."

Mama's Tuck is awfully important. When she does not go out in the evening, she comes upstairs and tucks each of us in, after we're in bed. When she has lit the night-light (she never makes us sleep in the dark if we don't want to), and kissed us Good-Night, and gone, we lie as still as mice, trying not to disturb the arrangement of the sheets around our necks. For that is Mama's Tuck, and as long as it is not disturbed we are "in"

it—as though it were her hands and arms about us. But
if we are restless, if there are crumbs in the bed, or we
have a "tickle," the Tuck may come undone; and then,
for the rest of the night we are not "in" it, and one dear
consolation of the long dark sleepless hours has vanished.
Now the nights Mama goes to Henry Irving's First Night,
or Augustus Harris's evening garden-party reception
to Mascagni, she is not there to tuck us in at all. So then
we ask if we may "get into her Tuck" for ourselves;
we cannot do it without her agreeing to it, and we have
to be very careful to tuck the clothes round well as soon
as we lie down, for it is only the First Tuck that "counts"
as Mama's. It is not an easy thing to arrange securely,
but it is better than nothing.

She stoops to kiss me Good-Night, with her lovely sweet
face, and blue-green-grey eyes, and fair brown hair as
fine as spider webs, and the soft cheeks I loved to feel—
they were as soft as, well, it was a funny thing to think of,
but you know when a white balloon gets tender, and you
can feel and press it silkily between your fingers, well,
Mama's cheeks felt like that to me.

"Mama, I do like 'nubbling' your cheeks like this!"

"You chump!"

"MAGGIE!" There's Papa shouting up the stairs.
He has gone down already, and the cab is there, and Mama
mustn't keep him waiting.

"Good-Night, my darling!" She kisses me and runs.
The door has banged. Empty, empty house! I go upstairs to Harry, to see if I can lure him to play TAR.
That shuts out all loneliness, all emptiness, all everything
but itself, as long as it lasts.

But the evenings she doesn't go out, we go into the
drawing-room; and if Papa is at the Club, or writing

something, so that there is no reading aloud, Mama gets
out her guitar and sings to us, or if we ask for a story she
says very seriously:

"Once upon a time there was a Giant! And he had
Three Heads!! And he lived in a BRASS CASTLE!!!"

"I don't mean *that* story!" frets Bertie, and if she isn't
quick he will be in a temper. So she quickly suggests
a game, Magical Music, or Forfeits, or Statues.

She opens the piano, and thumps the only tune to
which Statues can be played;

Round the room march Harry, Nellie, Joe, and Bertie,
and when Mama, on the last two chords, sings: "STATUE!"
like a command, they halt transfixed in attitudes, classic,
grotesque, fantastic, pulling faces in accordance with
their poses. Mama swivels on the velvet piano-stool
(with its precarious tendency to swivel right off its screw)
to look, laugh, and applaud. Secretly each of us hopes that
she thinks our pose "the best." Without disturbing
our postures, we slither glances at one another. "Joe's
is a good one, isn't it!" (Joe is to be an actor and a dancer

—why else is he named Jefferson, and none of the rest of us?—and his grace is proverbial). "I say, look at Bertie!" (Bertie is apparently tied into knots; he is capable of surprising contortions of which he is fearfully proud.) "Oh! Harry's face is *awful*—Bother!" For here Nellie, who has probably tried to "be a fairy," stumbles; she never *can* keep her balance; she always aims at "being beautiful," and always ends by "being awkward." Oh dear! But Mama praises all, dubs none "best," and swivelling back to the keyboard of the old walnut grand piano, sets the Statues in motion again.

"Now let's have the music-box, can we, Mama?"

It isn't quite bedtime yet. Mama draws the rosewood box from under the sofa, lifts the lid, sets it playing, and returns to her rocking-chair beside the fire. Out with the gas! we'll dance while the flames flicker, now in light, now in shadow.

The round of tunes goes on—the tune from *Maritana*, the Polish Mazurka, "Save oh save the Troubadour," the lovely Strauss Waltz, the first bars of which *will* sing themselves in my mind to the foolish words "O Jemima! O Jemima!" I don't know why—round and round they prick, the sweet, thin, glass-cased tunes, and round and round we dance in the light and shadow, till the musical box runs down.

"To-night in bed I am going to begin a lovely think about Apollo. I don't care if he *did* shoot Niobe's children. She oughtn't to of boasted.

"Sometimes I very nearly remember Charlie.

"Mama oughtn't to of spanked me for pushing Florrie Canton in the gutter. She ought to of known I couldn't *bear* Florrie to take hold of her hand instead of me, because Florrie *looked* at me when she did it, and I

knew she did it because she knew how I'd feel, and
Mama ought to of known that was why. It was so dreadful
when Mama sat in that little chair and made me lie
across her knees. I cried dreadfully. I was glad that
Mama didn't have the gas on. I don't like people seeing
my face when I'm crying. I think she was too.

O Jemima! O Jemima!

"What a horrid name Jemima is!

"I wish Harry'd let me be Alice *or* Jo when we play
TAR. Being Meg and Professor Bhaer and the White
Queen and the Mock Turtle doesn't make up, because
he's got Laurie and the Red Queen, and the Gryphon,
and the Carpenter, and Jo and Alice are much the best.
I'm glad I'm Aeneas and not Achilles, though. I don't
like Achilles, even if he was the best hero. And it wasn't
wrong of Aeneas to go away from Dido, because the Gods
said he had to, and you must do what the Gods say.

"Uncle George Rowe's face is always rather sad.
Once he was alone in the drawing-room when I came in,
and I sat on his knee and he kissed me, and looked very
sad.

Save O save the Troubadour!

"I wish they'd let me go in the kitchen and cook, but
they won't because of catching colds. I hate having a spoon
down my throat, and I won't. Harry doesn't mind.
Young Dr. Wilby tries to make me, but old Dr. Wilby
doesn't. He said Why-should-I-make-the-child-dislike-
me?

"At the Queen's Jubilee, we made gold paper crowns
and sceptres, and walked round the garden. Little Marie
Barnes *would* be Queen Victoria, so we let her. The

sceptres were the sticks Papa holds the flowers up with, bat the gold paper on them came unstuck, and hung all loose in curls.

"The Barrymores have gone away, to America or somewhere. The last time Ethel came we were reading 'Up the Moonglade,' and we didn't want to stop, so she had to listen, too. There's a new lot of people in 'Up the Moonglade,' they are King Arthur and his Knights.

"We haven't seen Ethel and Lionel for a long time. We don't see Lal Edouin any more, either. He's dead. He was a darling little toy. He lisped. Before he died his throat was bad, and he wanted something and couldn't say it, so Aunt Alice gave him a pencil and paper, and he drew a bottle and glass on it. So she asked: Do you want some water? and Lal shook his head. Then she asked, milk and lemonade, and he kept on shaking his head till she said Sarsaparilla. Then he nodded, so she gave him some. I've never had any. I never want to. I wrote to Aunt Alice about Lal on my small pink note-paper, but one day I found it in Mama's desk. I suppose she forgot to send it, but I did want to tell Aunt Alice and Uncle Willie I was sorry Lal was dead. When people die, you don't see them again. One day Papa and Mama will be dead. Oh, *don't!* Oh, *stop!* If that's my think to-night I'll cry and cry. Apollo! Apollo! Apollo! Apollo——

"We are half-American because of Mama. Harry says he is all American, because he was born there and could be President one day. Whenever people come from America they are lovely. I have an Uncle there who is younger than me, he is my Uncle Boll, but I have never seen him, and so hasn't Mama, though he is her brother! We haven't seen Grandpa either, and we haven't seen

Grandpa Lockyer, who is our *Great*-Grandpa. None of our friends are Great-Grandchildren, like us. When Grandpa Lockyer writes to Mama, he says 'Dear Tiddie,' and he sends us messages. So does Uncle Bill Warren. One day we'll see them both."

O Jemima! O Jemima!

The Musical-box runs down.

* * * *

No, we should never see them, any day. I went into the drawing-room and Mama was crying in her rocking-chair, with her head against Papa and a letter in her hand. Papa said, "Be very kind to Mama to-day." Soon we knew that Grandpa Lockyer was dead. Now we would get no more messages in the thin spidery writing from America; we would never see the perky little apple-faced old gentleman whose Carte de Visite was in the Photograph Album. We had lost more than that. We were no longer Great-Grandchildren.

But what concerned me most was my darling Mama's tears. I had never seen her so unhappy before, and I wondered how long it would last. Would she be unhappy for ever? This was death. Did one ever get over it?

Uncle Bill Warren, too.

Mama has put five pounds into each of our savings-books.

There's Grandpa left.

* * * *

Of course she's a tease. When we are little she plays

"Peek-a-boo!" with us in turn, hiding us behind the
rocking-chair while she sings:

> *"Peek-a-boo!*
> *Peek-a-boo!*
> *I see you hiding there!*
> *Peek-a-boo!*
> *Peek-a-boo!*
> *Come from behind that chair,*
> OH YOU RASCAL!"

And suddenly her funny face looks over the rocking-
chair-back, or round one side, you never know which,
you only know it's coming, and when it does you give
a little shriek of delight.

She loved planning a joke. When Mr. Renaut, the merry
little secretary of the Royal Academy of Music, was on
holiday with us in Trimmingham, we heard sounds of
mirth coming from his bathing tent one morning. Mama
had stolen his very respectable bathing-suit, adorned
it with ribbons of every colour, and folded it carefully
so that he should suspect nothing till he came to shake it
out. He was a good sport, and donning the gaudy
garment, issued from his tent chanting the Toreador
Song; down to the sea marched the bathing party, singing
Carmen at the tops of its voices, while from knee and elbow
Mr. Renaut's streamers flew on the breeze.

She teased Papa too. One Census-Paper-Night he
had us before him in turn, making a joke of every question
before he filled in the form. Then Mama's turn came.

"Nationality, Maggie?"

"American Citizen," said she.

Papa's pen remained in air. "British Subject by Birth!"

"American!" said she.

He went on to the rest of the questions, and when they

had been satisfactorily answered—"Now, Maggie, state your nationality."

"American Citizen."

She looked so funny, her head tossed up, her mouth primmed and her cheeks dimpled, that we laughed. Papa finished with the children and the maids, and for the third time returned to the attack. "Nationality, Maggie?"

"American!"

We went to bed, leaving them at bézique. My room was over the dining-room, and I could hear sounds through the floor. On my long sleepless watches, which generally lasted till three o'clock or so, I used to lie and listen to make sure that all went well below. Rippling and jovial sounds made me sigh with relief; there were sometimes louder tones that made me suffer. To-night, however, all the sounds were good; but they went on and on until I slept.

"What time *did* you go to bed, Papa?" I asked next day.

"Four o'clock," he laughed. "She wouldn't say it."

Say she was a British Subject, indeed! On the Fourth of July she sat among her flowers receiving her presents, with the American Flag stuck in her hair, and on the 22nd of February she let off a Japanese firework in Washington's honour.

* * * *

She was prone to displeasure, rather than anger; her cold, quiet disapproval was worse to me than Papa's noisy rage. It had its foundations in something that came from opinion, or from deep-seated fastidious instinct, not impulse and unreason, and was a far harder thing than temper to disperse, for when the displeasure had passed, the disapproval lay dormant still, not dead. Gentle though she was, she had a will, one face of which was obstinacy.

But her will could not control certain fears she had. She hid from thunderstorms, and was one of the women who really had hysterics at the sight of a mouse; if one ran across the floor of her room, she would fling herself on her bed and scream and kick. Heights were her terror too (one she transmitted to me); she could not look down the well of a staircase without wanting to throw herself over the banisters; and acrobats on the trapeze, or maids sitting on high window-sills, half-in and half-out (for bidden in our house, but always done) made her hands and feet grow clammy; even to speak or think of heights produced this effect in us both. After a murder-trial, she tried not to know the date of the execution, and if she did, lay awake the night before, sick with apprehension for the condemned man, or slept and had nightmares. She was afflicted always with bad dreams, and a faint high fearful whimper was the signal for somebody to wake her hurriedly. Dark rooms she avoided as if they held ghosts—as indeed, for her, they did. She was the prey of every superstition; all the accepted ones of tradition she bowed to, and at some she really shuddered. If a picture-wire broke and the picture fell, or if a bird got into the house, we did everything in our power to keep her from knowing it; and if she did know it, she was nearly always able to point a day or two later to the tragedy of which she was sure it was a portent. That fear at least she transmitted to none of us; and we used to try to laugh her out of her trivial fetishes by inventing others more trivial still.

"Don't you *know,* Mama, that it is very unlucky to

eat buttered crumpets at four o'clock on the second of
December?"

The clock struck four; the date was the second of
December; the danger of *this* was that Mama might put
back the buttered crumpet in the dish, and never touch
one on December the Second again. She kept the rule of
the new moon inviolate. One evening when about to
call on a friend, she saw the new moon from the doorstep, turned her money, bobbed, and rang the bell.

"I felt so *foolish*," she told us when she got home;
"a strange maid opened the door and waited for me to
say something, but of course I couldn't speak first, it
would have been unlucky. We stood there looking at one
another and she *wouldn't* speak!"

"What did you do, Mama?"

"I smiled and pointed to the moon, and I think she
thought I was mad. At last she said, 'Who did you want
to see, ma'am?' and then I could ask if Mrs. Loveday
was at home."

And if, after dark, the question was asked that was a
perpetual refrain in our house and set us running fruit-
lessly up and down stairs, "Has anybody seen my bag?"
—it was we, not she, who searched the unlighted rooms,
where, for Mama, the spirit of Tilly or the Indian Doctor
lurked behind the curtains.

* * * *

She does not like to be kissed on the mouth; she turns
her head a little so that you kiss her cheek mostly, and
she fends off demonstrativeness. But if you cry, "Ha,
ha, proud beauty! 'tis useless to struggle, no help is near!"
like the Villains at the Adelphi or the Princess's, she starts
laughing, and goes all helpless while you kiss her, till

she gets her breath and says "Don't be a chump!" and pushes you away.

When she laughs she is lovely, but once we had to stop her. Papa was going to read us a Frank Stockton story called "*Our Archery Club*"; it began "When we started an Archery Club in our village——"

He had read no more than this when Mama began laughing. Papa waited for her to stop, and read the first words again: "When we started an Archery Club in our village——"

Once more Mama went off into a fit of laughing. We didn't know why and she didn't know why. We couldn't help laughing because she laughed. Papa laughed too. Then he said, "Stop it, Maggie!" and began again—— "When we started an Archery Club——"

It was no good. She pealed and pealed with laughter, the tears ran down her face, and now when Papa said "Stop it!" she couldn't stop. It went on till we were almost frightened; Papa put the book away, and very gradually Mama's laughter stopped, and that evening we had no reading, but played a game. The next night at reading-time, Papa got out the Frank Stockton book, and read aloud: "Our Archery Club."

"Ha-ha-ha! ha-ha-ha! *ha-ha-ha!*" from Mama. He quickly took up another book, and Mama listened quite calmly with the rest of us. But for years after that, one of us had only to say carelessly, "The Year we started an Archery Club in our village——" and away she went into a stream of mirth. There seemed to be no accounting for it.

We had never heard of the lovely Miss May, her great-great-grandmother, who died of laughing. I wonder!

HARRY

"I AM NOT A BOY," he said, "I am a Being."

He knows that Right is *right,* and Wrong is *wrong.* He knows that White is white, and Black is black. He does not know there is such a colour as grey, or such a thing as compromise.

Law is his habit, habit becomes his law. Such-and-such an hour *is* Bedtime, such-and-such a chair is *his* chair, such-and-such a joint of chicken *his* joint. What he has done once he is in danger of doing for ever. Because he began life in petticoats he revolted against knicker-bockers. For weeks Mama was obliged to dress him in both. Only when the knickerbockers had become a habit was she able to wean him of his little frock.

* * * *

"I never had any trouble bringing you up," said Mama. "I left that to Harry."

And it was true. Whatever pains and penalties, what-ever joys and pleasures, were dispensed to us by the parental powers in the Dining-room and Drawing-room; whatever our fears of Papa's irritations or Mama's dis-pleasure; whatever solace or stability we derived from their approval—in the Nursery there was one Law-Giver who made the Laws: our eldest brother Harry.

For him, there was no gradation between Honesty and

Dishonesty, Truth and Lie, Fair and Unfair. Our behaviour, our morals, and our ideas were in his keeping;
he invented rules and codes with Spartan strictness;
if they were to be enforced, he enforced them; if relaxed,
only he might relax them; and if we obeyed him without
dispute, it was because he was as strict with himself
as he was with us.

No doubt he enjoyed managing us, and inventing
regulations, games, and treats, for he was a born organ-
iser, had a fertile invention, a whimsical mind, and
among us was able to exercise his gifts up to the hilt. But
authority cannot be enjoyed without responsibility;
that too, he shouldered, and if there was occasional
kicking against it, his belief in the Law's integrity remained unshaken. The only serious rebel was Bertie,
who no doubt knew, in his heart, that he was black with
wickedness—until time taught us all inevitably that
Harry's Right-and-Wrong could only be Right-and-
Wrong for Harry himself. It was a lesson harder for him
to learn than for the rest of us: but when experience had
broadened him, and time brought a truer perspective,
when wisdom as well as power had been added to his
astonishing intellect, and generous understanding to
his self-contained nature: it left him unique as a character which still applied to itself the old code of right-and-
wrong, yet relaxed it, without condemnation, for his
fellows. He began as an autocrat and ended as the
staunchest, sanest, most self-suppressing friend that anyone could turn to; his power ceased to press, and
became only a support.

* * * *

In our Nursery he exemplified Plato's "benevolent
despotism" with so much benignity, entertainment, and

impartiality, that we began life by accepting it without question.

He could not lie. So terrified was he of being caught, by chance, in a false statement, that as a small boy he acquired the habit of adding "perhaps" to everything he said.

"Is that you, Harry?" Mama might call from the drawing-room.

"Yes, Mama—perhaps."

"Are you going upstairs?"

"Yes, perhaps."

"Will you see if I've left my bag in the bedroom?"

"Yes, Mama, perhaps-p'r'aps-paps!"

"Perhaps-p'ra'ps-paps" was a triple tag rapidly uttered, lest, in a given conversation, the saving qualification had once lapsed. The habit developed to such undue proportions, that frequently he would spend a spare moment or so murmuring under his breath a whole string of perhapses, unattached to any statement whatever; banking them, so to speak, as securities against accidental falsehood. When this last phase set in, Mama very gently took him in hand.

I remember walking with her and Harry, one summer night in Margate; I think it was when Harry was about eleven years old. As usual, he had replied to everything with his habitual tag; and presently a little heap of perhapses spilled off his lips as pearls dropped out of the Good Girl's mouth in the fairy-tale.

"Harry," said Mama stopping, and taking his hand, "try to break yourself of saying perhaps so often. Don't be so afraid of saying what isn't true, by mistake. Look at the sky; we know so little about the stars up there. We can't tell the truth about everything, because we don't know it. We can only *try* to tell the truth about things; and you know, dear, saying 'Perhaps' doesn't really make any difference to you telling the truth or not. As long as you mean to tell the truth, that is enough; your 'Perhapses' are becoming a troublesome habit. Try to break yourself of it, dear."

Mama so seldom said anything of this sort that it made a deep impression on me; especially as it was addressed, not to me, or Joe, or Bertie, with all our faults, but to our Nursery Monitor! I have never forgotten that starry night, and her gentle smiling voice. Harry was silent. But from that night the perhapses diminished in frequency; the Banking Account was closed; by degrees his sentences lost their ridiculous tag, and 'Perhaps' no longer worked overtime in his service.

* * * *

Harry's intregrity was unassailable. If by error he over-shot a penny bus-ride, on the next penny-occasion he brought a twopenny ticket, thus regulating the accounts of the unconscious City-Atlas Omnibus Company, and enriching with their full dues the shareholders' dividends. And of course the Nursery must be as honest as he was.

As he and I walked through a turnip-field near Cromer, I pulled from the ground a young round tender turnip. I *might* not have pulled it with the farmer in sight, but I did not feel those stirrings in my heart which told me I was criminal. Harry's brow clouded; he stopped; I stopped; he looked reproof; I munched on; he pulled out his purse, extracted a penny, and laid it in the hole that should have held a turnip. I hope the farmer found it; or, if he did not, was not brought to beggary.

There was that May in 1890 when Harry and I went

to the Zoo together. This was one of our frequent
pleasures, and for some time we had been allowed to go
alone, Papa providing the sixpences, Mama the picnic
in a paper bag. The ticket-man knew well the pair of
small spectacled visitors. Harry's birthday fell on the 6th
of May; and it may have been on the 8th or 9th that we
made another excursion to the Zoo. Harry tendered the
usual sixpence for nine-year old Nellie and, beside it,
put down a shilling for himself. The ticket-man pushed
the sixpence back at Harry; and Harry pushed the sixpence back at the ticket-man. "I was twelve the day before
yesterday," he explained. The ticket-man grinned:
"I think we can forget that this once," said he. The
sixpence re-crossed the little counter, and we passed,
half-price both, through the turnstile. But I don't think
Harry was pleased; nor did it, I fancy, happen more
than "that once."

                            * * * *

In our Nursery, where "The Greeks" were rampant,
I turned to Athens while he swore by Sparta. Apollo
of the Golden Bow and imperfect morals was my ador-
ation, while Harry's ideal was Pallas Athene. (I never
liked that woman.) When we were both too small to
write to her ourselves, Papa sent Mama, during a rare
absence, pictures "from Harry and Nellie—Harry says
you must excuse one of his roses, because it is not quite
perfect." Young as he was, I am sure this imperfection
irked him. Things had to be just so.
Even his Diaries took longer to fizzle out than any
other child's. Their contents were so inviolate, that I
hardly know how one famous line comes to be handed
down: "Got up. Felt sick. Had a Banna. Was sick."

For if Harry *knew* that anybody had looked in his diary, read one of his letters, or even perused a postcard addressed to him, retribution followed.

"How did you know that about So-and-so?" he might ask.

"Why, it was on the postcard he wrote you this morning."

"Did you *read* the postcard?!"

"Yes, I did."

Harry reflected. Then: "I won't tell you *anything* about So-and-so for a month," was the verdict; the sentence, delivered impersonally, would be carried out. It was rather like a fine imposed by the Customs; if your silk frock cost you ten pounds, you must pay all the more dear for not mentioning it.

* * * *

Was it his penalty or his compensation that among us he was not a boy, but a Being?

It came perilously near sacrilege to doubt him. Joe and I, being "good" children, suffered less under Harry's Benevolent Despotism than Bertie, a "bad" child. Among our many "writing-games" was one in which we composed couplets about each other, anonymously; Mama opened them haphazard, and when she had read them aloud, the guessing began.

> "He is a *Boy*
> Without a Toy."

The Subject was Harry; the Writer, Bertie, getting one in under the Being's guard.

* * * *

But if you accepted the rule you were born under, what delights were prepared for you, from Monday to Sunday!

His mental make-up, intricate and eccentric, was more like Lewis Carroll's than any other's I can think of. His interests were unlimited. He seemed able to grasp any subject in a moment, master it in two, and give it out, in his own way, in three. He absorbed every sort of book from Plato to Wisden, and had the faculty of quickening their elements into Nursery games. It was almost impossible to be bored, under Harry's régime. Harry it was who invented our elaborate pastimes, indoors and out, active and on paper: The Stocks-and-Shares game, the Hoop Game when we were Greeks and Trojans all round the street-block, to the danger of staid walkers on the pavement; the Yacht-Races during the days of Lord Dunraven, with marbles rolled down inclined boards; the "Paper-Ships" game, when coloured fleets waged war on the smooth surface of the Nursery table; the Voting-Game, when Nursery decisions or choices must be made, or some embarrassing lark enacted by one of us; the Anker-Brick game, in which Classical Cities were built and beleaguered by special methods, or mountains climbed by Halma-men under special rules, or objects hidden among secretly constructed catacombs, to be discovered under particular conditions; the Grocer-Shop game, when Harry's big shop was stocked from the kitchen tins and jars, and each of us was allowed to buy so many "pounds" weight of groceries while we "kept house" on different corners of the table—the pounds were reckoned by toy-weight, and paid for in the Nursery Paper Currency; the Cycle Tours Harry arranged for himself and the boys, as they grew older; the "Giftie

Rhesuses" at Christmas, which I simply cannot attempt to describe (they ended in wonderful multiple gifts for everybody, acquired by various ingenious means); the Thousand-Word Tales we wrote, and the "Mr. Bacon's School" game we played, with Nina and Adrian, our closest friends.

He would spend Saturday arranging a "Sunday Fair" which lasted all day; with games and sports and competitions of all sorts, and booths where our possessions could be bartered for Paper Money. As I remember it all, we quarrelled very little; and few of those difficulties which beset parents to-day were present to ours. Harry solved our problems, settled our difficulties, was arbiter, controller, entertainer all in one. He had a miraculous gift for *materializing illusion*; games under his ægis came alive; within these epics and sagas, strictly as he controlled the rules and the stop-watch, he did not limit our play of personality. But never mind how fascinating the pastime, or how he, as well as we, might pine to play beyond appointed hours, as bedtime came, our part in everything ceased. For he sent us to bed, like clockwork, himself included.

NELLIE

I CANNOT REMEMBER being without a headache; I
cannot remember one night of restful sleep.

* * * *

I can't imagine what I seemed like to others. "You
were a *queer* little thing," says a cousin of the Leveaux,
who knew me slightly; and Nina, who knew me intimately, draws a picture of me as "a most attractive and
graceful child of extraordinary intelligence, a little Pandora. Your writings, and especially your poems, were
wonderful for a child. Then you danced charmingly,
and had a sweet voice which gave us pleasure, and which
you neglected all too soon. You could draw and paint too.
As a young girl you were loving and lovable. I never
forget that it was *you* who smiled at me and tried to
console *me* in your first great sorrow—and mine—dear
Uncle Ben's, your dear Father's, death. I came into a
room all darkened, but full of flowers, and you showed
me these, and comforted me."

* * * *

But when I try to make a picture of myself, it seems
to me that I was a dreamy, timid, sickly, lachrymose,
painfully shy, sensitive, greedy, ill-regulated little girl;
not selfish on the whole, very affectionate and desirous
of affection, almost as unwilling to inflict pain as to suffer
it (I was a coward in most respects), and intensely absorbed
in my writing, my raiding, my family, and my imaginative
life. I never wanted to venture outside my home-door;

everything that mattered to me lay behind it. At home I was spontaneous and unselfconscious. In other houses —selfconscious to a degree—I dared not let myself go, and hoped to be passed unnoticed. I knew I wasn't pretty. If I was "clever," I wasn't sophisticated, and, however forward I was in imagination, socially I developed at snail's pace.

"Doesn't it seem to you as though the world was made *for you*?" Bertie asked me once.

"Not for me more than for anybody else," I answered truthfully. I never felt I *could* contain within my own limits what was outside me; I had far oftener the sense of being lost in *it*—whatever "it" was. I never particularly wanted to "have" or to "understand"; I was always very ready to "be" or to "become." Possessive experience was less to me than shared experience; and perhaps it was because Harry exercised this sharing power so profoundly that my life was deeply complicated with his; so that the inevitable loosening of those early ties was one of the most difficult things I ever had to face.

* * * *

I think my earliest memory is of the time when I trotted round the field in Cobham with Harry, at the age of three or four The field was immense; under a big tree, near Rose Cottage, Mama sat in a sunbonnet shelling peas from a peck-measure. We had arrived a few days before, and sat down to tea in a dark sitting-room, and Louie Shearman had brought in the boiled eggs in a round stand, and whispered to me to offer old Mrs. Shearman a certain one. So I said, "That one's yours," to Mrs. Shearman and waited eagerly to see her crack it, for Louie and I were in a conspiracy. She cracked it—

ha-ha-ha! it was an empty egg-shell, turned the wrong
way up! What a joke on old Mrs. Shearman, wasn't it!

It was sunny in the meadow, and I was happy. Harry
and I were whispering together, some game (not yet
TAR) absorbed in it and each other. Suddenly through the
hedge some rude boys looked in and laughed at us.
"Abraham and Sarah!" they jeered. We hastened on.
When at last we reached the shelter of the big tree, I
would not walk round again, but stayed with Mama and
helped her shell the peas.

* * * *

I did not care for dolls much. I loved blowing soap-
bubbles, best of all out-door games; I loved snow-scenes
in glass globes, and tiny "tortoises" with fluttering feet,
in small sealed glass boxes, kaleidoscopes which shifted
magically, musical boxes with tunes that never seemed
near, glass paperweights with visions of Pegwell Bay,
and cuckoo clocks, where the bird appeared and disappeared. I was fascinated by things that came and went,
things I couldn't quite touch, or really find out; the
silver road on the sea to the sun on the horizon, the moon
and her star, the rainbow and its reflection, the shafts of
light drawn almost down to earth from a bright-edged
cloud, the spot of light at the end of a green arcade of
trees. I did not love the darkness of a tunnel, in which
the bad-egg-taste of smoke made me still sicker than I
always was on train-journeys. At the re-appearance of
daylight I breathed with relief. But my most intense
sensation on a train-journey was fret because the telegraph-wires *would* not disappear. I longed for them to
rise out of sight and fly away and be free, I knew not
where. I sat in my corner-seat watching for them to go.

Higher and higher they rose, there were but two or three left—now quick, quick! be off before the next telegraph-post appears to pull you down. Almost invariably the post flashed past before the last wire vanished, and down swam the whole stave, to begin their weary climb again. If ever they did all escape, it was but for the merest instant. Their coming-back almost *hurt,* but I had to watch them. At least they took my attention off the sick-headache, which began with the fuss and turmoil on the platform, the fear of being lost if Mama vanished, Papa's fuss and flurry with the porters, and the pain in my ears, and shock to my nerves, of the express-train running through before *our* train came.

* * * *

My Awake-at-Night Game, which began after my very first Sanger's Circus at Margate, was almost contemporaneous with the beginnings of TAR, the day-game played in co-operation with Harry. The power to change, almost at will, flat thought into three-dimensional fancy, turned my sleepless nights into hours of glory. To the Lady in the Circus I quickly began to add a figure or a person here and there, until, with years, I had a glittering medley to play with. My Greeks came in very soon; above all, my two favourites, Apollo and Diana. Others dropped out of my "thinking," and new characters flowed in from life and reading; but Apollo and Diana had always to be incorporated somehow. I allowed them, god-like, to take on human shapes, keeping secretly their immortal attributes unknown to those they lived amongst; I gave them as son and daughter to Warwick the King-maker, whom I adored after reading *The Last of the Barons;* and Diana (still Warwick's daughter) ended as the beloved of Amyas Leigh, who had for years my heart. But for Apollo, nobody was good enough. He loved his sister better than any woman, and he and Amyas were the most tremendous friends. As for his looks, I could hardly see him in my thoughts, for radiance. He was like his own description in that marvellous broken ending to *Hyperion*:

> "Soon wild commotions shook him, and made flush
> All the immortal fairness of his limbs. . . .
> . . . so young Apollo anguished;
> His very hair, his golden tresses famed
> Kept undulation round his eager neck.
> During the pain Mnemosyne upheld
> Her arms as one who prophesied—At length
> Apollo shrieked;—and lo! from all his limbs
> Celestial . . . .

From all the young Apollo's limbs celestial streamed a light that bathed my imaginings for ever after. Even to-day, when Mnemosyne lifts those prophetic arms, and the commotions of memory are scarcely bearable, he stands before me with his gloomless eyes:

> "Apollo is once more the golden theme!"

Keats took me whole, when I was about thirteen; but for long nothing quite equalled *Hyperion* for me; and so much more glorious was that name than Phœbus-Apollo, that I transferred it bodily to my young god. Apollo in my night-thoughts was now known as Hyperion (though among men he was "Dick" Neville, son to the King-Maker). Even now, in certain states on very dark, quiet nights, or when I walk rapidly by day in noisy streets, I can bring my shining god to life again. Noise is a wonderful insulator. I found it useful in another way. Pressed up in the far corner of a City-Atlas, as we rattled to our dancing-lesson at Mr. Crompton's in Berners Street, I could beyond the noise create an orchestra, which played through any favourite piece of music I knew well: Mascagni's *Intermezzo* and most of *Hänsel and Gretel.* As long as the bus rattled, and the street-noises enclosed me, that orchestra sounded as truly as the figures in my Night-Game moved; the instant the bus pulled up, the fiddles were mute, the horn held its breath —till on we rattled again. I still recreate that musical illusion with the *Meistersinger* overture, every phrase and instrument of which is impressed on the wax record of my uneducated musical sense.

* * * *

Schooldays I had none, and next to no Nursery-Governess Days. Miss Milton, of the pale red hair, took me and Harry through our pothooks and hangers, our *Reading without Tears,* our *Little Arthur's History of England,* and *Guy's Geography;* and showed us the portraits of the Kings and Queens of England, in proper order with their dates, in a small primer of which I forget the name. After that, she took us out for our walk.

Pothooks and hangers did not interest me, the reading matter that could be acquired without tears did not capture my imagination (if a book did that, I was only too glad to weep with it); the dates of Kings and Queens became a sort of dutiful nuisance, but I liked the pictures of the "nice" and "nasty" kings. The artist was a man with healthy prejudices; King Richard the First was plainly a Hero, King Richard the Third as obviously a Villain. As for the Morning Walk, it is a fact, which Papa and Mama noticed with amusement, that Miss Milton

first found out the way we wanted to go, and then took
us the other. Perhaps it was the Governess's lesson in
Discipline. If so, it was the only sort of discipline I was
ever subjected to by my elders, and it did not last long.

* * * *

From the régime of Miss Milton onwards, I was writing
and reading for myself, and the dull hours spent with her
were of no importance beside those spent exploring Papa's
enormous bookcase, or scribbling in the marbled exercise-
books which I, like my brothers, crammed with stories,
poems, pictures, and plays, finished and fragmentary.
When I was seven, Papa introduced me to the delights
of his typewriter. I soon began to use it regularly for copying, but not for the act of creation. For the poems, which
Harry and I were producing industriously, Papa bought
a special book, into which we copied them by hand.
Inside the book-cover Papa had written

> "*This book belongs to*
> *B. L. Farjeon*
> *196, Adelaide Road*
> *South Hampstead*
> *N.W."*

That was in case the book ever got lost; because, incredible as it was, *Papa would rather lose a Pound than
lose that book with Harry's and my Poetry.* Mama had
told us so. A Pound! the Most Money there was.

* * * *

Before I was eight, Harry passed on for a term to Percy
House, and Joe and Bertie joined the Pothooks-and-
Hangers classes. Harry's brief school-experience had one
beneficial result for him and for me. The teachers sent word
that he could not see what was written on the black-board.

Harry was taken to Harley Street to have his eyes tested by Anderson Critchett, and I was taken with him. Harry's were pronounced unsatisfactory; when it came to my turn, and Sir Anderson's bland, kind voice said, "Now let us see what the young lady can do," I stood at the end of the room staring at a card on which I could see nothing whatever—not even the top big letter. It was spectacles for both for life; and a visit every six months; and stringent orders from Sir Anderson as to the size of print permissible for our reading. "Don't let them read too much," he said to Mama.

"But I can't keep them from it," said Mama, "and Nellie is always writing."

"Then, don't let her sew or use her eyes in any other way," said Critchett; "if you had left her for another year, she would have gone blind."

My astonishment when the spectacles came home! I looked at a different world, a different room! I saw patterns on the wallpaper, things in our pictures, which I had never known were there! Even then my glasses left my sight far behind the normal level of others. My eyes were not only short-sighted, but so weak that they could not have stood continually the strength which would have brought them up to normal.

The restrictions as to the print were sometimes agonizing. A certain book I longed to read was only obtainable in a type below the regulations. On our next visit to Harley Street, I carried the precious volume under my arm. When the examinations were concluded, and we had admired the latest pictures of Sir Anderson's children (Monty and Dora were always on his desk, and occasionally we went up to the drawing-room and saw them in the flesh), and Mr. Carton's last play had been talked about,

Mama said smilingly, "Nellie has something very special to ask you."

"Well, little lady?" Sir Anderson turned his kind smile on me.

"May I read this?" I asked anxiously; "it's smaller print than you let us."

He took the book; it was Sir Philip Sidney's *Arcadia*. I remember the odd look he exchanged with Mama.

"And do you want to read it *very* much?" he asked. I nodded. "Very well—but only a page at a time; then rest your eyes. Hold the book upright, with the light behind you."

I'd do anything, as long as I could read my Sir Philip. He had captured me in the little anthology given me one Christmas by Mr. Lestocq. Such *lovely* songs! "My true-love hath my heart, and I have his"; and a sonnet that became my earliest anchorage when I thought of death.

> *Since Nature's works be good, and death doth serve*
> *As Nature's work, why do we fear to die?*
> *Since fear is vain, but when it may preserve,*
> *Why should we fear that which we cannot fly?*
> *Fear is more pain than is the pain it fears . . .*

I read that sonnet till I had it by heart; I recalled it in my tremors at night, and *knew* it was the truth, even if I could not always *feel* that it was. But it altered very early my conception of Death and Fear. It did not render me brave and unafraid at once, but it helped me more than anything else to become so.

In the front of each volume of my secret journal, scribbled prolifically in shiny black-covered books, I wrote, as my motto, "Fear is more pain than is the pain it fears." And to this presently added a quotation from

Milton, which struck me with the same force when I first read it:

> Nor love thy life nor hate, but what thou liv'st
> Live well; how long or short permit to heaven.

Of course, I found myself quite at home in *Arcadia*; the Elizabethan medley was all of a piece with the living tapestry of my fancies; chivalrous and decorative knights were assimilated with my Greek gods and heroes. These, first met in Hawthorne, had come completely clear for me in Cox. I was still, at six or seven, in the world of Andersen and Grimm, Kate Greenaway, Caldecott, and Mother Goose—when I was told by Harry that one of the books on the red plush cover of the octagonal table in the drawing-room was worth reading. "It has lovely tales in it," he said. I tried them; and absorbed the Wonder-Book from cover to cover, skipping the tiresome conversations between Eustace and his little listeners. It was the tales I wanted, not this sententious New-Englander. Pegasus and Pandora, Perseus and Philemon, rose on my horizon, outshining even Snow-White and Cinderella in my pet story-book. A Pitcher that poured milk for ever, a Horse with wings, a Box of Gifts that turned out to be Troubles, a Dragon with the heads of a goat, a lion, and a snake. A Giant who held up the sky. A Golden Apple-Tree upon a magic isle. More fairy-tales, more fairy-tales! the best I had read yet, but some of the names were rather difficult, like Epimetheus and Bellerophon. Oh well, you just said them how you could. Was there no more of this transcendent stuff?

As always when he saw my fancy captured, Papa began to talk to me about the Greek legends, and hunted his shelves and the sales-rooms for what might please me.

He gave me the Tanglewood Tales, to add to the Wonder-Book; and Tales from Homer and Virgil, with a new sort of picture in them we called "Flaxmans." Straightway all the Greek and Trojan Heroes marched into the Nursery, and were divided between us; their cities were apportioned too; Harry's, of course, was Sparta, mine was Athens—and for once I preferred what had fallen to my lot. Then Papa brought home one night Fénélon's *Telemachus,* a curious old edition, with an account of the world's mythologies at the end. I took no heed of the Hindus and the Norsemen; but I dwelt for hours on Calypso's Isle amid queer woodcuts, and browsed for longer hours on the Major and Minor Deities on Mount Olympus. One evening as I sat reading in the drawing-room, Papa came in with Uncle Jim Mortimer. I didn't look up till I heard Papa saying, "Which would you rather have, Nell, *Telemachus* or a diamond necklace?"

"*Telemachus,*" I implored, clasping it, with a horrid fear he might be going to exchange it for diamonds.

"You pretend to like it," teased Uncle Jim, who petted me more than any other "Uncle," "but you couldn't tell me the names of the nine Muses."

Pooh! he might as well have asked my nine-years-old tongue to repeat the A B C.

"Clio-Muse-of-History,   Polyhymnia-Muse-of-Sacred-Song,   Erato-Muse-of-Love-Song,   Melpomene-Muse-of-Tragedy——" I ran through the list of the ladies and their attributes; but added, "Orpheus was Calliope's son, and he ought to have been Euterpe's."

"Why?" asked Uncle Jim.

"Because Euterpe was the Muse-of-Lyric-Song, and Calliope was the Muse-of-Epic-Song—and Orpheus didn't write epics, but he *sang.*" This has always seemed such a flaw to me in the myths, that to this day I incline to look on Calliope as the Muse of Lyric Song, or on Euterpe as the Mother of Orpheus. Could the old Greeks have made a little mistake? It's a point I shall argue with Homer one of these days.

Uncle Jim laughed, and did not clear up the point; but very soon after he presented me with Cox's *Gods and Heroes*. The brief and pure accounts of the beautiful tales knocked Hawthorne down for the count, and he never got up again. I had no more use for Tanglewood and the Wonder-Book. Here were my Greeks as true as words could make them. I began to speak of Narcissus as Narkissos. I did not drop my Grimm and Andersen; Mother Goose still plucked her feathers all over my pillow, and anything and everything in the way of folklore and poetry took hands around the Nursery mulberry-bush. Except for *A Midsummer Night's Dream,* I did not yet read Shakespeare very much; but then, Papa read him to me, telling me about one or another play, and reading the very loveliest bits from each. Some of the bits went home to me for life.

> *Oh it is excellent*
> *To have a giant's strength, but it is tyrannous*
> *To use it like a giant.*

and

> *Man, proud man,*
> *Drest in a little brief authority.*

and

> *The poor beetle that we tread upon*
> *In corporal sufferance finds a pang as great*
> *As when a giant dies.*

These made an indelible impression on my mind. (Oh, the terrible hurt of tiny things, whose soundless sufferings could only be known by a state of identification!)

And best of all:

These cloud-capped towers,

to the conclusion, somewhere in those skies where all
imagination was released:

*We are such stuff
As dreams are made on and our little life
Is rounded with a sleep.*

This was Papa's favourite bit of Shakespeare; it was
mine too.

* * * *

He placed in my way everything he thought I was ready
for; Longfellow, or *Undine and Sintram,* the lovely
Egyptian novels of Georg Ebers, and everything by
Juliana Horatia Ewing. I had periods of certain authors,
to the exclusion of others—there was the Dickens period,
the George Eliot period, the Lytton period, the Charles
Kingsley period, when Amyas Leigh collared my young
heart; above all there was the Dumas period, which has
never passed. But I think, up to my twentieth year, the
three outstanding "revelations" in the worlds of poetry,
music, and pictures, came instantaneously from *A Midsummer Night's Dream, Hänsel and Gretel,* and Turner.
These gave me a new mind, new ears, and new eyes:
a new vision of life.

* * * *

Of course, I "liked" pictures very much indeed.
Every year Papa took me to the New Gallery, to show me
the lovely pictures of Mr. Burne-Jones. And Grandpa
painted very beautifully, and had sent each of us a real
big gold-framed oil-painting of our own. Mine was
a picture of the dashing sea. And Uncle Nicholas
Chevalier's house in Sydenham was crammed from top

to bottom with his beautiful pictures of New Zealand and Taheite and Madeira; we had two of them in the dining-room, and one by Ernest Parton, who painted tender birch trees. I loved Mr. Parton dearly. He had the American accent which always rang so sweetly on at least one of my ears. Papa and Mama took me to his Picture Sunday every year. I had on my prickly starched petticoats under my best muslin frock, and under *them* my flannel petticoat, embroidered in floss silk. My hands were forced by my nurse into tight little kid gloves, and my hair was washed and brushed without mercy to get out the tangles, and I felt very stiff and stuffy when I started to walk with Papa and Mama to Acacia Road, in squeaky shiny uncomfortable new boots. But when we got there the pictures were beautiful! I gazed and gazed and didn't know what to say. There was one that was as good as poetry. "Well, dear, do you like them?" said Aunt Alice Parton, a handsome lady in a fine white fichu, who gave me tea and tit-bits at a dainty table. I nodded and whispered "Yes." It was as difficult to praise as to be praised in company. I would always rather look and not have to say anything. We came away, and after we had been to see Mr. Marcus Stone's ladies sitting on stone seats under rose-bushes, we went home and I hurried to my room, got into my everyday pinafore, and wrote the poem that Mr. Parton's picture was.

I ran downstairs, shoved it under Papa's door, and ran away again. Soon I heard him coming up, and felt, as usual, awful in case the poem was a bad one. He came in smiling. It was all right—he liked it, and was going to send it to Mr. Parton! I hadn't thought of this, but I was pleased, and pleased too that the poem was "good enough" for the Poetry-Book.

Papa typed the poem, and sent it off to Mr. Parton, and I took the manuscript to copy in the Poetry-Book. I hadn't written one in since January 22nd, 1890, and now it was April. The one before was a larky one, and I'd made a tune for it. It was called "Oh! I'm a very gay fellow." Mr. Parton's Poem was called "Happy Springtime."

The reply to the poem was brought by Mr. Parton himself. I heard myself called downstairs a day or two later; there was the thin, sweet-faced, gentle-voiced American waiting for me with Papa and Mama. He kissed me and said how pleased he was that I had written such a nice poem for his picture. "Look Nellie, what Mr. Parton has brought you," said Mama. She pointed to a table, on which lay a lovely little picture of a stream flowing through bushes. For me? I stared entranced. A real artist, who had his pictures every year in the Royal Academy, had painted it for *me*. I hugged Mr. Parton, not knowing what to say. Thereafter Mr. Parton and I were devoted friends, and I made a point of writing him a poem every year, on the Picture-Sunday picture I liked best.

* * * *

What a medley was my upbringing, and how undisciplined my occupations. As nothing was ever imposed on me I did not have to suffer from one of childhood's common difficulties in undoing an accepted religious outlook, and finding it again in a new form. We were never obliged to believe anything. Once only, when I was about eight, I asked to go to church (I don't know why, unless because Harry had been, and I wanted "a different same"). Mama took me. I found the whole affair excessively boring. I never asked to be taken to church

I. MAMA

2. PAPA

3. HARRY

4. 'BUTTON'S SWEETHEART':
NELLIE, AGED FIVE

5. NELLIE

6. HARRY

7. JOE

8. BERTIE

9. THE EDITORS OF *Farjeon's* Weekly AND *Farjeon's Fortnightly*:
JOE AND BERTIE

10. THE GORING THOMAS SCHOLAR: HARRY

II. NELLIE

again, and grew up calling myself, as soon as I knew the word, an Agnostic. But my agnosticism was not painful, and remained for me a mental term instead of a mental process. Then, rather early, browsing in the little dusty bookroom, I unearthed Locke, and found in him something which satisfied my mind of the continuation of the spirit after death, but I recall this satisfaction as comfortable to my fears, rather than illuminating to my instincts. My spiritual response was to poetry, wild-flowers, woods and fields, and the sky—the sky most of all. It was an imaginative pageant that created for me a world dazzlingly vague, bewilderingly suggestive. It was there I found my first "intimations," long before I had read of clouds of glory,

All the same, I was afraid of Hell and the Devil. Nurses saw to that.

I said my prayers every night, because I had been taught to say them; the same simple prayers that Maggie Jefferson had said, "to be on the safe side." If I had omitted them, I should have felt uneasy; but it was the fairies, not the angels, who really controlled me. I invented "Fairy Games" for Joe and Bertie, I wrote them mysterious letters in gold and silver paint on small pink note-paper—no easy matter. The blobby but gleaming script invited them to attend certain "Fairy Revels" the nature of which I forget; only they began with dressing-up in coloured muslins, there were inspirational dances of sorts, and, no doubt, a feast. I clung to these effects long after I had ceased to "believe" in Fairies, because that belief had been my most transcendental experience; and I am sure that in my earliest, most credulous years, I never "believed" in God, or even the Devil, as firmly as I did in Santa Claus.

JOE

H E WILL GO to Heaven when he dies.
Whatever happens to the rest of us, Joe will quite
certainly go to Heaven.

("Now mind!" said he, forty-five years later,
"I hold a Watching Brief on this book of yours.")

I am sorry, Joe; I am trying to tell the truth, and you
had the least selfish nature of any child I have ever known.
You were so sensitive about the feelings of your family,
so eager to spare anybody pain, so ready to do anything
demanded of you by somebody else, (yes, Bertie! I *do*
mean you), in short, you were so good, that Harry
(I believe) used to add to his prayers a private plea to
God not to let you die. You looked like an angel, too.
I am speaking of the days before you and I had tussles
about the respective size of our noses, when yours (which
has outgrown mine) was small and charming, and your
hair, dressed in long curls down Mama's finger, the
brightest purest gold, and your eyes as dancingly brown
as Papa's own. Even your brand of temper didn't imperil
your soul; those flushed, excited bursts of indignation
were nearly always in the cause of somebody else (yes,
Bertie, I still mean you). You adored us all, but Bertie
I think you'd have died for. You were nearer my age than
his, but by natural division, when the Nursery fell into
halves, it was Harry-and-Nellie the elders, and Joe-and-
Bertie the youngers. (They called themselves "The
Chums.") This held you back unfairly; though you took
up the cudgels on his behalf, you were more like Bertie's

twin than his elder brother, and his forward mentality kept pace with your intelligence, so that the gap between you seemed hardly to exist, when he was seven years old, and you were eleven. You fell into step beside him. It ought never to have happened.

* * * *

We were a united and a devoted family.

We had, of course, our personal mutinies, and resentments that for some of us went deep. Our Nursery was not an Eden of Perfection, but a glass-house in which we breathed and re-breathed the emotional air.

We did not hide our feelings. Among ourselves we expressed our affections as liberally as other people their antipathies. We shared enthusiasms; we loved each other and said so; if one suffered, the others suffered too; we were not ashamed of laughing together, so why should we be ashamed of crying together?

So I still don't know why, if one has a heart, one should not wear it on one's sleeve, if one has a sleeve; or why being sentimental is less desirable than being cynical—if you must be one or other. Victorian Sentiment may have covered up many a raw truth, but it did express, in its own way, its feelings. What else is Cynicism but a covering that hides, in its own way, its feelings to save its skin? Why should one save one's skin? It isn't as valuable as all that.

Quite true! this *is* a bit of Special Pleading—a plea for Sentiment, without which any record of our childhood would be false. I cannot look upon it like an analyst; I cannot dissect, I can only try to present it, to re-live parts of childhood as they felt to me. I see us, as a group, affectionate, "original," over-sensitive, crude, and unformed, rather bashful socially, but not blasé. Experience was preceded by too little knowledge; but we did not begin life with a finished view of it. Perhaps it is just as easy—or just as difficult—to step backward as to step forward to experience; in any case, the advantages or the drawbacks of a generation depend on what each individual makes of them. Cynic and Sentimentalist are on a par if they cannot do more than accept the mould of their time. The advantages and drawbacks of the Eighteen-Nineties are as unsuited to the Nineteen-Thirties as those of the Thirties would have been incredible to the Nineties. It tickles the Thirties to call the Nineties Naughty; for what the Nineties would have called the Thirties, you would have to search the Old Testament.

In themselves, the Nineties were not comic; no period is, but by comparison with another. They were very real and far from being stupid. If the Nineties were Naughty, we did not suspect it. We did not even know they were Sentimental.

* * * *

As for this vexed question of Goodness, why does one hesitate to speak of it? From fear? Why do we not mind speaking about Badness? Only a species of cowardice makes us readier to say "Bad" than "Good." One does not comfortably laugh at Goodness—at Badness, for some curious reason, one does, and easily commanded laughter is a social asset. The simple respect which Goodness commands is not so sure of its company, and may thrust its expresser into isolation. But as Sentiment, it affords outlet for the social snigger; on such terms, Goodness may be safely mentioned. Let's laugh at all costs!

I am not mentioning it on such terms. Joe's nature was the loveliest element in the Nursery. And I cannot laugh at it.

* * * *

Joe was very ill. It was Diphtheria. We were bundled out of the house to Crossfield Road, where I spilt ink on the red tablecloth. (Fifty years of tablecloths and carpets are signed with my spilt ink.) These family breaks and interruptions were dreadful; besides, Joe was so ill that he might die. Why, he didn't know Mama when she sat by him! Of course she came to see us every day, and when we said, "How is Joe?" she tried to smile once as she answered, "This morning when I went in to him he waved his hand and said 'Go away, David!'" How funny for Joe to call Mama David! why, we didn't know any David at all except the one who killed Goliath. We were just going to feel amused when I looked at Mama, and suddenly a flush was all over her face, and her eyes were full of tears before she could turn her head away. Then one day we were told we were going home, *next* day. Baby went back with Fanny, but Papa came for Harry and me, and took us first to see Buffalo Bill's Wild West Show. It was a terribly exciting show. I was sure the Indians and Buffalo Bill would come into TAR. Papa bought us each a ball of pop-corn, and then we went back to 196. When we saw Joe, he was very thin and pale, but he wasn't going to die.

He was delicate though, perhaps because he *wouldn't* eat vegetables. Well, really, whatever the doctor said, he *couldn't*. Not any cooked sort, except potatoes. He liked raw peas. And cooked fruit he couldn't eat either, or any raw fruit with stones in it. The doctor said he ought to, and he tried and tried. Mama would put six peas on his plate, and he would wrap them up in mashed potato and try to swallow them. Then he was sick. It was so awful for him, and gave him such tight feelings in his head, that Mama gave it up.

* * * *

He was the only one of us called Jefferson. We rather minded this, and Harry so much wanted to be Jefferson, that when he had a Post-Office Bankbook he wrote his name in it "Harry Jefferson Farjeon." This is perhaps Harry's nearest approach to a lie. Because he was Jefferson, Joe was going on the stage. Mama got some leather and some dark red doth, and made Joe a "Rip" suit, just like Grandpa's. She did things to make the stuff look shabby and worn; and she made an old black felt hat and tore it rather, and made a blue cotton shirt, and a red-and-white cotton tie; and Papa got a gun and a little horn cup. Then Mama taught Joe the health Rip Van Winkle always said when he drank to his friends:

> "Here's your good health and your family's, and may they all live long and prosper."

Only what Joe said, when he lifted his horn cup, was: "Here's your good health and your family's, and may they all live long and *proper*!"

Aunt Alice Edouin used to chuckle when he said it. We always "did" our things for her and Uncle Willie.

When Mama had to take Joe to Margate by himself, till he got over having ringworm, she took the Rip Suit too, and he was photographed by Mr. Stoddart, the best photographer there was anywhere. The pictures were a great success with everybody; they went to Grandpa in America, and to all sorts of other people in England who had seen Grandpa play Rip. Mrs. Kendal wrote back; "Everyone is *delighted* with that Darling's picture."

Because of his acting, too, Joe learned dancing. He went to Mr. Reginald Crompton's in Berners Street, and had special step-dancing lessons; and then I and Bertie went too, for waltzing and quadrilles and Lancers and the Barn-dance. Harry wouldn't. He thought dancing undignified; a Being didn't dance. When he came to watch one of our classes, and Mr. Crompton asked him what he thought of us, he said, "I think they all look rather silly."

I learned a skirt-dance with Elsie Rathbone. It was to a Gavotte tune called *Immer Wieder, and* we had accordion-pleated skirts like Kate Vaughan. People said I was more graceful than Elsie "going round the room," but Elsie was much neater in her steps, and she never forgot what came next, as I almost always did. I rather liked the dancing-lessons, though, because you didn't have to meet lots of strange new children every time, and have to think what to say to them, as you did at parties. That was the worst of dancing with boys at parties, you had to think what to say, and the only thing I thought of talking about was my typewriter, which didn't seem to interest them much. After the class, Joe stayed on for his special lesson. He did a Spanish dance, and a Russian dance, and a Jester's dance, and the Hornpipe. Sometimes little Gerrie Somerset's lesson came right after Joe's, and then we made every excuse to stop and see her. She was Mr. and Mrs. Sala's tiny niece, and her father was Charlie Somerset, who came to our house for poker; and Gerrie was the littlest, prettiest thing we had ever seen. She was *precious,* and very seldom allowed to spend a whole day with us, because her mother made her practise and take her dancing much more seriously than Mama made Joe. We adored Gerrie like something out of another star. Joe wanted them to be sweethearts, and Gerrie let him rather, but not exactly. I was not surprised at either of them; Gerrie was almost too special to be a sweetheart. When William Terriss's pretty daughter Ellaline was

going on the stage as Cinderella in the Lyceum Pantomime, Gerrie was actually in the Pantomime too! She
danced a Fly, and Mr. Espinosa was the Spider. Gerrie
was the tiniest thing ever seen, running down to the foot-
lights and crouching while she played her fingers before
her face, like a fly with its front-legs. It was dreadful when
long hairy Mr. Espinosa caught her. Of course Papa
took Joe to the First Night, and Joe came back fonder of
Gerrie than ever. But as Gerrie was more and more in
the theatre, we saw less and less of her; and presently
she was just a dancing memory.

* * * *

Like all of us, Joe wrote notes and letters to the family;
we could not be away from home without writing to
each other, and to Mama and Papa; and if one of us was
ill, and separated from the rest (we all had shocking, very
catchable colds) the Sickroom post was kept busy.

(Pencilled on pink paper, aged about 6)

DEEAR. PARPE I. HOUP. UR. WELL, I. AN, MUCH. BEPTIE.
I AME. SO, SORRY U. CAN NOT GOT UP I HOUP U WILE GET
UP, TOMOROW
TO. DEEAR PARPE   FROM, DEAR
Joe.

(All the "I" s in the text are pictures of eyes, complete
with eyebrows.)

A year or two later, a long letter, in "real" writing,
and in ink, to Mama in Bournemouth, where she had
taken Harry and me one March. Susan was then our
Nurse, and Bertie and Joe were to be consoled, turn and
turn about, by sharing with her the enormous six-foot-
wide walnut bed, which was now in the night-nursery.

My <u>dear</u> Mama

I will be <u>ever</u> <u>ever</u> so glad When you come home. Please do let me tell you that I have slept with Susan first and do stop away an <u>odd</u> Number of days, because you see, I wan to sleep with Susan last. Well we have put enuf about "bed" for I am not going to bed for—let us see—8 hours—No not 8, But 8 hows and 10 Minits. Now Miss Newmann sais to me, "Put in your letter to Mama that I hope you are having better weather in Bournmouth than we are haveing in London."

Tuesday Night, I and Ber—— No Bertie and I, had 6 pounds of the Grosesshot!!!* Tuesday Afternoon papa read A Chapter of "Alas and Wonderland" No! No! I mean "Through the looking-glass" I think I an The Headliss man."† I want to ask you some questions——

I Have you seen the "punch and judy man?

II Are you enjoying yourself?

III Are you weell? (That comes nearer the ent this time)

IV have you A nice house, or Hotall?

V Have you been on the sands yet or have Harry and Nellie grown too old for it?

VI have you been in the "Pleiseure Gardens?

Answer me in your next letter to me, papa read us another chapter of "through the looking-glass," on Wednesday—goodbye I am <u>realy</u> your—at least I hope so—loving

PS Waat a long letter this is.

Joe

Ten ordinary kisses, and one super-kiss, breaking into an epidemic of tiny kisses, like stars from a skyrocket, adorn the last page of this letter. Joe's inheritance of the Jefferson name carried the Jefferson spelling with it.

* Grocer's-Shop. In Harry's absence the food-allowance had evidently been raised.
† *The Headless Man,* Mr. Wyndham's current farce at the Criterion.

Another note, that never was delivered:

Dear Mr. Bray
                          I would like the notebook for 2d. you
showed me today. Would it do if I gave you 1d now and
the other penny on Saturday? Please do not do it if it
inconvenients you."

This was found by Mama on the stairs, written on
a minute scrap of paper. Mr. Bray, the local stationer,
never received it; Mama called Joe, gave him the penny
he was short of, and told him never to try to buy what he
couldn't pay for. The tiny note she folded and kept in
her jewel case. After her death I found innumerable
tiny mementoes of us tucked here and there in corners
of bags and boxes, where a chance opening, once a year
perhaps, might let her eye light on some early nursery
recollection.

* * * *

Joe adored music. On him Harry first exercised his
later gift for teaching, with regular lessons on the piano
and "Elements." I had refused to learn; my musical
inferiority made me awkward if I ever tried to play with
Harry in hearing, and when Mama offered me piano-
lessons from Dr. John Storer, I didn't want to, and no
more was said. I have always regretted that.

Going to concerts meant much more to Joe and me
than it did to Bertie, who couldn't, or wouldn't, even sing.
Joe had, like me, a small sweet voice, and we learned
Mendelssohn Duets for the "Miniature Concerts"
Harry got up among us.

As soon as music began to play its part in our lives,
Papa dashed off to the City and bought the score of
Haydn's *Toy-Symphony,* and all the instruments neces-
sary to its performance. The Symphony was beyond, not

our powers, but our numbers; so Harry composed others within our limits. When we had practised one of these to perfection, we drew up a programme in which it was the Pièce de Resistance. Other items were a group of Harry's last piano-pieces, a Solo by Joe, Duets by Joe and Nellie, a Recitation by Bertie, and Harry's last setting of a Psalm, or a lyric by Goethe, sung by Nellie. The Programme was delivered to Papa and Mama. After tea the Nursery was arranged, with chairs for the audience. I put my blue Venetian beads round my head. We all felt nervous, as great artists should. Bertie I think took the tickets at the door; the Best Seats cost 2d., and so did the Worst Ones. Papa and Mama mounted the stairs; he came in his opera hat, she in white kid gloves. Joe and Nellie stood up with pains in their stomachs, and sang:

> *"I would that the lo-ove I bear thee*
> *My lips in one wo-ord could say——"*

losing their breath in the wrong places, and finishing their phrases rather wheezily. But Harry's accompaniment was impeccable, and he controlled our performance and covered our fears. The Concert was an immense success. As soon as we had a completely new programme we gave another.

Then, Joe abed, Harry would sit down to the piano, and give a "piano-recital," with the doors left open. Chopin, Schubert, *the Intermezzo,* whatever was Joe's special favourite, floated in to him in the dusk; and later, through the floor to me, descended the Evening Prayer from *Hänsel and Gretel,* which it was such a torment to try to pick out for myself.

* * * *

Joe's grace and agility, as he grew up distinguished

him from the rest of us. He was good at games, and
excellent at "gym," where he and Bertie joined a youthful
class at the Hampstead Swimming-Baths, on Tuesday
and Friday Afternoons. Their Drill-Master was an ex-
Sergeant, Mr. Biggs. Joe became the star of the small
class; he vaulted the "Horse," and climbed the Ropes,
and swung the length of the Rings, more nimbly and
expertly than any other. At "gym" the Chums began
to meet young friends known dimly to Harry and me;
particularly Olga and Hilda Antonietti, two strikingly
beautiful children who spoke English without accent, and
carried their race in their eyes and their complexions.
Hilda and Joe became gay rivals on the Rings; but at the
end of the summer term it was Joe who carried off the
little silver medal bestowed by Mr. Biggs on his best
pupil. He accompanied the presentation with an ex-
Sergeant-like exhortation, informing the Prize-Winner
that he now had his foot on the lowest rung of the ladder
of Fame, and must climb steadfastly to reach the top.
This done, he called Joe forward to the middle of the vast
drill-hall, and pinned the medal on his Gym-jersey.
Inspired by the occasion, Joe's small voice rang through
at least a portion of the Hall:

"Three Cheers for Mr. Biggs! *Hip, hip, Hooray*——"

Not a child chimed in. Whether because he had taken
his class-mates unawares, or because they didn't see
why they, who hadn't their foot on even the lowest rung
of Fame's ladder, *should* cheer Mr. Biggs for giving Joe
a medal—they left Joe's small "Hooray!" to wander
solitary up into the rafters. He didn't make any attempt
to complete the cheers; with two of the triplets still-born,
Joe, a trifle flushed, returned to his place, his little medal
shining on his breast.

BERTIE

WILL HE GO to Hell? We hope he won't, but it
looks awfully like it.

As Harry prayed to God not to let Joe die, I prayed
more than once that Bertie might not be damned by his
passionate temper.

* * * *

There's a new Baby! Oh *dear.* Mama *promised* me I'd
see it before she took it out of the flower. Harry was born
in apple-blossom, and I was born in a snowdrop, and Joe
was born in a geranium How *tiny* we must have been,
before we were lifted out of our flowers. Then we suddenly
got as big as babies. *But just the very second before that,*
we were as tiny as fairies And Mama had *promised* me,
because I'd made her, that if another baby came in
a flower, she'd let me see it before it was lifted out. And
here the baby was, and they'd forgotten to call me.
I didn't see how he *could* have fitted into the lily-of-the-
valley he was born in. It was a shame of Mama. What
was his name going to be?

"Bertie," said Harry.

Nellie agreed eagerly.

But Mama and Papa didn't seem to think so. Harry was
determined. Some things, he always knew, did *have* to be.
And when he knew they had to be, they were. Mama and
Papa did not like the name much—but then, they did
not feel as we did about Bertie, the Captain of the Gay
Volunteers in *The Babes.* Harry said, "He *must* be named

Bertie"—and he cried. Then Papa and Mama said, "All right, we'll call him Bertie." They gave him the name of Herbert, so that he could be Bertie for short, as I was Nellie for short of Eleanor, and Joe was Joe, for short of Joseph Jefferson. Harry wasn't for short of anything. Some people thought it was for short of Henry, but of course it wasn't. Harry was *Harry*. Well never mind the Herbert, the baby's name is Bertie.

* * * *

I never stole Baby's bottle as I did Joe's; I was six now, and wouldn't have, even if I'd thought of it. But in Mama's room one evening, when Mrs. Whittaker was filling a lovely warm bottle of milk, I asked, "Can I have one too?" So Mrs. Whittaker filled me a bottle just like it, and I walked downstairs, sucking it contentedly through its long rubber tube. Papa was in the passage below, and looked up and laughed at me through the banisters. "Hullo, you big baby!" he said.

* * * *

Baby's tempers are terrible, His screams give me headaches. They make Papa angry, because he can't work. Sometimes he shouts, "Keep that child quiet!" and sometimes he goes out of the house, banging the door. He goes away as far as the Club not to hear Bertie yelling. Once he went as far as Paris. When Baby has reached a certain point of passion, nobody *can* stop him yelling, he can't stop himself. As he gets a little older, and starts one of his tempers, I watch fearfully for the point where he will slip over the edge, and try to divert his attention first. But once over the edge it is too late; he goes first

red, then crimson, then almost black in the face, and can't
get his breath. It is frightening. When Mama had to be
in Margate with Joe, Papa got in a temper with Fanny
Dodd, because of Bertie's crying. Then darling Fanny
left us. Mama felt even more badly about it than we did—
and that was bad enough.

* * * *

He is beautiful, the most beautiful of any of us. Harry
and I aren't, of course, and I thought nobody could be
more beautiful than Joe. But Bertie is glorious. His face
is proud and haughty, his hair is very silky and rich brown,
gold at the ends as mine used to be; Mama makes it
into long curls down her finger, like Joe's. They try to
make my hair curl, but it won't stay in after the first
setting; Joe's and Bertie's are "naturally curly" and
bubble all over their heads. Bertie's eyes are the best of
all; they are big and dark, with long lashes, and every
lady who comes to the house says, "What Beautiful
Eyes that child has!" He expects it now. Once a lady
came, and we were called downstairs to see her, and after
she had kissed us all she just went on talking to Mama.
So before we went upstairs again, Bertie toddled up to
her and said, "I's got Boo'ful Eyes!"

* * * *

"Go back! go back!" cries Mama from the garden.
Her face has gone as white as death. Bertie has somehow
climbed to the night-nursery window at the top of the
house; he has seen Mama under the cherry-tree, and is
leaning right out, waving to her. "Go in, darling," calls
Mama more calmly, "I'm coming up to you; go right

in and wait till I come." She can't get into the house and
upstairs fast enough; all the way she does not know if
Bertie has gone in or has fallen into the garden. When
she finds Bertie sitting on the night-nursery floor, she
clasps him, feeling ill; she cries; then he screams, and
they cry together. Nobody scolds him for screaming,
but I think Nurse got scolded for leaving him alone, and
bars were put up.

Another time he was lost. He got downstairs by himself, and out of the front gate. We couldn't find him anywhere. Mama was nearly out of her mind. We ran round
the streets looking for him and asking. Presently he was
found in King's College Road, between two poor little
children. He wasn't lost at all, he had run away. After
that, a gate was put at the top of the Nursery Stairs.
But soon it isn't hard to undo a gate.

* * * *

"What shall I *do-oo*?" cries Bertie, in one of his
fearful fits of boredom. "I don't know what to *do-oo*!"

"Sit on your thumbs!" says Mama laughing at him.
Bertie scowls, and sulks.

"What shall I do-oo?! don't mean Sit-on-my-
Thumbs-and-that!" he wails next day.

* * * *

We can all do things when people come and we are
called down. Harry can play, I can sing, Joe can dance.
Only Bertie seems to have nothing special, though he is
very, very intelligent. Then he finds out something he can
do that none of the rest of us can. He can Bend.

It is because he has double joints. He can put one foot
in his mouth and hop round the room. He can rise on his

toes, and sort of *curl* over and lie flat on the floor with one smooth movement. He can lie on the floor with *both* feet, crossed, in his mouth, and his arms hooked under his knees, till he is like a sort of ball, or a frog, and then he suddenly begins to roll round and round the room, turning over and over. Aunt Alice Edouin laughs till the tears run down her cheeks.

So now when people come in the evening, and Harry plays something he has made up on the piano, and I have sung "Bread-and-Cheese-and-Kisses" (Papa wrote the words for Miss Fanny Josephs) and Joe has sung "There *was* a little man called Captain," with actions, and then danced the Hornpipe, Bertie waits for Papa and Mama to say, "Now, Bertie, will you Bend for us?" They don't always say it, and if he isn't asked to Bend, Bertie is miserable. Of course, if *he* says, "Shall I Bend now?" everybody says Yes, and then he does; but some of the people Mama thinks mightn't want to see Bertie bend, as much as they want to see Joe dance, I don't quite know why, because really it is what almost nobody can do.

* * * *

Sometimes when he is in a passion, he throws things. Once he threw a knife across the room at Joe. We saw it coming, and Joe shut his eyes and forgave Bertie, in case it killed him. It cut Joe on the temple, just missing his eye. I clasped Joe tight, because he might have been killed. Bertie was carried screaming into the Night-Nursery. Harry was very stern. He decided that when Bertie did things like that he must be sent to Coventry.

* * * *

Mama has found a little note left on her dressing-table.

T N

"I don't like Dancing. Bertie." So Bertie goes no more with us to Mr. Reginald Crompton's in Berners Street.

* * * *

There are children in the gardens on both sides of us. Little Marie and Paula Lutgen in 198, Alice and Eddie Franc in 194. They are really Joe's and Bertie's play-mates, not ours, and are among the youngest children now at our Christmas Parties. There's a big family in the Lutgen's house; the Grandmother, Madame Raimondi, teaches Harry Italian. There are two grown-up daughters, Henriette and Chérie, and four grown-up sons, almost all musical. Henri, Marie-and-Paula's father, plays the Violoncello at the Empire, Charles plays the violin, Alec, the youngest, and the one we know best, plays the violin too; Gustave fences. Joe and Bertie have fencing lessons from Gustave, and Bertie learns the violin from Charles. So now we will all be musical. We can all sing, except Harry, who never sings out-of-key, but has no tune in his voice.

* * * *

My dear darling Mama
            I hope you are well. Please tell me you are. Have you been out. If so have you been in the Dog Cart. If so do you like the pony. Has Mr. Willard immetated Henry Irving. The birds are well. Last night Papa let i and Joe stay up half an hour later. I have just finished my practice and I had to practice Half an hour because I did not have time to the day before yesterday.
            With best love bertie Farjeon.

An inverted pyramid of kisses fills the rest of the page, balanced by two hearts containing the legend we always

added to our letters to Mama: "Please Kiss this I have."
It was written when Mama had taken Harry and me to
stay with Uncle Ted and Aunt Rachel Willard in Banstead.

Joe, in a similar letter, carefully corrected "I and
Bertie" to "Bertie and I, but "i and Joe" in Bertie's
note stands its ground. It is also noteworthy that in
Harry's absence, Papa allowed the boys more licence than
would have been permitted by our Nursery Law-Giver.
"6 Pounds of the Grosesshot!" and staying up "half
an hour later" would have been rare liberties under our
régime. Papa, of course, had no régime at all, and when
the cat was away, the mice played.

Poor little Bertie. How much did we add to his suffering,
I wonder? His letters and notes, treasured by Mama—
from his first inky scrawl ("Did you miss the post all
my lets that i sent you are by myself") to older letters
written although "I don't know what to write about.
This is a letter of words but not news"—are as expressive of affection as mine and Harry's and Joe's. He
thanks Mama *very* much for the nice present she gave
him, he liked "the 'twelf-night'" *very* much too; he
is full of messages for the sister who prays for his soul
(though he doesn't know it): "Is Nellie better?" "Tell
Nellie i am going to buy her something." "Ask Nellie
to tell me in her letter to me if she has read My friend
smith or not" (in the Talbot Baines Read era). Kisses
in crosses and Loves in circles plaster every note. You
cannot love your family without suffering for it; and if
your family sends you to Coventry on the one hand and
prays for you on the other, you must be suffering more
than it allows for.

* * * *

Marna has found another little note on her dressing-table. "Can I stop learning the Violin? I make my ears ache when I practise. Bertie." So Bertie's violin-lessons with Charles Lutgen stop.

* * * *

Contact with the Lutgens does not stop, if music-lessons do. Cricket is in the air and to the fore. Harry follows the teams on paper and carries us with him. Bertie is Surrey, Joe Yorkshire. Papa Surrey, because of Tom Richardson, who bowls so fast and gets out for a duck with a grin. Mama obligingly becomes Middlesex. I from the first am Sussex (because of those Cambridge lights, Jessop and Ranji), though I have never seen Sussex in my life (or Cambridge). Harry, like Bertie, is Surrey.

Cricket becomes the most popular game in the garden. Bertie determines to make one Century in his life. This is where Marie and Paula come in useful. He gets the little girls over the garden-wall, he sets up the stumps and goes in first to bat. Neither Marie nor Paula is a Tom Richardson. He keeps the wretched mites bowling at him till he has compiled his hundred. Then he declares. At teatime he tells us casually that he has made a Century to-day.

Harry and Joe and Bertie go to Lord's; I too endure long days on a hard narrow seat with a packet of sand-wiches. I learn to look on the game as the epic it is. I learn how to score for our home-made table-cricket games, played in all manner of ways. I thrill when Joe writes effusively to G. L. Jessop, and gets a letter back, "I say, my dear chap, draw it mild!" Jessop helps Joe and me through many a bad Boatrace Day.

* * * *

Joe and Bertie are inseparable. They call themselves "The Chums"; as Harry and I have our elaborately-prepared games, they too prepare elaborate games for each other. They give each other Nursery Parties, and before the holidays spend hours making up "prize-packets" for each other to open during the long train-journey up to Cromer. The prize-packets, of all shapes, sizes, and colour, contain all sorts of things: presents, jokes, books, games, sweets and things to eat. Each Chum gets Mama and Papa and Nellie and Harry, and anybody else they can rope in, to add to their store of packets for the *other* Chum. It is their ambition to be able to present 100 Prize-Packets apiece! On the journey they divide the time by the packets, and with luck are able to open a packet every three minutes.

* * * *

Joe defends Bertie; Bertie imposes on Joe. When they come home from Gym, Bertie throws himself lazily into a chair in the dining-room, and says, "Run upstairs and get my shoes for me, Joe."

Without thinking twice, Joe flies up the two staircases. Not till he reaches the Nursery does he begin to think once. He returns to Bertie, shoes in hand, demanding, "*Why* do I go upstairs and fetch you your shoes?"

"Oh, well, you don't mind it as much as I do," drawls Bertie.

Then if Joe is seized with one of his funny fierce tempers, he cries, "Oh, you little—you little——"

"Little what?" drawls his Chum.

"Oh, you little—*Bertie!*"

* * * *

But they are bound with a bond that nothing in life can sever. They have invented an absurd tune for themselves. When they leave the dining-room after a meal, they go upstairs abreast, arms twined round each other's waists, chanting:

> *"Chums are going up!*
> *Chums are going up!*
> *They won't come down until they've Sponged—*
> *Chums are going up!"*

In a few minutes, from the top of the house we hear the verse repeated with a variation:

> *"Chums are coming Down!*
> *Chums are coming Down!*
> *They* may *come down because they've Sponged —*
> *Chums are coming Down!"*

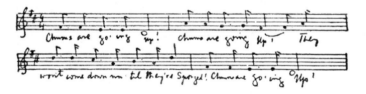

If you want to know what "Sponging" was, you will find it included in our Code of Nursery Laws.

* * * *

When Nursery Governess days came to an end, and Joe and Bertie became day-boys at Peterborough Lodge, the Preparatory School just started by our Mr. Linford in Finchley Road, a sudden change took place in Bertie's character. What it was due to I have never known, but at the age of twelve or thirteen he suddenly lost his temper. It did not seem as though he had learned to control it, but as though it had exhausted itself completely. In school he was good at his books, and good at cricket. He was one of the best bats, and a tricky slow bowler. Mr, Linford said, "That boy bowls with his head." Peterborough Lodge was so keen on cricket that young batsmen who forgot to keep the left elbow down were given lines, by a certain zealous master, for sending up unnecessary catches. That schooling should come second to cricket, seemed to Papa absurd—almost as absurd as schooling itself, a thing he held to be practically unnecessary. It was largely due to Mama's persuasion that the two boys were among Mr. Linford's first scholars; and Joe, to her regret, was removed after a year. What did Joe want with Greek and Latin, asked Papa, if he was going on the stage?

* * * *

Stamp-collecting was, of course, the rage. Bertie was assiduous with his Stamp-Albums, his Gibbons, and his duplicates. I learned how to look up plate-numbers, and to distinguish between Rose-Madder on Carmine, and Carmine on Rose-Madder. As Papa also interested himself in the collection, Bertie's box of duplicates passed the bounds of mere swopping.

"I say, you chaps!" he announced one day in school, "have you seen those frightfully good packets of stamps they've got at Bray's? They're awfully cheap, too, only twopence a packet!"

In the dinner-hour, he obligingly convoyed Stanley Woodhead and Og and Mog Frankenstein to the stationers' shop, and pointed out the desirable display in the window. The sale of a few envelopes resulted, and Bertie lingered on to split the profits with Mr. Bray, who had agreed to sell packets of Bertie's duplicates on a sharing-basis.

This is the only instance I recall in which any of us exhibited a trait attributable to our connection with the Merchant of Tunis.

* * * *

LIST of the 20 THINGS I LIKE BEST
(By Bertie Farjeon. n.d.)
1. Sneezing
2. Mother

The remaining 18 seem hardly of importance.

NURSERY LAW AND
NURSERY LORE

"NURSERY CALL

This is the Nursery Call. When you hear Harry play it on the piano, come at once. It is for something Important.

On Important Occasions of your own, you may play it yourself, to assemble the others.

"SO-AND-SO"

Any Person being physically annoyed or interfered with by any other Person can say "So-And-So!" at the Persecutor, who shall instantly stop persecuting. The Genesis of "So-And-So" is best expounded in drama.

BERTIE: Those are *my* Bricks.

JOE: Well, I'm only playing with them.

BERTIE: Well, you're not to. Harry, Joe's touching my Bricks.

HARRY: Play with your own Bricks, Joe. Stop touching Bertie's.

BERTIE: Harry! Joe's touching my elbow.

JOE: I'm not touching your *Bricks*.

BERTIE: But you're touching *me*.
HARRY: Stop touching Bertie, Joe.
BERTIE: He's touching me some more.
JOE: *I'm* not touching you, my pencil's touching you.
HARRY: Joe! Stop touching Bertie with *any*thing.
BERTIE: Now he's touching my bricks with his pencil.
JOE: Well, *I'm* not touching your *Bricks* or *You,* so there!

The Law-Giver takes thought. The following Rune is evolved:

"You mayn't touch Me, my Clothes, or Anything of Mine, with You, your Clothes, or Anything of Yours."

It worked like magic. Once pronounced, the pronouncer was exempt from that particular session of annoyance until "Next Time"—an indefinite period, honourably observed.

But the Rune was found to be not brief enough. During its utterance by the Irritatee, the Irritator could indulge in an orgy of "Touching." The Law-Giver considered again, and reduced the Rune to the comprehensive "SO-AND-SO!" The Nursery accepted and adhered to it. So much for the Law of Personal Rights.

"ONE-TWO-THREE-N!"

This is the Test of Truth. Any Person making a statement doubted by any Other Person can be challenged by the Other Person to repeat the Statement, followed immediately by three taps with the Right Forefinger on the Doubter's Left Shoulder, during which process the Tapper shall say: "One! Two! Three! N." But "N" shall not be tapped on. Anyone employing this Formula correctly for a False Purpose will lose the Confidence of the Nursery for ever.

Nobody ever did. But the complicated procedure, which must be carried out exactly, admitted of infinite misapplications which, if committed by the Tapper and unnoted by the Tappee, provided routes of escape for a good round Lie. *If you could get away with it,* you could not be brought to justice. (This is, of course, the Weak Spot of every Law ever made by man.) You had, as in later life, to be nippy about it, whether you wanted to utter, or to detect, a fib. Long before we knew anything of the legal system, we discovered for ourselves that a Law, when evaded cleverly enough, becomes the Wrong-Doer's protection.

JOE (bursting fiercely into the Nursery): Bertie!
BERTIE (drawling, suspecting what's coming): What?
JOE: You've torn my book!
BERTIE: I haven't!
JOE: Yes you have!
BERTIE: I tell you I haven't!
HARRY (looking up from minting new supplies of Paper Money, for Nursery Trading): Ask him One-Two-Three-N.
JOE: Didn't you tear my book One-Two-Three-N?
BERTIE: I didn't tear your book One-Two-Three-M.
JOE (surprised, but convinced): Oh.
NELLIE (looking up from *Jackanapes*): He said M not N.
JOE: There! you *did* tear my book.
BERTIE: No, I didn't, One-Two-Three-N.
JOE: You tapped on the N!
BERTIE: Oh, *all* right. One-Two-Three-N.
HARRY: You changed to your middle finger on Three.
BERTIE: Oh, ALL right! I did tear it then.

JOE: Oh, you little——! You little——!!
BERTIE (lazily): Little What?
JOE: You little——Bertie!!!

So much for the Law of Truth.*

SPONGING

This is the Law of Cleanliness. It was instituted less in our own interests than in those of the Nursery Piano, to Harry sacrosanct. After every meal, when you had received your permission to "get down," you must go straight to the Night-Nursery, and sponge your palms and fingers.

NELLIE (*perched on the green "Don Quixote" with pictures by Doré, jerking her short-sighted eyes up and down between the piano-keys and the "Schubert Album"*):
"Sah' ein Knab' ein Röslein steh'n——Röslein . . . auf . . .
Oh, bother!
(*She begins again, entirely forgetting what key she is in*)
"Sah' ein Knab' ein . . . ein Knab' ein Röslein——"
HARRY (*entering the Nursery*): Nellie! Have you Sponged?
NELLIE (*who nearly had it right, and now it's gone again*): Y-yes, I think so, didn't I?
HARRY (*running up a scale, and surveying the sticky keys with disgust*): No, you haven't. Go and Sponge at once.
[*Exit NELLIE, into the Night-Nursery, where, having sponged, her attention is probably distracted by her painting-things, and she sits down to paint a cardboard Troubadour with "A Merry Christmas" on the ribbon fluttering from his mandoline, for Papa's Christmas Card. When it is half-finished, she abandons it to write a Troubadour-Song. Harry*

---

* Should a Farjeon ever be subpœnaed as a Witness, let the Usher present said Witness not with a Bible, but with his Left Shoulder —and let Opposing Counsel jolly well look out!

wets napkin in his glass of water and wipes the keys, and as NELLIE *DOES not come back, sits down to practise his Czerny.*

PUTTING-AWAY

This is a Law of Order, instituted by Nellie, on Joe's behalf.

She had very little order herself, but, though she kept her shelf in the Toy-Cupboard in a shocking muddle, she never expected anybody else to put her things away for her. "Putting-Away" was not a popular job; Bertie particularly objected to "putting away his things when he had done with them."

He is reading a book in the Nursery, and is just about ready for a change of occupation.

Enter Joe. He comes and leans over Bertie's shoulder and looks at a picture. Bertie sidles away, leaving Joe looking. Bertie lugs out his Stamp-Album. Joe moves towards the piano. The book remains, un-put-away, on the table.

NELLIE (*laboriously gumming a shiny-black-paper wallet for Mr. Toole to take on tour with him, fondly believing he will really do so*): Put your book away, Bertie.

BERTIE (*with ill-concealed triumph*): Joe looked at it last.

JOE: What!!!

BERTIE: Yes, you did.

JOE: I only came and looked at the picture over your shoulder.

BERTIE: You looked at it after I did, and you've got to put it away.

JOE (*is speechless with indignation*).

NELLIE (*is vocal with indignation*): You *know* that's unfair, Bertie!

BERTIE: No, I don't. If Joe looked at the book last, it's fair for him to put it away.

NELLIE (*forcing her pointy in* JOE'S *cause*): Do you *really* mean that if Joe had been reading for an hour, and *you* happened to look at a single picture as he got up, you *honestly* think you ought to put the book away, and not Joe? You're *sure* you mean that?

BERTIE (*seeing no farther ahead than the moment*): Yes, I do.

NELLIE (*laying aside Mr. Toole, and tearing a half-sheet of note-paper*): Will you sign a paper saying so?

BERTIE (*uneasily*): Yes, I suppose so.

NELLIE (*scribbles hard, and pushes result across the table*): All right! sign this.

> Bertie says that if Joe has been using one of his (Joe's) books, and he (Bertie) looks last at one picture in same, it is his (Bertie's) duty to put it away.
>
> Signed: Bertie
>
> Witnesses: Nellie.
>
> Joe.

Joe put the book away.

Whether this document did more than supply us with a moral victory, whether it was ever brought out for enforcement, I don't remember. Even if occasion arose for it, it is more than likely that Joe continued to Put-Away for Bertie.

"*DIPPING-IN*"

This is a Law of Table-Manners. It is an indulgence, the relaxation rather than the institution, of a Rule. It would not do to dip your bread-and-butter in your tea *every* day—but what an agreeable difference it made to tea-time! Never to "dip-in" would be hard on Joe and Bertie, who valued the privilege particularly. For some reason unfathomed, "Dipping-In" became permissible on Tuesdays and Fridays, after the two boys had come home from "Gym." The Law-Giver did not invent this rule, but saw that it was duly carried out.

OXFORD AND CAMBRIDGE

The Nursery shall be divided into Oxford and Cambridge. Fairness shall be observed in the division. Harry began life Oxford; therefore, Nellie was born Cambridge. The next child (if any) must be Cambridge, and the fourth child (if at all) Oxford. Mere turn-and-turn-about would not be fair; for then Oxford's numbers would *always* be either level, or in the ascendant. Oxford though he is, Harry is too just to countenance a system that would not give Cambridge the chance of a majority. The Rule came into being after Charlie's death; in due course, Joe was born Cambridge, and Bertie Oxford. It advanced no further, but receded to our parents. Mama obliged by consenting to be Oxford, and Papa was accommodatingly Cambridge.

Of course, Joe and I were awfully glad we were Cambridge, because there is not the least doubt that Cambridge *is* the Best; but what we had to suffer in our youth, on Boatrace Day after Boatrace Day, hardly bears thinking about. Triumph was mercilessly charged with gibes; a low level of wit was indulged in, and humiliation rubbed in very hard. So hard, that in these latter years I do not hesitate to get my own back. Too many bitter Boatrace Days demand their compensation; woe betide any Oxford-man who comes within earshot now, upon a certain Saturday in March. I gibe, I jeer, I say, "N'yah! n'yah!" in your true Nursery style. The splendid part of it is that Destiny spared me the taint of having been born Oxford. There is no doubt whatever which is the superior University.

Reader! if you don't agree with me, n'yah! n'yah! Silly old Oxford. Well, never mind! perhaps they're good at Spillikins.

OCTOBER THE 11th, 3 O'CLOCK

On October the Eleventh, at Three o'clock, each member of the Family shall take special note of what he or she is doing, and, if they are separated, shall tell each other.

"BEING IN REACH"

You are "In Reach" of any Event, when it will take place To-morrow or the Day-After-To-morrow. To-morrow is "The Nearest in Reach," the Day-After-To-morrow is "The Furthest in Reach." Thus, when Christmas falls on a Friday, on Wednesday you cry joyously: "We are In Reach of Christmas!" (i.e. The Furthest in Reach). On Thursday you are the Nearest in Reach.

But note: by a blessed dispensation, you may also be In Reach of Being in Reach. On said Wednesday, you are not only the Furthest in Reach, you are also the

Nearest in Reach of being the Nearest in Reach ("To-morrow, it will be Christmas To-morrow!"). On the Tuesday, you are the Nearest in Reach of being the Furthest in Reach ("To-morrow, it will be Christmas the Day-After-To-morrow!"); as well as being the Furthest in Reach of being the Nearest in Reach ("The Day-After-To-morrow, it will be Christmas To-mor-row!"). And on the Monday, with Christmas four inter-minable days away, you can still say: "We are the Furthest in Reach of being the Furthest in Reach of Christmas!" This is the first dawn of hope.

The wistful and desirous child who mooted that one might even be In Reach of being In Reach of being In Reach, was squashed. And rightly.

"THE SNEEZING & HICCUP CHAMPIONSHIPS"

Hardly need explaining. The records in both events were usually held by Joe or Bertie. Your "break" in either ended after a lapse of (I think) a minute. Joe was the last holder of the Hiccup Belt with a run of 126 to his credit.

THE VOTING GAME

Invented by Harry for Family Entertainment during the Holidays, this game turned from mere Lore into Law, being put into operation when certain decisions had to be made. It was simple to play, but is rather complicated to explain. First you chose a subject to be voted on: The Loveliest Piece of Music, the Theme of the next Holiday Competition, or a Foolish Action to be performed by some unfortunate member of the company, said mem-ber to be elected by a second poll. Each Voter was sup-plied with a small heap of papers, about three inches square, on which he entered four contributions to the Pool of Candidates, giving three papers to his pet suggestion, two apiece to his second and third favourites, and one to his runner-up. When the six of us were playing, this formed a pool of 48 papers, from which each Voter then drew four at random. Of these, he tore up the one he liked least, duplicated the one he liked best, and returned them to the Pool. Four papers were then destroyed blindfold by Fate (in the shape of Harry), and from the reduced Pool you again drew four papers, and repeated the process of destruction, re-duplication, and reduction; when the Pool fell below 24, you drew three papers only, then two, and they were proportionately destroyed. Popular subjects soon came to the fore, while others were extinguished completely. Eventually a single subject remained in the Pool, and was adhered to.

"'Harry and Nellie are somewhere giving a little boy fivepennyworth of suet.' What do you mean? Why Suet?"—writes Papa from London to Mama in Overstrand in 1902, quoting from her last letter to him. We were summering in Norfolk that year, while Papa stayed at home without a holiday, I don't know whether because of work, or worry, or expense. "Why Suet?" Why? Because the Voting-Game had decreed so. We had each contributed a penny towards the purchase, and voted for the two victims who must perform the idiotic action. It fell on me and Harry; and nobody who hasn't tried it can imagine the difficulty of buying *exactly* fivepennyworth of suet in a village where you are known, and finding a small boy to give it to. Small boys, without elders in the offing, were peculiarly rare. Sweets? easy!—but what East Anglian Mother would eye without suspicion two strangers, both over twenty, who were foisting a horrid little bundle on her offspring *sans* explanation? We wandered far afield, and at last, in a remote lane, found two little girls in chargé of a toddler in a pinny. Hope revived—but pinafores are a-sexual. Beaming on the elder girl, we asked, "Is this your little brother?" "Yes'm." (*Thank heavens!*) "There, little boy!" we said benignantly, thrust our package into his hands, and fled before he had time to investigate it. We felt highly embarrassed on our own account, and horribly guilty about the baby's disappoint-ment—but the Voting-Game had been honourably observed.

HOLIDAY COMPETITIONS

"A Good Honest Cake!" was Papa's verdict over High Tea in Cromer, 1892. The Cake had been baked specially for us by a local worthy; we had looked forward to it, sampled it, and then Papa pronounced what might have stood as its obituary notice—but "I'll give a prize of a shilling for the best poem on this Good Honest Cake," he added. We were allowed a week to write our poems in, and on a given evening the anonymous results were read aloud by Papa, who did not himself compete. A vote was taken on the merits of the verses, and the prize awarded or divided as the case might be. I forgot who won the prize on the first occasion, but the Competi-tion proved so popular that another was set for next week—it may have been on the Donkeys, which took, or didn't take, us to our famous picnics on the Roman Encampment; or on the Melons, which Papa bought by the dozen, and ripened in the sitting-room window with great art, because Mama was passionately addicted to them; or to the Cornelian which we hunted on the beach for hours, giving each other "Benefit Days," when everybody's findings went to Joe, or Bertie, or Mama (Joe's Cornelian and Agate Collection swelled into thousands after a few years); or to the Circus in the Meadow outside our cottage, when Bertie, having wept bitterly in the afternoon for the death of Black Bess in *Dick Turpin's Ride to York*), wept just as bitterly in his bed at night, when the Circus Band repeated the moving strains which told him Bess was dying all over again.

From 1892 the Weekly Competitions became a regular feature of our holidays for years, and of all our efforts I find only one preserved, oddly enough by Mama, whose forte was not literary composition. The subject was "Fishing," set in 1894, when we had a chalet on the Thames at Bray. Local topics were of course the popular ones; we had already written poems on "The Punting Championship," over which family feeling ran high, the four younger Farjeons being ardent adherents of the noble William Haines at Windsor, while the elder Farjeons supported the inferior William Morris of Bray. (Let me place it on record, *en passant*, that there never was, is, or will be a Professional Punter to equal the immortal William Haines.) And now Fishing was in the air. Mama, her father's own child, adored it. She couldn't put on her own bait, and she couldn't take off her own fish, if she caught it (which she never did); all she wanted was to be moored safely in the punt in a nice quiet backwater by Gilbert the boatman, with a rod in her hand. Here she sat contentedly by the hour, watching her float, and if it bobbed she hauled it up excitedly—and then Gilbert put on some more bait. One day we decided it was time she caught a fish. When she was nicely established, Gilbert passed her her rod, already sunk in the stream;

for a little while she sat there dreamily, then some passing weed in the undercurrent pulled the float under and Mama jerked up her line—"I got a fish! I've got a fish!" she cried thrillingly, and hauled into mid-air a splendid kipper, which Papa had bought in Maidenhead. So it was fitting that when "Fishing" was the theme, Mama should, for the first and only time in her life, carry off the prize with the following contribution:

> She never caught her fish,
> But let the barbel like a worm i' the hook
> Feed on her little bait. She fished and thought,
> And with a brown and yellow fishing-rod
> She sat with patience in a punt
> Waiting for fish. Was not this sport indeed?
> Others may row more, punt more: but indeed
> Shows are more than will; for still she proves
> Much in the river
>   But nothing on her hook.

"GOOD-NIGHT, GOD-BLESS-YOU, DEAR PAPA AND MAMA"

This is one of mine; I made it up, and nobody else does it. When I have said "Good Night" to Papa and Mama, I must run upstairs starting with the Left Foot, pause on the Eleventh Stair with my Right Foot suspended, and call over the banisters, "Good-Night, God-bless-you, dear Papa and Mama!" I must not change my position until they call back; then only can I run up the rest of the stairs. If anybody is on the staircase while I do it, I must go back and do it all over again. American Uncles, having discovered this, keep me running up and down a dozen times by stepping on the stair just before I can get clear. The feeling then is rather like the Telegraph-Wires, pulled into sight again. But back I have to go, and back, and back, till Mama calls, "Stop it, Boll! Stop it, Willie! Let the child get to bed."

BED-TIME

This is fixed for all of us by Harry at half-hourly intervals. When Joe and Bertie go to bed at half-past eight Nellie goes at nine, and Harry at half-past nine. It is a Law that must be as positively observed as Curfew. Why Joe and Bertie had a common bedtime is not clear; perhaps from attachment—spiritually they are Siamese Twins. Joe "minds" this secretly, but for years is too self-suppressing to put his point. When he does, Bertie "minds" openly.

At twenty-five minutes past eight, Harry takes out his silver watch, and lays it beside him on the table. His eyes consult it frequently, because he will no more mulct you of your last second than he will extend it. At half-past eight exactly he announces: "Bedtime, Joe-and-Bertie!" Joe and Bertie perhaps are playing Ludo. They may be excitingly near the finish, their men trotting up and down final corridors.

"Can't we just——" Joe begins.

"It's half-past eight. Good night."

Loiteringly they relinquish the game, and go.

Nellie looks up, expectant. Harry says, "We'll have half-an-hour of TAR. Where did we get up to?" Nellie tells him.

They begin. An episode of particular thrill is in progress. Nellie, for the moment not herself, but M. le Comte de Guiche, or Hermia, or Prince Ravna, for twenty-five minutes is rapt away from earth, while she and Harry

walk round and round the table, talking and being, suffering and rejoicing. When they get giddy, he wheels and
walks the other way, and Nellie follows, scarcely aware of
the change of motion. At five minutes to nine, out comes
the silver watch; Harry holds it in his hand as they per-
ambulate. Now Nellie is only half-absorbed in one of her
multitudinous Other Selves; in four minutes, three
minutes, two, in *one* more minute, the knell will sound.
Back goes the watch in the pocket. "*We're Harry-Nellie-
Joe-and-Bertie!* Good night, dear."

"Oh, Cola! *Please.*"

"Of course not. It's your Bedtime."

Nellie kisses him, and goes. Harry returns to *Zanoni* or
David Copperfield. At twenty-five minutes past nine, out
comes the watch. He places it where he can see it from
his page. Up and down, up and down, he blinks, the
thickest lashes boy was ever blessed with brushing his
strong glasses. The instant the minute hand reaches half-
past nine, let Zanoni exercise what magic he may, let
Dora be at her last-gasp-but-one, let the very sentence he
is reading be unfinished—bang goes the book. Zanoni's
spell must hang upon the air, and Dora's life by its precarious thread, till Harry's Reading-Time to-morrow
night. He sends himself to bed, as he sent us. The queer
boy has no appeal against himself. That is why we do not
appeal against him.

It should be added, that these Nursery Laws were made
for us three younger members. Harry, who owned and
adhered to them as strictly as he expected us to, submitted us to none of the physical persecutions which demanded the protection of SO-AND-SO! and under all circumstances would have told the truth, without assistance
from ONE-TWO-THREE-N! Perhaps now and then, jokingly,

he might cast some mis-statement on the air which demanded the administration of the Nursery Oath; he then,
in carelessly obvious fashion, might tap our right shoulder
instead of our left, fail to tap at all on "ONE!" or amuse
himself indefinitely with the teasing evasions we had discovered to be possible. But his evasions always *were*
obvious, and had we been so blind as to miss them, the
mis-statement would not have remained extant. That
Harry should perpetrate anything that could be distantly
called "a fib," was as inconceivable to us as to himself.

One result of these adhered-to rules was that quarrelling
was, on the whole, far less frequent, and far more easily
put down, in our Nursery than in most others. Another
result was, that when friction did occur, slight quarrels
loomed big, out of all proportion. We might have been all
the better for a few healthy storms to clear the air, and
thought far less of such things in later life. Only those
Nurseries which suffered from outbreaks can say.

CHRISTMAS CARDS FROM
THE CREMERS

A MONG OUR BENEFACTORS were Mrs. Benedict and the Cremers.

Mrs. Benedict was a large rich widow. She lavished on us, from time to time, at unusual seasons, and for no understandable reason, quantities of unexpected things, such as rich red silk sashes and nonpareils in cages. I have not the very slightest idea who she was. My recollection of her ends with her dim benevolent figure, and her gifts.

The Cremers are a little more definite. Mr. Cremer kept the best toy-shop in Regent Street, There had been a Mrs. Cremer; there, were two Miss Cremers. As long as old Mr. Cremer continued in life, Christmas brought us cases full of the most fascinating toys. The Major and the Chinaman came from Cremer's. The Major was mine, the Chinaman was Harry's. They sat on the mantelpiece and nodded at us. One day we discovered that their heads lifted out. We looked inside them, and found packets of sweets. After this, we looked inside them every morning. Other packets of sweets were always there. Harry's superb Noah's Ark came from Cremer's too. One night he launched it on his bath, and left it floating. Where it sailed to by night, who shall say? In the morning it held a cargo to delight a child. Whenever he left it hopefully afloat, his hopes in the morning were not disappointed. Above all, Dobbin came to us from Cremer's. He had two simple green rockers, and a brown-hair coat. How we despised, later on, the unreal, varnished breed of rocking-horse, with horizontal action back-and-forth, instead of the authentic up-and-down! Dobbin was *real*, you fondled his ears, and wore his smooth neck smoother still with kisses. One day we discovered that his horsehair tail pulled out. We explored his stuffing, as far as small fingers could poke. In the days to come, we began to find "things" in Dobbin; like the Major, the Chinaman, and the Noah's Ark, he became a yielder of treasures. I recollect jewellery of the "Bong-Bong" order (we called your Christmas Crackers Bong-Bongs then). How many of the wondrous toys in Papa's study came from Cremer's? When Papa took us into the study it meant a treat of some sort. The richest treat was Papa's Coloured Paper. He had a huge packet of it in a cupboard, good square sheets, exquisitely tinted a dozen different colours. He would deal us out so many sheets apiece—dark blue, pale green, rose-pink, grey, orange, purple for Harry, light blue, deep green, mauve, crimson, yellow, and brown for Nellie; we returned to the Nursery stored with material for endless ingenuities. Or else, we stayed in the Study, and were shown some magic toy. Papa took apart for us the beautifully-glazed coloured Indian boxes, box within box within box, from two inches high to something too infinitesimal to open. Or he produced a set of carved ivory tubes, strung with silken strands in brilliant hues; he drew a tube the length of the harp-like strands, and the twenty strings had dwindled to two! he drew another tube along the two, and they spread themselves into a row of ten; another—there were sixteen multi-coloured strands, then four, then twelve, in bewildering succession. Where did they vanish, how did they reappear? It was a Chinese mystery.

Most magic of all, he showed us the square box with the

glass top that never came off. The box was lined with
shiny silver paper, on which, in little heaps, lay tiny
curious objects: midget, loose-limbed men, with bodies
painted scarlet, purple, or with blue and pink stripes:
purple beetles and yellow butterflies, bigger than the
men: a tiny crane, with white wings and red legs and
beak: three balls, yellow, green and purple. Black and
quiescent they lie about their silver floor. Papa takes up
the worn red-leather "rubber"; he rubs, swiftly, lightly,
squeakily, the glass lid of the box—we watch, holding our
breath. A midget lifts a red leg, one waves a blue arm, a
purple beetle skims the air and flops, the balls begin to
bump upon the glass, the crane rises, remains, and
flitters half across the glass before it falls. Suddenly the
whole minute troupe goes insane; the little men run,
leap, spread-eagle themselves over the glass, hang on by
one limb, climb one another's shoulders, totter about,
here there and everywhere; the skittering beetles fall on
and attack them, the crane flutters and hops, the three
balls behave madly. Then, one by one, the troupe drops
prone. We name the one we think will last the longest.
Sometimes, when he seems dead, a midget man will
twitch a feeble limb, but is powerless to leap to the glass
roof again. Sometimes a butterfly shudders convulsively.
A ball rolls half an inch. Then all is still—till the Magician
makes his wizard passes once again with the Morocco
pad.

From the Cremers came the dolls I never cared for, but
the best tea-set which I valued for tea-parties for ourselves, not for the dolls, came from the unaccountable
Mrs. Benedict. It was big enough to put things on the
plates; and the teapot poured out.

When Mr. Cremer died, the two Miss Cremers went to

live in the Isle of Thanet. At Christmas now "The
Cremers" meant cards only. But they were always the
first Christmas-Cards we received—dear little robins
perched on babies' cradles, dear little girls in bonnets,
with bunches of holly, "To dear little Harry—dear little
Nelly—dear little Joe—dear little Bertie—with love from
the Misses Cremer." They came like heralds, early in
December, when Christmas was three endless weeks away.
Mother's voice calling: "The Cremers' Cards have
come!" brought us running. We looked, and knew that
Christmas was coming too.

But posts are so uncertain, and Thanet and London not
quite next-door, you know, and it would be dreadful to a
pair of fond, remembering spinsters should their cards
ever arrive a trifle late. To make quite sure, they began to
despatch their Christmas-cards in November.

"Children! the Cremers' Christmas-cards!"

"Already?"

Christmas is not yet due for a full month. We run to
collect the precious firstlings.

And years pass, you grow older, the things to be done,
the occasions to prepare for, press a little more irksomely
each year on ladies who, if they cannot still send cases of
toys to little Harry, Nellie, Joe, and Bertie, must *never*
disappoint dear children of their Christmas Greetings.

"The Cremers' cards!" calls Mama, somewhere
about Guy Fawkes' Day.

We return, one September, from the summer holiday.
The golden weeks beside the sea have waned, but London
streets are sunny, it is weeks yet to the time of fog, and
fires.

Laughing too much to speak, she appears waving an
envelope. "*No!*" exclaims Harry. But there they are,

the Cremers' cards have come. "To dear little Harry—
dear little Nelly—dear little Joe and dear little Bertie——"
The robins, and the little girls in bonnets.

Two of us at least are over twenty, and to-morrow it
will be October the First.

That was the last of the Cremers' Christmas-cards
Then time went back on them.

TAR

"**W**HAT DO YOU REMEMBER?" I asked Alice, no longer Franc, after a separation of thirty years.

I remembered that when the Leveaux left us neighbourless on the right hand; and we no more saw daily Freddy, a rather thrilling friend, because legend said he had eaten poison in his infancy and so he *might* have died, instead of merely speaking as though his mouth was full of fluff; or Monty, much our elder, dark-eyed, handsome, and deeply admired by me; or little Bibsy; or Violet and Daisy, whose enormous doll descended on me one Christmas, a shiny plaster person with horrible joints, real hair that matted, and a dark-red, shot-silk dress, a perfect White Elephant of a doll, that I had to pretend to like: the Francs replaced them.

The two small children, Alice and Eddy, concerned us most. It was not long before we were appearing circumspectly through each other's front gates, and less circumspectly over the dirty wall at the end, where their rockery" gave you a leg-up or down. Little Eddy, and Alice, square and sturdy, with big round eyes, were soon members of Joe's and Bertie's cricket team.

Mr. Franc I barely remember; but kind Mrs. Franc, discovering I loved Schiller, invited me to read German with her every week; and once a charming young Fräulein Toni was staying there, who, when she heard that Harry was "musical," said *she* had a cousin who was "musical" too, and played the viola. Privately I didn't suppose that Fräulein Toni's cousin, Mr. Tertis, was anything like Harry. Such wisps are all I remember of the Francs, the lucky owners of the next-door pear-tree.

"What do I remember?" said Alice. "Bertie bit me."

"He wouldn't now."

"Well, he bit me once. Joe and I consulted about it. We didn't want to tell Harry and have Bertie really punished, but even tender-hearted Joe felt that bite couldn't be passed over. We decided Bertie must say he was sorry or be spanked. He wouldn't say it, so Eddy and I sat on him while Joe did the spanking."

"What else do you remember?"

She began to laugh. "I remember the very first time we saw your Father. We'd only just moved in, and Mother was resting in bed. The door-bell rang violently, and an excited stranger rushed into the house, brushed the girl aside, ran upstairs into Mother's room, knelt down by the wall, and began to smell the floor. Then he got up, and apologized to Mother, who was lying there in helpless amazement, thinking a lunatic had got into the house. He explained that Mrs. Farjeon was ill, and he had noticed a bad smell that made him anxious, but couldn't trace it under *her* floor, so he thought it must be under ours. However, it wasn't, so he went away, leaving Mother to wonder what sort of neighbours she'd got. Then I remember Joe and Bertie taking me to the theatre two nights running to see Henry Irving—*two nights running.* I was fearfully proud that they wanted to, because you Farjeons gave me a terrible inferiority complex, you were so darned clever." She began to laugh again. "I remember you and Harry walking round and round the houses, he a little ahead, you trotting at his elbow, arguing and arguing with your heads together. I never knew what it was about, but I *never* saw you two walking in the streets without arguing."

So that was how it looked from the outside. We were not arguing, Alice; we were playing TAR.

* * * *

It was, I know a comic little couple in spectacles, her hair never too tidy, his hair always too long, that set forth daily, sometimes twice a day, from Adelaide Road, on adventures nobody dreamed of. For ten years we faced the secret smiles and open jeers of the neighbourhood. Our absorption was almost complete, though sometimes the "Git yer 'air cut!" of the arabs annoyingly destroyed our self-hypnosis. Once when this happened Harry marched up to the offender. "There is an H in my hair!" he said severely, and passed on.

We were surprisingly indifferent to externals; all we wanted was not to be interrupted. Friendly smile or mocking grin rolled off us like water off a duck's back, and greeting and gibe were equally unwelcome when we were playing TAR.

There were two crossing-sweepers on our beat; the nice old one, who smiled and called Joe "Curly," and the ugly nasty one who made gross noises at us. I always wanted to get this one out of consciousness quickly, and was surprised one day to see Harry slowing up.

"What are you going to do?" I asked.

"I've decided to give him a penny."

"What for?"

"To see what he will do."

As the first coarse words were launched on us, Harry calmly took out his purse, and laid a penny on Ugly Crossing-Sweeper's knee. His leer disappeared in astonishment, hoarse gratitude replaced his sneer, and the next day he did his best to smile at us. It wasn't a nice smile, and I did not like him any better for two or three years. Then his wretchedness conquered my distaste with sympathy. He had only one leg. But at that time all we cared about was that we had laid an enemy low, and could play out-of-doors with one less interruption, talking and talking with our heads together.

What was TAR?

* * * *

TAR was the usual child's game of pretending to be somebody else; but I think in our case it was extended to a degree of intensity, complexity, and accomplishment never equalled. This game began when I was about five years old, and for more than twenty years it continued to be the chief experience of my inward and outward life. The creative imagination we had inherited from Papa's side, the sense of impersonation that must have come from Mama's—and that fluid element of our dual being, which made me alive, at its inception, to Harry's wish— enabled us to secrete ourselves in a world of illusion within which we became, not one, but fifty persons at once (by changes of thought and mood so swift that the machinery of the drama never creaked). Harry had only to say "We are This Person and That," and we instantly *were* those two, till some movement in the drama necessitated an exit or another entrance; then "We are So-and-So and Such-and-Such" he murmured (like a stage-direction in italics)—it was enough; once more we were those two. I could not "be" anybody till Harry said so; he could move freely about my one personality of the moment, because the course of the play, and its stage-management, lay somewhere in the recesses of his mind. I waited only to know who I was next; and guided by his unrevealed direction, I played my part, emotionally absorbed. Harry must have been in the position of the Creator watching his puppets, even allowing them to affect their own destinies when they did things he had not quite prepared for. So actual, so exciting, so fascinating was this twin-gift of ours, so much more marvellous was the life we could make for ourselves than the one we had found made for us, and so fertilely did the gift develop as we grew older, that the game of childhood had no excuse for dropping away with our growth. My own development took place far more within the boundaries of TAR than within those of life. At an age, and long past it, when life's horizons should have been widening, they kept their narrow circle, while those of TAR widened increasingly. I had no desire for new adventures, friends, or experience, outside this powerful game. When I should have been growing up, it was a harmful check on life itself, for its imaginative extension did not include natural knowledge. Because of it, I was never aware of my own sex till I was nearly thirty years old, and it took at least ten years more for emotional crudeness to get abreast of mental ripeness.

But if it checked me on the one hand, I acquired through it on the other the power to put in motion, almost at will, given persons within given scenes, and see what came of it, and I think I owe to TAR, more than to any other element in my life, the flow of ease which makes writing a delight.

* * * *

It was essential that nobody should know what TAR

was. TAR was an inviolable secret. *I must not tell.* I never did. So absolute was this seal of secrecy, that I wonder I am not struck dead by thunder-and-lightning as I break it now.

Of course, domestics and parents knew we played some absorbing game by the hour (though they did not know of the orgies that lasted a week, when we moved among them disguised as Harry and Nellie); and Papa and Mama, if not our nurses, had an inkling of its elements. But even Joe and Bertie, who were, as Nursery Denizens, initiate, and had their birthright of a name apiece in the game (where ours were legion)—even they never enacted *à quatre* the magic we achieved *à deux*. They soon slipped out of the game, except for an anniversary occasion to be recorded; and Harry and Nellie went on existing, by themselves, in a setting as remote as that seen in a crystal globe.

Hold the globe very still, gaze as you will at the little house, the tree, the church, the castle; ponder as you please on the nature, purpose, and sex of the figures within; you cannot mingle with the life you look on. You cannot climb that hill and enter that castle. You cannot hear what these people say to each other, or dream what they are feeling. You will never even see their lips or limbs in motion while you gaze. Foiled, you may seek to exert power over them by shaking the globe and raising a blizzard round them; the futile demonstration will but hide them from your sight, the little people will vanish in the flurry, and all unseen will mount the hill and run into the castle for one eternal moment. When the white snow-storm settles silently, there will they be, the two untouchables, just as they were, a problem to you still. What they have seen and been you can only guess at—wrongly.

Let Mama and Papa smile, let nursemaids shrug, at
Harry and Nellie "playing their game of pretending"—
pretending endlessly, hour after hour, week after week,
year after year: smiles and shrugs were both far from the
mark. TAR was more than a game, it was an existence.
Harry was Glendower, calling spirits from the vasty
deep—and they *did* come when he did call for them;
Harry was Prometheus and I his figure of clay, till he
breathed into me the stolen fire. Like a medium I flowed
into, or was possessed by, other streams of being, imagination released from all check was set vibrating and took
astonishing action, TAR was not something that replaced
life for me, TAR was life. All other calls remained green
when they should have been fruitful, frustrated when
they should have been fulfilled. Everything that might
have happened to me in the world—love, adventure,
tragedy, comedy, sport even!—happened to me when
Harry and I played TAR. I had *become*, for days on end,
creatures in Wonderland; I had lost and won duels and
battles, committed crimes and heroisms, achieved
nobility, endured accident, died many times in many
ways, plotted against my king, rescued my king, had
mistresses, and been them, triumphed and been defeated
on cricket-field and tennis-court, followed the Grail,
felt danger and delight, starved and been rich, loved
and been loved, hated and been hated, been beautiful
and ugly, strong and weak—lived through a phantas-
magoria of experience that life could not have offered me
at that age, if ever. It is common for two or more children
to units in imaginary games, played with intensity; and
still more common is that solitary existence the child
does not speak of, where he exchanges his personality
for another. But I know of no other case in which the

game of two was continued for more than twenty years with increasing richness; and I doubt whether, among children, there have been many capable of following their leader as I followed Harry to the last time he said "We are D'Artagnan and Porthos" from the first time he said "We are Tessy and Ralph."

───────

I was five and Harry was eight. We had been to our Second Theatre. Our First Theatre was *The Japs*, when I was four. Aunt Alice and Uncle Willie Edouin and Uncle Lal Brough were in it, and also in our Second Theatre, which was *The Babes*. Uncle Willie was the Boy Babe, Aunt Alice was the Girl Babe, and her name was Tessy. She was the Best One. There were two Villains, the Bad Villain and the Good Villain; the Bad Villain was Uncle Lal Brough, the Good Villain had blue boots. He was called Ralph. His blue boots were most beautiful. There was the Captain of the Volunteers, called Bertie. "We are Gay Volunteers!" they sang marching in to bright music. "How we splash! How we dash!" sang Bertie, who was the *Very Best One*. He was a Hero. He was Miss Grace Huntley. One time in the play Aunt Alice who was Tessy pretended to be an Italian Hurdy-Gurdy Grinder, and she had a Monkey, and the Monkey was Uncle Willie. He ran about on a long chain, and was very *very* funny. In the end Tessy married the Boy in Blue Boots who was Ralph.

When we got home we would be them. Harry would be the Girl Babe Tessy, who was the Best One, so I would be the Boy Babe who was Uncle Willie, Harry would be Bertie who was the Very Best One and Miss Grace Huntley, but I did not care if only I could be the Boy in Blue Boots who was Ralph and married Tessy who was the Best One and Aunt Alice.

Harry said "We are Tessy-and-Ralph," and we *were* them. Then he said "We are Harry-and-Nellie," and we were Us again.

Every day Harry said "We are Tessy-and-Ralph." I waited for Harry to say it. The magic could not begin until he did. Sometimes he said we were other people in *The Babes*, but mostly Tessy and Ralph. Joe heard us. He had not seen *The Babes*, but he wanted to be in the game of Tessy-and-Ralph, so we let him be the Monkey who was Uncle Willie Edouin the Boy Babe who *I* was, but I was not the Monkey. Joe was too little *really* to play the game, but we told him about the Monkey. Joe called him "The Monk" and then just "Monk"; he ran about and made funny faces. That would do for Joe to be in the game. Now Harry said every day "We're Tessy-and-Ralph-and-Monk," and we were them; presently he said "We're Harry-Nellie-and-Joe," and we were Us.

The Baby. He hasn't got a name. He must be called Bertie, he *must*. It is the Very Best Name. Papa and Mama say No. Harry cries. Papa and Mama say Yes. The Baby *is* called Bertie, and he is Oxford. Harry says so, so he is. Harry's Oxford, and I'm Cambridge. Harry said I was, so I am. Then Joe had to be Cambridge, because it must be fair, and in turns.

(I will never, never, *never* let *anybody* know, *ever* — but I wish I was Oxford. Not because Oxford wins, and not because it is the Best One, but because Harry is Oxford. But he shall never know this as long as he lives.)

Now Bertie is old enough to know what Oxford is, and he is it. He is the worst at jeering of all. Listen! he's screaming. Papa is shouting up the stairs for him to stop. What *is* the matter with Bertie? He is sobbing, "I want to be in Tessy-and-Ralph." If you are old enough to know about Oxford, you are old enough to know about Tessy-and-Ralph. What will Harry do about it?

Harry is fair, he decides that Bertie ought to be in Tessy-and-Ralph, but there is nobody left in *The Babes* for Bertie to be; he does not tell Bertie this, but I can see he is thinking.

Bertie is screaming, "I want to be a Monk like Joe."

"You can't," says Harry, "there was only one Monk."

"Then I want to be a Doggy!"

"All right," says Harry. "We're Tessy-and-Ralph-and-Monk-and-Doggy."

Bertie is crying harder.

"What is the matter?" asks Harry. "I've told you you're a Doggy."

"I want to be a Doggy-Woggy."

"All right. We're Tessy-and-Ralph-and-Monk-and-Doggy-Woggy."

Bertie is simply yelling.

"Didn't you hear me *say* you were a Doggy-Woggy?" demands Harry.

"I want to be a Doggy-Woggy-Woggy. I want to have the longest name in the game!"

Harry says very firmly, "We're Tessy-and-Ralph-and-Monk-and-Doggy-Woggy-Woggy-Woggy-Woggy-for-ever."

Bertie stops crying. He is pleased, because now nobody can ever have a longer name in the game than he has. Tessy-and-Ralph goes on. We *are* them.

Presently Harry says "We're Harry-Nellie-Joe-and-Bertie."

We're Us again.

Harry whispers, "Never let Bertie know that Doggy-Woggy wasn't in *The Babes*." So of course I never will.

* * * *

When people ask "What *are* you playing, dears?" we do not answer. The name of the Game is secret. They must not know. But suppose they heard me say to Harry "Let's play Tessy-and-Ralph?" then they would know. Harry has a splendid idea. "We will call it T. A. R., and we will say it like TAR. Then nobody will know." So some people know we play TAR, but nobody knows about Tessy-and-Ralph.

* * * *

Grimm's Fairy-Tales. Some of them shall be in TAR with the Babes. Harry is the Boy who is turned into a Fawn, and I am his sister who married the Prince. Fawnie becomes very important, and he is very strange and magic. Because he can speak like a boy and an animal, he has most curious ways.

Little Women. Mama is reading it to us. We like Papa's reading best, it's more exciting, but Papa said Mama would read us Little Women because of the American. Harry is Jo and Amy and Laurie. I am Meg and Beth and Professor Bhaer.

Alice. Papa reads us that one, and it is the Best One. Harry is Alice and the March Hare and the Queen of Hearts and the Cheshire Cat and the Gryphon; I am the White Rabbit and the Hatter, and the King of Hearts, and the Cook, and the Mock Turtle.

It is wonderful! Alice is finished—and there is another one of her! Now Harry is the Red Queen and the White King, and the White Knight, and I am the White Queen

and the Red King and the Red Knight. Of course Harry
must be the Fawn Alice meets in the Wood, because of
Fawnie.

Lots of ones are coming into TAR.

* * * *

We go to the Adelphi and see *The Harbour Lights*. It's
a new sort of play. Miss Jessie Millward comes on in
a pink dress on a sunny morning, and someone says
why is she so happy, and she clasps her hands and says,
"David's coming home to-day! David's coming home
to-day!" I should think she would be happy, for David
is William Terriss who comes to play poker with Papa.
He is handsome, just like a hero. He is an officer. People
think badly of him, and he saves another lady at the
bottom of a cliff where the villain put her with the tide
coming in. Then people think well of him. His faithful
one is Tom, who is a sailor, and Johnny Shine plays
him; and *his* sweetheart is Peggy, who is Miss Clara
Jecks. They are a funny pair of sweethearts, and make
you laugh. They quarrel a lot. When we get home,
Harry says they will be in TAR. I am Miss Jessie Millward
and Tom, and Harry is Will Terriss and Peggy. We like
being Tom and Peggy best, and the others drop out.
Tom and Peggy have a mountain-climbing game with
Halma Men and the Anker-bricks; Harry piles up
mountains of bricks with one upright on top; Tom is
a black Halma Man, Peggy a white one, and there are
ten red guides. They have to go up the mountain, hopping
from stone to stone, in turn, till they reach the top
without falling. Once they fall, they are "out." You
must jump them fairly, and not *put* them from stone to
stone. It's very hard to get to the top. They never do.

We play this again and again, and we *always* play it now
on Christmas Eve. It is one of the regular rules that we
must be "Tom-and-Peggy-and-Monk-and-Doggy-Woggy
Woggy-Woggy-Woggy-for-ever" on Christmas Eve. We
never break it. It is a Nursery Law.

* * * *

I have shown Harry my green-covered *Midsummer
Night's Dream.* Yes, I was right, they will come into TAR.
Harry is Lysander, Helena, and Titania. I am Deme-
trius, Hermia, and Oberon.

"We're   Hermia-Lysander-Monk-and-Doggy-Woggy-
Woggy-Woggy-for-ever!"

We are them.

"We're Harry-Nellie-Joe-and-Bertie."

We are Us.

* * * *

Harry is reading some stories I haven't read, and
don't want to because a man is scalped in them. I saw
the bit about him with the top of his head off, and it
made me feel ill. Harry tells me about the people in the
tales, because he is going to be them in TAR, as well as
the "Dream" people who now we mostly are. The people
are called Hawkeye, and Uncas, and Ching-gak-gook (it
sounds like). Uncas and Ching-gak-gook are Red Indians
and Hawkeye always gets the best of it. These dreadful
people come and disturb the heavenly Dream. "We are
Hermia – Uncas – Monk – and – Doggy – Woggy – Woggy –
Woggy-for-ever." Hermia and Helena are carried off by
Red Indians. Harry lets Lysander and Demetrius *not be
strong enough to rescue them.* Hawkeye rescues them. This
is terrible, and there is somebody called Hurry-Harry
who is stronger than Demetrius. I can hardly bear this

period of TAR, when Alice and the Fairy-Folk and Tessy-and-Ralph have dropped away, and my lovely Greeks are being always worsted by these violent scalpers and bronco-busters. How I hate Hurry-Harry. "We're Harry-Nellie-Joe-and-Bertie."

We are Us.

Of the older lot, Peggy and Tom remain, on Christmas Eve.

* * * *

We are both reading *The Three Musketeers*. Oh, which *which* of these wonderful men will I be? I cannot ever hope to be D'Artagnan. I am Porthos. I love him. I love him more than anyone I am. I love boasting like him, and being vain like him, and stupid like him, and making love like him, and having an enormous appetite like him, and being the third-best fencer in the world, and the very strongest man. The Musketeers take the world of TAR by storm. They appear in a Wood in Athens, and on the Red Indian Prairie. They down simply everybody. Demetrius and Lysander, pale ineffectuals, fade away before them; the Red Indians and Hawkeye are routed for good and all. Harry allows Porthos to fight Hurry-Harry with his fists, and to conquer him! Harry brings in Hercules for Porthos to fight, and Hercules loses! Porthos is stronger than Ajax, who I was in the Greeks-and-Trojans game! Porthos is the *very strongest of all*. At last I am one thing in TAR that is The Most. Nobody that ever was, is, or will be, will be allowed to be stronger than Porthos. Only two other fencers in the world will be allowed to be better fencers. These of course are D'Artagnan (Best) and Athos (Second-Best). Aramis is equal with Porthos, but even here Harry is generous. Porthos shows up better than Aramis with the sword a shade more often. When Harry is Mousqueton, I can bully him. I am the other three lackeys. I make a good thing out of Planchet, and I enjoy being Grimaud. Bazin is nothing much. Farewell, our Greeks! Love-affairs with Hermia and Helena dwindle away; these ladies are too pallid for our Musketeers, though they have a shot at them. En route for Paris, messieurs! for Fontainebleau! Have at the Cardinal's Guards! Corbleu! Morbleu! Parbleu! Our Nursery language bristles with French oaths. Our Nursemaids wonder if they should be corrected. I refer over dinner casually to the King's Mistress. Papa looks at me oddly, and Mama is amused. Papa says, "I wouldn't say that anywhere else, Nell, if I were you." Why ever not?

"We're D'Artagnan - Porthos - Monk - and - Doggy - Woggy-Woggy-Woggy-for-ever!"

We ARE them!

(Oh please make Harry forget to look at his watch! make him not remember it's time to turn back and go home! make him not remember it's time for me to go to bed! Oh let me go on being Porthos and De Guiche and La Vallière for another half-hour—ten minutes, five! Sometimes, very very rarely, Harry smiles, and yields to my importunate pleas.)

But at last: "We're Harry-Nellie-Joe-and-Bertie."

And we are Us.

* * * *

Joe and Bertie have been discovered in a corner; we overhear Joe whispering illicitly: "We're Monk-and-Doggy-Woggy-Woggy-Woggy-Woggy-for-ever."

I look at Harry, and wait. Will he permit this? *Can* Joe arrogate to himself this power to be those two whenever he pleases? Harry considers—and leaves it alone;

he knows well that Monk and Doggy-Woggy have no real place in TAR now, which has entered its final, longest, and most glorified phase. Let Joe and Bertie carry it on as they will. They very soon drop it, and go to their own games; Harry and I to ours.

In Runton, when I was fifteen, a new person came into TAR, the Devil in disguise. He was to be a powerful element of evil, and when he appeared in the Court of Louis XIV, took on a human shape and another name. Harry said, "He is called Hyperion."

I stopped short as if I had been shot. No, never, never, never!

"Cola," I said, "he must have another name."

Harry looked at me. There must have been something in my tone which made him realize this was a life-and-death matter to me. He asked no question, but said, "He is called Hypernos."

We walked on by a red wall I can see now. I felt as though I had safely crossed an abyss. What would I have done if Harry had not consented to make the change? Or had asked why? Hyperion was *my* inviolate secret—the secret I would never tell anybody. (And of course I never will.)

For ten more years TAR goes on gathering its cast from all sources: from books and plays and legends, from the gods and heroes of sport, from Harry's own eccentric imagination. There was in King Louis' Court a M. de Fleury——

Mais non, messieurs-mesdames! No Fleury French Historian ever dreamed of.

He was the most peculiar person who ever existed. Let us leave it at that.

* * * *

And still, on every Christmas Eve, after tea, just before, or just after the final touches are put to secret preparations; to writing on family cards in disguised writing, and piling them on the hall-stand for sorting over breakfast in the morning; to hanging up limp stockings with safety-pins on the nursery guard; to running to the front door, each time the carol-singers knock, with a penny and an orange for everyone; to listening at the door of the drawing-room, locked this past fortnight, with Santa-Claus-sounds going on by day and night, and now and then a trumpet blowing softly; to arranging our presents for everybody on chairs, and preparing each of us a special Christmas Game the others know nothing about; to tacking up the last ivy round the doors, and setting a bower of laurel behind Grandpa's statue as Bob Acres—at some time during these and other excitements, the Nursery Call sounds on the Nursery Piano, and wherever we may be about the house, I and Joe and Bertie run to obey. A mountain of stone bricks is on the table, the Halma Men are out——

"We're   Tom-and-Peggy-and-Monk-and-Doggy-Woggy-Woggy-Woggy-for-ever!"

And we *are* them.

"Come along Tom!"

"Come along, Peggy my lass! I know I'll get to the top *this* year!"

"Oh, Tom! I don't think you will, Tom!"

"Shiver my timbers, Peggy, but I will!"

"Well, mind you don't *put* it, Tom!"

Down goes guide after guide! down goes Peggy! down goes Tom!

The mountains are built and re-built for half an hour.

* * * *

Then, year by year, the mountains are re-built for about ten minutes only.

* * * *

At last, one mountain, and a very small one, and only Peggy, Tom, and two red guides, maintain the Law of Tar on Christmas Eve.

———

In 1933, the year my Mother died in Fellows Road, the first Christmas I was not to wake there, I had things to do on Christmas Eve in Hampstead which kept me out till midnight. I returned to my own cottage near the Heath as Christmas came in—and on the doorstep stood one stone Anker-brick, one black Halma Man, and one red one.

Then I knew that, some time during that evening, we four, scattered over London, had been for one moment Tom-and-Peggy-and-Monk-and-Doggy-Woggy-Woggy-Woggy-Woggy-for-ever; and that an instant after some-one had said:

"We're Harry-Nellie-Joe-and-Bertie."

And we were Us.

THE SWISS DRESS

I WAS ALWAYS SHY at a party. Little girls *were* shy when I was a child, at least, most of them were. Now perhaps a few of them still are, but most of them are not. But forty-odd years ago, which was my little-girl party-time, I never knew whether I would come home having enjoyed the party or not; and I was quite sure of not enjoying it *before* I went, because I always had a stomach-ache on party days. I wasn't pretty, and I knew I wasn't; also, I wore spectacles at a time when spectacles on a child made the grown-ups say, "*What* a pity!"

In my make-believe games by myself, and in my "thinks" at night, I always had the most successful parties. I was all of a sudden quite pretty, and I didn't have to wear spectacles, and when I was asked to sing, my tiny voice didn't dry up in the top of my throat, but came out as clear and easy as it always did when I was singing to myself; and everybody clapped, and I came home happy. This is how I always *hoped* the next party was going to be, I always *hoped* to enjoy it more than last time, I *hoped* I would somehow be as gay and popular and petted as Olive Routledge, who wore lovely frocks, went to heaps of parties, and danced like a fairy. For me, Olive was the radiant spot in any party we were at together. Once Olive had come to tea with me (another agony beforehand), and had proved so merry, and so full of ideas about my toys, that the agony subsided in the first five minutes, and did not return afterwards, in memory. Usually I lay awake at nights for weeks after a tea or Christmas party, in a state of shame at the awful blunders I had made, or the embarrassing silences I hadn't known how to get over. For Olive these didn't exist; she danced through every occasion quite sure of herself, and when she came to tea all by herself she made me equally care-free. Oh, for Olive's confidence!

I never longed for it more than in the January of 1890, when, besides the family Christmas-tree party, and one or two of the simpler sort given by my everyday friends, I was invited to two of special grandeur and terrors. One was the party given by Mrs. Charles Wyndham at her big house in St. John's Wood Park. This was long before her enchanting husband (I was among the enchanted) had received his knighthood, for in those days actors weren't knighted, not even Henry Irving, for whom I would have laid down my life. But Mr. and Mrs. Wyndham were very rich, and their house was very grand, and had one of those slippery floors that I couldn't keep my feet on gracefully. And though I knew Mrs. Wyndham very well, and wasn't a bit afraid of her, I remembered that her parties were crowded with strange and brilliant children, before whom I would be terrified to make a fool of myself by falling down on that polished floor. This party was a pleasure to which I had to steel myself once a year, and till now it had been my greatest ordeal. But this year—worse still!—a sudden invitation had arrived for a party at Mrs. Labouchere's. Mr. Labouchere was an editor, and in Parliament, and a friend of Papa's, who knew everybody who wrote or acted in London. But I didn't know him, and had hardly heard of him. Mr. Labouchere wasn't one of the ones who came to the house for card-parties, those card-parties which started early enough for me to run down to kiss "Uncle'

Willie Edouin, and "Uncle" Lal Brough, and even handsome Mr. William Terriss. Unfortunately for me, Papa and Mama had "happened" to meet Mr. and Mrs. Labouchere out somewhere—perhaps at one of Henry Irving's wonderful First Nights, which were always followed by a box for a Morning Performance for me and my brothers, with ices after Act Three. Anyhow, Mrs. Labouchere had "happened" to be giving a party soon, and to say to my mother, "You must bring your little family." And, oh dear! had remembered to send the invitation next day. Here was another grand house, and a completely unknown hostess and company for me to face. And this was not my new-party-dress year, either. Once every two or three years my home-made velveteen or China silk was replaced with a "real" dress bought at Whiteley's or Peter Robinson's. I enjoyed it in prospect, imagining that this time it would give me confidence among the other little girls. But my last party-dress was two years old, and had been lengthened to make it "do" for this year.

Suddenly, to my joy, two days before Mrs. Labouchere's party, Mama said, "Papa says you're to have a new party-dress."

We took the dark green City Atlas bus to Oxford Circus. My feet in my tight buttoned boots felt cramped and cold, in spite of the straw in the bottom of the bus. But I bore contentedly the tedious journey, enlivened only by the transparent pictures of Lamplough's Pyretic Saline stuck inside the windows, which I knew by heart; and I did not mind as much as usual the dangerous slipping of the horses' feet on the icy road—sometimes, where it was *very* bad, they had to led carefully by the conductor, just the same as in fogs. The thought of the dress that awaited me in Peter Robinson's was a charm that tided over the frequent stoppings and slippings, the dress that would help me through the coming ordeals at Mrs. Labouchere's and Mrs. Wyndham's.

* * * *

The dress was a salmon-pink surah silk, with cream silk trimmings. There was another in blue silk, pretty, but not *so* pretty, and half a sovereign cheaper. I tried both on, while Mama and the shop assistant twitched the dress about, and told me to stand still and not fidget, and to hold my shoulders straight, and walk away a little and turn my back. I was sure it would be the blue one. When Mama said, "Now try the pink one again," my heart leapt, and when she smiled into my excited eyes and said, "We'll have this one," I could have hugged her.

The salmon-pink surah was ordered to be sent, and I went home full of hopes for the best. The frock arrived next day, and wasn't taken out of its tissue paper till the evening of Mrs. Labouchere's party, when my stomach was behaving worse than usual. It was some comfort to slip the pretty dress on over the stiff, scratchy petticoats that were one of the minor tortures of my life. So was the hat elastic, which left a red mark under my chin, and when slipped behind my ears for relief, made my head ache. So were the tight little kid gloves worked down my fingers till I could get my thumb in. So were the bronze boots now being buttoned over two pairs of stockings, cashmere underneath and silk on top, so that I shouldn't take cold; because of this my insteps were pinched, and my feet were icy. But the new dress *did* look nice, and my uncle in America had sent me for Christmas a tiny gold ring with three real garnets in it. So I hoped that, in spite of my plain, straight hair and spectacles, I might pass among the gay little girls as though I were one of themselves.

Luck was not with me. I found myself clinging to Mama's side in a strange and overwhelming room crowded with unfamiliar faces. I knew nobody but my own brother, and all the other children seemed to know intimately everybody but us. I dared not enjoy myself freely at supper, and was chiefly supported by rumours that after supper there would be a Christmas tree. This, if true, would not only be nice, but would take up a lot of time. Our standard of Christmas trees was measured largely by Papa's. His lavishness was famous; he was buying things for the tree all the year round, at home and abroad, and half the party was occupied with children choosing gift after gift, turn by turn, till they went home with the empty cracker boxes, provided in advance, stuffed with necklets and pencil-cases, Indian scent bottles, French purses, and Swiss chalets, as well as all the big things that wouldn't go into the boxes—telescopes, microscopes, dolls, books, boxes of soldiers, bricks, animals, and *everything*. There never were, there never had been, Christmas trees like Papa's. But all Christmas trees were exciting and full of promise.

The rumour was true. Supper over, the children were taken to another part of the house, and marshalled in a line which filed slowly through a corridor and past the tree, where two elders with scissors were presiding. You did not choose your present; the gifts had been decided in advance, and each child's name was announced as it drew level. The present was snipped off, one of the ladies said, "There, dear," and the child said, "Thank you," and passed on. When I came within sight of my turn, I saw on the half-empty tree one of those objects so precious and desirable to a child—a lovely folding leather writing-case, with, doubtless, an endless supply of pockets for stamps and stationery, perhaps even fitted out with penholders and pencils in their round leather bands, and blotting-paper clipped with leather corner-pieces. At each step forward I expected to see this prize awarded to one of my predecessors, who were all jollily addressed by name by the ladies with the scissors. I could hardly credit my luck when my turn came, and one of the ladies, cutting the string that tied the writing-case to the tree, put it into my hands, saying, "There, dear." I stammered my "Thank you" and moved on. The party suddenly was a *lovely* party! All its agonies, past, and perhaps to come, were compensated by this unlooked-for treasure. I would not dare to examine it fully here, but I foresaw the joy at home to-morrow of arranging notepaper and envelopes in the compartments, and begging a few extras, such as elastic bands, pen-nibs, and correspondence cards, and perhaps even a stick of sealing-wax, to make my outfit rich.

Then:

"Wait a moment, little girl. There seems to have been a mistake. *What* is your name?"

I whispered it.

"Oh, yes, dear, *this* is your present."

The writing-case was removed from my hands, and and in its place was put a calendar, bound in blue and pink satin ribbon, criss-crossed into diamonds.

The other lady added, "The writing-case is for you, Olive."

And from behind me came the fresh, enthusiastic

voice of Olive Routledge: "Oh, *thank* you. It's perfectly *lovely*." The ladies laughed and chatted with Olive for a moment—she was such a favourite!—and my crimson cheeks, and my muffled second "Thank you," went unnoticed. I got away, with Olive at my heels.

"Hullo, Nellie! I didn't know you were here."

"No, I didn't either."

"It *is* a big party, isn't it! What did *you* get? Oh, how *sweet*!"

Olive praised the calendar as warmly as she had her own writing-case. I tried hard, by agreeing with her, to cover my own shame and disappointment. I slipped back as soon as I could to Mama in the drawing-room, where children were beginning to perform. Flossie Lancaster, a big girl, quite sixteen, sang "The Garden of Sleep," which I also could sing. Other children did other things. Presently little Dora Labouchere recited a French tale in which a spoiled, babyish girl said "*Oh, maman!*" for a dozen different reasons in a dozen different inton-ations. During the acclamation of the elders—"the child really is a marvel!"—I wondered *what* I would do if they asked me to recite. I was learning a rather silly poem with my governess, that began:

> *A pound of tea at one-and-three,*
> *A pot of strawberry jam,*
> *Some new-laid eggs, some wooden pegs,*
> *And a dozen rashers of ham.*

The poem was about a little girl going shopping for her mother; she goes over her list, thinks of other things, and repeats her list, with variations, at intervals through the verses. In the end she is in a perfect jumble, and asks the grocer for:

A pound of three at one-and-tea,
A pot of new-laid ham——

and so on. I disliked the poem, and, anyhow, I hadn't
got it by heart yet. I shrank into Mama's dress and
whispered, "Don't let them ask me, Mama."

"I don't think they will, dear."

They didn't, and the dreadful party came to an end
and I curled into the corner of the hired brougham with
relief, clutching my satin calendar and wishing I *had*
been asked, and had recited my poem so amusingly that
somebody had said: "The child really is a marvel!"

* * * *

The memory of the Labouchere Party had not ceased
to fill me with hot feelings of shame (for it somehow
seemed to be my fault, as well as my misfortune, that I
had tried to receive a treasure meant for somebody else),
when Mrs. Wyndham called. It was just an afternoon
call, and had nothing to do with her party, which was to
take place next week. Mrs. Wyndham was a kindly,
homely little person, and I was sent for to come down
just as I was. "Just as I was" chanced to be rather
gorgeous, for I was "dressing-up" in the charming
Swiss dress which Papa had brought me from Interlaken
in the autumn. The dress was a real little girl's festival
dress; in Switzerland little girls at their parties really
did wear scarlet skirts, black velvet corsets embroidered
with silver flowers and laced with silver cord, white tucked
chemises with full sleeves, and adorable black velvet
collars, from which hung sets of silver chains, ornamented
with beautiful filigree roses. I clinked as I came running
to kiss Mrs. Wyndham, who said, "*What* a pretty dress!
You must wear it to my party, Nellie."

I looked enquiringly at Mama, who said, "Well, I don't know. It is not a fancy dress party?"

"Oh, that doesn't matter! She *must* wear this. Mind you do, Nellie. It is such a pretty dress."

"Would you like to, Nellie?" asked Mama.

Though I adored the Swiss dress for my dressing-up games, I would much rather have worn the salmon-pink surah for the party, but I always found denial difficult, and weakly murmured, "Yes, Mama."

"That's a promise then. Now see she does, won't you, dear?" said Mrs. Wyndham. And away she went, leaving me committed. I didn't like to tell Mama that I would prefer to wear the surah again, and on the day of the party I put on the Swiss dress, and let them lace the black-and-silver bodice over the pain in my stomach.

Mrs. Wyndham's big rooms were filled with many children whom I knew, still more whom I didn't, and a few I was "just coming to know." Among these were the Gunns, a family of noisy, brilliant Irish children, rather wild in their manners. I found Kevin, the eldest boy, rather frightening, but also rather attractive; I would have liked to be on laughing terms with him, as Olive was. Olive was even prettier than usual, in a lace dress like frostwork over a pale blue slip. It was easily the prettiest frock, and Olive the prettiest child, there. But mine was the most noticeable dress. Nobody but I was wearing "fancy dress," and I felt conspicuous and singled out by my scarlet-black-and-silver, and my clinking chains. However, the elders praised it, and the children accepted it, and after a scrumptious tea with crackers, I began to feel easy, and thought this *might* be one of the parties I would enjoy—if only Kevin Gunn, who liked sliding rowdily up and down the polished floor, and bumping into the little girls on the way, didn't choose me for one of his victims.

After tea there were some games, and then the usual requests for some child to "do" something began. There were songs and recitations, and Olive was asked to dance. She complied as readily as she always did, picking up her lace skirts and floating like a snowflake over the shiny surface on which I could hardly keep my footing. Oh, Olive was lovely! In every lovely thing I saw material for my make-believe games, and I decided to write a play about a fairy princess, and get Olive to act the chief part in it. I was lost in this blissful plan when the dance came to an end, and I heard Mrs. Wyndham's voice saying in my ear, "Nellie, I'm sure you know a little piece to recite to us."

I came out of my dream with a start. The moment had come which I always dreaded. Could I get out of it, or would I *have* to? I heard Mama say, "Can you say, 'A Pound of Tea,' dear?" It was no good. I would have to. I knew Mama knew that I had got "A Pound of Tea" by heart at last, and was now learning "It *was* the Schooner Hesperus." I couldn't do anything but get up and walk uncertainly along the treacherous floor to to the end of the room, which seemed very big and full of people as I stood there trying to feel like a little girl going shopping. Olive would have said it with lots of expression, but though I used lots of expression in my games at home, I never dared let myself go at a party. So I wetted my lips and began in a monotonous little voice:

> "*A Pound of Tea at One-and-three,*
> *A Pot of Strawberry Ham,*
> *A . . .*"

Oh, horror, I had said it wrong! The jumble didn't
begin till the Third Verse, and I knew how silly it must
sound to the children who at present knew nothing about
the poem, or that it was *going* to be a jumble. It only
sounded like a silly mistake of mine, and, of course,
it was one. I was not pretending to be a muddle-headed
little girl, I *was* a muddle-headed little girl. I began
again, hastily:

> "*A Pound of Tea at One-and-three,*
> *A Pot of Strawberry Jam . . .*"

There! I had managed the First Verse all right. The
Second Verse was different, and I got through that too.
In the Third Verse, the jumble began. But which jumble?
My nerve was shaken by my bad start. There were three
jumbles altogether, each worse than the last. I launched
desperately on one, and knew it was the wrong one. The
children didn't know, but I did. I hesitated. Every
line, every word of the poem went out of my head. I
stared blankly in front of me—Mama was too far away
to prompt me, she was halfway down the long room, which
was growing horribly misty.

"'A Pound of Tea' . . ." I faltered, and stuck.

Somebody said, "She's forgotten it, poor little thing."

I burst into tears, slithered along the floor-polish with
my chains clinking, and sobbed in Mama's lap. She
tried to comfort me and remind me of the lines (as if I
could ever go back!); some of the elders patted me and
said, "Never mind, dear," and another child got up
and recited something competently. I kept my face hidden
against Mama. Oh, how awful it was! Would anybody
ever clap me as they were clapping Bronnie Albery,
who had just said "The Psalm of Life" without

forgetting a word? Oh, if I could only go straight home!

But the party went on. There were more games, and I had to play them; and there was "Sir Roger de Coverley," and I had to dance it—with my tear-stained face, in my Swiss Fancy Dress. Everybody couldn't help noticing me. All the strange children who didn't know my name knew my dress. And how Kevin Gunn was grinning as he pulled me off my balance when it came to the "Both Hands" bit. I would never get over this, I would suffer for it every night of my life. If *only* I had on the Surah Silk! Among all the other little girls in silk and lace dresses I might presently have been lost, and my shame forgotten. But wherever I went my black-and-scarlet proclaimed me, and whenever I moved my silver chains clinked mercilessly, announcing to everybody: "This is the little girl who forgot her piece and cried! This is the little girl who forgot her piece and cried!"

BOTH SIDES OF THE CURTAIN

"WHEN WILL YOU BRING THE CHILDREN to see us?" says Henry Irving, tired, smiling, gracious, taking leave of Papa and Mama after one of his First Nights. The Lyceum has rung with such applause as never tried to burst the roof of any other theatre; the Paying Public has dispersed; the Distinguished Deadheads have remained chatting in the stalls, until the genies behind the curtain have dressed the feast. They then troop round to a stage set with tables loaded with delicacies, wine, flowers, and cigars. Champagne flows freely; the ladies hover round the plovers' eggs, the gentlemen loiter near the boxes of Havanas. It is help-yourself-to-what-you-like. Papa (who smokes all day long, but only affords himself the cheapest Swiss sticks, except when Aunt Mary Albery sends him a hundred Coronas for Christmas) lights and appreciates his fine cigar, and fumes to see some of Irving's guests quietly extract their cigar-cases and fill them from the boxes lying open. If Irving sees it too, he gives no sign; he is a prince to his guests. "Bring your darlings soon," breathes the most adorable actress that *ever* breathed, kissing Maggie Farjeon on both cheeks, while Becket the Saint or Iachimo the Sinner adds, "Let me know, Ben, and Bram will send you a box."

"The darlings" pounced early next morning on Papa and Mama in bed. "What was it like? Was Henry Irving good? Was Ellen Terry good? Was William Terriss good? Was Genevieve Ward good? Was it a Success?

What did you have to eat? Who did you see behind?
When are we going?"

We did not often wait long for that Royal Box for
a Morning Performance. Lyceum days were our theatrical
red-letter days. For us, there was Going-to-the-Theatre
and Going-to-the-Lyceum. Very very nearly equal with
the last was Going-to-Ada-Rehan, and she came under
one head with Henry Irving and Ellen Terry, which was
Going-to-Shakespeare. I adored Going-to-the-Theatre,
but Going-to-Shakespeare was—oh well, you couldn't
say what it was. It left you blissful and unsatisfied. You
came out of the theatre into the dusk or the night longing
to do things that would somehow prolong the vision, and
make the magic last for ever and ever. Until Bernhardt
and Opera were added to our fare, there was *nothing* in
the world to compare with what we saw played by Henry
Irving's and Augustin Daly's companies.

The day was quick with anticipations, the journey in
the cab seemed never-ending. There was a moment's
pause in the Foyer when a big genial Irishman, with
a reddish beard, beamed down on us enquiring, "Well,
is it to be Tea and Ices after Act Two or Act Three?"
We thought after Act Three, please, Mr. Stoker. And
we passed up the broad staircase to the Box we shared
with Royalty, where Princes and Princesses ate *their*
Neapolitan ices, when we left them free to do so. It never
occurred to us that we *could* sit anywhere in a theatre
but a box. And we preferred to be very early, because if
one had not the time in which to master the details of
the endless cast of characters, and the multitude of
scenes in the Five Acts, it seemed quite certain we should
never get them straight after the curtain went up. Oh,
how long the curtain was in going up! Hush! at last!—

and a stageful of Lords and Bishops one would *never* get straight! Yet miraculously the mind soon ceased to be troubled with un-mastered details. He, or She, appeared upon the scene, and the magic began.

The magic began when I was four years old, and my first theatre-curtain rolled up after dark.

                              * * * *

"Go to sleep, Nellie," said Fanny Dodd, taking me up to my room in the afternoon. It was because I was to have the strange experience of driving out at night with Papa and Mama. I had driven with them by day, and stopped in Hyde Park to have a drink of milk warm from the cow, which they told me would be nicer than other milk; but I disliked it. What I thought I was going to see, as I lay obediently on the bed, not sleeping, I cannot remember. I only knew that Uncle Willie and Aunt Alice Edouin would be there, and Uncle Lal Brough. When dear funny Uncle Willie, with his red carbuncled face, came to "Fairhaven," he made us laugh. Papa kept hens in the garden, and was so excited about getting eggs from the hens that he seized the dinner-plates from under our noses, peppered the scraps violently, and rushed out with the peppered food to the henhouse. When Papa boasted that he got nine eggs a day out of eight hens (and it was true!) Uncle Willie accused him of peppering their tails, till they laid out of sheer temper, and when even pepper didn't bring the eggs quick enough, he said "Ben" *squeezed* the hens, though I had never actually seen Papa do this. And when the poker-party was over, very late, Uncle Willie went waddling down the front steps flapping his coat-tails and clucking just as though he had laid an egg. Another time he said he wanted to

borrow the big garden-roller, and he pushed it half up
the road at four o'clock in the morning, and when he saw
a Policeman coming he shouted to Papa, who was laughing
at the gate, "Well, good night, Ben! I won't take it to-
night after all!" And he went on with Aunt Alice,
leaving the roller rocking in the middle of the road.
Papa had to go out and roll it home, out of the way of the
milk carts, under the Policeman's eye. . . . And then
there was that time at Christmas, when we came downstairs to see the big people at the grown-up dinner-party,
and I showed Uncle Willie my blue-and-white doll's
trunk, and he held up the clothes in it and said, "And
what are *these?*" and I said "It's her drawers," and
everybody else laughed, but I didn't know why . . . And
that other time when he brought a very poor man, who
acted very badly in his company, to play poker for the
first time with Papa and Mama, and before he came
Uncle Willie said to them and Uncle Jack Barnes, and
Mr. Johnny Morris, "Look here, Chevalier hasn't
a bean, and he doesn't know the game; when he bets,
don't 'see' him." So they all made a little plot not to
let Mr. Albert Chevalier lose, but instead of that they
couldn't stop him winning. I often heard Uncle Willie
and Aunt Alice chuckle with Papa and Mama about the
night when Mr. Chevalier "held all the cards," and
"saw" them every time, and "took every pot," though
he had never played Poker before. Nobody ever told that
poor man about the plot, and I never quite got over the
feeling that you had to be very sorry for Mr. Albert
Chevalier. . . . And then, at dinner, before he ate his
asparagus, Uncle Willie pretended it was a pen, and
wrote his name in the air with such funny flourishes . . .
and I opened my eyes, and Fanny came and put on my

cream cashmere frock with crimson velvet trimming to go and see *The Japs*.

In *The Theatre* for October, 1885, Clement Scott said:

> "Regretfully enough I can say nothing good of 'The Japs' . . . It is sad to see Mr. Brough, Mr. Edouin, and Miss Alice Atherton wasting their talent on such dreary childishness."

Ah yes! but if it had happened to be Mr. Scott's First Theatre, and if he had been four years old, and if Fanny Dodd had carried him to his cot in broad daylight and said, "Go to sleep, Clemmie!"—because a few hours later he was actually going to drive out at night in a carriage with his Papa and Mama, to see his funniest Uncle doing still funnier things than writing in the air with his asparagus—and if, for the first time in his life he had sat in a red plush box with his arms on the ledge, and leaned over to stare, and listen, and wonder, and not realize, till the curtain came down for the last time, what a pain he had in his chest, where the box-edge cut across it—he would have gone home half-asleep in his Mama's arms, to dream as he had never dreamed before; and he would have written something like this about *The Japs*:

"It was very very glittering, and lovely music, and half the soldiers were in bright blue armour and half in bright red armour, and Aunt Alice had saucy skirts and her hair in plaits, and she sang 'Eyes of English Blue' which I can sing too, and she did a bubbly laughing-song, and Uncle Willie came right down to the corner near the box and said 'Hullo Ben!' to Papa, and then he began to cluck like a hen; and going to the theatre is better than any thing else there is, and *The Japs* is the best play of all."

Through my first experience of the enchanted world behind the curtain, illusion and reality became indistinguishably mingled for ever. What wonder, when our own back garden got mixed up with that sparkling world, and the sparkling world got mixed up with our own back garden, where Harry and I were always finding bits of it to enact again? And at night, when I was in bed, and ought to have gone to sleep, the most wonderful things began to happen all by themselves, in which appeared the people I knew and loved on both sides of the curtain.

Many another play was to contribute to that neverending pageant of the night and day, but *The Japs* was the first, the curtain-raiser to the piece; and it has never ceased to glitter like a star in my memory.

After *The Japs* came *The Babes* (which must have been a revival on the failure of that entrancing play); and in *The Babes* were Tessy-and-Ralph, who changed the course of my life.

* * * *

One afternoon Papa took me on his knee in his study, and told me a lovely tale about a queen who pretended to be a statue; and he read some lines out of a book to me as he told the tale, and that night the hired brougham came again to the door to take Harry and me to see Miss Mary Anderson in *A Winter's Tale*. But when we got to the theatre, everybody was coming away; Miss Mary Anderson was ill. Harry and I looked anxiously at Papa; the disappointment was too big to bear. Papa said to Mama, "What about the Pantomime?" And before we knew it we had driven on to see our first pantomime. It had started when we got into our box. Mr. Harry Payne was the Clown. We went home feeling we had missed

nothing; very soon after we went, on another night, to
A Winter's Tale, and Miss Mary Anderson was almost
too beautiful to be true—especially as Perdita, so flowery
and dancing. That was my first William Shakespeare
play. Not *very* long after that there was my second
Shakespeare play, *The Taming of the Shrew,* with Ada
Rehan in a red velvet dress sweeping everything before
her in a temper, and at the end being humorous and
gentle in white-and-gold. The play was *very* funny.
Afterwards Papa asked me which of the two Shakespeare
plays I liked best, and I said Ada Rehan's one; and he
looked disappointed and said, *A Winter's Tale* was a *much*
better play, and told me why; and I went away feeling
miserable because I had chosen the wrong Shakespeare
to like best—but all the same, I went on liking it best,
for quite a long time. It wasn't the first time I had seen
Miss Rehan. I'd seen her in some plays like *A Night Off*
and *Nancy & Co.,* the first plays in which people did
not sing and dance. Afterwards in the lobby we met
a lady who turned out to be our Aunt Mary Daly, and
I heard Mama say to her, "Perhaps it's rather a dry play
for the children." When I got home I said, "I like wet
plays best." "What *do* you mean by wet plays, Nellie?"
laughed Mama. "Plays with music in them," I said.

* * * *

One night, when I was seven, Florrie Canton was
staying with us. We had a box for a theatre, and I don't
know how it was; either there wasn't room for Florrie
in the box, or her Papa and Mama didn't let her go to the
theatre at night, but she stayed at home with Fanny
and Joe and Baby, while Harry and I drove off with
Papa and Mama. The play was *The Dead Heart* with an

actor and actress we had never seen before—his name was Henry Irving and hers was Ellen Terry, and *what* a play! The only person I knew in it was Uncle Teddy Righton, and *that* couldn't take off from the strange and thrilling horrors. I was fascinated and affrighted. Shall I ever forget the storming of the Bastille, and the dragging from its depths of the ghastly, incoherent figure in rags that had been gay young Robert Landry in the Prologue? When he did get his speech back, in the next acts, he was gay no longer; he was stern to the beautiful lady he had loved, who had married another thinking he was dead; and he fought a wonderful duel with Mr. Bancroft, who was an Abbé, and killed him; and he was going to send the lovely lady's son to his death. The son was as beautiful to look at as the mother; and I heard Papa say to Mama "How good young Craig is!" Well, the lovely lady came to plead for her son's life with Robert Landry, but his heart was dead, because of the Bastille and her marrying another; and it seemed as though she must plead in vain. And then, suddenly his heart came alive again; but it was too late to do anything except take the son's place and be killed instead—so he did; and the last thing you saw was Robert Landry on the guillotine, and the stage seemed dark, but his face was shining. as the curtain came down you knew you had enjoyed yourself tremendously, but your heart was torn within you all the same. Then, instead of going outside to the carriage, we followed Papa and Mama down curious stairs to such a funny place. It was the wings of the theatre, it felt like a carpenter's shop, and men were scurrying about the stage, taking away the guillotine, and the curtain was down; and there was the lovely lady fluttering with her hands out to Papa and Mama, and there sitting on a chair was Robert Landry, smiling such a lovely smile; and he took me on his knees and stooped to kiss me—ugh! his face was all over shiny greasy stuff, and I just had to put up with it; all the same, I loved him from that night, and for ever after.

To make it up to Florrie, we went two days later in the afternoon to see Henry Neville in *The Royal Oak;* he was much *handsomer* than Henry Irving, and the play though exciting, wasn't terrifying—but between the two Henrys I did not make the mistake of preferring the one who shook the air of the theatre to the one who kindled it.

* * * *

Mr. Toole's face wasn't greasy like Henry Irving's. When you went to *him* behind the scenes, hugging the big box of chocolates he had sent in to you (it was always chocolates if it wasn't ices), his face was not the same colour as when you saw him in Pegwell Bay, but the red on his large rather flabby cheeks was dry, and you didn't mind them touching you when he kissed you. His cheeks were soft and warm. Like Uncle Willie Edouin, he called out things to Papa and Mama in the play; when they were carrying him out to duck him in a pond, he screamed "Save me, Maggie! save me!" and waved his hands at her. When actors do that, they're gagging, and we can't help enjoying it, though we know it isn't right, and it takes away the magic feeling at once. Still, Mr. Toole hadn't the same sort of magic as Henry Irving, great friends though they were. Before Mr. Toole went to Australia, there were all sorts of parties given for him. There was a supper-party for him that Papa went to, in Henry Irving's Beefsteak Room, and a luncheon-party the ladies gave him, where they got a florist to make a wonderful globe of the world in moss and flowers, on a tall wire stand. After the lunch Mr. Toole gave it to Mama to bring home, and it stood for a long time in the drawing-room, and when the flowers were dead and the moss was dry, the wire globe and stand went up among the trunks in the attic, where whenever I came across it, it reminded me of the lovely black-paper pocket-books Harry and I had made for Mr. Toole to take round the world with him. We were sure he would find them useful in Australia. Then he came back, and we saw him in *Walker, London*, but it ran a long time before we went, so that at last he wrote to Papa:

"You are one of the few men in London *and* the Provinces who have *not* seen 'Walker London.' Why not come and see it *don't* be pointed at by everybody as you walk through the streets."

So Papa and Mama went one night with Harry, and they all came home talking about young Mr. Hicks who was so good as a young doctor who pretended he wasn't excited about passing his examination, but was awfully excited when he found he had. Then I went to see it too, and agreed that Mr. Hicks was a very good actor. For if you think we didn't know how to draw lines, you're wrong. Even Henry Irving was sometimes bad and sometimes good. In *Cymbeline,* when Ellen Terry was at her best as Imogen, Henry Irving was at his worst as Iachimo. The best thing in *Cymbeline* after Ellen Terry was the lovely way young Mr. Craig and young Mr. Harvey knelt by her and said "Fear no more the heat o' the sun." And yet, you know, even when Henry Irving was bad, the magic was there.

* * * *

There were glamorous experiences, not quite of the theatre, when you spent long hours in "Venice and London" and "Constantinople in London." You glided in strange barques on romantic waterways and were yourself a part of the scene you looked on, hovering on the verge of an adventure that did not happen.

* * * *

There was *The Harbour Lights* at the Adelphi. Our Mr. William Terriss was the hero; we were used to him as a King or a Lord with Henry Irving, but at the Adelphi he was a soldier or a sailor or something like that, and spoke so heartily, like when he came to Papa and Mama's poker-parties. He was nearly always the last one to arrive and first there seemed to be a breeze in the hall, and then the door was flung open and Mr. Terriss came in with his arm out crying, "Ha, Ben! the grasp of an honest hand is worth more than gold or silver!" One time he and Mr. Beveridge arrived together, and Mr. Beveridge went into the drawing-room ahead of him, crying: "Give me your hand, Ben! for the hand of an honest man is better than a fortune." So Mr. Terriss walked in very quietly, and just said "Good evening" to everybody, and they laughed because Mr. Beveridge had "stolen his entrance."

Before the poker began, we used to come downstairs to see them all, and when there was time we did things for them, though Mama wouldn't let me sing all *five* verses of "Bread-and-Cheese-and-Kisses." Mr. Terriss gave Joe some advice about going on the stage, which Joe was going to do because he was called Jefferson. "Take your hands out of your pockets, Joe," he said, "or you won't know what to do with them when you're acting." And he always asked to see Joe's last dance. The time it was the Hornpipe, there were such a lot of poker players sitting round that Joe said "I don't think there's room to dance in." "Yes there is," said Mr. Terriss, "remember, Joe, whatever size your stage is, you've got to fit your performance to it." And he made Joe dance the hornpipe in a very little circle.

I liked the poker-parties, because they broke up too late for the maid to clear away. When the last guest had gone, and Papa and Mama had come upstairs, and everything was quiet, I waited; and at about four o'clock in the morning I slipped barefoot downstairs into the dining-room, and made a swift round of the supper-table. A sandwich here, another there, the three-cornered edges just slightly curling with the first loss of freshness; an anchovy egg, a tart—and up I crept, lifting my laden nightdress in front of me.

"Why don't you eat your breakfast like a good girl?" demanded my nurse, four hours later. "Have you got another of your headaches?"

"Yes," I said languidly. But I knew the headache was my own fault this time.

* * * *

Mr. Terriss's letters were just like his talking. He wrote to Papa from the Lyceum Theatre:

Dear Ben Farjeon,
                                Do we meet for a sparkle at your house on
Sunday? Aye or nay?

                                                            Thine
                                                        Will Terriss

The wife says, oh! what a good man Mr. Farjeon must be by his writings—over! and over! again!

And to Mama from the Adelphi:

> "Oh! woman you are our curse and our
blessing combined. But he that finds a good wife finds
a blessing of The Lord"

And from his own house he sent a Postal Order for the
Cot I collected money for in *Little Wideawake,* where I won
my first competition for an essay on a pet. My pet was
"Pop," the little sparrow I found tumbled out of its nest in
Margate, that died though I nursed it for a lot of days
first. I cried while I wrote the story about Pop, and I
won Ten Shillings, and gave it to the Cot in Pop's name;
and a lot of people gave me a shilling for the Cot, but
when William Terriss heard about it he sent me Five.

> *2 Bedford Rd.*
> *Bedford Park*
> *Chiswick*

My dear Ben Farjeon

Above is address Make a note of it—it
will always be a pleasure to see you and yours within
its humble walls—irrespective of the honour you confer
by the presence of so able a man as yourself. Will you
ask the little girl to accept the enclosed 5/–for her little cot
—With all good wishes

> believe me
> Sincerely yours
> Will Terriss

June 3. 91

So when that fatal knife went home, on December
16th, 1897, and Papa came into the drawing-room saying,
"Good God, Maggie! Terriss has been stabbed at the
stage-door!" it shook the Nursery as much as the
drawing-room.

* * * *

There were the gay Criterion Comedies, with delightful Mr. Wyndham and delicious Aunt Mary; there were the smart ones at the St. James's, with Mr. Alexander. We knew Aunt Mary and Mr. Wyndham long first. When I was five I sent Mr. Wyndham some things from the Christmas Party, and he must have liked them very much, because he wrote:

"Dear Miss Farjeon,

I am playing all day with my toys till the nurse has stopped me because the trumpets make her head ache.

I am therefore now going to turn to the cake and the orange.

Yours truly
Charlie Wyndham.

He wrote the letter from the Criterion Theatre, so I suppose he played with the toys in his dressing-room. His plays were funny ones, but he didn't gag like Mr. Toole and Uncle Willie Edouin. Still, when he played *The Headless Man,* something from *our* side of the Curtain got behind it, because at the end of Act Two a carriage went across the back of the stage, and Boy, Aunt Mary's lovely Collie with the white ruff, ran barking after it, just like real.

Mr. Alexander we knew first as a holiday companion. We had never been to any of his plays when we at last deserted Margate for Cromer, and he took the next house to our one at The Meadow. His house was bigger than ours, had a tennis-lawn, and Papa went in to play tennis quite often, and all sorts of gay parties happened.

One afternoon Papa said: "Alexander wants us all to go in to tea; Alfred Capper is coming to read our bumps." So we went. Alfred Capper was a sort of

magician; Mr. Alexander did not tell him who anybody
was, and one after another the people sat in a chair, while
Mr. Capper felt their heads, and told the company
everything about them. Mr. Alexander introduced Papa
and Mama as Mr. and Mrs. Smith, and Mr. Capper got
Papa's head all wrong; Mama he said had a most determined will, and always got her way, because of her
square jaw; about Harry he was terrifyingly good. I
saw my brother read under my eyes. "Now, little girl!"
said Mr. Alexander. I shook my head.

"Come along, Nellie, come and be read, too," he
said, kneeling by my chair.

"No, I'd rather not."

"But why, dear?" He knelt there quite a long time,
trying to coax me; he put his arm round me, but still
I wouldn't. Give myself up to the hands of that magician,
who would tell everybody my thoughts and feelings?
Never, never, never! It was very difficult not to yield
to Mr. Alexander, and impossible to say why I wouldn't
be read. But when the tears began to flow he whispered,
"Never mind, Nellie, we'll ask somebody else." So they
did, and I didn't mind who it was as long as my own
inside-me was left alone. It may have been Mr. Oscar
Wilde, who was staying near by that summer, because
he was writing a play for Mr. Alexander; I saw him
driving in a dog-cart, but if he was at that crowded tea-
party, I was too busy protecting my personality to heed
anybody much. I wouldn't have wanted to heed him
anyhow, because the first time he drove past, and Papa
and Mama bowed, Mama said to Papa, "Well thank
goodness he's driving and I can't shake hands with him!"
"Why don't you like shaking hands with Mr. Wilde,
Mama?" I asked; and Mama didn't seem to know

herself. All the reason she could give was that she didn't like the feel of it.

As for Alfred Capper, we all decided that he wasn't infallible. For instance, he had said Mama had a strong will, and always got her way. Now, when there was anything she wanted, we teased her about it. "Square your jaw, madam, square your jaw!" laughed Papa. And Mama smiled a funny little smile.

After this holiday we began to see all the plays that Mr. Alexander did; *The Prisoner of Zenda*, which Papa had read us as soon as it was written, we saw more than once. It was one of the plays Joe and Bertie acted by themselves, doing all the parts. Joe was Mr. Alexander as Rudolph, and Bertie was Mr. Waring as Black Michael. Mr. Waring had a way of throwing his chin up and breathing with a curious sound; so Bertie threw up his chin and snorted in those bits. The snorting got worse and worse, till it sounded as if Bertie was a horse being strangled. This unpleasant noise came to represent Mr. Waring to us for good and all. I don't think Mr. Waring himself was ever allowed to hear it, when he came to the house; but it was one of the things that made Aunt Alice Edouin gurgle. She was born laughing, I think; and Bertie made her laugh more than any of us.

* * * * *

Of course, as well as *Liberty Hall* and *The Prisoner of Zenda*, we saw some of Mr. Wilde's plays, which Mama liked, though she didn't like him; and once he got mixed up in a joke of Papa's on Mr. Wyndham. One day Mama had written suddenly to ask if she could come to the Criterion, and Mr. Wyndham sent this telegram on three sheets of paper:

"The heart that does not respond to such an appeal is unworthy of anybodys consideration but the anatomists very good box alas is gone but the whole staff have become inspired with their managers enthusiasm and are prepared on her arrival to throw themselves at Maggies feet and place box or stalls or whatever available she wishes at her disposal Telegraph box office or come early."

Papa wired back "Expect us Non Corpus Non Habet."

"What does that mean, Ben?" asked Mama.

"I haven't the faintest idea," said Papa, who couldn't speak Latin, and didn't see the use of it anyhow.

In his dressing-room, Mr. Wyndham asked the same question, and Papa laughed at him for not knowing Latin. Afterwards they all went to a big restaurant, and while they were at supper, Mr. Wyndham looked at the next table and there was Mr. Wilde with another party. "Aha!" cried Mr. Wyndham, "the very man! Oscar, *you* can tell me what this means!" And he pulled Papa's telegram out of his pocket, and laid if before Mr. Wilde. Mr. Wilde read it, murmured "Non Corpus Non Habet! Non Corpus Non Habet!" and shook his head and handed it back again. "What!" cried Mr. Wyndham delighted, "are you stumped too!" Mama and Papa both seemed to think he was, for once or twice during the evening he wrinkled his forehead and whispered, "Non Corpus Non Habet!" All that was long before the time at Cromer.

Then presently there was a case about Mr. Wilde in the papers. For several days Mama and Papa always seemed to be talking about it, and always stopping when I came into the room. I gathered that I mustn't even ask what it was about; and I was not enough interested in newspapers to take time off from Keats and Shelley to read them. But I did, in an idle sort of way, notice that if I had wanted to read the papers, they were never lying about; and I knew something funny was up. "I don't suppose I'll ever know what it is," I thought, and decided to try to remember the date, and find out when I was grown up.

That, for me, was the end of Mr. Wilde.

* * * *

In pantomime, it was Dan Leno first, and the rest of the field nowhere. Of course, I liked it all, but I knew the difference. We generally did at least two pantomimes a year, the one at Drury Lane and the one at the Islington: where we saw Dick Whittington in the year of Lottie Collins. Harry fell for her. She and her Ta-ra-ras became *his*. I liked, but not adored her; and of this pantomime, apart from her big hat and tossing skirts, I chiefly remember "clapping" a song by the Principal Boy— well, one clapped everything, didn't one? The song was called "Oh What a Difference in the Morning!" I didn't understand it much, but it had a lively tune, and there was a lot of grown-up laughter; so naturally when the song was done I clapped. Over my shoulder came Papa's warm firm hand; he was sitting behind me. His fingers closed on mine, and held them still for a moment on the box-ledge. I looked round enquiringly, and he smiled at me, and took his hand away. I asked no question, and did not clap any more.

* * * *

Bernhardt came early with us. We didn't understand a word. We didn't need to. It was enough to look at her, to listen to her. We saw her first as Marguerite Gautier.

Her languid tones in the death scene haunt my ears. *Tosca* they wouldn't take us to, because of the torture scene, but even through the poor plays, like *Izeyl* and *Gismonda*, we sat spellbound by her presence and her voice. Going to see Sarah Bernhardt came into the same air as going to see Irving, Ellen Terry, and Ada Rehan.

* * * *

Ada Rehan spoke Shakespeare matchlessly. I have since seen one lovelier Rosalind, but never such a Viola or Katharine. Her visits to England meant personal joys to Mama, because they brought Mr. and Mrs. Augustin Daly with them, and when Mama was Tiddie Jefferson in America Aunt Mary Daly had been Mary Duff, sister of Mama's very great friend Maggie (but her best friend of all was Katie Holland, whose chestnut hair she kept in her big wardrobe, and whose ring with diamonds she often wore). So there were lots of messages and old-time talk, when Mr. and Mrs. Daly were in England. Mama and Aunt Mary Daly laughed about "The Cousins" Duet. Mr. Daly took one of my poems back to America with him, and printed it on one of his pink satin programmes, that had verses and anecdotes on them to amuse the audience. It was called "A Faded Flower," and it was the one Uncle Warren Edwards set to music and sang to his harmonium. I wrote it when I was ten, and I and Uncle Warren Edwards and Mr. Daly ought all to have known better.

Daly's Theatre
New York
Nov. 27, 1891

My dear Farjeon

Here is a programme of our Opening Night in the Home Theatre—with your little one's poem. I have heard it charmingly commented upon. In a few days I expect to have a satin programme of the opening with her poem, and I shall send her a copy.

I wish I had seen more of you during my London Season—but our hours of leisure (?) did not agree I fear. I hope you are all quite well—and more than all I hope you will come some day back to New York, that I may return you some bit of the pleasure which Mrs. Daly has enjoyed in Maggie's society and yours and your most lovely childrens.

Tell Maggie I have not yet seen her father—but I hope to soon after Christmas when I shall tell him how bright and happy I found her.

Very sincerely
Augustin Daly.

* * * *

Before Mr. Daly built his own theatre in London (there was a great occasion made for the laying of the foundation-stone), we followed Ada Rehan from the Gaiety to the Lyceum and once, I think, to Islington. We loved going behind to see her after the play, and lean against her, holding her hands and squeezing them, while her fascinating not-a-bit-pretty-really face was turned to Mama, and her golden-humorous voice asked anxiously, "Now tell me, do you think the red lining to the grey is a mistake?"

"Don't *think* of changing it," said Mama, "the effect was wonderful."

It wasn't Shakespeare that time, but a play called *The Last Word*, that made you cry more than anything did, ever, except Charles the First saying good-bye to his children. In *The Last Word* Miss Rehan was a Russian Lady with an accent, oh such a *lovely* accent (as fascinating as Mr. Mansfield's in *Prince Karl*), and she twisted everybody

round her little finger, in different ways. When the Son
was being against his sister (who was the Countess Vera's
friend) she went to talk to him in a grey cloak. And when
he was haughty about it, she was furious, and raged up and
down the stage (not quite like the Shrew, because that was
the biggest temper you ever saw), and her grey cloak
flew open, and it had a scarlet lining. The red whirled
all round her while she walked up and down. So he wasn't
quite so haughty, and fell in love with her. So then the
Father was angry with him too, and she went to see the
Father, and told him to beware of the last word he ever
heard from his children's lips, because he would never
forget it. Then she told him about her little brother that
died, and she had refused him something just before.
She cried, and everybody in the theatre cried, and I
thought of little Charlie and cried, and the cruel Father
cried, and forgave his daughter for wanting to marry
somebody else (who was the Countess Vera's brother),
and then the Son came and made it up with the Countess,
and suddenly she was all different again, so comic and
dimpled that it was not surprising that Mr. John Drew,
Aunt Georgie Barrymore's brother, wanted to marry her.
Ada Rehan belonged to Harry first; but after the young Rip
Van Winkle photograph she was Joe's, and used to write
to him. So she turned to him and said, "What does my
sweetheart think about it?" And Joe said the red was
lovely. Our eyes were nearly as red as her lining with
crying, and our handkerchiefs were sopping. You wouldn't
think you *could* cry any more than that at a theatre.

And yet you could.

* * * *

Uncle Ted Willard didn't make you cry. He did other

things to you, but just not that. He played all sorts of
parts; we saw them all, and I don't think he was really
bad in any of them, and in some of them he was very very
good. His smile in *The Professor's Love-Story* was just
like Harry's smile as Mr. Bacon. And though he didn't
gag like Uncle Willie Edouin, he did, when the Professor
was trying to remember his first sweetheart's name,
say "Her name was Maggie Watson!" instead of Millie.
He was masterful, and intellectual, and full of humour
and pride; I think he kept a passionate temper under
control. I heard Papa say to Mama, "If Ted had one
touch of heart, he would be a great actor." We didn't
know him, and his lovely, erratic, impulsive wife, our
Aunt Rachel, till we were quite old—I was nine when
I saw him first in *The Middleman,* and after that he began
to come a lot to our house, and so did she. She had a
lovely fresh complexion, and wavy grey hair, and beautiful
bright eyes, and she was full of whims and fun, and you
never knew where to have her. She wore floating veils
and scarves, and perfect colours, and roses lived longer
for her than for anyone I ever knew, and she pulled door-
bells when she was out and ran away, and if the maid
came too soon pointed down the street as though a naughty
little boy had done it. She took us for picnics on Hampstead Heath. Sometimes you saw her every day for a week,
and then not at all for ever so long. She wrote, and loved
poetry. Her name when she wrote was Rachel Penn, but
her real name was Emily, and Uncle Ted spoke of her
as "Rachel-Emily or Emily-Rachel" and at last only as
"Remily." She dedicated *Cherriwink*, her book, to me.
She and Uncle Ted were two of those who gave their
confidence to Papa and Mama. We loved them, and, still
more, loved Quilt, their Collie. I have said there is one

apple and one rose in childhood; there is, I am sure, one
dog. Quilt was ours. She taught us how intelligent and
loving a dog can be. She would come to us in the dining-
room and stand looking longingly at the biscuit-box. "Go
and ask missis," Papa would say quietly, and off ran Quilt
to Aunt Rachel, chatting in the drawing-room with Mama.
When she came back barking joyfully, it was to tell us
that Aunt Rachel had said "Yes"; then she got her
biscuit, but wouldn't dream of touching it if you said
"Trust!" When Aunt Rachel was telling Mama anything sad, Quilt threw back her head and whined with
sorrow. And if, to tease her, Joe lay on the sofa, and put
his face in his hands, and pretended to cry, she would
lay her paws on him, trying to comfort him, and then
run distractedly to Aunt Rachel, and tug her skirt; and
if she did not come. Quilt ran back and forth, back and
forth between the weeper and the one who might console
him, till it was too much, and Joe looked up laughing.
And then Quilt bounded with joy. She bit me once. It
was a perfect accident. We were playing in Uncle Ted's
garden in Blenheim Road, and I tossed something for
Quilt to catch; her up-leap met the down-fall of my hand,
and her teeth caught my wrist. At the sight of the blood
I ran quickly in to Aunt Rachel. The place was bathed
and bound, and my alarm died down; but there was no
comforting Quilt the rest of that afternoon. She followed
me about dejectedly, and though I hugged and "loved"
her would not forgive herself.

* * * *

When Uncle Ted left St. John's Wood for Buff House,
Banstead, we sometimes went and stayed there with
Aunt Rachel. And when he went to America, and was

very ill with typhoid in Chicago, it was on Papa and Mama both he and Aunt Rachel relied in a special sort of way. Later on, in the Spring of 1899, it was Papa who was ill—far more ill than we children knew, Mama was in a very anxious state, and Uncle Ted would have helped her if he could. Papa had gone for one of his rare holidays to Monte Carlo with Uncle Ted, Aunt Rachel, and one or two others. There was a dreadful carriage accident, from which they only just escaped being killed, and all of them were badly shaken. It affected Papa more than he told us, when he came back. Uncle Ted was very much concerned. He wrote Papa the cheeriest of letters on one day, and on the next invited Mama to the theatre, so that they could discuss between the acts "what ought to be done with Ben." It was just at this time that Papa pencilled some sheets, and put them away in one of his nests of drawers.

* * * *

The curtain rises and drops, rises and drops; behind the footlights people with inappropriate figures and divine voices fling open a new world to us. "If the boy is musical," said Augustus Harris, "he must hear all the Opera he can." As a consequence, every season, two or three times a week, stalls or a box arrived, to be used if we liked. I think we heard whatever and whoever was worth hearing, from the best available places in the house. One night Harris apologised to Father because he "only" had a top box for *Romeo et Juliette,* when Melba and the two De Reskes were singing. I preferred (wrongly perhaps) the romantic and passionate Alvarez to Jean de Reske; and (rightly, I'm certain) Pol Plançon to Edouard, whose vast bass voice seemed drowned in its own volume. I still think that Plançon had the most purely beautiful bass ever heard in Opera, and to that perfection of tone he added his handsome presence, and his splendid French panache. The supreme beauty and greatness of singers like Van Rooy and Chaliapine was of a different order of genius entirely; they were to become gods to me, like Irving; yet for quality Plançon could match either of them. And Emma Calvé! Calvé rather than Melba any night! for acting meant as much to me as music, and it was of her Carmen Grandpa wrote to Mama: "She is so great an actress that it would not matter if she could not sing at all." Ah, but *couldn't* she sing! and wasn't she beautiful! She enslaved, and thrilled, and made you wonder and shiver as Irving did, and Sarah. And hadn't she tantrums too! I remember a night when she and Alvarez sang Carmen with the cold and beautiful Emma Eames as Michæla. They weren't friends, those two Emmas, and in the curtain-call at the end Calvé snatched her hand away like a bad-tempered child, and Alvarez, who was very tall and strong, took the dark and the fair Emma's hands, and held them forcibly as they made their bow. We loved those moments of footlight drama, and missed none of them.

Wagner? A bore. He meant only *Lohengrin* and *Tannhäuser* to us in those days. It was the Frenchmen and the Italians we loved; it was a long time before I thought there *could* be a more beautiful musical air than the "Misere"; then, than "Salve Dimora"; then, than the "Intermezzo." Mascagni took us and the barrel-organs by storm. We grieved over the story of his poverty; of his winning the Competition in Italy with his wonderful opera, and being refused admittance, at the first performance, by the doorkeeper, because he was in rags. When Augustus Harris brought him to London, and Papa and Mama went to the great reception in his honour at "The Elms" in Avenue Road, with its large and beautiful garden, we besieged our parents next day for news of the poor Italian genius. As with poor Mr. Albert Chevalier, I never quite got over being sorry for poor Signor Mascagni. It was long before we would allow Leoncavallo to be his equal. Papa took Harry to the first performance of *Pagliacci* and wrote about it to Mama and me in Cromer. "Melba sang like an angel and acted like an elephant." I heard it soon after, but not even De Lucia, singing "Vesti la Giubba," ousted the beauties of the "Intermezzo."

* * * *

Once, Augustus Harris rather hurt our feelings by sending, at a late moment, two Amphitheatre Stalls for *Rigoletto*. *Could* one sit in the Amphitheatre? (Even the Dress-Circle was *infra dig* to us free-born box-and-stall-holders!) However, we hadn't heard *Rigoletto* yet; and as the cast included Melba and Victor Maurel, for the first time in our lives we grudgingly accepted the comedown of those elevated seats. A pair of little snobs panted up the endless stone flights from Floral Street (*our* entrance was the Foyer and Grand Staircase); but it didn't take us long to forget ourselves. But until Papa's death, I can't remember ever sitting in Gallery or Pit.

* * * *

Hänsel and Gretel. That was one of my young "revelations." I went with Papa to the First Performance at Daly's; and it was not only because it presented one of my beloved Fairy-Tales, not only because Jeanne Douste was so delightful, and Marie Elba a Hänsel never (I still

believe) really equalled for clumsy, naughty, and gay
boyish charm, that I swam away into one more new
world. I got my ears for myself on *Hänsel and Gretel*; I
heard the movements and parts of the orchestra, as something distinct from the too-sweet melodies of Gounod
and Co. For me it was a doorway to new delights. Papa,
noting my rapture, saw to it that during the long successful
run of the piece I went to hear it seven or eight times.
I came to know *Hänsel and Gretel* so whole-heartedly
that I could time each number in it by the clock; and at
home I lay in bed singing the different songs as their
hour came round. I was given the piano score, and
suffered agonies (for I refused to learn the piano) trying
to pick out some likeness to the music I heard so clearly
in my brain. I "insulated" myself in bus and train, and
compelled the orchestra to play the overture for me
beyond the clatter of hoofs and the roll of wheels. *Hänsel
and Gretel* was *mine*.

Mrs. Upcott Gill was calling, on one of Mama's At-
Home days. "Come here, Nellie," she said good-natur-
edly. "Who do you think I met last week? Jeanne
Douste."

"Did you?" I said almost indifferently.

"She says I'm to bring you to tea with her one day.
You see, I've told her all about you, and how much you
love her."

I thanked Mrs. Upcott Gill. But I didn't want to go to
tea with Jeanne Douste. I loved my Gretel, and I loved
my Hänsel, and had not the least desire to meet them
over tea-cups. That never was a part of my hero-worship.
I managed to avoid the tea-party, and kept my Hänsel
and my Gretel intact.

* * * *

Henry Irving was going to be knighted. We were all overjoyed. I knew, from hearing Papa and Mama talking, that he didn't particularly care about the title. "It was for the sake of the Profession," Papa said. Well, whatever that might mean, we thrilled for him. He was giving just then that perfect cameo performance of the old corporal in *Waterloo*. He wasn't for the moment devilish Mephistopheles, saintly Becket, gay Benedick, sly Richelieu, sinister Louis, unforgettable Shylock, or heart-rending King Charles; he was a gaunt old wheezy figure whose first-and-last idea was "The Dook." "The Dook," when Corporal Brewster got his medal, told him "The Country's proud of ye." I sat down and wrote to "Sir" Henry Irving that the Country was proud of *him*. "Love and affectionate greeting and hearty thanks for your sweet letter," he wired. What occasion we four children had to write him a joint letter in 1891 (when Bertie was only just four!) I can't imagine; whatever it may have been, it wasn't inspired by our elders. Letters of thanks were dutifully committed; but we wrote to our gods out of our own impulses. Irving replied to Papa from Grafton Street.

"My dear Farjeon
            Greeting and my best love to Harry, Nelly, Joe & Herbert.
    Tell them what delight their sweet little letter gave me.
    It is easy to see that their hearts are in the right place and that they gather the virtues as they come down the generations."

There was not one occasion where our small inconspicuous lives met his, that was not touched by him with generosity and courtesy. Let my last curtain-memory be of Him and of Her.

* * * *

It was a Morning Performance of *Charles the First*. The house was so full, that you didn't have the Royal Box that time; you, Harry, Joe, and Mama sat in a smaller one. You had the ices and tea and cakes just the same though, after the act in the tent where William Terriss betrayed King Charles, and Charles loved him; and when he heard what his friend had done, he turned on him a look so hurt and loving, and suddenly the joints of his bright armour gave a tiny click and he *almost* bent his knee—it was as though he was going to kneel to his friend as much as to say, "How could you do this to me when I loved you? "Suddenly all the lords standing round made a tiny startled movement together, the armour of Mr. Haviland and Mr. Howe clicked too, like a tiny shock; and at the sound Henry Irving did not kneel, but drew himself up and was a proud unhappy King and not a wounded friend. It was all very sad, but strong in a way, so you could eat your ice without salting it with tears. In the very next box to us was Olive Routledge and her Mother. We could lean round one corner of our curtains and talk to Olive in between the acts. Olive always laughed and chattered, but after Act Three we didn't laugh or talk. Then came the last Act, and it was Whitehall, and King Charles was going to be beheaded; and the Queen put by being a Queen and pleaded with Oliver Cromwell so that you forgot your history, and thought he *must* let King Charles live. But he would not. And then the children were brought in, and King Charles took them on his knee, and said things to them, and really what he said I could hardly hear, for the crying began worse than it ever had been in a theatre before. Of course, Harry and Mama were crying too; but by the time it came to "Remember!" I was just lying against her shoulder on one side, and Joe was lying against her shoulder on the other, and we could not move. The curtain came down and went up and came down and went up, and we only lay and sobbed and wet her dress. The clapping stopped at last, the audience began to go away, Harry got on his things, and Mama tried to get us into ours; but Joe and I couldn't lift our heads from her shoulders. Mrs. Routledge looked round the curtains and said, "Mrs. Farjeon, you've no *business* to bring children like yours to the theatre. Look at Olive! she hasn't turned a hair." Mama didn't answer, but kept her arms round us and tried to help us to stop crying.

And then the door of the box opened, and there was a rustle behind us, and a lovely voice said, "Oh those poor *dear* children!" And Queen Henrietta Maria's arms went round us, and she kissed and comforted us till we did stop crying. But talking was out of the question for Joe and me; if you tried to say a word it wobbled into lots of syllables, and our noses were stuffy and shiny, and our eyes bulged with crying, and our heads ached. And of course it was heavenly to be comforted by Ellen Terry, but in spite of her clothes she wasn't any more the Queen whose King had said "Remember," and that is what had made us cry and went into our feelings for ever. So that for a long time I could not think of Henry Irving saying *Remember* without tears falling; and I cannot now.

A BAD DAY FOR NELLIE

IT HADN'T been one of my "good" days. I knew it as I pulled off my things unhappily and went to bed. It wasn't that I had been bad myself; I knew quite well when I had been naughty, and I didn't make the mistake of calling my naughty days "bad" days. Naughtiness was my own affair, and not the fault of the day. No, the bad days were those on which all sorts of things had gone wrong, or fallen flat, or not been understood aright by other people. Not naughty things at all, but things which began in my mind by being delightful or important, and ended in other people's minds by being—well, somehow quite different. And then there were other things, that didn't begin in my mind at all, but just occurred by themselves, as though this "bad" day had suddenly thrust them upon me out of sheer spite, leaving me helpless, and foolish, and fallen in the eyes of the world.

The worst of it was, the day had come to its end with Mama out of the house.

When she wasn't at home, home wasn't itself to me. To me Mama was—well, you know. You can't really talk about it, and most of the time you don't exactly think about it. But when Mama went out at night to a theatre or a dinner-party I knew—as soon as the front door banged.

Life was no more perfectly secure. If doubts and fears came and sat on my pillow, it would be of no use to cry in the hope that she would hear and come and comfort me. Somebody else would come without the power of knowing what I wanted—and even if they did know, what I wanted was Mama's arms, not theirs. A doubt, of a new and alarming nature, was hanging over me as I shut my bedroom door. Was I really Papa-and-Mama's child? Not long ago I found a picture-book up in the fusty attic, and, squatting behind one of the huge trunks, absorbed the story of a little girl who was only an adopted child, and did not know it. Suppose I also was an adopted child? Suppose one day a strange lady and gentleman appeared, said "We are your Papa and Mama!" and took me away?

I tried not to think of it. Before Mama went out I had asked as usual, "May I get into your Tuck to-night?" and she, as usual, had said, "Yes, you may."

I kept my mind on this, as I pulled off my clothes on the night of the specially "bad" day I had just gone through.

* * * *

It had begun to go wrong before breakfast.

There had been a mouse in the Day-Nursery trap. Harry and I always looked for these prisoners, and were glad when there were none, gladder still when the trap was shut, but empty, and the little hook denuded of its bait. *Some* mouse had enjoyed itself in the night. A year or two ago, Harry had gone the round of the traps at dawn, setting free any captive he might find. When this was discovered, he was told he mustn't let the mice out; it was pointed out to him why. His reason was convinced, but not his heart; and now he and I did what we could to make the pathetic little mite's last moments happy. Finding my mouse, I bore it tearfully to Harry, still in the one-piece swansdown-calico sleeping-suit which Mama made for our nightwear on her sewing-machine.

They made us look like clumsy little pierrots.

"Harry! there *is* one!"

Harry's dark eyes were troubled.

"Can't we let it out?"

"You *know* we mustn't. Go down and get some sugar and some cheese."

I crept down to the dining-room cupboard, and returned. Harry and I fed the trembling prisoner through the bars. At first it was too terrified to respond, but we kept very still as we offered morsels of loaf sugar and cheese, and our woe was a little assuaged when it began to nibble. Poor little criminal! On the morning of execution, it had what it liked for breakfast. I tried to forget it, as I went in to my own.

* * * *

Harry was now a day-boy at Percy House; I and Joe and Bertie remained to Miss Milton. She came at nine o'clock to give us lessons and take us out for a walk.

Miss Milton had reddish hair, rather a high complexion, and was thin and ladylike. Being ladylike was very important to Miss Milton; and ladylikeness, as she gave me to understand it, seemed particularly to reside in one's hands and arms. Gloves out walking, and how you carried your shoulders, and how you arranged your fingers as you lifted your cup of tea to your mouth, and how you managed your elbows at table—these things marked you as a real lady, or as not a lady at all. And brown hands and forearms after the holidays, of course. Miss Milton, after a month at Herne Bay, could come home with fingers as pale as when she went. She spoke of a party she had been to where one of the young ladies in short sleeves and a "round" neck had distinctly shown the sunburn-line in both places. "It looked very badly," said Miss Milton, "so unladylike. I was quite ashamed."

She blushed very easily. One morning Papa came into the Nursery while we were at lessons, and wished each child "Good morning, dear!" with a kiss. As he was leaving the room, Joe said, "Say Good-Morning-Dear to Miss Milton." Papa obeyed, with the pleasantest smile and nod (what else *could* he do?) Miss Milton turned scarlet to the roots of her hair. We giggled. Papa went out. We were reprimanded. But whether she was pleased or offended, who could say? One never knew how Miss Milton felt, only how she behaved.

We admired her for her musical accomplishments; her repertoire consisted of a few ravishing "pieces" with watery names: "*Cascade*" and "*Rippling Brook*," full of arpeggios, trills, and runs in the treble.

We found her tiresome when we went out for a walk; she first found out the way we wanted to go, and then gently discovered some nice reason for going the other way exactly. We did not love, but I don't think we disliked her. We took her for granted.

Miss Milton taught us Spelling, and "Copies," and the Capitals of Europe, and Tables, and Dates. There was no magic in these things as she taught them.

"Give the name of the capital of Sweden, Nellie."

A slight pause. "Copenhagen?"

"No, dear; Copenhagen is the capital of Denmark. Stockholm is the capital of Sweden. Repeat that."

"Stockholm is the capital of Sweden. Copenhagen is the capital of Denmark," I repeated.

"You'll remember that next time when I ask you, won't you, Nellie?"

"Yes, Miss Milton."

But though I thought I would *say* it the next time Miss Milton asked me, I didn't think I would really *remember* it. Remembering was something quite different. You remembered things that lay in the corners of your mind, and you came on suddenly like your old toys, or Mama's Maltese lace head-scarf that had such a lovely faint smell when it came out of the drawer—it took you on a little perfumed wave back to all sorts of feelings and thoughts, you didn't quite know what. You remembered things because there was something *else* about them, as well as just themselves, something happy, or sad, or beautiful, or hurting, or wonderful. But there was nothing else about Copenhagen the capital of Denmark; it was just itself, it wasn't lovely, or ugly, or joyful, or miserable, or anything; so it might just as well have been the capital of Sweden after all, except that it merely happened not to be.

And then the dates——

"What is the date of the Constitutions of Clarendon?'
"Eleven-hundred-and-sixtyfour."

"Quite right. You know that now."

"Yes, Miss Milton."

But what exactly did I know, when I knew that? "Constitutions of Clarendon, Eleven-hundred-and-sixtyfour"; just that. Was that *knowing*? I didn't know what "Constitutions of Clarendon" was. Was it to do with somebody's health? Who was Clarendon? Or perhaps with the way red wine was made—or with the blowing of gold trumpets every morning at a certain hour. What *was* Clarendon? Miss Milton never told me, and I never asked. Miss Milton was not one of the people whose answers ever succeeded in satisfying me; somehow they seemed to go against everything I wanted to discover. Just the same as when she took us for walks.

To-day Miss Milton settled us as usual with our copy-books. Bertie had pothooks and Joe had letters to copy; but I had a proverb in beautiful copper-plate at the top of the page, to be copied six times on the lines underneath. I disliked copying, and wanted this bit of the lessons to be over.

Miss Milton said, "Don't dawdle, dear. Copies must be done by half past nine."

My Proverb this morning was a funny one: "How Far That Little Candle Throws Its Beams." What little Candle, I wondered, and what were its beams like, and how far *did* it throw them, and where to? Oh, bother! a blind "e"—not quite blind, though. The tiny white spot in the middle suddenly irritated me—I simply couldn't endure it! I filled it in. Now the humour of the black blobby "e" tickled me, and as I finished each "copy" I blobbed the "e"s in every word with care. The Little Candle couldn't possibly throw its beams very far, if the "e"s were black, like the dark shutters at the photographer's. How I did hate going to the photographer, and being told to hold a bunch of flowers and to smile at a spot on the wall. Almost as much as going to the dentist—worse, in a way, because you *had* to be photographed, but on the dentist's doorstep Mama *promised* you you needn't have your tooth out if you were too frightened when you got in the chair, so you believed her and went in. In the chair you were too frightened, after all, and Mama said, "I'm very sorry, I must take her away; I promised her I would"; and the Dentist was cross and said, "You ought to make her have it out"; and Mama said again, "I'm sorry, but if I did she would never believe me again." So we came away, and I knew I could always believe her. Soon after that I didn't mind much going to the dentist; but it was another dentist.

"Have you done?" said Miss Milton at half past nine precisely.

"Nearly, Miss Milton. What is the Little Candle?"

"What little candle?"

"In the proverb in my copy?"

"Oh. It's not a proverb, it's a quotation. Nellie! just look at all these blind e's! You naughty girl! You made them blind on purpose."

I couldn't deny it. "They're funny," I explained.

"They are *not* funny," said Miss Milton crossly. She turned the page to "All is not Gold that Glitters." "Do that page." I looked at her gloomily. I'd *done* my copying-lesson. "Not a single blind e, mind!" she said.

Oh dear, oh dear! lessons were going to be horrid to-day. My fingers ached round the thin penholder as it crawled down the page.

"There, you see! you *can* avoid making blind e's when you really try, can't you?"

"Yes, Miss Milton."

She blotted the copy-books, put them away, and brought out the Spelling. To-day we did things like "Through" and "Threw," "Bread" and "Bred," and "Would" and "Wood."

"They *sound* just the same," explained Miss Milton, "but you *spell* them differently. Do you see?"

"Yes, Miss Milton." But really and truly I didn't see very much.

At twelve o'clock it was time to go for a walk.

"Let's go to Regent's Park," said Joe.

"And take some bread," added Bertie, giving the show away. Bread meant the delight of ducks and water.

"Wouldn't it be nicer, dears, to go to Primrose Hill? It is such a clear day, and I can show you Saint Paul's from the top."

We disliked Primrose Hill, the grass was so bare, and the trees were so dull, and you never got away from the feeling of iron railings, and however clear it was *I* couldn't see St. Paul's and, even if I could, I didn't want to. However, when Miss Milton said firmly, "Yes, we'll all go for a nice walk to Primrose Hill," we knew there was no hope.

However, if we took our hoops we could play the game of Greeks and Trojans which Harry had invented for us, after the Iliad had been shared out fairly among us.

Each of us had so many Trojan heroes and so many Greek ones, that we could "be" in the Game of Hoops. And each had so many Great Heroes and so many Lesser ones. In the Hoop Game you all went apart and decided in your mind who to be. Perhaps I decided to be Aeneas of Troy, and bowled my hoop to meet Joe, who announced himself as Menelaus of Greece. Then we fought, beating our hoops against each other, and because Aeneas was a Great Hero I could fight my strongest, and because Menelaus was a Lesser Hero Joe was on his honour not to fight his best. Then all depended on Bertie, bowling into the fray with shouts of battle. If he happened to be Diomed of Greece he backed up the weak Menelaus, and I would have my work cut out to keep my hoop from falling. But if Bertie was Glaucus of Troy, he sided with me against Joe—and then, small hope for Menelaus! As soon as a hoop fell, that Hero was dead for the rest of the morning. Away went Joe, to re-appear in a new character.

"Hail, Stranger! Who are you?"

"Agamemnon of Greece. Who are you?"

"I'm Ajax of Greece. Who are you, Bertie?"

"I'm Troilus! I'll fight you both!"

"You mustn't fight your hardest for Troilus, Bertie, he wasn't one of the greatest ones."

The Greeks and Trojans Hoop Game was our outdoor favourite. But Miss Milton thought we had better leave our hoops at home.

* * * *

On the walk I was seized with a lovely plan for the afternoon. It had to do with Mrs. Brace the Florist's. Mrs. Brace had a narrow greenhouse window in Adelaide Road, wedged in by the fire-station. The window was filled with rather wide-necked glass vases with cut flowers in them. Her flowers were always the drawing-room sort of flowers, like gladiolas and roses and smilax and carnations. I loved the window, and was always glad when Mama took me inside the little greenhouse to buy sixpenny-worth of flowers for the middle of the dining-room table. Behind the vases of cut flowers, pots of spiræa and azaleas stood on the greenhouse shelves, and behind the greenhouse itself a narrow strip of yard ran back into which I never penetrated, where I was vaguely aware of Mr. Brace busy with pots and boxes. I didn't really know Mr. Brace; but I knew Mrs. Brace quite well, from going in with Mama.

The thought of the flowers took hold of me entirely, and a desire to have lots of them filled my heart. I was constantly filled with quick little desires, I felt intensely the desirability of all sorts of things through the day: suggestions and possibilities of something new—something delicious, or beautiful, or romantic, and different.

Flowers were never bought for the nursery, only for the

dining-room table downstairs. How lovely it would be to
have flowers in the nursery! As soon as I got the idea, I
began to want the flowers tremendously. I could hardly
wait to get home to look in my brown leather purse, that
had been Mama's till Papa gave her a new grey one on her
birthday, and Mama gave the old brown one to me. It was
shabby, but still quite sound, and full of delightful
"extra" places—places for stamps, as well as several for
money, and a special flap with little pockets in it for
sovereigns and half sovereigns, two sizes. Of course, I
never had even a half sovereign to put in the small-sized
pockets, but I knew I had a sixpence in the safest middle
part of the purse, and some pennies in the outside compartments.

As soon as I got home I rushed and counted it—altogether I had one-and-a-penny! It was more than Mama
ever spent on flowers on ordinary days, only when she had
a dinner-party she sometimes spent more than a shilling.

My desire increased; how lovely if I could spend *two*
shillings on flowers for the nursery! I could get four or
five different sorts, and the nursery would be different
and beautiful, a sort of princess's bower.

After lunch I cornered Joe and Bertie and sprang on
them my vision of the bower. When I was ardent about
anything I could get a response from both the little boys,
and they offered, almost before I suggested it, to contribute between them the rest of the Two Shillings. Joe had
sevenpence ha'penny, and Bertie about sixpence, but
we only let him give fourpence, and Joe made up the
remainder.

I slipped out in great excitement. Miss Milton had gone
home for the day, the nurse was in the kitchen, so except
for Papa's study, the coast was clear. I didn't quite know

why I wanted the coast to be clear, for I didn't *think* I was doing anything naughty. All the same, I went as inconspicuously as I could past the study door, and returned breathless with joy, my hands full of colours, pink, blue, red, yellow, white and green.

I got upstairs safely. The little boys were in the night nursery making Surprise Packets for each other to have after tea, while I was at Harry's first School-Party at Percy House, which wasn't far away.

I opened the white paper in which the flowers were wrapped, laid them out on the table, and fetched vases and a big jug of water, and scissors to cut the bass round the stalks. I wouldn't call Joe and Bertie till the nursery was a bower.

I had filled one vase and put it on the mantelpiece, and was beginning to fill another, when Papa came into the room.

"What is all this?" he said.

I knew at once, and had suspected all along, that I had done something certain of disapproval.

"I got the flowers at Mrs. Brace," I said, looking and feeling guilty as I said it.

"What for?" asked Papa, evidently ruffled.

I simply *couldn't* explain.

"What did you give for them?"

"My shilling and—and some of Joe's and Bertie's."

"Maggie!" shouted Papa.

Mama came upstairs.

"Nellie's been spending the children's money on flowers. She must take them back, and tell Mrs. Brace she has made a mistake."

I looked from Papa to Mama in dismay. It seemed a quite impossible thing to do. I felt I would die of shame before Mrs. Brace if I had to do that. Papa went out of the room, and tears began to roll down my face.

"Oh, dear," sighed Mama. "Don't cry, get your hat."

"Must I?" I whispered.

"Yes, or Papa will be cross. You shouldn't have done it without asking, dear. Wipe your eyes. I'll go with you and explain."

"C-can't you g-go alone?"

Mama thought better not.

The next ten minutes were dreadful. In the little shop, while Mama "explained" to Mrs. Brace, I stood behind her crying all the time, and didn't try to get out a word. Luckily Mama didn't try to make me. Mrs. Brace took it very calmly, and made no bones at all about giving back the two shillings, and putting the bunches of flowers back into the glass vases.

* * * *

Parties were still my trials, especially if I didn't know some of the people. At Percy House I knew nobody but Harry, though I had once seen his chum Charles Brock at tea. My velveteen frock felt tight in the sleeves, and had rucked up under my coat, in spite of twisting a handkerchief round the cuffs as I pulled the coat on. When I got the coat off, in the stuffy crowded little cloakroom full of the boys' sisters, I couldn't get my sleeves comfortable again, and I wondered rather forlornly however I was going to find Harry.

A tall lady stooped over me and said, "And what's *your* name, little girl?"

I whispered it.

"Oh, yes," said the lady, and told me where Harry was, and to my great relief he really was where the lady said he would be.

The party was very confusing. Things happened for reasons I wasn't clear about. We were all jostled into another room and sat on benches in rows, while the big people talked, but I hadn't the faintest idea what about, and there were some presents given to a few boys, while people clapped. But I didn't know why. Presents for everybody out of a bran pie, I would have understood. Harry didn't get a present.

After this we were all jostled downstairs into still another big room, with tables at the end, and things to eat on them. The children sat on chairs against the walls, but a lot had to stand, and a crowd of grown-ups moved about giving the children spoons and empty plates, and after a time cups of weak tea which were hard to manage on their laps. I had a chair, and Harry stood very close to me. He was a shy boy too, but of course this *was* his school. In the crush Brock was pushed against us, and Harry said:

"Hullo, Brock."

"Hullo, Farjeon," said Brock.

That was all they seemed to have to say to each other. I hadn't even as much as that to say.

Another tall lady came up to us, and looking at my empty plate said, "And what would you like *now*?"

I hadn't had anything yet, and didn't know what there was to have. I looked between the people at the tables as well as I could, and saw dishes of something pink and something white.

"I'd like some ice-cream," I said.

The lady burst out laughing. She turned to another lady and said out loud, "This little girl wants some ice-cream, and there isn't any."

The other lady laughed too. My cheeks burned with shame. My bad eyes had played me false again. The first lady brought me some pink-and-white blanc-mange, but I could hardly eat it. I hoped nobody would notice me or talk to me any more at the party, and I hoped Harry didn't think I had disgraced him, and I hoped Brock didn't despise me. But I was afraid that I had, and that he did. My spirits were very low.

The party went on being stuffy and crowded until it was time to struggle into my coat and go home, with rather a headache.

* * * *

Bertie was in bed, and Joe was still in the day nursery. He was building Thebes with the Anker Bricks, very carefully and thoroughly. Thebes was his city in the Anker-brick game. Corinth was Bertie's, Athens mine, and Sparta, of course, Harry's (who was also Achilles in the Hoop Game).

"Will you help me make this?" asked Joe. "I want two White Longs now, and a red Thick."

We had given names to the different sorts of bricks, so that they could be easily asked for.

I began to find the kinds Joe wanted, and as I looked at his clear little face and gold head bent over the model a wave of love for him broke over me. Joe was a sort of angel, I thought. How *lovely* he would look in a white dress—so much lovelier than me with my plain straight hair. Why shouldn't he be an angel—or a fairy? A delicious idea was born, more magical than a nurseryful of flowers.

"Joe."

"What?"

"Wouldn't it be *lovely* for Bertie if he saw a *real* fairy!"

"Yes, but how could he?"

"Well, if he *thought* he did it would be the same. Oh, do lets!"

"What?"

"Let you be a fairy and go and stand by his bed."

"He'd know who I was, wouldn't he?" said Joe, rather puzzled, but trying to follow my new vision, which was evidently another ardent one. And Joe, for love, was always so willing to help me out with my visions.

I said, "He wouldn't know you if you were all draped in white with a white veil, and a silver wand and crown and wings, and if you just stood for a moment by his bed and waved your wand over him, and then flitted out."

"Silver wings?" said Joe.

"Yes. We'll make them with cardboard and silver paper, and we'll cover a stick with the silver tinsel from last Christmas, and there's all that butter-muslin in the dressing-up box for the dress. Let's make the wings *now*—we'll just have time before you go to bed."

"All right," said Joe, catching my eagerness.

We dragged out a litter of our possessions, and I rapidly cut the wings in cardboard, and while Joe pasted on silver paper I twisted a tinsel crown and wand. Then with lots of pins I draped Joe in muslin, and fastened the wings at the back, and put on the crown, and gave him the wand. The effect was all rather hasty, and the wings hung down too much instead of spreading in flight as I had imagined them, and the dress was rather bunchy here and there, but all the same Joe *did* look lovely, with his fine little features and golden hair all in a maze of white and silver.

"Come very softly," I whispered. "The night-light will just make him able to see you."

"What shall I do?" asked Joe.

"Just hover above him and say 'Bertie' softly."

The night nursery door was ajar. Joe went in and stood by Bertie's bed in the dim light. I watched breathless with joy through the crack.

Bertie wasn't asleep. He heard something, turned over, looked, and uttered a shriek. Joe dropped his wand. Bertie shrieked again, and I rushed in while Joe tore off his tinsel and muslin as fast as he could. "It's me, Bertie, it's me," he kept on saying, and I kept on crying, "Bertie, darling, it's only Joe being a fairy for you." And Bertie kept on shrieking.

There was a commotion on the stairs. Papa and Mama and Susan came running as fast as they could, and Harry hurried in from his little bedroom, where he had been reading *Paradise Lost* without skipping. ("Skipping and looking at the end" were minor crimes.) They found me with the screaming Bertie clasped in my arms, and Joe dreadfully upset, with the torn fairy dress hanging from its pins about him, and the tinsel crown crooked on his head.

The explanation was a muddle of eager self-defence, remorseful self-reproach, childish terror, and noisy efforts at comfort. For some curious reason, Papa was hardly cross, and Mama rocking Bertie in her arms, had a funny look on her face.

Presently Bertie was quieted, and Joe went to bed beside him, promising him that he really *had* been a fairy all the time, and *not* a ghost, and Harry went back to Milton, and Papa and Mama drove away in a cab.

Then Susan said to me, "You'd better go straight to bed too. You've done enough silly tricks for one day, I should think!"

* * * *

I thought so too, as I went to my little side-slip of a room next to the day nursery, and undressed myself. It had been as bad a day as I could remember, for a day that wasn't actually a naughty one. All my lovely hopes and plans and visions had gone wrong. I hated myself for frightening Bertie so. I lay down in bed so unhappily that I forgot about the first tuck being Mama's, and realized too late that I had only lightly and scantily pulled the sheet about my shoulders. A movement would shift it, and I was lying in an uncomfortable position. I tried to think, but the "thinking" wouldn't come real; no, even the young Apollo wouldn't come properly. I could set him up in my mind, but it was like setting up a toy on the table; he didn't begin to move and speak on his own, and I couldn't get lost in my thinking.

Sound ceased in the house. Time crawled on. I was used to not sleeping for hours, but without entertainment night was unendurable. This was going to be a long one.

The thoughts crept in that I had tried to shut out. Apollo would not come near me, but a strange lady in a cab drove up to the door. I was called down to the drawing-room, where Mama and Papa stood looking very sad. "You must say good-bye to us, Nellie, you are not our child after all. This is your mother——"

The pillow began to grow wet under my cheek. Things had happened on this dreadful day which I would never forget, and never get over. The happiness of life was all finished. I shook with grief, and the sheet moved out of position. Mama's Tuck was destroyed. At this I buried my face in the pillow, and sobbed my heart out.

Then the door opened softly, and I felt the only two arms in the world go round me, and heard the only voice in the world say, "Nellie *dear*. What is it, what's making you cry so?"

I clung to her with all my might, and sobbed in her sweet-smelling lace instead of in the pillows.

"Oh, Mama! I did want you! I *did* want you!"

"Don't cry so, darling, it will make your head ache."

"I am *really* your child, aren't I? I'm not adopted or anything?"

Mama looked at me with her funny face. "You little chump! of course you aren't adopted."

Comfort came stealing back.

"Was it a nice theatre, Mama? Was Henry Irving good?"

"I'll tell you all about it in the morning. Mr. Irving says you must all come and see it soon. Now lie down, darling, and I'll tuck you in."

I lay down, and I felt the dear hands turn my pillow, and smooth my sheet, and then draw the clothes all snuggly round my chin and shoulders. And Mama wiped my wet eyelashes, and kissed my heavy eyelids, and went out. . . .

And the two little Sanger Princesses came riding on their cream ponies; they'd a long way to ride because the Old Crossing Sweeper had just come to tell them that Alice was in great danger and must be saved, but it was all right, it was all right, because there was the young Apollo come to help with his glittering bow and his hair like golden fire. . . .

MY SWEETHEART

I HAD A SWEETHEART.
How did it begin? We both too well remember how it ended. But how did Button and I begin to be Sweethearts?

To-day small children don't declare their sweethearts. In our time, infant sweethearts were quite the thing, and, thinking back, I cannot remember Button in any other light. But at what point did he declare himself—or I?

Retracing my steps among the forget-me-not-beds of the Eighties, I seem to see this one planted by our parents. "Nellie and Button are Sweethearts." It was one of our earliest axioms. From the age of four or thereabouts, I accepted the fact that he was the nicest little boy I knew (and he *was*), and that I therefore loved him more fondly than any other little boy (and I *did*—Harry always excepted). Button, I believe, was sure that I was the nicest little girl. The situation was never allowed to languish. If there were errant moments on both sides, the bond held firm until a certain summer day, in 1891, when I deliberately broke his heart. I took this step to save myself, and possibly him (though I am not sure if I took that into consideration), from tragedy in the future. But let me not anticipate the end of this Love-affair of the Eighties.

Button, Bronnie, and Bay. The three brothers were almost sons of our house. Their brilliant father—such a dim memory—died when we were all small. I remember him vaguely. Under my eyes is the torn half of a letter, beginning, "10 large Queen Victorias—1 middle sized

Empr. of Russia—4 Prince Wales, full size—2 small
sultans and one very little pope." The son of a man who
could compile such a catalogue was clearly the boy for
me. Besides, apart from his own virtues and those of his
father, Button had certain unusual values. He had swallowed a button in babyhood, and survived; also, a needle
that had once broken off in his shoulder, re-appeared
some years later through the sole of his foot. Suppose it
had made its re-entry through his heart! These things,
which Button bore with a perfect modesty, made him a
bit of a hero in our eyes. He was a generous and unselfish
boy, and from our Christmas parties, when all the other
children went away loaded, he would have gone empty-
handed, for he parted with anything to the first hinter.
But Aunt Maggie and Uncle Ben took particular care
that Button's box was re-filled with the best that remained
on and under the gigantic tree, which fifty greedy
children could not despoil.

With Button's father is bound up my first sharp recollection of a telegram. It startled our Margate holiday one
August day in 1889. I see myself in the sitting-room at
6 Royal Crescent, and Mama and Papa with the telegram.
Mama told me gently that Papa was going to London to
help Aunt Mary, because Button's father had died. I was
seized with anxiety for the prettiest of all our courtesy
aunts; would she have to wear that old-person's colour,
black? "She won't look nice, Mama!" Mama assured
me, "She'll look beautiful."

Papa went away from Margate, and came back again.
I heard him telling Mama about the funeral; Button rode
in his carriage, and kept by Papa all the time, and held
his hand very tight. "Mary was wonderfully sweet and
brave." I recorded the facts that Telegrams were Bad

News, and that Mourning need not make a person ugly.
I found with relief that what Mama had said was true;
Button's young mother looked beautiful in black.

Her struggle began. My parents had been her devoted
friends from the time of her marriage, at the age of sixteen, to a husband thirty years her senior. She was nearer
in age to her first son than to her husband; she had
become a mother at seventeen. What was she to do with
him and his younger brothers, when Mr. Wyndham gave
her the part on tour which sent her running to Ben and
Maggie, clapping her hands? Who'd keep an eye on
Button and Bronnie and Bay, if not my parents? Were
not they Button's parents-in-law-to-be? And so, though
we did not live under one roof, our nurseries were linked,
and our trysts were constant. Our nurses left us to go to
Aunt Mary's boys, they had the reversion of our governesses; Fanny Bagge (successor to Fanny Dodd) only
stopped putting Bertie to bed in Adelaide Road, when she
began putting Bay to bed in Melina Place, and Miss
Milton, having taught us to Read Without Tears, repeated
the same process upon them. They were the only little
boys I wasn't shy of. I loved little Bay like a brother,
and Bronnie *very nearly* like a brother; but Button was
my Sweetheart.

On every Christmas-party-day for years, he entered
the drawing-room with a little bouquet of flowers, and I
sat on the hired red-cushioned rout-seat, my feet still
several inches off the floor, awaiting, in embarrassed
expectation, the presentation which would create our
elders' smiles. Button's face was red, he held his head low
as he advanced and poked the little bunch at me. Once
indeed he held his head so low, that he poked the bunch
by mistake at the wrong little girl. Georgie Catling had

got *my* bouquet! My eyes were round with astonishment, his face burned with mortification, the elders this time not only smiled, but laughed. And what were Georgie's feelings when the flowers were rescued? What Button's, as he did his duty over again, and thrust the bouquet into my cream-cashmere lap? And what mine? Had it *really* been all a mistake?

Then, or later, I must have had doubts of him. Something palpitating occurred before my seventh birthday. On February 13th came his birthday present, a slender blue-cloth volume, stamped in silver: "THANKFUL REST, by Annie S. Swan." All was well, then. Button loved me still. I sat down instantly and indited a Valentine Verse for him, the first complete poem from my pen.

KEEP TRUE TO ME
My heart has never beat before,
As it did beat just now;
I want you but to keep to me,
And I'll give my hand to thou.

I'll never turn away from thee,
If always you keep true;
But if you always turn away,
I will not keep to you.

But I will go out far away,
And find a lover true to me;
But if you never turn away,
I'll never, never turn from thee.

You've turned away from me just once,
But if you won't again;
I'll give you all the love my heart,
Will ever and can contain.

I cannot now remember whether a certain insistence in the verse is attributable to Georgie Catling or to Phoebe Carlo, who for one dark moment cast a shadow on our troth. Harry and I had been taken to a performance of *Alice in Wonderland*. In the book-world, Harry had long claimed Alice as *his,* and out of the theatre he now drew Phoebe Carlo, delicious beyond compare, across the foot-lights, also to be *his* for evermore. We went to a second morning performance of "Alice," and this time Button, who was staying with us, sat in our box. The next day, at midday dinner, he proclaimed his love for this most adorable Alice.

Harry rose up in his place like Nemesis. His brow was black. It wasn't that Button encroached on his preserves —at least, it wasn't *only* that. How *dared* Nellie's sweet-heart pledge his heart to another, in Nellie's presence? He emptied his glass of water on Button's head.

In a moment the two were rolling on the carpet. I stared aghast. Harry, who *never* fought! Harry fighting Button, because of me! (Was it because of me, Harry?) "Mama! Papa! Harry and Button are fighting one another!" Elders hastened in. I forget the immediate sequel. But presently peace was restored, Button returned perforce to his allegi-ance, and Harry remained in possession of Phoebe Carlo.

But if he ever needed my forgiveness, I, too, upon occasion needed his. Our courtship gave rise to a still more famous battle.

We had come over from Margate to them in Ramsgate. I was perhaps six. I remember a walled-garden behind their house. We all had tea together in the garden-room. During tea, some quarrel or other arose between Button and me. We hurt each other's feelings, I know not how. Tea over, we were sent to play in the garden, until it was time for us to be driven home, He, ever sweet-natured, lurked about me, trying to make it up; it wasn't possible that we should part, unforgiving, unforgiven. I vouchsafed him not one glance. I summoned his younger brother. "Let you and me walk round the garden, Bronnie!" Bronnie only too willingly complied; wounded, Button retreated out of sight. I didn't care! I walked deliberately round the garden with another. As we reached the door of the room again, Button sprang out, fell upon Bronnie, and thrashed him. I wept.

When justice had been administered, he turned to me. I stood, fallen from grace, awaiting my verdict. But when was Button not magnanimous? He held out his hand.

"Come into my room, Nellie," he said, "and I'll let you see me change my shirt."

I followed, meekly grateful. I looked on while he stripped (to the vest) and exchanged his soiled shirt for a spotless one. At parting we kissed as usual.

These are the only painful episodes in our six-years' love-story. Few enough, as love goes. But we were growing up, and I was beginning to think.

* * * *

I was ten, and allowed to drink tea instead of cocoa. This advance had been promised me since I was nine, and still too young for tea. Mama could not think why I wanted to drink "the horrid stuff," but for me it was a stride towards grown-npness. I had been drinking it, grown-uply, for fifteen weeks, when my three brothers developed whooping-cough together. I was packed off to Margate with Miss Milton, till it was certain whether I had or hadn't "got" it.

Before I went to melancholy exile, Papa took me into his study and gave me a beautiful new book. lit was *A Midsummer Night's Dream,* by William Shakespeare. As usual, when he gave me anything special, he told me

something about it, and turning the pages read magical
lines here and there, lines of the loveliest fall:

> *"I know a bank whereon the wild thyme grows ..."*
> *"The course of true love never did run smooth ..."*
> *"In maiden meditation fancy-free ..."*
> *"Philomel with melody ..."*
> *"Are you that merry wanderer of the night? ..."*
> *"I was with Hercules and Cadmus once——"*

Oh, my beloved Greeks! I beheld their pictures as we
lingered over the heavenly passages, mingled with pictures of my beloved fairies. With these, and Miss Milton,
for companions, I left home.

My miserable quarantine in Margate was relieved once
only by a visit from Mama. One morning came a telegram, for *me*—— Good news, not bad! "Coming to
Margate arrive 1.30 Mama." I was in a quiver of excitement; I would not lose one instant of her presence; I
would be at the station at twenty minutes past one.

At one o'clock, Miss Milton took me for a walk—the
other way.

Of course, we were late at the station; the train had
come in, and Mama was standing outside, looking for us.
I ran with the little dusty bunch of flowers I had picked
for her, eager to show her my new discovery, the pim-
pernel. She gave Miss Milton the afternoon to herself,
and we had it blessedly to *our*selves. There were letters
and messages from Harry, Joe, and Bertie, and Papa. She
told me the boys were getting better, and Joe whooped
the worst and was the best patient. When he began to
whoop, he stood up in bed, holding out his hands for her
to grip, and whooped and whooped with the tears running out of his eyes. She eased my loneliness by saying

that soon, instead of staying in far-off Margate, I would come back to be in Melina Place with Button and Bronnie and Bay. Then I could see Mama almost every day, till it was safe for me to come home again. She told me, too, that I would see, when I came back, my American Uncle Joe, who was coming to England for his honeymoon. He was about to marry a beautiful girl called Blanche, who had acted Meenie and Lydia Languish with Grandpa. They would stay in Adelaide Road, as Albert and Viney had done, and darling Aunt Josie.

This was a great excitement; people from America were like rainbows in an ordinary landscape. I cried a little as the train took Mama away, waving to the last; Miss Milton drew me from the platform before her handkerchief vanished. But I felt I could live through the rest of my quarantine.

Apart from this visit, I took refuge, and had incessant delight, in my *Midsummer Night's Dream*. The pictures were numerous and beautiful; it was past anything I had ever read or dreamed of. It was far better than *The Taming of the Shrew* or *A Winter's Tale*, the only two plays I knew well of Shakespeare's. I read and read and read it, and would not be parted from it; I slept with it, physically and mentally. The miraculous combination of fairies and Greeks was for me a wholly natural union. I had no difficulty in harmonizing them. I had done harder things than that in my "thinking" at night. I longed to get back to Harry, to share this new world of beings with him, to see how they would find their way into TAR. I knew they would! And I wondered which would be "his" and which would be "mine." And then, there were Uncle Joe and Aunt Blanche in prospect. And before that, Button, and Melina Place.

Button! Ah, there it was! The course of true love had not run perfectly smooth. I had reached an age when I must make a decision.

"Button and I are sweethearts! *Why* are we sweethearts? It can't be helped, but we are—and sweethearts marry! Oh goodness! If I don't do something *soon,* I'll have to marry Button presently. I don't want to marry Button, I must break it off! Whatever they say, I won't marry him. Oh dear! What *can* I do to break it off?"

* * * *

I was safe now, I wasn't going to have whooping-cough; for three weeks I was happy at Melina Place. I was not shy. In the bedroom, Fanny Bagge helped me to do up my buttons again; in the schoolroom, "Mademoiselle" taught us French verbs, just as she did at home. The house was romantic, the garden "windy-walky"; I controlled the nursery games with Bronnie and Bay, my youngers, and tasted the strange power of playing them *my* way (in Adelaide Road we played them Harry's way). Pretty Aunt Mary, much occupied with people from the theatre, was so affectionate; her sister, Aunty Fan, so comfortable; garden-parties and gay little dinners sent their echoes floating up to our rooms, just as at home.

On an evening I ran through the windy walks with a butterfly-net. I had lately been taken with a fancy for "Natural History," so I caught butterflies, looked at them, and let them go again. A well-known actor and author of the day, who also came occasionally to 196, saw me with two white fairies in my net. "So you collect butterflies, eh, Nellie?" He took the fragile things out of the net, and before I knew what he was doing, chopped off their heads with his pocket-knife. I stared in horror as he snapped his knife and said, "Now you can put 'em on pins." I ran away, and was sick. I tried to forget those headless fluttering wings. I cried that night, with longing to go home. Aunty Fan heard me, and came to find out what was the matter.

"Are you ill, dear?" I shook my head. "Has Bronnie been teasing you?" No, it wasn't that. What was it? tell Aunty Fan. How could I tell her what the dreadful man at the party downstairs had done? "Are you homesick, Nellie?" Well, that was true enough, at any rate. "I want Mama, I want Mama!" I sobbed like a baby. I never used my butterfly-net again.

* * * *

It was an easy walk from St. John's Wood to Swiss Cottage; we took it almost every day, passing our favourite crossing-sweeper by the church, the old smiling one who called Joe "Curly." At 196, though I might not go in, Papa and Mama came out upon the steps, and Harry, Joe, and Bertie waved from the windows. One morning two more people came out on the steps with Papa and Mama. One was a ravishingly lovely girl, and one a tall, half-shy, delightful uncle, who stooped and kissed me, saying, "So this is my English niece." I was enraptured with him, and with my Aunt Blanche. Uncle Joe, when he spoke to Mama, called her "Maggie-May."

I walked home in ecstasy at the thought that I would soon be seeing them every day. "Isn't she *beautiful!*" I cried ardently.

There was a brief silence. Then Bronnie burst out— "Do you fink she is more beautiful van my Muvver?" (He and his brothers could no more pronounce "th" than I and mine our R's.) I did think so, but hesitated. Then I said, "They're both very beautiful." Bat I said it a shade too late. Bronnie wouldn't speak to me the rest of the way back.

And you, Button, where were you? You now went to school, where the name by which I called you was all unknown. (Not for your school-fellows to suspect that you had swallowed a button as a baby.) You were another person, and so was I. Bronnie dropped a hint about some-one called Una. On one of your returns, I taxed you with her. You admitted that it *had* been so, but wasn't now. Would I forgive you? You had no doubt I would. I saw my chance, and took it. I refused to forgive you.

Indeed, indeed, it was not what you thought, not jealousy or anger or revenge; I was still fond of you, and when your eye roved could have overlooked it. Nothing less than concern for both our futures made me seize on "Una" as a pretext. Those startled thoughts would leave me no peace till I did so. I must not be moved by your bewildered looks, your wounded tones.

"But, Nellie, won't you make it up?"

I wouldn't.

"I didn't know you could be like this," said Button bitterly. "I wouldn't have *thought* you wouldn't say you'd forgive me!"

(*But if I do, I'll have to marry you, Button!*)

Nearly as wretched as you, I stuck to my guns. The sweetheart days were ended, the true-love-knot severed once and for all. Vows were taken back, Valentines would be composed no more; the forget-me-nots withered in their heart-shaped bed. Ah me!

> *For all that I could ever read or hear*
> *The course of true love never did run smooth.*

* * * *

Dear Button! I forgave you sooner than you thought. And you, how long did it take you to forgive me?

Was it the day, not quite twenty years later, when you asked me to be Godmother to Jessica Mary?

THE NEW GOVERNESS

MISS LILY NEWMAN stood in the drawing-room of 196 Adelaide Road, taking leave of the mother of her prospective pupils. The interview was over. She had just "been seen" by Mrs. Farjeon, but she herself had seen none of the children. All she knew was that there were three of them: two small boys and an elder sister. There was another boy, the oldest of the family, with whom she would have no concern; he had a private tutor downstairs, her dominion was the Nursery on the second floor.

The door burst open. An impetuous gentleman, with curly black hair and sparkling brown eyes, darted into the room, and looked her rapidly up and down.

"I like the look of you! You're not to teach them anything they don't want to learn! The girl has headaches. Leave her alone!"

Young Miss Newman, blunt, good-hearted, and readily tickled, went home and gave her mother an account of the interview.

"You can but try it, Lil," said her mother.

* * * *

In the Nursery, all we knew was that the old régime was over, Miss Milton, with her pale face, her mole, her red hair and eyebrows, her pothooks and hangers, her dates of Kings-and-Queens, her *Brewer's Questions,* her *Guy's Geography*, and her *Reading Without Tears*: Miss Milton, with her musical accomplishments and her nice knowledge of what was ladylike: Miss Milton was going. Miss Milton was gone.

The departure of the First Governess, like the departure of the First Nurse, creates a Nursery cataclysm. They are *The* Nurse, *The* Governess, as our parents are *The* Parents. Could there be others? These were the life we knew. Was there another? (What if *The* Parents one day departed too?)

In the interval between governesses we wondered, and some of us feared. Harry was passing on to Mr. Linford, a home-tutor; one he looked up to, and whose opinions he quoted, on all occasions and subjects. "Mr. Linford says——" this. "Mr. Linford says——" that. Papa was rather annoyed. "Mr. Linford *says*!" indeed. On some subjects, at least, he thought he knew better than Mr. Linford, with his Greek and his Latin, and his mathematical formulas: Papa had little use for the Dead Languages and for formulas, and did not encourage Mr. Linford's suggestion that Harry should study for a Scholarship in Mathematics. Harry had one of the finest brains a tutor could hope to chance on. But Mr. Linford had to abandon those hopes of a brilliant private success; the boy was going in for Music.

Divided, in lesson-hours, from our President, we knew we must sample, in his absence, an unfamiliar law. What would the New Governess be like? It was a time of suspense for Nellie (aged 11), Joe (aged 9), and Bertie (aged 5).

One day a sinister figure mounted the stairs and came to the Nursery Door; a thin queer formless figure draped in black, with a shapeless hat swathed in a heavy veil that darkened the visitor's features, and black kid gloves protruding from a strange mantle. Visitor? Rather, a visitant wandered out of a bad dream. It stood in the doorway, announcing in a squeaky voice: "Well, dear children! I'm the New Governess."

We stood appalled.

The creature minced into the Nursery. A howl rent the air, and Bertie burst into tears.

Shaking with merriment the figure flew at him open-armed. Light flashed upon me; I darted at the horrid image, tore the veil from its face, and screamed, "It's all right, Bertie! it's all right! It's Mama!"

The Nursery was loud with lamentations and laughter. Bertie, still yelling, shrank from and clung to the skirts of the New Governess, who cuddled and comforted him in Mama's voice, brimming with fun, brimming with self-reproach. Joe was overwhelmed with his concern for Bertie; while I was torn between appreciation of Mama's funny trick, sympathy for Bertie's terror, which I had for a moment shared, and a curious horror of the things Mama had done to her darling face. The cheek-bones, and even the tip of her nose were liberally reddened, and she had burnt-corked her eyebrows, which were naturally so fair as to be almost invisible.

When at last Bertie had been calmed, Mama assured us that the New Governess would not be at all "like that."

But it wasn't a propitious prelude to Miss Lily Newman.

* * * *

She wasn't like that. Miss Newman, unlike Miss Milton, never "behaved," and one always knew just what she thought about anything. She was forthright, cheerful, incapable of tyranny, able to get our obedience, because we had no idea that we were obeying her. True, we were not, except for Bertie, an unruly trio. I was dreamy and lacka-daisical, Joe docile and unselfish.

But Bertie—well! Bertie bit. He threw things. He kicked and fought. His tempers were of the kind that drive fathers out of the house. They were the kind that begat tempers in others. "MAGGIE! *keep that child quiet!*" Nothing kept Bertie quiet; his passions went over the edge beyond pacification. Poor mite! there were no Psycho-analysts in those days to say, "Give the child Glucose"—and I would not, for worlds, have been the Psycho-analyst who tried any such dam'-nonsense on Papa. Miss Newman had a secret worth two of that.

She adored Bertie. She picked him up and sat him on her knee, all through "lessons." (They must be quoted; never were lessons less so.) She refused to be told that he was a naughty boy. She had a flat, optimistic power of contradiction. "Bad? He isn't. He's an Angel!" She stuck to her guns, and does so to this day. Those guns must have been Bertie's secret stay. How had he con-quered her? No doubt with his "boo-ful eyes," when he strutted up to her, on introduction, and announced: "I've been alive five years, Joe says I haven't, but I *have.*"

The first remark she heard from Joe was: "I'm fascinising!" (This sounds to me more like Bertie, but she won't have it so.)

From me: "I don't like sums. Can I do German?"

German, I knew, was among Miss Newman's accom-plishments. It wasn't Otto's Grammar I was after, but Schiller.

To sweeten the grammar, Miss Newman copied out in plain script Schiller's *Semele,* page by page, and word by word made me translate it with her every day. I took the script away, and next day gave it to her in English blank verse; and, for the sake of Schiller and my Greeks, cracked the hard nut of Otto's German Grammar.

Apart from this I dawdled; because of my headaches

and almost sleepless nights, I was allowed to sit at the
piano as long as I liked, muddling out Schubert and
Mendelssohn accompaniments, while Joe and Bertie
got on with the lessons set for them. Lessons were set for
me, too, in history, geography, grammar, and sums; but
the first three I was already absorbing ignorantly and
copiously from my reading, and as for sums, I never really
knew, and don't quite now, just what the two little brackets
were for in Long-Division. I still listen resignedly if the
simplest formulas of x and y are explained to me, or if
someone tries to tell me the meaning of the term which
sounds to me like one-over-the-eight. Then my mind re-
jects it all, and continues to reach its own results rapidly,
and not too inaccurately, by private methods. I never
learned how to learn from other people; I hated being
obliged to follow any other mental process than my own.
But I tackled German Irregular Verbs without a pang,
because they were a road to *Wilhelm Tell*.

* * * *

If Miss Newman supposed she was not to be concerned
with the eldest boy, she soon discovered her error. Our
President could not leave his realm undisputed. Up to the
Nursery he came, to keep an eye on his people (and his
Prime Minister?).

"Bertie! get off the table."

"Why shouldn't he be on the table, bless him?"

"Don't tip up your chair, Joe."

"Let the child tip his chair up if he wants to!"

"Nellie, have you sponged?"

Impregnably good-humoured, Miss Newman shook
her fist at him. "Go away, Harry! you're a Disturbing
Element!"

"And you're a Demon!" was his parting shot.

The names stuck. As long as Miss Newman taught us, Harry was called by her The Disturbing Element, and she The Demon by everybody in the house, from Papa and Mama down. Soon she became known as Demon, *tout court.* "Where's Demon?" "Has Demon come yet?" "Who's going to take us to Gym to-day, Mama?" "Demon."

Perhaps, as she and the boys were about to set out, the front door flew open when they were half-way down the steps, and an impetuous gentleman with curly black hair and sparkling brown eyes shouted, "Come back! there's an East Wind! They can't go out to-day!" For Papa's anxieties about Mama's lung had descended upon us all. So we were muffled and cosseted out of all hardiness. No windows open at night—no tops of buses in winter-time— no venturing out without umbrella or goloshes if it looked like rain—no going out at all if it had started to sprinkle— and coats buttoned tight to the chin, and thick scarves and silk handkerchiefs over all. Miss Newman would have un-stifled us if she could, but against some things there were no appeal. All she could do was to bring the disappointed gymnasts in again—and on the next occasion watch for a moment when Papa was out of the way, and slip out quietly, East Wind or no East Wind—"Now run!" and the three of them pounded it to the corner.

On the other hand, Papa would explode into the Nursery on a sunny morning. "What are you all doing here on a bright day like this? Lessons? Take 'em all out for a walk, Demon!" And out they had to go. I now took my morning walk with Harry alone, but when the boys took theirs with the governess, *this* governess always found out which way they wanted to go, and went it.

Or perhaps Papa suddenly decided to "do his work" in the room where we were supposed to be doing ours. Then it was all *hush-hush* ("Keep those children quiet!") until Mama peeped in and made faces at us that summoned us into the passage: "Demon, you'd better take them all to the Zoo to-day."

Such was our education.

———

NOTE.—To this day Miss Lily Newman is Demon, not only to us but to Georgie Wood, once "Wee." His stepfather being the stepson of Miss Newman's sister, it practically made him our blood-relation, didn't it? Well, if not quite, we share a Demon in common.

THE AMERICANS

OVER THE WATER came the Americans.

When a letter said that one of them was coming, Mama's face was alight with happiness, and our world was rainbow-coloured. There was something about the Americans that brightened the air. They brought a radiance with them. A first visit kindled life with expectations; a return visit made it glow with certainties.

Of course, we knew all about them. We knew we belonged to them, and they to us. When Mama sang the broken-Dutch and Darkie songs on her guitar, she told us tales of when she was a little girl in Paradise Valley and Hohokus (where Harry was born); and what a darling Uncle Charlie was, and what a bad boy Uncle Tom was (so that "Tom" became a bad-boy's name for us), and what a fine old gentleman Uncle Bill Warren, and how Grandpa Lockyer took her to church to make her forget the convent; and she told about "The Cousins" duet with Maggie Duff, and how they walked barefoot in the stream at Paradise, and how she played "Bertie Ray" in a performance, and how Katie Holland, whose chestnut lock I was holding, was her dearest friend, and how silly Mr. Beebe was one of her "beaux," and how she and Uncle Charlie gave the Valentine to the teacher, and Uncle Tom sucked Josie's orange for her, and how "Tilly" and the "Indian Doctor" frightened her when the medium slept in her room; and she told us all about the Civil War, and John Wilkes Booth, who was so fascinating, and was our Aunt Dolly Morgan's

uncle; and how Aunt Josie "wished" on the very silver
bangle whose knobs I was rubbing, and how Grandpa
had cut a fish-hook out of her hand when she was just
about as old as me. I wrote to Grandpa myself when I was
eight, and then that Christmas I got a letter of my own
from him with ten pounds in it! This was the letter:

Washington D.C.
Dec. 10*th* '89

My dear Nellie

                I was much pleased to get your letter last
September, and would have written to you before but
I thought I would wait till near Christmas time so that
I might send you and your Mother a little something to
spend during the holiday time. So I enclose along with
a draft for your Mother another one for you in your own
name and I want you to divide it between yourself and
your brothers.

We often see friends from England who have seen all
of you and it is pleasant to hear of your health happiness
and talent.

I would like much to see you and hope to do so some
day give my love to your Father and Mother and your
brothers and accept the same from

Your loving Grandfather
J. Jefferson.

That was the first of many letters from him, the grandfather whom I had never seen. He might have remained
an imagined figure for me always, but for the chance
which carried us to America the year before he died. He
belongs, in his own person, to days when I was a child
no more; but over our Nursery he loomed like a wonderful presiding genius, linked with Mama's delicate
happy personality as with threads of gossamer. Shining
strands floated off from her to a world, a life, which lay
outside our experience, yet was delightfully our own.

When we heard, in 1890, that Aunt Josie was coming to
stay with us in London, we shared Mama's joy and excitement, though all it meant to her we could not know.

The little aunt arrived. Not sweetly pretty, like Mama,
but so sweetly merry. She walked with a little twist, but
I don't think we noticed it for long. She brought presents
for us all, and when I went very shyly up to her for mine,
her starry eyes twinkled; "And a little box for Nellie,"
she said, putting in my hand a tiny cardboard box. I
opened it—and there was just cotton-wool in it. I did
not know what to say or do, but I did not like to think
Aunt Josie would see how disappointed I felt. So after
I had said "Thank you," I murmured, "It will be nice
to put things in."

Aunt Josie, who was giving Joe his present, looked
oddly at me, and said, "Why, dear, haven't you found
your little brooch?" And Mama lifted up the cotton-
wool, and there was a beautiful little gold bar, set with
two pearls and a sapphire. How pretty it was! how red
I got! how Josie shook with mirth, saying, "Oh the poor
child!" and how different was this laughter and Mama's
laughter, from any other laughter I had to endure. You
had to laugh too, and very quickly you weren't shy any
more with your merry little Aunt Josie. But for years that
"Nice to put things in!" stuck to me, when a present
did not come up to expectation.

Aunt Josie stayed about six weeks, and if she was ill
during that time, if she had any of those dreadful spasms,
because of which Tiddie used to keep a spoon in her
pocket, we knew nothing about it. Her coming opened
up that other world over the water for us; life was happy,
and Mama never so happy, as while she was with us. It
was during this visit that Papa and Mama took Aunt Josie

to see "poor" Mr. Albert Chevalier in his new coster songs at (I think) the Pavilion Music Hall. All London was raving about him, and they came back saying how wonderful he was when he sang "My Old Dutch." He was not going to be "poor" Mr. Chevalier any more, and I was able to stop feeling sorry for him. That same night Mr. Augustus Harris had sent some tickets for *Lohengrin,* so while they went to the Music Hall I went to the opera with Miss Newman. I thought Wagner was dreadfully call. He was not like *Trovatore,* and *Faust,* and lovely music like that. Aunt Josie brought all of us presents from Grandpa; I had a marvellous book of American flowers, and Joe a box of minerals of untold worth, and Harry a pen-and-pencil-set with moss-agate handles, and Bertie a knife-fork-and-spoon with cornelian ones.

Before she went back to America, Aunt Josie bought pots of flowers for us all from Mrs. Brace, pots of spiræa, and azaleas, and cherry-pie, and musk. The Nursery was beautified; with Jeffersons in it, 196 became like the transformation scene in pantomime. Then she must go to Liverpool, and Mama went with her, and came back with red eyes; but never mind, Aunt Josie left us each five shillings, and in the new Japanese sort of shop in Fitzjohn's Parade I had seen something so beautiful for Mama's birthday. I came to Harry in great excitement, and proposed we should get it together. He went with me to see it, and was enraptured like myself. It was a white painted easel, and on it was a landscape in real oil-colours, of trees and water, and flowers, and one corner of the picture was draped with buttercup-yellow silk. It only cost four-and-elevenpence. We clubbed, and carried it home, breathless with pleasure; and, as a great secret, revealed it to Papa.

Papa said nothing much, but went to Mama. "The children have got you something simply horrible," he said; "what can we do?" He did his best to describe it.

"Couldn't we put it somewhere in the drawing-room out of the way?" asked Mama.

"Wait till you see it," said Papa. He showed it to her when we had gone to bed, and they consulted, how to spare our tender feelings.

Next day Papa came to us and said, "You know, that picture is rather too big for the drawing-room, and Mama wants some vases *very* badly. Let's take this back to the shop and see if they have any we can change it for."

Harry and I felt just a trifle crushed, but we did not suspect that our choice of a present had failed. Papa somehow convinced us without hurt that to change it was advisable. We went with him to the shop, and bought a set of harmless little vases, which cost five-and-sixpence; Papa paid the extra. But really, do these shop-keepers know their business? The three little pale-pink vases were, of course, exquisite, and very likely a bargain at the price; but they were *nothing* to the relinquished masterpiece at four-and-eleven, easel, yellow silk draperies, and all!

* * * *

Grandpa had written his Autobiography. It was a tremendous success, in England as well as in America. Mama gave each of us a copy, and wrote in it for us; and the benevolent and mysterious Mrs. Benedict sent me the Edition de Luxe, bound in white; and Papa had dozens of copies from America, and Mama wrote in *them* for all the actors and actresses who loved and admired Grandpa, and the doctors who saw us for nothing in Harley Street.

(*A week before her death, in* 1933, *I found and bought in Charing Cross Road the copy she had given old Mrs. Keeley.*)

We learned a lot more about Grandpa from that wonderful book, but nothing about Mama or Uncle Charlie or Uncle Tom, because he never would make his private affairs public. But there were pictures of him and our great-grandfather and great-great-grandfather, but not our great-great-great-grandfather who was the Yorkshire farmer's son. (*Him* we discovered excitedly in a set of Theatrical Magazines, bought by Papa at an auction; and there, in the *Dramatic Mirror* for 1804, was a steel engraving of old Thomas Jefferson, with the "Jefferson nose," just like Mama's and Grandpa's.)

In his book, Grandpa told tales of when he was a little boy, and once on the Fourth of July he had to sing "The Star-Spangled Banner" in a theatre, but when he had got as far as "Oh, say, can you see——" he forgot the words. His mind was a blank, just like mine when I forgot "A Pound of Tea" at the party, and he began again and forgot, and the audience hissed, and he ran off the stage to his mother in the wings and threw himself into her arms, and cried—just like me. And *he* was a real actor!

* * * *

The next Americans to arrive were Joe Jefferson the Fourth, aged twenty-one, with his beautiful little nineteen-year-old bride. Blanche was as sweet and almost as spoiled as a baby; you had to adore and pet her, and, when she made herself sick before meals eating candy, forgive as you scolded her. When she went shopping with Mama, she always bought a box of candy and carried it along to the next department, and ate it while she bought her stockings and gloves. Then she would push the box across

the counter and say, "Have some!" to the assistant, and
the girl would get red and say, "No thank you, Madam";
and Mama would tell Aunt Blanche afterwards she
mustn't do that, because if the shop-girl were seen eating
candy with the customer perhaps she would be dismissed.
This was beyond the baby's understanding; in America
the shop-girl would have taken the candy. "How can I
go on eating it without offering her some?" she pouted;
"it makes me feel so *mean*."

Uncle Joe gave me a shilling every day to sit and tickle
his feet after dinner, till he went to sleep. All Jeffersons
loved having their soles tickled, and their forearms, and
their heads stroked. We were quite used to seeing Mama
kick off her little shoes, and say invitingly, "Who'd like
to tickle my feet?" and then I would sit on the hassock
with her feet in my lap, and tickle one sole till she said,
"Now the other! I can't feel that one any more." I
couldn't bear it myself, it made me shriek. Joe was the
only one of us that liked it, I suppose because he had
Jefferson in his name. Now Uncle Joe found, as Mama had
also found, that his English niece had rather sensitive
fingers, and was a very good foot-tickler.

He was a dreadful tease, but a tender-hearted tease.
He couldn't resist singing "Poor Cock Robin!" in a
tuneless voice at Bertie, to see if he would howl. The
three words were enough to set him off, and then Maggie-
May scolded Uncle Joe, who begged Bertie's pardon and
did it again next day.

The young honeymooners went; and two years later
came a second visit from Aunt Josie, full of joyous
recognition.

This time she did not bring us presents from America,
but asked what we would like? I said "A desk," Bertie

said "Some goldfish," Harry a watch, and Joe a rocking-horse. I thought of a desk to go on the table, like Harry's; instead, a beautiful little Davenport arrived. Bertie thought of a globe with three red fish in it; instead came a big aquarium, with fish of many colours, shells on the floor, and waving weeds, and coral. Joe's rocking-horse was half as big again as Dobbin, of beloved memory; Harry's silver watch was as good as works could make it. Desk, goldfish, rocking-horse, where are they now? The silver watch is intact.

* * * *

Out of America came the First Gramophone, to 196 Adelaide Road. Grandpa had sent it, with two records of his voice in "Rip Van Winkle." With our own ears now we heard him say, "Here's your good health, and your family's, and may they all live long and prosper!" He said it through a wheezy, scratchy sound, but Mama made him say it again and again.

* * * *

In 1896 Willie came over, the Uncle who was christened at Stratford-on-Avon, and whom Mama hadn't seen since he was a baby. He was just twenty years old.

It was full summer when he landed, and we were already on holiday at Manor Farm, East Runton, which belonged to Farmer Abbs. Mama went up to London to bring Willie down to us, but he had one night by himself in London first, and he went into Romano's to have supper. On the table was a dish of peaches, and at the end of the meal he whiled away the time by eating five of them. Then came the bill, with an item: "15s."

"Say, what's this?"

"Fifteen shillings, sir."

"Yes, but what for?"

"The peaches, sir."

"The *peaches*!" exclaimed the astonished youth from the land where peaches are fed to the pigs.

"Yes, sir, they are three shillings."

"Three shillings for five peaches!"

"Three shillings apiece, sir. Fifteen shillings for five."

"For the Lord's sake, Maggie," said Willie, when they met, "don't let the boys know about it, or I'll never hear the last of those English peaches."

He took her shopping; bought golf-sticks and a croquet-set for the country, infinite exquisite coloured silk shirts for himself, presents for all of us. (No wonder his money ran out before his return. "Send Five Hundred Dollars," he cabled his father. "What for?" cabled Joe Jefferson. "For Willie," cabled Willie. The Five Hundred were sent.)

Never was the American rainbow so bright! Willie was the liveliest, funniest, most lovable uncle imaginable. We didn't call him Uncle very long; there was only a couple of years between him and Harry, and five between him and me. He wore the highest collars we had ever seen, and the longest-pointed shoes; but if in town-attire he was a dude, in the country he took off more clothes than was our decorous habit, and lolled in an old string hammock drinking cold tea, while I tickled his feet by the hour for him—for love. It was a blazing August, one of those summers when farmers prayed for rain. Old Farmer Abbs went about the fields with a strange look in his deep-set piercing eyes. Though a small man, he was the Viking, not the Saxon, type of East Anglian. The churchyard had its Abbses, drowned at sea. Willie, tickled by the funny little name, came down to breakfast one morning scratching himself.

"What's the matter, Willie?"

"I guess I've caught an Abbs in my bed," said he. After that, none of us ever had fleas; we were only bitten by Abbses.

The heat, the farmer's anxiety, was our festival. We played comic croquet on the roughest of odd-shaped lawns, and were taught golf on "The Bump," a hillock in the meadow at the back. All the usual games, picnics, and sea-bathing of holiday, had a heightened joyousness because of Willie. He played jokes on us all, but Mama was a Jefferson too, and got back on him. We children followed him about like shadows, and Papa was as fond of him as we were. Then why one day did Papa look up from his book after I had come in from tickling Willie's feet as he lolled in the hammock, and say very kindly, with just a tinge of embarrassment, "Nell, dear, I wouldn't pet Willie quite so much, if I were you"? Mama was in the room; I glanced at her, and realized that they had been talking about something that had to do with what Papa had just said.

"All right," I said briefly. "He's just gone to play golf with the boys."

"Well, run along and play too," said Mama.

"No, thank you, I think I'll read."

They said no more about it; neither did I; I did "pet" my young uncle a little less, and he himself appeared to notice no difference. I had to work the puzzle out by myself, and was so unsophisticated that I couldn't do it —so unsophisticated perhaps Papa was right to speak— so unsophisticated that he had not the least need to do so!

* * * *

One night, rather late, when it was dark outside, and
we were sitting round the lamp-lit table playing games,
Papa lifted up his head and said, "Hark!"

There was a pattering on the earth outside. Suddenly
it rushed into a torrent of sound. The next moment the
outside door of the sitting-room burst open, letting in
the darkness and the smell of the heavy hot wet air.
Into the shadowy room strode Farmer Abbs, his bare
chest under his dark red shirt was damp, his deepset
eyes were blazing. "D'ye hear it? d'ye hear it?" he
cried. "The rain has coom! The Lord has sent the
rain!" He raised his shaking arms above his head, like
Noah invoking a blessing, not on the ceasing, but the
coming of the rain. Tears streamed down his seamed oak-
tanned face, the room throbbed with the emotion he had
brought into it. Papa got up and wrung his hand. "Sit
down," he said, and fetched some bottles of beer; and
Mr. Abbs sat in our midst, drinking to the coming of the
rain, and Papa drank with him.

When the old farmer had left us, Papa said, "That is
one of the most tremendous things I've ever seen." And
I remember now, as a moment of great drama, equal to
some amazing effect of Irving's, the entrance of Mr.
Abbs, out of the dark wet night, into the lamplight,
crying to all the world that the rain had come.

* * * *

On his arrival in Boston, Willie was met by an assortment of brothers. Before he could land, they were shouting from the quay: "Hey, Willie, what's the price of
English Peaches?"

THE THOUSAND WORD TALES

THE AFTERNOON was all set for the "Thousand Word Tales." Irene and Cola di Rienzi were awaiting the arrival of Nina di Rienzi and Adrian di Castello. To-day marked the start of a new series of the romances which were kept going, four at a time, by those noble Roman families, whose names were drawn out of Bulwer Lytton's novel. From the moment when Harry had read *Rienzi*, and recognized elements of himself in the Roman Tribune, he became "Cola" to us in the Nursery, and to our two great friends outside. I never thought or spoke of them by other names than Nina and Adrian. In the romance, Nina was the Tribune's wife, and Adrian my lover; I, of course, was Rienzi's sister Irene. Joe became Walter di Montreal, and Bertie the young Angelo Villani; but as in TAR, they were Honorary rather than active members of the company.

The system adopted for the Thousand Word Tales was that of the ephemeral paper-games we played in the evening, when a line or two of verse, or the beginning of a story, was scribbled on a slip, and passed round for continuation by other hands. But the Thousand Word Tales were none of your ephemera; they were epics, lasting for months. Each of the four authors wrote the first thousand words of his tale, according to taste, and once a week a meeting took place for the reading of the instalments, which then passed in given order from hand to hand. Nine weeks concluded the tale, so that the originator began and ended his own, and had a chance in the middle to control its course. When a series had been brought to its conclusion, a new set of tales was started. The first session was exciting, for then the scenes were set in which our thoughts would wander during the next two months.

Until the Opening Day, we kept inviolate the place and period of our themes. Irene's was pretty sure to be your Fairy-Classical, Cola's your Whimsical-Ingenious, Nina's vein was your Tragical-Emotional, placed possibly in Poland, a nation to which, largely because of Chopin, she had abandoned her passionate heart (she drew Irene's tears with those heart-moving Nocturnes), Adrian's perhaps your Comical-Prosaic; but we all leaned to the romantic, with a tendency to "perchances" and "methinks." Each Thousand Words had to be strictly counted, and you broke off in the middle of a sentence, if obliged to.

The readings took place round the Nursery fireguard, and the room was debarred to outsiders. If we met before tea, we arranged an hour that gave us a clear run before Susan *must* lay the table. The presence of "the Boys" was permissible, as long as Angelo and Montreal kept quiet; Papa and Mama knew better than to intrude; unexpected visitors little suspected the degree of their unpopularity.

As I took a last glance through my MS., I did not suffer my usual anxiety when any composition of my own was to be made public. I hoped for the approval of my fellows—but they *were* my fellows. Between us four existed an understanding which spelled security.

The bell! They had arrived. We flew downstairs to greet them coming up, Nina grumbling at the weather, Adrian chuckling over some vile pun which she and her Uncle Ben had perpetrated in the passage. Adrian made even worse puns than Papa, recited humorous parodies, "did" imitations of Henry Irving to admiration, and was unfailingly cheerful, sweet, and undemanding. Nina, one of the most restless, impatient, brilliant creatures ever created, was always in some torment of emotion. She swung between agony and ecstasy. She adored and hated. Music, her great gift, exhausted her. She was demanding and devoted; love was her loyalty. She would really have stood up to be shot for a cause or a person to whom her heart was given. Her temperament had that incalculable touch of genius which would have made her sweep an audience away, if only it had not swept her away first. She could not control it, and when she sat down to perform, her gifts, two times in three, were the prey of her nerves. The third time was electric. We loved and admired her, but teased her when she grumbled, and her Aunty Maggie took her gently to task for the excesses of hilarity and suffering which frayed her feelings. Just now she was in a fury with the weather, which gave her chilblains.

Before the Romans could settle to the business of the afternoon, the Farjeons were called down for a moment to see the Misses Hands, who were "just going." Nina redoubled her grumbles, and we promised not to be long; it would have been unthinkable for those sweet elderly ladies to have travelled all the way from 11 Laura Place, Clapton, to Adelaide Road, and not to have had a glimpse of "the dear children."

Ben Farjeon had never lost touch with the three old maiden daughters of his schoolmaster. Miss Mary Ann, the oldest, was stone-deaf, and could only be visited in Laura Place, where she presided, looked up to by her sisters. Prominent on the hat-rack in their virgin hall, hung their father's ancient broad-brimmed beaver hat— to affright burglars. It adorned Miss Susie's hall as late as 1930, when there was no majestic Miss Mary Ann, no sprightly Miss Bessie, to share or soothe her fears. She spoke of them as "my dear ones," with love in the tender, pale, round blue eyes that were to the end as innocent as a baby's. For years before her wits began to wander, at ninety, she spoke quite simply of "the dear angels whispering to her"—she really heard those angels. Once she had ventured into a tube-lift—"But never again, my dear Eleanor!" And in her youth, like Miss Matty, she had had a little faded love-affair—"But it was not to be."

Miss Susie was oh so proud of her friendship with Mr. Farjeon, so doubly proud that it was *her* dear Father who had loved *my* dear Father as his best and brightest scholar. She had literary aspirations of her own, and used to write kind mild little books, for which she was "thankful" to receive a five-pound note outright from the religious society that published them now and again. Overcoming her trepidation, she would venture to bring her manuscripts to Papa for advice; she would have been "*so* glad" of slightly better terms and a *little* more publicity for her stories. Papa's advice, given with a twinkle in his bright brown eye, was: "Put a little more devil into them, Miss Susie."

"*Oh*, Mr. Farjeon!" The dear creature was fascinated and horrified, as he knew she would be.

Having delivered himself of this impossible counsel, he became kindness and helpfulness itself; he was quite ungrudging of his time and assistance to anyone poor, simple, and in need; he knew all about poverty, and his heart was especially quick and tender to elderly women. All the poor people in our street knew and loved him, he did much more than give them pence, he left behind him fun and a moment of warmth. Old country folk, in villages where we spent our summers, would do anything for him, would give him without thought of compensation the fruit and flowers from their gardens, and bits of old china from their mantelpieces—only Papa always contrived that they got their compensation, in a way that did not injure the grace of the gift.

So now, he would not let the straitened maiden ladies depart without one of the pleasures they had counted on, the pleasure of kissing young Ben Farjeon's children, and praising the last verse of "the little Poetess." When could her dear Mama bring her to tea with them in Laura Place? A date was settled, and they returned to Clapton to pinch their resources in advance, that they might provide more tea-cake and plum-cake, more pink-sugar fancy biscuits and macaroons, than ten little poetesses could have accounted for.

Back to the Nursery, and our semi-circle round the fire. Cola consulted his watch. Still plenty of time.

"Who will begin?"

"Won't you, Cola?"

"No, I did last time. It's Adrian's turn."

The moment had come. Adrian cleared her throat, with a slightly-comic "Ahem!" We settled down, expectant, to

THE SULTAN'S DAUGHTERS

"There were three of them—Princess Zuretta, Princess Hasura, and lastly, little Princess Leila. Daughters of a proud, fond father and mother——"

The Nursery door opened, and Susan poked her head in, "Miss Gerty Hall."

Consternation round the fireplace.

Irene got up to greet the unwelcome intruder.

Gerty Hall was one of a rather big family who lived near by. We were all "friends," and exchanged annual parties, but we were not knit into each other's lives. Gerty had never come to see us out of the blue before, and why she had come now I couldn't think. Some special reason, which, a message delivered, would mean her speedy withdrawal? No, it appeared that Gerty had merely come to "see" us.

I did my best to be nice to her. Cola was chilly, and Nina and Adrian sat saying very little. It was only too plain to me—and it amazed me that it wasn't also to Gerty —that the Nursery was waiting for the guest's departure. She seemed to have no intention of departing; she sat on, and I sat by her on the sofa in the window, while the remote trio by the fireplace looked on with disfavour. Perhaps I deserved it, perhaps it *was* my fault, for the colder the atmosphere, the warmer I tried to be. Adrian was looking glum, Nina was pettish, Cola was quietly consulting his watch again. The precious private hour was frittering away. It would all too soon be tea-time, and *then* we would have to ask Gerty to stay to tea. Cola put his watch back in his pocket, and advanced to the sofa.

"Would you please go now, Gerty?" he said. He was polite, but final.

She looked at him astonished and confused. I wanted to be under the sofa instead of on it. Gerty, very red, got up and said Good-bye. I was aware of Nina trying to suppress hysterical giggles. With a glance of mingled reproof and relief at my brother, I accompanied the routed guest downstairs, stammering some sort of explanation. "You see, Gerty, there is something very particular we do."

"Oh, yes," murmured Gerty.

"I do hope you don't mind?"

"Oh, no."

We parted at the door, highly embarrassed. I watched her down the steps and flew back to the Nursery, where I was greeted with cries of "Come on quick! Sit down."

"Cola, how could you?"

"She was spoiling the afternoon. She had to go."

"Yes, but how *could* you? I felt simply awful."

"Oh, shut up, Irene, and sit down, there's a dear!" Nina pulled me down upon my chair. "Start again, Cola, we've wasted enough time already."

The semi-circle re-formed.

THE SULTAN'S DAUGHTERS

"There were three of them—Princess Zuretta, Princess Hasura, and lastly, little Princess Leila. Daughters of a proud, fond father and mother, who thought there was nothing too good to give, or to say of 'their dear ones,' as they called them when they spoke between themselves— and, let me add, *that* was pretty often.

"Now, two of these maidens both possessed some special quality or characteristic—but, mind you, *one* only —that was all; they lacked everything else——"

(*Gerty Hall passed out of every mind. . . .*)

"—I am very pleased you didn't choose Zuretta or that dazzling Hasura. For my part——"

Adrian broke off. This was the limit of her Thousand Words. Her tale was to pass to me, and for a moment my mind was preoccupied with Things Oriental.

"Your turn, Irene!"

I moved a little westward, and began my tale of

THE ARCADIAN SHEPHERD

"On the fairest of the Arcadian hills, there dwelt a shepherd.

"Not in one of those rudely-built huts that you might suppose, but in a green bower, which he only needed for sleeping, and often used it as a shelter from the hot sun; for all the rest of the time did he stay in the air, even eating there, and ever watching his flocks.

"And in a towering palace of marble, a lordly mansion, forsooth, there lived his master, Mechanitis.

"And Phillomeis, as was the shepherd called, loved a maiden, by name, Cytheroea, fair and beautiful as the sun, and whose laugh was clearer and sweeter than the heedless rivulet, as it flows, in its joy, unto the arms of the sea.

"But alas! Mechanitis also loved her, and what chance, think you, had he, poor shepherd, against this great and noble lord? And he knew not that once had Mechanitis loved a maiden, Basilea, and who now wondered at his cold and heartless treatment towards her."

(I hadn't read my Sir Philip Sidney for nothing. . . .)

"I would try to escape if it were not for Cytheroea——"

From this point, the musings of Phillomeis would be in Adrian's hands, and it was Nina's turn to read.

THE WAYS OF TYRANNY
Poland
"How long, O God, shall men be ridden down,
And trampled under by the last and least
Of men? The heart of Poland has not ceased
To quiver . . ."
ALFRED TENNYSON.

"The facts which I am about to relate, took place about twenty years ago, when I was a boy of fourteen. I was the son of Polish peasants and was born during one of our bitterest persecutions by the Russians. My parents (Casmir and Masha Kowiatowski), gained their living by breaking stones and cutting wood. Strange to say, my father by no means resembled his class. His features were both handsome and refined, and he carried himself with a certain air of grandeur, which seemed at some variance with his station."

(*Just like Count Naganowski, an aristocratic Polish exile of our acquaintance. . ..*)

"Your mother belonged to a powerful family, and being very beautiful had many suitors, foremost amongst which were myself and another Count, Paul von——"

It was for Cola to carry on with Count Paul, in exchange for

THE COURTSHIP OF BLANCHE AND PINTANTO

"In one of the fairest of the Italian kingdoms, the soft evening peculiar to Southern Europe was just deepening into night, as the beautiful Princess Blanche sat by the window of her chamber. She was accustomed to sit thus at the Death of the Day, when everything seemed to combine to minister to her fancies, which were extremely poetical."

(*She is therefore ripe for the appeal of the "sound of the guitar" which reached her ears; the following verses are a specimen of what she heard:*

> "*In the early moonlight*
> *By the palace wall*
> *The troubadour goes singing*
> *His mistress fair to call.*" . . .)

"He was slain by the great Gostitito. Well, this celebrated man will meet me soon, for the purpose of killing King Habart. Swear to me that you will be faithful to your best——"

The readings concluded; they had just been got through by tea-time. Approval of the new beginnings

were rife; Irene and Adrian exchanged Mss., Cola and
Nina did likewise. A date was set apart for the following
week. Susan brought in the big tray. Soon we were sitting
down to Nursery tea, writing our names in treacle on our
bread-and-butter, and discussing the book we were
reading, the last-seen play, the last-heard opera or concert.

"I'm reading *Adam Bede*," Nina confided to me, "but
I hide it in a drawer when I hear Mama coming."

"What for?" I asked.

"She says it isn't fit for me to read yet."

"Why?"

"Because of a certain incident."

"Which one?"

"Hetty."

"Oh," I said, uncomprehendingly. I had read *Adam
Bede* myself, it was a very great favourite of Mama's, and
if there were things in it I didn't understand, well, I knew
there *were* things I didn't understand.

For instance, that time at *La Dame aux Camélias*. In
spite of a "Témoinage de Satisfaction," written in ornamental script by Mademoiselle, I couldn't understand a
word of French when spoken. In the box, before the
curtain went up, Papa described sketchily what I was
going to see, and Mama happened to mention that it was
the same story as the opera *Traviata*.

"What does Traviata mean?" I asked.

"It means a bad woman, dear," said Papa.

"Bad?" I looked enquiringly at him, supposing he
would say she was a thief, or a murderess, or something;
but I saw he was hesitating how to describe her.

"Do you mean bad in a special sort of way?" I asked.

"Yes, Nell, in a special sort of way," said Papa, ex-
changing that glance with Mama which always told me

he wondered what I was thinking, and there was something more to know one of these days—yet what it was left me incurious. As incurious as the "incident" about Hetty, in *Adam Bede,* which Nina's Mama didn't want her to read.

I turned to talk to Adrian, and presently heard Cola "aggravating" Nina.

"Eroica!" he said tauntingly.

Nina had evidently just made some exaggerated statement, which Cola was promoting to a fib.

"Another False Sophist! Eroica!" jibed Cola.

"*Will you shut up with your Eroica?*" cried Nina, flying into one of her tantrums.

In an unfortunate moment, she had once declared she had heard the Eroica Symphony, and it transpired that she had not (but had merely mistaken it for the No. 2). A mis-statement was nearly as good as an untruth to Cola, and the Tribune taxed his wife with uttering one. Thereafter, "Eroica" became synonymous with a fib, and was relentlessly applied to any exaggeration Nina uttered. "False Sophist" was the name for a liar in our Nursery, where Truth was Socratically run to earth. Now, when Cola repeated "Another False Sophist!" Nina screamed at him, and snatched up a knife in a frenzy.

"Put that down at once!" said Susan sternly. "I'm surprised at you carrying on like this, Miss Nina. If you don't put it down, I shall go and fetch Mrs. Farjeon."

Nina dropped the knife, gasping, "Well, then, you shouldn't aggravate me, Cola."

"We will play 'Mr. Bacon' after tea," announced Cola; and the Nursery calmed down.

We delighted in the "Mr. Bacon's School" game, which had the advantage of including Joe and Bertie.

When the square mahogany table was cleared, and Susan had left us to our own devices, we sat round it in class, with pencils and paper. The table-cloth was swept off, so that we could write properly. Mr. Bacon, the schoolmaster, sat at the head; the class consisted of Brown (Irene), Isaacs (Nina), Jones (Adrian), Smith (Joe), and Green (Bertie). Mr. Bacon rose in his place, said, "Good morning, boys!"—and BEAMED. No letters are big enough to describe that beam. It spread like a Cheshire Cat's all over his face, showing two rows of superb white teeth; the effulgence of that broad good-humoured smile overcame us. A breeze of mirth bore our "Good morning, sir!" to our master's ears.

Then lessons began. I forget what they were, but they were all very brief, very ingenious, and highly absurd. Sometimes we had ridiculous problems to work out, sometimes ridiculous questions to answer. Marks, of course, were given. With all due modesty, I think Brown usually topped the lot; but then, in addition to being rather bright, he was also in great favour for being "good"—which Isaacs, an equally bright scholar, was not. Bad marks were given for petulance and disobedience, and of these Isaacs collared his share.

Presently: "Dinner-time, boys!"

We laid down our pencils and turned eager eyes upon him.

The menu was preposterous; one disappointing announcement succeeded another, each one accompanied by the "Mr. Bacon smile," and the hungry boys had to ejaculate "Oh, sir!" in tones of groaning gratitude. "And for dessert, boys"—(tense expectation, under the irresistible smile)—"one sniff of the cloth in which a Christmas pudding has been boiled." "*Oh*, SIR!!!"

We had hardly resumed lessons, before the door opened, and in tripped Papa and Mama. Our pencils paused, for an explanation of the interruption.

"Please, sir," said Papa in a small-boy voice, "we've come to your school, please, sir."

The class looked enquiringly at the master. Mr. Bacon turned his gracious beam upon the newcomers.

"Very well, boys. What are your names?"

"Samuels," said one.

"Phillips, please, sir," said the other.

"Very good, boys! Samuels, sit there by Green. Phillips, sit here, by me."

The class was resumed. We soon became aware of a rebel in our ranks. Samuels proved to be a model scholar, but Phillips—— Phillips was *awful*. He sneaked, he disobeyed, he carneyed, he gave wrong answers on purpose, he even objected to the fare at supper.

"PHILLIPS!" thundered Mr. Bacon. "*You are Expelled!*"

"OH, SIR!!!" from the class. Such a thing had never happened before.

"Please, sir, let me stay, sir, I won't do it again, sir!" said the horrid new boy, half-whimpering, half-grimacing at his horrified but secretly-fearfully-delighted school-fellows. Mr. Bacon relented, but alas! the nasty little fellow was past reform. Eventually he really was expelled, and went, making faces at us.

Order was restored in class. Mr. Bacon had us well in hand. But ever and anon, in future games, we glanced at the door, hoping for the abominable Phillips to sneak in and take his place among us; and ever and anon, he did not disappoint us. Expulsion was his invariable fate.

REVOLT

ON THE TWELFTH OF FEBRUARY, 1897, the night before my sixteenth birthday, I found myself alone with Papa and Mama. To-morrow night, of course, there would be a party, and Nursery rules would be relaxed in my favour. On Valentine's Day, my bedtime would be advanced, according to law, by five minutes—from twenty-five minutes to half-past nine.

Suddenly I looked at Papa and Mama, and asked:

"Why does Cola send me to bed?"

"Because you let him," said Mama.

"All right. I won't."

I knew, by the amused glances my parents exchanged, that they were not horrified by these seditious words, and that whatever battle lay ahead of me would be purely a duel.

My birthday came and went. I was sixteen years old. On the evening of Valentine's Day I took my book into the dining-room, and sat down on one side of the mahogany table. Harry, with *his* book, read opposite me. Papa, in the big leather armchair by the fire, was reading the *Globe,* and sucking his handkerchief. Mama was doing wool cross-stitch on a pair of carpet-slippers for Papa's next Christmas.

I felt horribly nervous, and glued my eyes to a page I could not read. Presently, out came the silver watch, and was laid on the tapestry cloth at Harry's side, where he could keep his eye on it, till the exact second. All too soon:

"Bedtime, Nellie!" The watch went back into his pocket.

"Oh," I said casually, "I'm not going."

"*What?*"

"I'm not going to bed yet," I repeated.

Harry got up, came round the table, said "Good night, Nellie," kissed me, and went back to his place. Nothing had happened! Could it really be all right, after all? A few moments later I addressed some remark to him. He did not answer. I spoke again. He took not the least notice. I knew him so well (I have always read him swifter than anybody else, and understood looks and words and kinks of thought in him which for others have to be translated) that in a flash I realized the line he had taken. It was a line popular with the War Office, when soldiers in England were technically in France. At half-past nine precisely Nellie had gone to bed. Therefore she was no longer in the room. Therefore, if she spoke, she could not be heard, and if she could not be heard, how could she be answered? I felt baffled and miserable, and for two pins I would have agreed that I was upstairs, undoing my plait for the night. But I sat on; reading nothing, I am sure, and, for all my determination, not daring to outsit Harry's own bedtime. After a little while, I rose and kissed Papa and Mama good night. The amused, but very kind, smile was on both their faces. I think they wondered whether I would keep it up.

I did keep it up; and so, for about a fortnight, did Harry. He never made a single comment on the case, but at half-past nine exactly, he said "Good night, Nellie," kissed me as usual—and after that I ceased to exist for him.

I hated those evenings. Harry, whom I loved so dearly,

with whom I was more knit-up than any being on earth, was being hurt and offended by me—and it was very difficult not to believe with him that I was wrong. Presently, I don't remember how or when, something I said to him after nine-thirty p.m. received an answer. Had Mama spoken to him? Had be come of himself to realize that it is not enough for Benevolent Autocracies to be benevolent? I don't know. But my act marked an epoch for us both; and perhaps it was on that Valentine's Day in the Year of the Diamond Jubilee, that my Nursery of the Nineties began to totter.

FARJEONIANA

HARRY FARJEON

HARRY FARJEON started writing late in life. Owing to delicate health, his studies were held back, and it was not till he was about seven that he began to be proficient in penmanship. The fallow period was not without its advantages. By the time he was able to write, he was mentally and orally a fluent creator, with a fund of ideas, and a technique, that enabled him not only to produce poems and dramas rapidly, but to finish them. He left fewer fragments than his sister Nellie, who could read and write almost contemporaneously with her eldest brother, but, through faults of youth and temperament, rarely completed a major work till she was eight. For a short time Harry contributed regularly to the Ms. Book in which B. L. Farjeon requested his children to copy the poems they scribbled on odd scraps of paper. Harry's first known poem, *The Stag,* shows a freedom of rhythm which at this age his sister lacked, though in a few years she was experimenting in every metre from Lear to Spenser.

The Stag.

I

"The moon was bright
On Saturday night,
And onward still I bounded.
No notice I took
Of the trees and the brook
By which I was surrounded.

2
"For far behind
(He'd liked to have dinned
On ven'son for his dinner,)
Was a hunter tall;
I wished he'd fall,
For then I should have been the winner.

3
"There was a brook—
I with one look
Was over it safe and sure!
When I was there
I did not care,
For he was the other side of my door.
                              By Harry Farjeon
                                   March 1st 1889
                                        Bournemouth

But it is as a dramatist that Harry shone. Marbled copy-books are crammed with his plays; unfortunately, all that is available of a promising tragedy, *The Sunset,* is one sheet of note-paper.

Act 1.
Drawing room.
Olover with the "Times."

———

OL.: The Wonderful Sunset! Whoever thought of such a thing. I declair *I'll* try to find it.
 Enter MR. CURST.
CURST (*aside*): How *will* it be settled? (*Aloud*) Olover, please leave the room.
 Exit OLOVER. *Enter* MR. CLOVER.
CUR.: Here you are.
CLO.: Yes here I am.
 A pause of five minutes.

Could any situation be more pregnant?
Of the finished plays, only one can be given in full.

I have hesitated between the ominous *Half-Past Three,* and the informative *Harry's Tour,* in Act 3 of which Harry is discovered in "Switzerlant" at the foot of Mont Blanc. He observes, "I should like to climb this mountain. It is 15,732 feet high." In Scene 2 of this act, the young Excelsior has made the attempt; it is further up the Mountain, in the distance is seen a "monstery," and Harry is discovered lying down and shutting his eyes, covered with snow. "Enter St. Bernard dog with wine. He knocks Harry about," and is followed by three Monks, who observe respectively: "Le pauvre homme." "Il faut que nous le porte chez nous." "Oui, mon ami." In the course of Harry's Tour, the customs of Pirit Captains and Continental Lanlords are fully exposed, and after four more months in France, Germany, Italy and Russia, the Tourist returns to the bosom of his family, with a fortune, to be greeted on the Docks by his little brother Joe, who cries "Oh! he's come back and he's such a delightful young man!"

But on the whole I prefer the subtler elements of *Half-Past Three.* Written in 1888–9, when the Belgian Master was an unknown quantity in the Farjeon Nursery, this play combines Maeterlinckian qualities with those of the Bread-and-Butter School. The inner meaning of the three Burglars can only have been known to the author—if even to him. Clearly, Move stands for action, Fast for speed (note that this character appears as Quick in the cast.) But the crux of the play is undoubtedly embodied in the mysterious Still. This character is condensed into a name, two stage-directions, and a single speech, yet implicitly is so potent, that he lifts the drama from the plane of the tea-table into the region of ideas. Tom, on the other hand, is the most natural character in dramatic literature. The author's musical tendency is showing in polyphonic dialogue; and the student of technique may find worthy of notice the device by which Lucy is removed from the stage in order that Nellie may utter a few words not intended for her sister's ear (Act 2—Scene 2). Now let the play speak for itself.

HALF
PAST THREE
By Harry Farjeon
A PLAY

MOVE		NELLIE	
STILL	*Burglars*	TOM	*Children of*
QUICK		LUCY	*Mr. & Mrs. Flee*
MR. FLEE		RICHARD	
MRS. FLEE		CHARLOTTE *(Their Nurse)*	

ACT I SCENE I

A field with grass and a few trees. In the distance is seen a large, dark house.

NELLIE, LUCY, TOM.

LUCY: I belive that there is a *great* mystery connected with that house.

NELLIE: So do I, and I am wrather frightened of it.

TOM (*aside*): Just like girls, (*aloud, scornfuly*) Don't be so foolish; there is *nothing* to be frightened about a *house*.

NELLIE: There is.

TOM (*sharply*): I don't want an argument, miss.

[*Hits her. Enter* RICHARD.

RICHARD (*kindly*): What is the matter, Nellie?

NELLIE (*crying*): Tom hit me because——

RICHARD (*angrily*): Did he? Where are you, Tom?

[TOM *hides behind a tree.*

RICHARD: I'll give it to him.

LUCY: I shall tell Mama.

[MOVE *is seen in the distance to enter the house.* NELLIE *covers her eyes with her hands.*

NELLIE: Oh!

[TOM *quietly escapes from behind the tree in the opposite direction.* LUCY *turns pale.*

RICHARD: I think I had better take you home.

ACT 2—SCENE 1

[*A bedroom.* NELLIE *lying in bed very pale and ill. Enter* MRS. FLEE.

MRS. F.: Won't you tell me what it is, dear?

NELLIE: I would if I could but I can't for it is so dreadful.

MRS. F.: But couldn't I make it better if I knew?

NELLIE: No.

[*Exit* MRS. FLEE. *Enter* RICHARD.

RICHARD (*slowly*): I think I know what it is.

NELLIE: What?

RICHARD: The other day—(*excitedly*)—I declair I will go and see about them.

[*Exit quickly. Enter* TOM & LUCY & MR. FLEE.

LUCY: Are you better now?

TOM: I wonder what it is.

NELLIE: Yes. (*Aside*) I wish I was.

MR. F.: I am very glad.

ACT 2—SCENE 2

The same. Enter LUCY.

NELLIE: I am so glad you have come.

LUCY: You are frightened, not ill. You are frightened of the man.

NELLIE: Yes.

[LUCY *draws a chair close to the bed & sits down on it.*

LUCY (*ancusly*): I hope you will get well by Thursday, because if you are we are going to have a picnic. Do you think you will be well by then?

NELLIE: Yes, I think so.

LUCY: We are going to start at half-past twelve and get there by one. Then we are——

[*They here a step outside. Exit* LUCY.

NELLIE: If I am not better I will pretend to be.

[*Enter* LUCY.

LUCY: It's nothing. Then we are going to have dinner. After dinner we are going to play alone till four, and at half-past three some soldiers will pass.

———

ACT 3 SCENE 1

The field. A table-clorth spred on the grass with Mr. &
Mrs. Flee & the children seeted around.

RICHARD: Pass me the pepper please.

NELLIE (*passing* RICH. *the pep. pot.*): Please can I have some more meat?

RICHARD: Thank you, Nellie.

MR. F.: Yes, dear.

[MR. FLEE *gives her some meat.*

TOM: Get off! Papa theres a horid spider eating my dinner and I can't get him off my plate.

[RICHARD, *who is sitting next to* TOM, *takes it off.*

LUCY: Oh! look here! Heres an ant hill!

TOM: The ants will get all over the food.

[TOM *steps on it.*

LUCY: How *could you*?

RICHARD: It is very cruel.

———

ACT 3 SCENE 2

The same. Not with the table-clorth or things. TOM,
LUCY, NELLIE.

TOM: We must get ready for the soldiers.

LUCY (*laughing*): We will tell them to take you prisoner.

TOM: They won't do——

[*Enter* MOVE, STILL, *and* FAST, *armed with guns.* MOVE
rushes at TOM, STILL *lies down and* FAST *aims at* LUCY.
All the children run about.

FAST (*to* LUCY): You can't get away.

MOVE (*to* TOM): We have got you safe.

[*Enter* RICHARD *with gun. He runs at* FAST *who drops his gun.* RICHARD *gives it to* TOM. *Meanwhile* FAST *takes another gun and takes aim at* LUCY. *Tom throws down his gun.* FAST *shoots and kils* LUCY, RICHARD *turns from pusuing* MOVE *and shoots* FAST *dead. Then he turns and shoots at* MOVE *and kills him.* RICHARD *takes hold of* NELLIES *hand.*

RICHARD (*to* TOM): Keep by LUCY while I get Papa.

[*Exit* RICHARD *and* NELLIE.

TOM: I wish we had not come.

[*Enter* ALL.

CHARLOTTE: *Let's see. I do believe she is dead!*

ALL BUT RICHARD: *Dead!!!*

[STILL *slowly gets up.*

RICHARD: Yes she is dead! (*Seeing* STILL) Who are you.

STILL (*slowly pointing to* MOVE): I thing I am one of them!

CURTAIN

It is obvious, from the cast as first set down, that the author had some original intention which was not carried out. The soldiers who never appear were probably meant to turn up in the nick of time, and foil the Burglars; but from the moment the Burglars were first sighted in Act One, they proved too much for the dramatist. The artist recognised in them a problem which mere arrest by a Small Army of 5 Men could never solve; the drama had him in thrall, and moved to its strange yet inevitable conclusion. Lucy must die, the good and noble Richard must be left with questions to grapple with throughout his life. Whether Jack Mann, the eradicated Page Boy, might have stepped in as a Force of Good against a Force of Evil, remains unknown. In the original cast he dominates the trio of Burglars, but alas! whatever part was adumbrated for him by the author, he never emerged from his Limbo.

NELLIE FARJEON

Miss Farjeon's earliest recorded work is a story, and she was too young to record it herself. The authoress was about five years old when she dictated to her father

MY TRAVELS, AND WHAT I SAW
By Eleanor Farjeon

CHAPTER I
THE COMMENCEMENT OF MY TRAVELS

Once upon a time, when I was eleven, my mother and father said I could go on a travel. Cook made me a lot of nice things, and papa and mama gave me a little pocket-book, to write down all my adventures. So off I set.

CHAPTER II
MY ARRIVAL IN A WOOD

I did not go in a carriage, for I thought it would be nicer to walk, for I could look at things as I passed them. Presently I came to a field. I picked a pretty bunch of flowers. The field became thicker and thicker with ferns, and soon I came to a wood.

CHAPTER III
WHAT I DID IN THE WOOD

I made my bunch of flowers thicker with the flowers from the wood. They smelt sweeter and sweeter as I put more and more. Presently I became tired, and I saw a little hut and I slept in it till the morning broke out.

CHAPTER IV
WHAT I DID AND SAW WHEN I CAME OUT OF THE WOOD

After sleeping one whole night I thought it was enough, and so I began for my morning's travel. I thought I had been in the woods long enough, so I began my journey to get out of it. As I went to get out of it I saw a lot of little streams running into a lot of little brooks. I saw deer running. I caught one of them. Soon I became thirsty, and saw one of the little brooks and drank out of it.

CHAPTER V
HOME AGAIN

Presently I had a letter from papa to go home. So I knew I must go home. When I got there they said, "Nell, dear, did you like it?" I said, "Yes, mama and papa, I did like it very much."

THE END

At the age of five or six, when Miss Farjeon began to take down her own thoughts in Early Pencil Script (with the inverted N), she was chiefly engaged on a novel, *The Adventures of Reggie*. Unable to finish it at a sitting, she invariably began it all over again whenever she took up her pencil; and it was the first matter she attempted to type. She was seven when her father placed her at his own Remington, set the paper, instructed her as to the space-line, and left her to figure out the unusual alphabet for herself. He returned later, to find her typing busily, under the impression that she was at last bringing Reggie's Adventures to a conclusion. Alas! as she had no know-knowledge of shifting the carriage and paper, she had been typing on one space for at least half-an-hour, and the Adventures were being compressed into a solid block at the end of the first line. After this, Reggie was abandoned, and, like her brother Harry, Nellie Farjeon turned her attention to the stage. Her first subject was the story of Snow-White, which opens with the Good Queen at her embroidery frame.

QUEEN *works and pricks finger.*

QUEEN: I wish I had a little dauter with her skin as white as snow her lips and cheaks as red blod and her hair and eyes as black as my en-boradeere frame.

[QUEEN *dyes*.
Entter KING.

KING: Shes dead I must marry agayne.

[*Exsite* KING *and* QUEEN KING *marrys*.

The drama pursues its course to the second attempt on
Snow-White's life, and is left unfinished. For her next
play, Miss Farjeon chose an original theme. *The Fairy
Cave* is in Seven Acts. The Scenario runs: Act I, The
Fairy Cave. Act II, The Sea and an Island. Act III, A
Forest. Act IV, The same, but in the distance the Cave
all lighted up can be seen. Act V, Found. Act VI, A
Mournful Experience. Act VII, Buried. Through these
scenes, Mary, "a lost Little Girl," is persecuted by a
Wicked Little Gobling. In Act IV, as she approaches the
Cave all lighted up, this stage direction appears: "butler
comes out of the cave, drinking brandy, wiscky, &c."
Presumably he too is all lighted up. At the end of this
scene "butler gets mad and sawers." This horrid action
remains unexplained. It is the Wicked Little Gobling
who, in Act VI, "sticks a sowrd" in Mary, as she lies
asleep. Mary says "Oh" and dies; the least she could
do after such a "Mournful Experience." Act VII merits
fuller quotation:

> [*A garden it is night Enter* gardener *with spad, and with
> a gun* Jack, *and* fanny, *and* mrs. green, *and* santa clause,
> *And* Alice, *and* gobling, *and* w. fairy, *with a loaded gun,
> and* fairy queen *holding* mary *in white*.

JACK: poor mary.
santa: dig the grave gardener.
gar.: Il dig the grave sir

  [*digs a grave and* fairy q *puts* mary *in*
MRS. GREEN: I could never bear such a seen.
fanny: nor I tis very sad.

For simple pathos, this burial scene can only be compared with one in Shakespeare.

Rustic life made ever a strong appeal to the authoress. The following extract is from a story, written at the age of eight.

"A Use-ful Family

"Once upon a time, a man, who, kept a farm, fell sick. His wife, and children, knew not how to get bread, for they could not plough the feilds, nor grind the corn. I must tell you somthing about the farm, now, and go on about this presently . . . Meg, and Snow, the cows each wore a bell, so, if they were late from the pasture (which they seldom were) the bells tinkeled, so the *milkmaid* knew they were coming home. Cud, they had a lot, of, growing on the hills, and the cows enjoyed it very much."

Nellie Farjeon's first poem, composed on her seventh birthday, is quoted elsewhere. Of the same period is

THE BROOK
The Brook! it rippled loud and clears,
Singing to every human ear;
The birds! they bathed in the surface bright,
Hopping and twittering with delight.

2
The summer bright oh now did come,
And roses red came to their home;
The little fish laid down and died, ·
Oh fate, Oh fate, and the brook was dried.
Nellie Farjeon. March 7th 1889. Bournemouth.

By far the most considerable work from the authoress's pencil, before, at nine, she took finally to the pen, is the Shakespearian play of *Damon and Pythias*. She has not yet aspired to Blank Verse, but does not stint her Lords and Lovers.

DAMON & PYTHIAS
Characters

DANYEL	
HARRY	Friend to DANYEL ⎫
HENRY	Sutir to VILOT ⎪ Lords
ANTHONY	Sutir to VILOT ⎬
MITTI	Sutir to MIRIDA ⎭
MIRIDA	A Young Lady. Daughter to DANYEL
RICHARD	A Young Man. Sutir to ⎤ Children
	MIRIDA ⎬ to
VIOLET	A Young Lady ⎦ HARRY
KING ATOM	
QUEEN MIRIDA	
SUSAN	Mother to KING. A Wicked Old Dame.
	Soldiers, Servants, &c.

ACT I. SCENE I.

A Drawingroom in the Kings Palace.

Enter HARRY, MIRIDA, MITTI, *and* RICHARD, *and* HENRY.

MITTI (*aside*): I wish I could get to marry Mirida. (*Aloud*) Mirida I want to say som-thing in private to you.

MIRIDA: Well.

MITTI: I am very loath to ask you this, my love, but still I must.

MIRIDA: What is it?

MITTI: Harry, my dear, told me to ask you if you would marry Richard. I refused. He preesed me close to do so. But still I said I would not. At last I consented, and I wish to ask if you will take me instad.

MIRIDA: No. I cannot. I must have Richard.

MITTI: Have I come fifty miles to recive this answer? "Nay." Chose wisely Mirid. I am here to ask your hand.

MIRIDA: I cannot let you have it, for Richard is mine.

MITTI: Goodbye then. I leave you to yourself. (*Exit.*)

MIRIDA: Impertance of him. Fancy *me* to marry a brute like him. (*Blushes.*)

[RICHARD *comes up to her.*

RICHARD: Ha Mirida. Why looks thou so floushed?

MIRIDA: Oh don't.

RICHARD : Thou hast had a conversation with that Mitti.

MIRIDA: Yes.

RICHARD: And he wishes to marry you?

MIRID: Yes. Oh don't call your father.

RICHARD : Why not. *He* will settle it. Father!! (*Exit.*)

MIRID: I don't want to talk with *him*. (*Exit.*)

    [*Enter* MITTI, *and* HENRY.

HENRY: Well, what do you want of *me?*

MITTI: I want you to lay a trap for Mirid.
    [*Enter* HARRY.

HARRY: Where is Richard Mitti.

MITTI: I don't know. Oh *pleace* go away.
    [*Exit* HARRY.

HENRY: How shall I do it. *I* am in love with Vilet.

MITTI: Pretend to be in love with her. One day bring her to me.

HENRY: Yes.

ACT DROP. 8 Months ellacped.

ACT II. SCENE I.

A room in MITTIS *house. Enter* MITTI.

MITTI: I wonder when Henry will come. (*Knock at the door.*)

MITTI : Is that you Henry?

SUSAN: (*Without*) No. It is me, Susan.

MITTI: Come in. *(Enter* SUSAN.)

SUSAN: I have got a new plan for you getting Mirid.

MITTI: What is it?

SUSAN: You dusise yourself for when Mirida is coming
    (she is coming soon) and when you have got her,
    through it off and tell her you will do somthing to her,
    if she don't marry you.

MITTI: Yes. Thank you. (*Exit both. Enter* MITTI *disguised.*)
[*Enter* HENRY, *and* MIRIDA.

MITTI: My dear sit down. (*Aside to* HENRY) Get a knife.
[HENRY *goes to a draw and gets a Knife.*
[MITTI *Throughs off his disguise.*

MITTI: Now will you marry me.

MIRIDA: No!!! You have dicived me.

MITTI: Give me the knife Henry. I will kill you if you
do not. Will you?

MIRIDA: No!! I cannot.
[MITTI *raises the knife to her heart.*

MIRIDA (*sceaming*): Richard!!! Richard!!!
[*Enter* KING, RICHARD, HARRY, *and* DANYEL.

RICHARD (*rushing forward*): Stop!!! stop sir!!! let her
be!

MITTI: She is a lyair.

HARRY: She is not.

DANYEL: Don't you dare to hurt my daughter.

HENRY: Take your daughter then. And go.

KING: You go. Go yourself.
[*Exit all. Enter* QUEEN MIRIDA.

Q. MIRID: Who has been here? I wonder. I heard a great
noise just now.
[*Enter* MIRID.

MIRID (*faintly*): Oh they are coming. (*Faints.*)

Q. MIRID: What is the matter? (*Enter* RICHARD.)

RICHARD: No!! Out sir!!! out. (*Enter* MITTI.)

MITTI: They are having a jolly fight out there.
[RICHARD *goes out, and* MITTI *gets* MIRIDA *and Exit.
Enter* HENRY. *He takes hold of the queen and drags her
out. Enter* RICHARD.

RICHARD (*shouting*): There's no one in here. Where is
Mirid?
[*Enter* MITTI.

MITTI: She is in our van being carried away.

RICHARD: Oh. (*Exit. Enter* KING.)

KING: Harry—Harry—Harry. (*Enter* DANYEL.)

DANYEL: He is carried away with Mirida and the Queen, oh my Harry, my Harry.

KING: The Que—— Que—— Queen?

DANYEL : Yes. (*Exit. Enter* ANTHONY, *and* VIOLET, *arm in arm.)*

ANTHONY: Violet? I wish to ask if *you* know what they are doing out there?

VIOLET: Fighting.

ANTHONY: Goodbye then. I must go to fight.

VIOLET: Oh Anthony don't——

ANTHONY: I must. (*Exit* ANTHONY, *and* KING.)

VIOLET: Oh dear, I am left alone. I hope he will be back soon, because I don't like him to fight, and I want to be sure that he is not killed, *and the sooner he comes back the sooner the battle will end.*

  [ACT DROP. ACT III, SCENE I. *A battle feild. Enter all the lords exsept* HARRY, *and soldiers.*

DANYEL: Now!!! be careful and on the watch, or elce those bruts will get the best of it.

SOLD.: Yes sir. But if we happen to chatch sight of "Sir Harry" what shall we do.

DANYEL: Nothing. It will only do harm.

SOLD. : Alright sir. (*Exit* MITTI.)

DANYEL: Just   what   I   expected.   (*Listens.*)
  [*Enter* HENRY *and* MITTI.

MITTI (*aside to* HENRY): If we bring out Harry, we will be alright, because they are not going to try & catch him, so we will drown him in the river. (*Exit.*)

DANYEL (*aside, to himself*): We'l see. Oh arn't we though, I only said the soldiers.

  [*Enter* HARRY *and* MITTI.

MITTI (*to* HENRY): Now we will drown him.

HENRY: Oh indeed, (DANYEL *rushes forward.*)

DANYEL: *I am* going to fight for him, with *you* Mitti.

MITTI: Very well, (*they fight. Meanwhile* HENRY *takes* VIOLET (*who has just come on*) *and* harry *to prison.* [*Enter* KING

KING: Hallow what are you doing?

DANYEL: Five taken. Harry, Queen, Mirid, Violet, and er, let me see. No only four.

KING: Dear me. (*Exit,* DANYEL *blows a trumpet loudly. Enter* ANTHONY.)

ANTHONY: Oh dear. They are persuming Richard.

DANYEL: RICHARD? *Not Richard. It can't be Richard. Our cheif defender. It wont be Richard!*
[*Enter* RICHARD *with* soldiers *after.*

ANTHONY: *Richard.*

RICHARD (*panting*): I can't stop. I must, and will save my sister.
[*Exit With* SOLDIRS.

ANTHONY: My poor Violet. (*Exit.*)

ACT III.

A Prison. In it are VIOLET, QUEEN MIRIDA, MIRIDA, *and* HARRY.

QUEEN MIRID: I wish I could get out of here.

VIOLET: So do I. (*Enter* RICHARD.)

RICHARD (*laughing*): Your wish shall soon be completed. I'l come for you soon, father. (*Exit with* VIOLET, MIRID, *and* QUEEN. *Enter* DANYEL. *He unfastens chains from* HARRY.)

DANYEL: Come, Harry. (*Exit with* HARRY. *Enter* RICHARD.)

RICHARD: Wheres father. (*Exit. Enter* DANYEL *with gun. Places himself where* HARRY *was. Enter* RICHARD.

DANYEL: Hush! don't make a noise, (MITTI *is heard coming.*) Now my friend, you'l soon be lieing dead.
[*Enter* MITTI. DANYEL *fires and kills him. Enter* HENRY.

HENRY: What have——(danyel *kills him. Enter All exsept* SUSAN.)

HARRY: Susan is being hung, and now, in peace, Richard can marry Mirida, and Anthony Violet.

CURTAIN.

Plays, stories, and poems now flowed freely from Nellie's pen, but we have space to quote only two more examples. The first, written at the age of ten, is the lyric which appeared in print on pink satin under the ægis of Mr. Augustin Daly (*q.v*). She would gladly suppress it, but offers it as a public sop to her brothers, in mitigation of anything she has printed concerning them.

A FADED FLOWER.

1

Only a faded flower love
Only a faded rose
Living in bloom but yesterday
Now taking sweet repose.
Now it is wrinkled and old love
Yesterday fresh and young
Yesterday singing a song of Life
But now the song is sung.

2.

Only a faded flower love
Once 'twas a pride of mine
Now it is no more good in the world
No more its looks are fine.
Like a little old woman love
Once lighthearted when young
Once 'twas singing a song of Life
But now the song is sung.

3.
Only a faded flower love
Harmless and sweet and true
Sweet in both youth and womanhood
But now its days are through.
Learn a lesson from this love
Learn it while you are young
Now you are singing a song of Life——
Presently 'twill be sung.
        Nellie Farjeon. September 12th. 1891.

When she was eleven, Miss Farjeon chanced on a reference to Chaos, in an abstruse mythology, as the deity who had created order out of disorder. This novel view gripped her imagination; she felt it was time that the name of Chaos should be vindicated, and determined to do it on the spot. It was evening, and she was about to dress for a performance of *Richelieu* at the Lyceum Theatre, but the heat of inspiration must not be allowed to cool. Placing pencil and paper on her marble-topped washstand, she wrote with her right hand, while performing her ablutions, and brushing her hair, with her left. For the first time in her life she essayed blank verse, a medium in which she was able to write without pause; the epic was finished as the brougham drew up at the door.

To CHAOS
By Eleanor Farjeon

How wonderful the earth beneath us seems!
How wonderful the clouds that send us rain!
How wonderfully doth the ocean roll,
Rolling for aye, for all Eternity!
How wonderful that gently blowing breeze,
As though some unseen nymph draws in her breath,
Which is as perfumed as a thousand flowers

Plucked from the peaceful grounds of Paradise!
These are the gifts of Chaos. All the earth,
The rolling sea, the air, and fire withal—
Yea! for the elements, when all combined,
Form one, a mighty god. 'Tis Chaos' self.
To him we owe our lives. This peopled world
Through him exists; for until Chaos came
All was as night, the darkest, blackest night,
An unformed mass, without humanity.
Before the world was made what changes space
Each day, nay ev'ry hour did undergo!
The fire, the earth, the air, all reigned in turn,
And water oft in sweeping torrents rushed.
But Chaos leapt into unending space,
And unto each and every element
Assigned its place; with arms commanding waved
Each cloud, each torrent, and each flame away.
The wind was wild, and water loudly roared,
The earth all trembled, and in hissing flames
The fire sprang upwards. In the midst of all,
His work beginning, Chaos, mighty god,
Repels the darkness, and above his head
Appears the Zodiac in shining stars.
Next Chaos, taking of the sacred fire,
Forms the great sun which sends the light of day;
He stills the waters; makes the clouds more white,
And paints the sky to make it fair and blue;
He makes the air less thick, and forms the moon,
And then creates the world on which we live.
And others, too, he makes; each planet, all
By him takes shape, e'en ev'ry twinkling star
Which doth appear so small unto our eyne
Is made by him, as made is all the rest.
Thus Chaos doth divide the elements,
And each its duty does, his will obeys,
And thus this world, the planets, and the sun,
Through these an everlasting motion take.
And when the work is done the sun sinks down
In all its glory; tints the sky with gold,

And red, and purple. Rises then the moon,
And smiles upon this earth, inhabited
By man, and beast, and fish, and bird alike.
And when at eventide we're thinking o'er
The sorrows or the pleasures of the day,
'Tis Chaos must we thank for this fair life.
And thus continue all these worlds of his
In animation, health, and wealth, and joy,
Tasting the fruitful pleasures of the earth
Whose cultivation keeps us now alive.
But not for ever. Then will come the cry,
"Chaos is dead!" and all will be destroyed
That he has done. But now, and until then,
We'll live in peace, and love, and happiness.

Next day, *Chaos* was pushed, in the usual way, under
B. L. Farjeon's study-door, and Nellie Farjeon ran away
quaking to the Nursery. She has no recollection of his
comments; but he appears to have spent the day typing
copies of the poem, and sowing them broadcast. One copy
he carried to the Green Room Club, to inflict on anyone
who would listen to it. He was accused by several members
of having had a hand in the lines, to which he replied, "I
couldn't write lines like these to save my life."

48, *Abbey Gardens*,
S.W.

Dear Farjeon,
                    The poem is very remarkable. More so
perhaps in the extraordinary range of ideas than in its
literary quality, though quite astounding in that respect
for a child so young. I was not wrong in supposing that a
granddaughter of Joseph Jefferson, and a daughter of
your own, must have genius. It is a great privilege you
enjoy and a heavy responsibility you live under. Good
luck and great fortune to you and yours!
                    With hearty greetings
                                        Hall Caine.

JOSEPH JEFFERSON FARJEON

Joseph Jefferson Farjeon was intended for the stage, but, like his brothers and sister, devoted a good deal of his spare time to writing. Before he entered the field of journalism at the age of fourteen, he had already tried his hand at tales and verses, of which three early specimens are extant: a lyric, a ballad, and a very brief novel. The date of the last is uncertain; the poems were probably written between 1890–93, and the lyric, which preceded the ballad, shows, in line four, a very early leaning towards Man's Rights. For if a woman is raised to the status of "Lady" by marrying a "Sir," why should not a man be equally privileged, when marrying one who is already a "Lady?"

THE TRAVELER

I

I wandered through the woods alone
Thinking of her;
If she would but become my own
I'd be a 'Sir.'

2

Her name is Lady Marlow, now—
And she is rich.
She owns a horse—likewise a cow,
It makes me itch!

3

If she'll accept me I will ask,
And *now* I'll do't—
I hope she'll marry me
And take my suit.

J. J. Farjeon.

THE SHIP-WRECK

1

Some time ago a ship named wave
Was sailing on the sea.
The sailors on this little boat
Were less than twenty-three.

2

The sea was not at all rough then.
The sailors did delight
To see the sea so calm and blue
On such a lovely night.

3

There were three watchmen on the Ship
Who thought t'wood be no harm
To go into their cabins snug
Because it was so calm.

4

Into their cabins they did walk
Soon in their shelvs they lay
They thought the boat would be quite safe
Until the break of day.

5

But a little after midnight
The watchmen wished they'd done
Their duty, for a storm was there
A very nasty one.

6

The sailors then jumped out of bed
And quickly ran on deck.
The ship had run against a rock
It was a bad ship-wreck.

7
The sailors knew not what to do
The boat was sinking fast.
But then a man stepped out and said
We'el keep up till the last.

8
A ship went out next day to find
The boat, and it to save
But nothing could they find atall
But peices of the "Wave.
                                    Joe Jefferson Farjeon.

And now for the Novel.

Preface
Again he sprung up at him with an unearthly shriek, but, as before, he was flung back into the deep ravine.

The story
'Twas Christmas Eve, & the fire was crackling on the white marble fire-place. A man was pacing the room with long strides, & he had an agitated look on his old & withered face.

"By Gad!" he exclaimed, at last, "this must be the end! I can stand no more;" & so saying, he quitted the room.

Epilogue
Thus the year passed on, & the old clock, which had served its master so faithfully, hangs once more in its old place.

THE END
But it was as the editor of the first Nursery Magazine which exhibited any powers of endurance, that J. J.

Farjeon made his literary mark on Adelaide Road. Sundry earlier efforts had died stillborn, but with the initial number of

FARJEON'S WEEKLY

in 1897 a new era was inaugurated. The magazine, which ran to seven neatly typed quarto sheets, was issued at (I think) 2d. a copy, and the circulation ran to quite half-a-dozen subscribers. The make-up of No. 1 (followed fairly faithfully throughout the journal's life) was as follows.

Serial Story:

THE USURPER

By

J. J. Farjeon

Chapter I.

"Many years ago, an Indian Prince, named Kumar Shri Raja, went for a voyage round the world. While he was away his father died, and Raja's brother usurped the throne. Etc. etc. etc."

(*N.B.—Kumar Shri Ranjitsinhji was at this time the Farjeon children's idol.*)

Serial Story:

THE TRAVELLERS

By

Herbert Farjeon

Chapter I

"Harrold Fencer was going to try to discover the north pole, and every preparation needed was ready. Etc. etc. etc."

Short Story:

JACK'S TRIUMPH by J. J. Farjeon

Short Story:

THE LATIN SCHOLARSHIP, by Herbert Farjeon

A Poem:
"LIFE"
By Tommy Bee

(*N.B. This promising young poet's work was always handed in by B. L. Farjeon, and was usually accompanied by a personal letter of enthusiasm for the Magazine and its editor. The writer appears to have been about ten.*)

A page of Advertisements, and a fill-up called "The Odd Half-Hour" completed the issue.

A CAUSE CÉLÈBRE

The appearance of FARJEON'S WEEKLY gave rise to a Cause Célèbre in the Nursery, in which a scurrilous production calling itself

"THE RIVAL"

was involved. For a few days Harry and Nellie Farjeon were observed much closeted together, and before the second number of FARJEON'S WEEKLY was due to appear, "The First and *Only* Number" of THE RIVAL was anonymously distributed. In type, paper, and format it was identical with FARJEON'S WEEKLY; but where that was a publication of unimpeachable character, there was hardly a contribution to THE RIVAL which would not have involved its editors in heavy damages for libel, if they had come into the open. Horrible parodies of the manner and matter of FARJEON'S were bad enough; worse were the fictitious interview with J. J. Farjeon, the analysis of his paper with shady meanings attached to its noblest sentiments, and the insulting anecdotes which, in spite of allusions by initials and asterisks, plainly referred to every member of the Farjeon family—except Harry and Nellie. The issue created a sensation in high circles; which was intensified when the anonymous Editors of the Rag in question had the face to offer to advertise in the pure pages of the journal they had sought to defile.

I cannot do better than quote the editorial columns of FARJEON'S WEEKLY, No. 2.

A TRANSPARENT FRAUD

The following letter and advertisement have reached us. At first we were disinclined to give them the wide publicity guaranteed by our enormous circulation, but upon consideration we decided to expose the trixters responsible for the announcement that a second number of our contemptible RIVAL would appear. No second Number *will* appear. And why? In the first place, because the anonymous writers and editor of that scurrilous print *dare not* issue another; and in the second place, because the *small modicum of brains they posess* must be completely exhausted by the strain to which they have been subjected. We pity and despise the poor creatures.—*Editor* "*Farjeon's Weekly.*"

Sir,

Please insert the following advertisement in your paper, for which I enclose one penny. Let it be displayed as in this copy.

Yours Commercially,

Proprietor of "The Rival."

Look out for the Next Number
of
THE RIVAL.
Another Number will Appear,
In consequence of the Enormous Success of the First.
Everybody is asking for it.
THE RIVAL! THE RIVAL!!
THE RIVAL!!!
The Smartest Journal in the World
Read No Other,
And send your Subscription Immediately to the Office.

The following letter was sent to us a few days ago:

Dear Sir,

I was passing a scavenger's cart this morning when some sheets of paper dropped from the basket the scavenger had just filled from the dustbin. Picking up these sheets I discovered that they formed the "Only" copy of a journal entitled "The Rival." Of course the "Only" copy. The Editor would not dare publish another. And who is the Editor. He does not manfully proclaim himself, as you do, Sir, in your admirable Journal, the publication of which has marked a new Era in Literature. No, Sir. He hides himself under the veil of anonymity; he is ashamed to publish his name. As well he may be. A more disgraceful copy of your excellent Serial stories could not be made, but it is easy to gauge the quality of brain that produced it. Not like yours, Sir— no, not like yours. Lucid, elegant, accomplished, cultured effusions like yours are seldom met with. Go on and prosper, Sir; be not discouraged by the vulgarity, mendaciousnessness, and incapasity, such as is displayed in the pages of your weak-minded comtemporory. Long may Farjeon's Weekly continue to adorn and grace the Victorian age.

Your ardent admirer,
T-e P-i-c-of W-l-s.

The wish expressed in the Exalted Personage's letter (delivered personally by his emissary, B. L. Farjeon) was realized, THE RIVAL died the death it deserved, not surviving its first issue; and FARJEON'S WEEKLY reigned supreme until its Editor retired gracefully in favour of young blood, and FARJEON'S FORTNIGHTLY, edited by Herbert Farjeon, appeared two years later on the journalistic horizon of the Nursery.

HERBERT FARJEON

The youngest of the four Farjeons burst into verse at the age of eight, giving vent to a poem which combined the kindness of heart with the robust outlook of a Fighting Parson.

DON'T FORGET THE BIRDS

1

You get up in the morning
And with the birds do deal
And the sparrows, mourning
For their daily meal.

2

You put bread-crumbs on the window-still
And also small cherries.
The cherries with a plate you fill
And very small berries.

Chorus

Don't forget the birds, boys,
Don't forget the birds
Don't forget your task, boys,
Don't forget your task.

December 15, 1895.

Herbert Farjeon was at this time largely under the influence of the B. O. P., and suitable sentiments continued to flow from his pen.

CHRISTMAS

Summer's past with all its joys,
Now Christmas comes, with all its toys.
Santa Claus does dress the tree
And a stocking fills for me.
And the people look so gay.
In winter there's no making hay!

December 16, 1895.

FOR ENGLAND HOME AND BEAUTY

1

For England, Home and Beauty
The beauty of the land,
The soldier does his duty
To save all of England.

2

And not one single man does flee
Back to his homely land.
They fire their guns, and you should see
Them fight with sword in hand.

3

A shout, and then up with the flag!
The enemy retreat.
And slowly up the hill they drag
That's how they take defeat!
                                   February 5, 1896.

During the next two or three years, young Farjeon's creations were mainly embodied in various short-lived magazines, until, with the appearance of FARJEON'S WEEKLY (*q.v.*) he became a regular writer of serials and short stories. The experience he gained under the able editorship of J. J. Farjeon enabled him, in 1899 to assume editorship on his own account. From the outset he attacked his job with an originality and firmness which enabled him to carry this, the most notable of Nursery Magazines, into its Third Year. The motto he adopted, and printed on the front page of each issue, was

"*Non bonus, non melior, sed optimus.*"

This was exchanged, in the Second Year, for a sentiment from Keble:

"Onward and Upward till the Goal we win."

Both aspirations were fully realized by Herbert.

His first number, published on Wednesday, October

11th, 1899, included not only full measure of serials, stories, articles and poems (he had been far-seeing enough to offer a post on his staff to his old Editor and to Tommy Bee, the famous young poet of FARJEON'S WEEKLY), but it also printed the only personal interview with Eleanor Farjeon that writer ever accorded to anybody, and featured a series of

SPLENDID PRIZE COMPETITIONS

THREE PENCE IN PRIZES!

with effectiveness and tact. Rule 2 reads:

> "Each competitor shall put his or her name, age and address on the top of his or her paper; otherwise he or she shall be disqualified. But it is deemed proper that Mr. and Mrs. Farjeon, Mr. and Mrs. Linford, Miss Newman, Madame Louise, Mr. and Mrs. Corder and Fraulein Haeszler should be excused from putting their ages."

In the second issue (October 25th, 1899) Herbert Farjeon made his first appearance as a Dramatic Critic.

"KING JOHN," AT HER MAJESTY'S THEATRE

By

A Constant Playgoer

What would Shakespeare say if he could see this latest production of his play? Would he like it? Most assuredly he would! I can fancy his ghost hovering over the stalls at Her Majesty's, and murmuring:

"That's what I meant, that's *exactly* what I meant, only in my time there was no such thing as scenery, and no such actors as are before me now. And they have got all the right business, too. Clever of them, considering I have never written any stage directions to my plays. I can see, Mr. Beerbohm Tree understands me thoroughly."

It is indeed a fine and most impressive production. Never have a series of more beautiful historical pictures been presented to the eye. Tree's impersonation of the king is in some scenes really wonderful; notably when he discovers that little Arthur is alive. The hapless child is played in an exquisitely sympathetic manner by Master Sefton. Through the gloom and sadness there passes ever and anon, like a ray of sunshine, the handsome and dashing Falconbridge, acted—well as only an artist like Mr. Lewis Waller *can* act.

The ending of the play is intensely impressive, the white-robed figure of the dead king in the centre, in the background are the monks, and as the last words are spoken, the organ peals forth and they sing a solemn "Amen!"

And on December 20th the critic, after attending a performance by the Dramatic Class of the Royal Academy of Music, foresees, in a certain Mr. Nugent Monck, a Dan Leno of the future.

On February 14th, 1900, FARJEON'S FORTNIGHTLY published an authentic interview with Mr. Lewis Waller. The Editor had never met the Actor, but knowing that any words from this greatest of Matinee Idols must be a draw, had submitted to him a list of questions by post; Mr. Waller had good-naturedly returned them, to be written-up, unsuspecting that a little-known portrait of himself was to adorn the interview.

Everyone in London has heard of Mr. Lewis Waller, and a good many other people, also! His stately Brutus, his gallant Buckingham, his dashing Falconbridge, and his excellent Lysander, have, of recent years all tended to maintain and enhance an already fine reputation. It was therefore, not without some misgivings, and a keen sense of my own insignificance, that I knocked at the door of his house in Elmtree Road. I was shown into the picturesque drawing-room, where the great actor did not long keep me waiting. After the customary greetings I plunged boldly into my task, and asked Mr. Waller what had been his earliest aspirations.

"My tastes have always tended towards the stage," he answered.

"And how long have you been on the stage?" was my next question.

"I have been working at my profession since 1883, nearly seventeen years," replied Mr. Waller.

"At what age did you start performing?"

"I was twenty-two years old when I began acting. I am quite devoted to my work, and cannot imagine life without it."

"Do you feel nervous, when acting, Mr. Waller?"

"I used to suffer agonies of nervousness," he replied, "and do so still on all first performances."

"Where was it you made your first appearance?"

"It was made with Toole, at his theatre."

I should have been glad to elicit Mr. Waller's views upon the vexed question of the National Theatre; but he assured me that he had *no* ideas upon the subject. I now rose to go, thinking I had already trespassed too long upon Mr. Waller's valuable time; but the kindness and patience with which he had answered all my queries encouraged me to put one more question to him before I left.

"It would be of great interest to our readers, Mr. Waller, to know which you consider your best part."

"I don't think," said he, "that actors are the best judges as to their own work."

Perhaps Mr. Waller is right; in any case, he may feel quite safe in leaving the judgment of his work to the public, and can always feel quite confident that they will return a favourable and enthusiastic verdict.

A copy was in due course posted to the victim, who, on February 26th, wrote from Her Majesty's Theatre:

My dear Farjeon,

Many thanks for your letter and enclosure. I was delighted with the interview and portrait. What an extremely original idea is the typewriten picture!

I'm afraid the youngster is too clever to come to a good end, at least I *should* think so if I didn't know his father.

Give your son my best thanks for having dealt so mercifully with me and tell him that I am longing to make his personal acquaintance.

Very sincerely yours

Lewis Waller.

With the issue that completed his first year the editor enclosed a printed slip:

Dear Sir or Madam,

Will you kindly send me your opinion of "Farjeon's Fortnightly," as it would be convenient to me. And will you also convey to me by mouth or letter, whether you intend to continue taking in this paper.

I remain,

Yours &c.,

Herbert Farjeon.

The response was overwhelming. In the first issue of Vol. 2 the Editor printed the following tributes:

FARJEON'S FORTNIGHTLY

Opinions of the First Volume by its Readers.

Mr. Joe Jefferson Farjeon, who was the Editor of both "The Lancaster News," and the "Trimmingham News," writes,

I heartily approve of your bright magazine, and hope to continue its perusal for many years to come. The alternate Wednesdays would seem barren indeed, were there no "F. F." to fill the mind with healthy thoughts. May it long enhance the libraries of the wise, including that of

Yours truly,

J. Farjeon.

Miss Lily Newman writes of "F. F."

I consider it a most interesting and original periodical, combining instruction with pleasure.

I remain,

Dear Sir,

Yours faithfully,

Lily Newman.

Miss Nellie Farjeon sends us an interesting triolet.

Here we behold at a glance
One of the pow'rs of the age—
Proof of a nation's advance
Here we behold at a glance.
Poetry—science—romance—
Lore for the child and the sage—
Here we behold at a glance
One of the pow'rs of the age.

Nellie Farjeon.

Miss Dorothea Corder writes:

No library worthy of the name would be without a copy of this valuable paper. In the drawing-room it is indispensable, not to have it in the dining-room would be a crime! All trustworthy servants expect it in the kitchen, the children cry for it in the nursery, no school could complete the education of its pupils without it. It is my deliberate opinion after many years experience that for keeping the head cool and the mind clear, there is nothing like "Farjeon's Fortnightly."

Faithfully yours,

Dorothea Corder.

We intend to print some more in our next number.

The same number was signalized by an interview with a well-known author who had recently become known to the Editor; on this occasion the questions and answers were oral.

A Chat with Tom Gallon

It generally happens, when a journalist writes an interview with an author, that he tells his readers when the author was born, how old he is, what books he has written, and when he started writing. But in the case of Mr. Gallon this is entirely unnecessary; for it would be like telling the public that William the Conqueror ascended the throne in 1066, or that London is the capital of England,—because these things are already known; but it is *not* known what William had for dinner on his Coronation day, nor is it known what is Mr. Gallon's very interesting method of writing. But whereas the former will never be discovered, I am now going to let my readers into the secret of the latter.

"First," said the celebrated author of "Kiddy" and "Tatterly," in answer to my query, "I take three sheets of foolscap. On one of these I write the names of all the principal characters who are to come into my book, and opposite them I write their characters, so to speak, appearances, and anything about them. On the second piece of paper I write a synopsis of the story; and on the third, I write the headings of all the chapters, in proper order, from first to last."

This is wonderful enough; but it is not all. With this in his hand Mr. Gallon paces his room, and with the writing in the three papers alone as a basis, he dictates his story straight off to his sister, who, being a quick typist, takes it down on a "Remington."

Mr. Gallon has a certain complicated routine round the room, and says that he often works out his dialogue, so to speak, on the pattern of the carpet. He dictates fluently and easily.

"And," he informed me, "when I have once arranged the plot and characters, I can write a book in five or six weeks."

A book in six weeks! That is nearly nine a year. It is not all writers who can do this, but many would like to.

Mr. Gallon does most of his work in the morning after breakfast; he seldom corrects what he has once written. He is a passionate admirer of Dickens; and anyone who has read Dickens' works and also Mr. Gallon's, will see the effect the former has had on the latter.

"I was brought up on Dickens from my childhood by my father," Mr. Gallon will tell you.

One word of advice, readers. Read "Tatterly," so that, when you hear it discussed over the dinner table, you need not be ashamed of your ignorance.

That Mr. Tom Gallon considered himself "made" after this is evident from a contribution he submitted for publication in the following issue.

THE HALL-MARK
A Fable
By
Tom Gallon

Herbert (which, being interpreted, means, "He Enhances Reputations By Encouraging Real Talent") gazed afar from the battlements of Farjeon's Tower. There came to him, weary and spent, a Young Writer, who had been sorely mauled in heavy conflicts with certain hostile tribes of Critics in the plains of Literature.

"I see what *you* want," said Herbert, briskly. "You've come to me just in the nick of time. You want furbishing up. Come inside."

So the Young Writer went inside; and Herbert did great things for him. He Boomed him! Yea—and not only him; but also his Sister, and his Carpet, and all that was his!! In fact, he Boomed him like the very Dickens!!!

And the Young Writer came forth again, with the glow of youth on his cheek, and with his hair curled, and a step that was elastic. And the tribe of Critics, who had been waiting for him, bore down upon him. But they stopped; they recoiled; they bared their heads; they prostrated themselves in the dust.

"Touch him not," they said; "he bears the Hall-Mark! Speak well of him; be nice to him."

For, marked all over him, in a sort of delicate pattern, were the letters "F. F."—which stands for "Farjeon's Fortnightly." They (the Critics) bowed in the dust several times more.

For the Young Writer was all right now; this was Fame!

For another year the FORTNIGHTLY continued a firmly-established favourite; the Editor is, after the manner of editors, cock-a-hoop about it in the first issue of Vol. 3, and says in his "Editorial":

"'Men may come, and men may go, but I go on for ever.'
"This applies perfectly to 'Farjeon's Fortnightly.' No less than three magazines have come and gone whilst our periodical has been in existence. May it live to see three times three more!"

Alas! his wish was not gratified. Two numbers later the following stern NOTICE! concludes the issue:

"Certain personages who receive this magazine from fortnight to fortnight, are requested to pay up. It may be as well to add that in our next number will be a list of those who are behindhand."

The Editor had crowed a little too soon. Immediately after this, FARJEON'S FORTNIGHTLY, like many a less worthy publication, disappeared from view for lack of support. It was the last of the Nursery Magazines.

R.A.M.

THEY WERE SENDING HARRY to the Royal Academy of Music!

I stared the gloomy fact in the face. They were cutting our lives in half, Harry's and mine.

Oh yes, of course Harry must learn his music. But couldn't he go on doing it at home? For two years he had been doing so with Dr. John Storer, who made no difference to our intensive existence, and before that with young Landon Ronald, who tried to. That is, he not only came and taught Harry piano and composition, but laid out a sort of time-table for him to observe through the day. We were accustomed to making our own time-tables; we had the greatest admiration for young Mr. Ronald's gifts (his pianoforte accompaniment from memory to the whole of the delicious *L'Enfant Prodigue* was prodigious!) but what *did* he know about TAR? It wasn't allowed for in the time-table, and we had never been broken-in to any form of existence which did not leave you at least half your life to yourself.

After a year young Mr. Ronald was succeeded by Dr. Storer, who, in another two, told Papa that he had brought Harry as far forward as he could. It was time for the next step to be taken. We waited for Dr. Storer's successor to come to the house. None came. Something much worse happened.

Among Papa's friends was a certain Mr. Austin, who was connected with the St. James's Hall, the Crystal Palace, and organized Command Performances for Queen

Victoria at Windsor. Amongst our treasures were some of the royal programmes. To Mr. Austin, Papa wrote for advice; the reply was two stalls for Harry's first Richter concert, at which Mr. Austin said he would see them. In the Hall, he gave Papa a letter of introduction to Sir Alexander Mackenzie. He was the Principal of a never-before-heard-of institution, the Royal Academy of Music. Actors and authors were our familiars; musicians were a comparatively unknown race to us. Thanks to Augustus Harris, we heard opera galore, and thanks to Mr. Austin, concerts and oratorio. We were taken to most of the notable recitals. Papa saw to it that we heard Patti before it was too late, and Joachim, whom he admired above all violinists; when Paderewski stirred the world like a flame, he lit us up with a quality we conceded to very few—we called it genius, and recognized its high-spots in him, in Henry Irving, and in Sarah Bernhardt. For all our enthusiasms, we had dividing lines, and not many geniuses stepped over the border. We were sorry that Papa, who preferred violin and 'cello to the piano, considered "Paddy's" genius over-rated, and wouldn't call him anything but "Paderooski." He thought our Polish pronunciation an affectation. We thought his an insult.

The Hampstead Conservatoire, so close at hand, gave us many a joy; there we heard the Hallés, and, for the first of many times, Vladimir de Pachmann. It was long before the days of his well-known eccentricities. In this recital was included one of Schumann's exhausting major works. Pachmann left the platform amid a fair round of clapping. He did not return to make the customary bow. There was a long, long pause, prolonged far past the time for the next group. Everybody wondered what had happened. Then on to the platform came an embarrassed attendant, and announced: "M. de Pachmann is waiting for applause." The astonished audience broke into laughter and plaudits; the offended artist appeared and made his bow; in a little while he consented to finish the concert. But afterwards in the Artists' Room, where we were taken by Uncle Jim Mortimer, we found him in an effervescence of wrath. "I play like a god," he cried, "and zey do not onderstand! Ze Breetish Public is von beeg Peeg!"

Music? We ate and drank it, brought it home with us, and reproduced it there. We had been giving our own concerts, performing our own symphonies, and singing Harry's settings of the Psalms of David, for years. (I couldn't think why Dr. Storer had snorted with laughter at the first hearing of those Psalms, when, at various points, I had chanted "SELAH!" loud and triumphant. Those "Selahs" were cut out before the concert performance.) With Harry composing music for all he was worth at home, what need to go to the R.A.M. for it?—that never-before-heard-of institution of which the unknown Sir Alexander Mackenzie was the Head?

* * * *

Oh, it was dreadful! Even Harry had qualms. For all his self-confidence inside 196, outside it he was as shy as a boy could be. He had rubbed elbows too little with his fellows, and shrank from the thought of going up among strange boys and girls to a strange place, for a preliminary examination by strange men. When Papa explained Harry's unusual diffidence, Mackenzie stretched a point, and told him to bring Harry to his private house, where they could talk over the boy's work together.

After the momentous interview, Papa and Mama and

Harry consulted at home; Harry agreed to try a term at the R.A.M., but suppose he didn't like it, must he stay a whole year? Again Papa put this point to Sir Alexander. On Christmas Eve, 1894, his answer came:

> "Now, as to the boy. I have on one previous occasion let a student enter for one term (on trial) under somewhat similar circumstances. Therefore, see no reason why I should not do it again, if it will serve you.
> "I can't help thinking that, apart from music, Master Harry must get over this diffidence and shyness if he means to be happy in after life."

The upshot was that Harry was to become a student in the New Year, under Battison Haynes for Harmony and Composition, and Septimus Webbe for piano. It did not give me the happiest Christmas of my life. What would I do with myself while Harry was away, several days a week, pursuing a life I was unable to share? It left me blank.

I put no trust at all in that "Trial term." Something in me said that Harry was going to like it.

Well, perhaps I could make myself stick to my writing now, and really finish some of the works I began. Not finishing things was my besetting difficulty.

* * * *

He went. He liked his Piano Professor, Mr. Webbe, and to Battison Haynes he yielded his whole heart. He scarcely spoke to anybody else. He worked assiduously, and, owing to the diffidence which made Sir Alexander fear for his happiness, it was at least two terms before he began to know his fellow-students. At lectures, and the Fortnightly Concerts in the little old-fashioned hall in Tenterden Street, he sat by himself.

"Do you know what, Harry," said Joe, coming home from Gym. "At the Royal Academy they've nicknamed you the Genius."

How did Joe know that?

"Hilda Antonietti's Governess told Mama"

It transpired that Hilda's brother, Aldo, was the star violinist in the R.A.M.; he and others had noticed the small silent boy, always so regularly taking the same seat at concerts and lectures, and for quite a long time they did not know his name. "There's the Genius," they said, when he appeared. Presently that curious name became known, and Aldo recognized it as one borne by some of his young sisters' Gymnasium-mates—"Why, their brother's the student we all call the Genius." I thought it nothing less than Harry's due.

* * * *

Not share his life? They weren't going to shut me out as easily as all that. Battison Haynes held out hopes of Harry's having a song done at one of the "Fortnightlies." Well, songs had to have words, didn't they? I wrote a sentimental three-verse ballad "To Adeline." About the time Battison Haynes was to see it I was once more in bed. The boys were not allowed to come near my frightfully bad colds; Harry did his best for me by playing little concerts overhead, and Joe, who had been taken for the first time to the R.A.M., and happened to attend the lesson on "Adeline," wrote to me this account of it, in the evening.

My *dearest* Nellie

I am so very sorry you are not well, but I hope you will soon be better. We always hear your clapping, darling. I had a lovely time. First about the lesson. It was lovely!

There was a bench in front of the piano, so Harry and
Mr. Haynes (a short, not fat or thin & very nice looking
man) sat on the bench and Mr. Haynes played Harries
composition (To Adaline) & liked it very much. As for
me (or "I" (I don't know which, but I think it is "me"))
I sat up in one corner for about 10 Minutes & then Mr.
Haynes invited me to sit the other side of him. He *is*
nice. The whole of the lesson which took up about
I hower was about "To Adaline." (He didn't say anything about your words). Then we went to a place where
we had a luncheon for 1/6 each. We had a plate of Ver-
micelli soup each with some Chees sawdust looking like
to put in the soup! It was lovely! Then we had a
plate of whitebate each Then some Roast Beaf, Yorkshire
pudding, lovely *New Potatoes* and some Spinage. Then
some Chees! Wasent it Cheep? (1 /6 *each* you know.)

Then we went to Faust.

I did not like Faust much.

" " " " Marguerite,,

" " " " Sieble atal
        (Olitzka)

" " " " Valentine Much

I did like Mephi Rather

Martha was not bad

It did seem funy to look at my watch & see it was 20 to
3! And then to come out into the lite, (it wasn't very light
though). Oh dear! What a *very* lot of traffic, &, dear
Nellie (this is true) in one part, the pavements were so
crowded with people, that I could hardly see the pavements atall! It was simply Awful. I don't think I have
much elce to say, still I will try to fill up the paper. I hope
you will get a very good sleep. I am quite well. If there
is anything I can do for you I will be very happy to do it
& so please send word (If you can thing of any way of
doing so. Oh, I have had a lovely time. I am so sorry you
are not well & I do hope you be allright.

"You'll get round soon enough" as Doctor Gill would
say.

Oh, Yes! And Harry couldent find his hat after the

Opror was over and we looked under the seats & where do you think we found it? On a seat behind us. How it got there, none of us new. I also saw Mr. Webb, & he is Tall, but not very thin. He has a very nice face. Mr. Haines liked Harries "To Adaline" very much, though I think it was very nasty not to say anything about the words, but he didn't actually know they were by you, so it would have seemed funny to say anything about it.

* * * *

"To Adeline" was sung at a Fortnightly Concert by Gwilym Richards, the best tenor then in the Academy. The family went in a bunch to hear it. We were all nervous, but I think Papa's nervousness outdid everybody's except Harry's. The song, a tuneful one, was a success. The Platform Attendant, listening "without," said to Harry as he left the platform, "If you go on like that, you'll make your fortune."

"Tell Harry" (wrote Uncle Ted Willard from Chicago) "how delighted I was to get his letter and to hear that his first public appearance was a success. Tell him he must never be nervous: excited! interested! Yes, but Nervous No. Can't do yourself justice if you *are*."

After this, I made it my business to keep Harry supplied with ballads, and before long they were being sung regularly by Richards, a promising and popular young baritone called Ranalow, and a delicious girl called Isabel Jay. The lyrics were the worst stuff I ever wrote.

Harry, now making friends, loved the life and the Institution. His application was almost terrible; the next exam. was studied for, the next prize competed for, at the expense of his eyesight. Dr. Gill, our much-loved family doctor (he was the very spit of the first pictures of Sherlock Holmes in Vol. I of the *Strand Magazine*) warned Harry that his eyes would not hold out. That didn't matter; he *must* pass his Harmony Exam. with Honours, he *must* must take his Piano and Sight-Singing Medals, he *must* finish a Ballet Suite for the Charles Lucas Prize, and score a scene for the Goring Thomas Scholarship.

* * * *

The Goring Thomas was a Scholarship for Operatic composition, a difficult class of work for a student to reach a good standard in. It had been competed for, and never awarded. Harry selected a scene from Longfellow's "Spanish Student," which was presently completed, and sent in to await results.

* * * *

> *Buzzards Bay*
> *Massachusetts*
> *May 11th 97*

My dear Maggie,
    Your letter and Bens came together I need not say how delighted we all are at the phenomenal success of your dear boy. It must be a great comfort to his Mother and Father and they will make it a delight for himself. Nelly writes Josie that when she is asked who she is she will say that she is the Grand Daughter of Joseph Jefferson the Daughter of Benjamin Farjeon and the Sister of the Goring Thomas Scholar. But from all I hear, the above named Individuals will be equally proud of her. I can understand that the *imagination* of all your children will be highly developed—their Father is full of it and I have had a lively time in that direction myself. I lecture twice this week before the Contemporary Club of Bridgeport and the University Club of Boston so you see the older I grow the more I do.
    All join in love to you Ben and the Children
                    Your loving Father
                            J. Jefferson

A cheque for a thousand dollars followed the letter, to buy Harry a really good piano.

The Scholarship was granted for a year, to be extended at the end of the time if he satisfied the examiners with his progress in Operatic Composition. He did so with a second, more elaborate scene from Longfellow's poem.

* * * *

Why shouldn't *I* write an opera for him? I found a subject in a tale by Heinrich Zschökke, a youthful love-affair of Henry of Navarre's. Of course, I knew all about that Gascon and his mistresses long ago, from Dumas, and with no doubts of my ability to deal with him, sat down in my pigtails and my sixteen years to dramatize the first village maiden Henry betrayed. It was the most artless account of Henry ever written—yet perhaps this Floretta was actually no more artless than that other Floretta, as whom my Great-Grandmama, Cornelia Burke, had touched the heart of my Great-Grandpapa, the Second Joseph Jefferson.

Meanwhile, opera bring in the air, Harry wrote one for home-consumption only. In a number of the Academy Magazine, *The Overture*, he had found an amusing article by Frederick Corder, which laid out the scenario of a Grand Biblical Opera, *The Trombones of Jericho*, complete with suggestions for songs and choruses. This was the basis of the three-act work for which Harry supplied the lyrics as well as the music. He was also the Orchestra (on the piano); Joe, Bertie, and I doubled and re-doubled ourselves in the cast.

THE TROMBONES OF JERICHO
Music and Libretto by Harry Farjeon,
on a Theme by Frederick Corder F.R.A.M.

Miriam (An Israelite Maiden)	Nellie
Joshua (Her Father)	Joe
Koshru (A Native of Jericho, Miriam's Lover) .	Joe
Zanemi (Koshru's Sister)	Nellie
Jubal (An Israelite, Zanemi's Lover) . .	Bertie

Chorus of Israelites: Nellie, Joe & Bertie
Chorus of Zanemi's Maidens: Joe & Bertie
Act I: The Israelite Tents by Night
Act II: Zanemi's Boudoir in Jericho
Act III: Outside the Walls of Jericho

Harry produced and trained us, and his tuneless, but perfectly-pitched voice assisted the choruses from the piano-stool. The music was a cross between Gounod and early Verdi; Miriam (rather Light-Opera) had a spinning-wheel song of equal charm to the "King of Thule," and Zanemi (very Grand-Opera) an aria rather an improvement on "Fors' è Lui!" Both Joe and I had to take a great many long breaths towards the ends of our songs, when we brought down the house—but Bertie, who refused to sing at all, brought it down harder. His was a spoken, or rather, a muttered part, with melodies on the orchestra. Anybody off-stage supplied instrumental obligatos at crucial points. When, after a Romeo-and-Juliet Duet, Miriam was imploring Koshru to depart at dawn, because she heard the Cock, and Koshru valiantly swore it was the Owl, Bertie played the bird's part on the "Cuckoo" which was among the old Toy Symphony instruments.

Joe had his bad moment when, as Koshru, he had to be worsted by Jubal in a comic duel, fought strictly to

music; and Bertie his when, as Jubal, Zanemi descend
upon him with open arms, singing:

> *"How can I tell thee the rapture entrancing*
> *When I see Love from thine eyes softly glancing—?"*

Jubal edged away from his beloved with a scowl, mutter-
ing:

> *"How can I tell thee the rapture enthralling*
> *When thy sweet voice my soft praises is calling—"*

I enjoyed my own transports exceedingly; Bertie
loathed me heartily; and Aunt Alice Edouin held up the
show with peals of laughter.

Later, we acted it for the entire Corder family, the first
time they came to supper at our house; Dolly (the closest
and dearest friend that period brought me), Paul (a shyer
boy, if possible, than Harry), and their parents Frederick
and Harriet, the first enthusiastic translators of Wagner's
librettos. Mr. Corder was tickled with what Harry had
made of his scenario, but what he thought of the performers I haven't a notion.

For us, *The Trombones of Jericho* was our high-water-
mark performance.

* * * *

New friends enlarged our circle, people with a new
set of ideas, a new way of looking at things. I trotted
down so often to Tenterden Street, that I felt myself,
vicariously, a student; and though I wasn't qualified to
wear a red sash across a white dress on Prize-Days, Harry
set me down to an "Elements Paper" as a test, and without any tuition to back me up, I passed with honours in
the regulation two hours.

I made a little timid social progress. The Corders lived

near us, and we began to frequent each other's homes and parties. Fred Corder, the Curator of the Academy, and one of England's loveliest musicians, was devoting himself to inspiring (he did no less) a brilliant group of young composers. Of course in his house Wagner was the god, Wagner, to me almost intolerable! It was Dolly who first astonished me by preferring the *Preislied* to *Salve Dimora*. In a very short while I was abandoning *Salve Dimora* for the *Preislied*. Paul I was sure I'd never really know well. He had a dozen interests outside music, was an excellent photographer, carpenter, mechanician— and capable of inventing the telephone, though he shied at using it. Aldo Antonietti, with his golden-toned violin, was our admiration, and his tall person was even more handsome than his sister Hilda's. Whitworth Mitton, a still sweeter tenor even than Gwilym Richards, was the Royal Academy's hope and despair—his voice was the victim of his indifference to work. The Academy pianists of Harry's generation numbered three brilliant girls— Gertrude Peppercorn, Marguerite Elzy, and Vera Margolies. Vera, queenly as a rose on the stem, Marguerite, lovely as scattered rose-petals, brought the house down at a Fortnightly Concert in the set of Variations for two pianos with which Harry won the Charles Lucas Medal. The girls tossed to see which should play First Piano, and Vera had it. The "great" basses and baritones of the time were Radford and Ranalow—and just after them an immense, lovable fellow slouched down from Scotland, to win all hearts; his voice was almost too big to be controlled, his height almost too great to be upheld, and his name was Ernest Torrence. Of the many lovely girls who sang and made names, or sang and passed out of knowledge, the most enchanting of all was Isabel Jay.

She was the flower of one of those bright Academy-Picnic days, when everybody met at Paddington for Windsor; where a great launch was crowded with students and professors, and we steamed past lock after lode to the dark green velvet reach of Cliveden. While the long tables were being set by the water, we scattered over the lawns, and afterwards wandered up through the rich background of trees, till, from a little unsuspected church, sounds issued more moving and beautiful than those of the world's great organs. The music drew us inside—it was Battison Haynes, who had strolled away by himself, and finding the small church open sat playing the simple organ like an angel: the little man (not fat or thin) whose life had been crowned by the coming of a pupil he had dreamed of. Frederick Corder had a bunch of plumes in his cap; Battison Haynes had two—Charles MacPherson, who had left, and Harry.

The return home in the hot summer evening, when Boulter's lock *was* Boulter's Lock, my dears! and while we waited for a tardy exit among the crowd of launches and rivercraft, Mitton stood up and sang "Songs of Araby" as I never heard it sung before or since. His tone was as magical as the tender sunlight falling on the water, the lock was still under the spell of that voice, and when it rose to its last honey-note, such clapping of hands filled the air, such cries of "Encore," as would have flattered a star in Covent Garden. In the annual examinations of that summer, Whitworth Mitton did not take his medal. What became of him? All we who listened that evening remember him.

Windsorward we steamed, and out of the sunset in the water a little boy jerked a little fish; and Isabel Jay in her soft white chiffon blouse and flowery hat, leaned over the rail of the launch with a delicious gurgle—"Hurrah, boy! that's the first fish I ever saw caught!" She was on the eve of being tempted too soon from her studies, to make her debut as Elsie Maynard at the Savoy.

Papa was at his best on such occasions; he bought flowers and baskets of fruit for everybody, from pretty Isabel to old Miss Riedl, the matron who shepherded the girls so rigorously, and whose lover had been killed in the Franco-Prussian War. Sir Alexander was affable and witty (let none who knew him say again a Scot has no sense of humour); Mr. Renaut, the lively little Secretary, was primed with fun; and if Emil Sauret occasionally embarrassed a student with Gallic compliments, how tactfully Papa diverted his attention from the blushing girl. Little Irene Scharrer was getting sleepy, so were Joe and Bertie, in their Diamond Jubilee belts and hat-ribbons; Mr. Corder was filling the boat with mirth and comic song; Windsor again, and crowded carriages, and everybody asking everybody riddles, all constraint vanished, professors and students one great happy, laughing, yawning, family party.

*　*　*　*

I had long finished my part in *Floretta*; now Harry's was done, and shown to Battison Haynes.

The result was surprising. The Academy did what it had never done before—it took St. George's Hall, and performed in public the first opera ever produced by a student within its walls.

An exciting, crowded time lay ahead of us. Harry rose at six in the morning to copy parts, and I rose to read aloud to him while he worked. Composition and orchestration he had to achieve in solitude, but he had an

astounding faculty for listening to Charles Kingsley and
copying—and even transposing—music at the same time.
If I went too fast, he did not pause, but flung a crumpled
paper at me, and I slowed down. Occasionally he held
up the small dictatorial fingers that could barely stretch
an octave (he was saddled with Mama's narrow little
hand). "Wait a minute!" Hypatia ceased to orate in
the lecture-hall; Harry knit his brows over some point
among the Violins or the Bassoons; the hand fell: "You
can go on." Hypatia resumed her lecture, Harry his
orchestration. He worked till eyes and fingers could
stand no more, I read till I was hoarse; in one day, I
remember, I read aloud more than half of *Hereward*.

A buzz of rehearsals began, at home as well as in the
Academy. Real scenery was painted, real costumes hired.
Whitworth Mitton was Henry. He came to me and asked,
"What sort of dress did they wear then, Miss Farjeon?"
Miss Farjeon found him one among her Papa's 8,000
books. Ernest Torrence was Henry's worldly tutor; he
made his entrance reading a learnèd tome. "We'll want
some old-looking book for that, Miss Farjeon." Miss
Farjeon routed out a calf-bound Churchill. It worried
her that it was two centuries too young.

I enjoyed the rehearsals, especially the last ones among
the scenery in the hall. I thought Harry's music exquisite
(and it *was* very pretty); and I couldn't think why Mr.
Betjemann, who produced the opera, pulled my pigtails,
when Julia Franks, as the Comtesse d'Ayelle, sang:

> "*False butterfly!*
> *Oh, if thou for my beauty art athirst,*
> *That wish will soon be past;*
> *Thou hast kissed many. I am not the first,*
> *Nor will I be the last—*"

"Where did you get your knowledge from, young lady?"

But in the Nineties, when one was eighteen, one didn't know what sort of knowledge Mr. Betjemann meant.

The great night came. I suddenly felt sick. Papa and Mama were terribly excited. I went to my room, and began putting on a little tussore frock. Mama came in and said, "Don't wear that, dear."

"But I want to, it's Cola's favourite."

"Still, you had better wear your cream, with the pink stripe."

"But why, Mama?"

"In case you have to go before the curtain."

"Oh, no, I *couldn't*."

Mama smiled. "Still, dear, I'd like you to put on the cream frock." And I put on the cream frock, feeling sicker than ever.

But what a nice night it was! So strange and dizzy. There were a few mistakes; Mitton's hat fell off in the love-duet, and when he put it on Ethel Wood knocked it off again, so then they put it on the seat, and forgot and sat on it, and the audience burst out laughing: but on the whole the two acts ran out smoothly. The feeling in that small theatre wasn't quite like any other feeling I'd ever had in a theatre; everything was a little blurred, a little tipsy, one wasn't quite there at all—and it was lovely! Lady Mackenzie and Sir Alexander were so pleasant between the acts, and everybody was buzzing round Papa and Mama, and Papa was beaming, and Mama squeezed my hand, and presently Henry was singing his last agonized cry—

> "*Floretta dead?*
> *Oh, my God, forgive!*"

and the tender unseen chorus sang "off":

> *"The sunbeam has vanished, the bee is a rover;*
> *Broken-hearted the maiden, and fickle the lover.*
> *Die pretty flowers! your short day is over!"—*

and the curtain was falling while Mitton lay sobbing on the stage.

Somebody whispered, "Go behind to Harry," and I found myself being pushed into the wings, where Cola's hot hand gripped mine awfully hard, and presently we were standing on the stage, with the curtain going up. The glaring footlights made me feel like a moth, there was a strange dim sea in front of me, filled with noise. And as I made my little bow, right, left and front, I *still* wished I was wearing the tussore frock, which was my Cola's favourite.

* * * *

Friends were enthusiastic, the Press was kind (though one of them *did* refer to the "Theatre-Royal Back-Drawing-room").

And Henry Irving wrote: "My dear Nellie, I wish I could have been present at the performance of the Opera. Your father is so old and dear a friend of mine that the success of his children is very near my heart. With every good wish, and my love to all at home, Affectionately yours, Henry Irving. What night or morning are you coming to us?"

And Grandpa wrote: "Your letters and Maggies with the long and brilliant notices of the Opera have given us much pleasure. It has been a great triumph for both Harry and Nelly, and must have given great joy to you all."

And Joe and Bertie said to me, "You did make a funny bow!"

* * * *

That was in July 1899. A hot and dazzling summer. (Surely summers were hotter and more dazzling then?) Harry had taken all his medals and certificates again, and lots of other prizes, including the Blue Ribbon of the Academy, the Charles Lucas Medal for composition. We knew it was going to be a splendid Prize-Giving for Harry.

It was the year for the award of the Worshipful Company of Musicians' Medal, bestowed once in three years on the most Distinguished Student in the R.A.M. In the next two years it went in turn to the Royal College and the Guildhall. You had only about one chance of getting it in your studentship. We had hardly dared dwell on the possibility for Harry. As we took our seats in St. James's Hall, facing the orchestra filled with a great band of red-and-white girls, backed by a narrow black strip of boys, I looked up through my opera-glasses to find Cola. I knew he must be almost the first of the boys, because of the Charles Lucas. Then I saw he was the *very* first.

Papa had gone out, and come in again. His face glowed. He leaned over and whispered in Mama's ear: "He's got it! he's got it!" Mama flushed and breathed. Battison Haynes looked round at us, and nodded. His face was, if anything, more flushed than Papa's and Mama's.

Sir Alexander stood up to make his annual speech. We could hardly sit still till he came to the announcement of the particular awards not made public till the day itself: "And this year the Worshipful Company of Musicians' Medal goes to a student who——"

I didn't hear any more; everybody seemed to know what was coming, the applause was even more than at *Floretta,* and tears were standing in Papa's bright brown eyes.

(Oh, Father dear, you were so *proud* of us.)

In the artistes' room afterwards, where we had ices and strawberries with Lady Mackenzie, everybody was wringing Papa's and Mama's hands. It wasn't the thing for students to be there, and we had to wait a bit still to find and hug Cola. But Battison Haynes was there, identified at that moment with the pupil he loved.

* * * *

After the summer holiday, just before the autumn term began, Papa read aloud to Harry and me a letter he had had from Sir Alexander. It was to the effect that well as Harry had done at the Academy, he felt he would now benefit by a change of master. So he would begin the next term under Corder.

It was a wise decision. Corder could do for his pupils things no one else in the Academy could do. The change forged a bond that lasted more than thirty years, a personal friendship strengthened by pupil's and master's common passion for the R.A.M. itself. But Mackenzie's letter fell like a blow on the Nursery.

I very very seldom saw Cola cry. That letter almost broke his heart. It quite broke the heart of Battison Haynes.

FAILURE

THE YEAR AFTER THE DIAMOND JUBILEE, we had moved to No. 11 Lancaster Road. It was a more spacious, more interesting, and more expensive house than 196; the passages were not pinched, the staircases were not narrow, there was a wide hall with a double glass door, big "reception" rooms, and a smaller, but ample, study for Papa on the ground floor. Not that he stuck to it; he cluttered it with the materials of his "Cloisonné" Craze and his Gold Paint Mania. Pale biscuit-coloured pottery for enamelling was bought in quantities; jugs, plates, bowls, dishes, and vases; and box upon box of enamels, brushes thick and thin by the dozen, every variety of gold paint and "medium." He discovered that it was easier, if less economical, to gild his ware completely with great flat brushes, instead of creeping painstakingly with fine ones between the lines of the pattern on the plate. Then he had to wait for the gold to dry, before applying his colour-scheme in enamels, green, blue, red, terra-cotta. Meanwhile, here was a saucer of liquid gilt going begging. Ha! he seized the splendid White King and Queen from the ivory chessmen, ruined them with gold paint, and promoted them proudly to the drawing-room cabinet. He spotted black picture-frames with dots of gold, he put a gloss on every object within reach—I think he would have gilded the wooden spoons in the kitchen, if he had thought of it; his clothes and fingers gleamed, and his "Study," stacked with objects waiting sacrifice, and spread with newspapers to preserve

the furniture, reeked of turpentine. Meanwhile, Papa's
typewriter and current Mss. triumphed once more over
the dining-room table; and meals continued to be
squashed at one end. Mama hid precious objects from
his golden paint brush.

On the first floor there was at last a "real" spareroom,
an innovation full of possibilities. To my surprise. Mama
and Papa chose for their bedroom the back room next to
it, leaving to me the enormous bay-windowed front room
over the diningroom. A deep cupboard, under the central
staircase to the upper floor, connected my bed-sitting-
room with Papa's and Mama's bedroom.

I had never dreamed of such a room for my own. I had
my desk and typewriter in the window, and the reversion
of the good old-fashioned American furniture, the tall
chest with drop handles, the low chest with the gabled
looking-glass, the six foot by eight bedstead with its towering back. So spacious is the room, that in spite of the
enormous furniture I can walk, walk, walk incessantly,
up and down, round and round (in the maddening Farjeon
way), while I pretend that I am thinking out my stories—
but am really setting in motion my secret game. Oh, but
no! I check myself and set my teeth. Here I *will* work
at last, settle down in earnest, regulate my days, and
write, write, write! something to make Papa's "hopes of
me" good at last.

Upstairs are the book-room, the boys' two bedrooms
and—the Nursery?

We decide that we can call it the Nursery no more.
Harry uses it for his composing, and it is still the common-
room, but Joe and Bertie are turning into schoolboys,
the day of Nurse and Governess is past. My well-loved
German mistress, Fräulein Haessler, comes to my room;

upstairs only old M. Lambert gives us our French lessons—the gentle, impoverished gentleman, who is so poor that he walks to and from Dulwich, to save his fare. We are all sensitive to his necessity, when Mama can persuade him to stay to a meal before he returns to what must be the most meagre of lodgings, she contrives to have him served in a room alone, so that the well-piled plate need not hurt his delicacy, or he feel ashamed to wipe it clean with his bread.

Well then, we cannot call this room the Nursery. What then? The Common Room? The School-room? We agree to decide its name by the "Voting-Game." Each of us casts four suggestions into the pool, which, by Harry's intricate system, are re-duplicated and reduced till a winner remains. Drawing four names at random, I find myself tickled by the humour of one of them: "Harmony Gaol," the name out of *Bleak House*, peculiarly applicable to any room which Harry himself dominates. I plump for Harmony Gaol, and double it whenever I get the chance. It begins to outnumber its fellows. Joe looks anxious.

"There's one name I *hope* won't win!"

But "Harmony Gaol" has it. It was one of Harry's suggestions, and it goes through. Joe dares to protest.

"We can't call it that! It's so ridiculous!" he cries. "What will our friends think when we ask them to come upstairs to Harmony Gaol?"

No good. What's settled by Voting-Game becomes Nursery Law. Harmony Gaol it must be, and it is. We soon get used to it. The boys are reconciled.

The Nursery begins to fade out of our lives.

* * * *

The garden at Lancaster Road was square and pleasant,

less interesting to a child than the broken plots and paths of 196; it was, in fact, merely a good-sized lawn, bordered by a path, a flower-bed, and the square of wall. There were no memorable roses here; of the things that grew there the one thing I remember is a buttercup. Papa delighted in it, and forbade the gardener to pull it up; it grew in a few years to the proportions of a bush, and its seed is growing now in other gardens.

The lawn was almost big enough for croquet—big enough for our croquet, anyhow (how I disliked the game, with its squabbles and setbacks). Of course, we had to play it fair and square; we were, perhaps, the only Family Croquet-Players who never dreamed of cheating by a hair's-breadth. How amazed, then, was Uncle Boll—our own Uncle Boll, younger than me and Harry!—when, on his first trip from America, he found he was expected to play by the book. He was sixteen, a shy, intelligent, charming boy, with all the easy Jefferson sense of fun, when we first saw him; Willie, the bachelor of five years ago, had married Christie MacDonald, a pretty musical-comedy star, really musical, with a delightful voice. Like Uncle Joe, when he married our Aunt Blanche, Willie ended his honeymoon trip in England; and made a party of the whole affair by including the bride's sister and the bridegroom's brother.

That was another summer of delight; the American rainbow spanned our sky again. In Boll I found a fourth brother to devote myself to, and he played unmercifully on the relationship. "Nellie, come and tickle your uncle's feet!" "Nellie, run upstairs and fetch your old uncle's shoes!" Off I went, and did not, as Joe with Bertie, return demanding, "*Why* do I fetch your shoes?" I was ready to spoil up to the hilt the dear boy-uncle. We took to our hearts this youngest of Mama's brothers, whom she, too, saw for the first time in her life. But when, at croquet, he moved the ball in position surreptitiously, Harry pounced on him. "Stop, Boll! I saw you move the ball with your foot."

"All right, Cola, I'm caught. I'll go back a hoop."

"No, put it on the spot you moved it from. And don't cheat again."

These weren't Jefferson ethics. Anybody brought up playing croquet with Tom and "The Fluff" (everyone's name for Charlie now, the biggest child of them all), couldn't for his life have played the game without cheating. Willie, Boll, Sall and Beezie, Gene, Con, and Dot, the whole bunch of uncles, aunts, and cousins on Grandpa's estate at Buzzard's Bay—why, they all did it! It was your only chance; if you could improve your position with a little footwork, you did, and if you were caught you paid the penalty cheerfully. That cheating was Cheating, in the Farjeon sense, didn't come into it at all. But Harry's decision won the day again. The whole of Buzzard's Bay succumbed to the lawn in Lancaster Road, and Boll accepted a code he didn't understand.

The summer of 1901 I remember as the most radiant of all. The Fourth of July brought Mama's forty-eighth birthday, and "the Americans" made a day of it for her. She had superb birthday presents from everybody, and a gala tea with ice-cream in the garden. The Stars and Stripes were flown, fireworks (of sorts) let off. Music was in the air. Christie sang American comedy, and French light-opera songs. Our affection for Boll put the finishing touch to happiness. All too soon the American rainbow faded. My heart-ache was only lightly assuaged by a letter from Grandpa soon after, expressing his pleasure in the

success of Boll's visit. He and Grandma Toney were
"glad indeed that you all like Frank. It must have been
a strange experience for your dear Mother to see her
brother for the first time and for you grown up niece and
nephews to look up on a stripling of a Boy as your uncle
Bol. Both Will and Frank and Christie write glowingly
of their trip and the warmth of their reception amongst
you all." To Mama he wrote: "Frank is not usually
enthusiastic, but he feels deeply, and will never forget
the welcoming love of you and yours." And he sent a
hundred pounds for the summer holiday we were going
without.

* * * *

At Lancaster Road I began to be beset by doubts.
Doubts of myself, of my power, *ever*, to stand on my own
feet. I was troubled with a nervous sickness which lasted
more than two years, and was in a transition stage which
perhaps began when, at sixteen, I had broken some
shackles for myself, and found that they had spelt a
certain security. Without the support of my bonds, I
didn't know where I was.

Floretta had been produced, and I had written another
"book" for Harry to set, a comic one this time, on
pure Gilbertian lines, called *The Registry Office*. The
Academy spoke of doing it next year. But if they did,
this didn't hit my nail on the head. I had received my
first three guineas for a fairy-tale *The Cardboard Angel*,
printed in Hutchinson's Magazine. Papa had sown
copies broadcast, and Mama had given me her chased
gold ring to celebrate it, but I did not judge myself
by such results. I knew myself too well. To turn out a
libretto when Harry wanted it, some verses now and
then, and a tale or two—this wasn't writing as I ought

to write. I was still dawdling three-quarters of my week away in excuses and small self-indulgences. I knew I had no sucking-power that counted. My nests of drawers were full of beginnings, jottings, and ideas, and remained at that.

In 1899, the last year of the Nineteenth Century (or wasn't it? the inevitable discussion was beginning) I sat in the rocking-chair in my lovely room and sobbed. I had enjoyed my opportunities for two years now, and what had I accomplished? So very little. Some "lyrics" for Harry, *Floretta* (well behind me), another opera desultorily under way, but my "big" books all lay in my desk neglected: *The King of Yvetot*, the Dumaresque Romance, the "idyllic" country tale, the Epic Poems, none worked at, none completed. What was the use of opportunity? The fault lay in me, in my idle, procrastinating, greedy, self-indulgent, undisciplined nature. Every day I spent hours shut up in my room, hoping to delude the household into a belief that "Nellie was working." Actually I was calling up Hyperion, lolling endlessly, playing just one more game of patience, sucking sweets, and reading, reading—reading one more chapter, before I took up my pen. It had always been like that, and it was so still. Even though I bad, under pressure, put up my hair (corsets I stuck out against—my Greeks wore none), put it up so badly and self-consciously—it didn't help. Papa looked at me rather wistfully, and said, "You look like a boy, Nell." I knew he didn't like it. Neither did I. I wasn't pretty, I was painfully shy. At Haidée Gunn's party, when that boy I didn't know had said, over the table, "Shall I kiss you after supper?" I felt as though something frightful had happened to me. Haidée had muttered to him, "Shut up, you fool!"

Bertie, sitting beside me, had looked black. I longed to go home at once, but Mama, when I told her, pressed my hand gently, and persuaded me to stay a little longer. Then Harry wandered up, and Mama said, "I thought you were dancing with Miss Edwardes, Harry"—for she had seen him lead out one of George Edwardes's daughters.

"I was," said Harry, "but she said she'd rather sit it out."

"Where is she then?" asked Mama.

"Sitting it out," said Harry.

Pretty Tid Jefferson, in her element at a dance, must have sighed and smiled up her sleeve at the awkward way her son and daughter were mismanaging their social teens.

All those uncomfortable times came back on me now. I had no self-confidence, no foothold anywhere if it wasn't in my writing. And I could not, *could* not, compel myself to work. I believed I could write—if only I would work.

I sat and wept for my own futility.

The big cupboard door opened. Mama passed through from her room into mine. She was kneeling by me, saying anxiously, "What *is* it dear? What *is* the matter with you?"

I sobbed through my fingers, "I have wasted my life."

"Oh, *Nellie.*"

She put her arms around me. But her voice was no longer troubled. I couldn't say whether it was more tender or amused.

When I looked at her through my wet fingers, Mama was laughing at me.

THE NURSERY COMES TO AN END

IF WE SUSPECTED that the house in Lancaster Road strained Papa's diminishing means and waning hold on the public, we did not attribute to worry his increasing tempers, his more and more unreasonable irritability. We only tried to avoid, if we could not avert, them. I suffered almost as much for Papa as for myself, and more for Mama. Each subsiding storm left us throbbing, him most of all. His love for us came back on him like a boomerang; his pride in us, his generosity, his wish for us to be happy, was never changed. He would have died standing between us and outside hurt. But he was tormented, and could control less and less the electric outbursts.

I knew it was all dreadfully unfair. But I loved him so much, and he, I believe, loved me in a way that might have been turned to confidence between us. "What do you think Papa said about you yesterday?" Joe came and told me, with a certain amusement; "he said one day you'd be a noble woman." I treasured that in my heart, because he'd said it. Why, if he loved us so, why if he was so proud of us, must he make us and himself unhappy? I wanted things to be better; I wanted a different approach to him when they went wrong. I almost felt that I could *make* it different.

I broke an ornament he considered precious (it was in the famous mixed-china cabinet, and may well have been trash). Mama said, "We'll slip it away, and perhaps Papa won't notice."

"Mama," I said, "can't I go and tell him? I'd rather not hide things from him."

Her look grew worried. "No," she said, "that's never any good." Then, seeing me unconvinced, she urged, "*Don't*, Nellie!"

She may have been right; it may have been too late; long experience had taught her to hold her tongue. Whatever happened now, she only acted so that the next storm should pass as quickly as possible. One day he came into the dining-room where she was arranging some flowers in a vase. "Maggie! don't tear the stalks! Cut them, cut them!" he cried, and said passionately that it was cruel to tear the flower-stems. Mama fetched her scissors silently. I hated to hear him fume and to hear her say nothing, yet this time was in sympathy with them both, and when Papa turned to me saying, "Nellie, don't *you* ever tear the stalks of flowers," I said I would not—and felt like a traitor to Mama as I said it.

A trivial incident one day at dinner (which only I took with them, because my perpetual nervous sickness made extra feeding necessary for me, said the doctors) produced an explosion which made Mama burst into tears. She left the table hurriedly. Papa and I finished a gloomy meal. As soon as I dared, I crept up to Mama's room. It was dark; she was kneeling with her head buried in the counterpane, stifling her sobs. I touched her.

"Mama!"

"No, don't, dear, don't!" she whispered.

I left her, wretched because things couldn't be spoken out with either him or her.

My sleepless nights were intensified by listening, after I was in bed, to the tone of the talk in the dining-room underneath, where Papa and Mama sat reading, playing patience, bezique, or halma. If the murmur continued quietly till they came up to their room, I turned over and tried to go to sleep in peace of mind. But too often now the strong voice grew excited, and the gentle voice silent. Then I did not sleep till nearly morning.

* * * *

Papa was very ill, but we didn't know it. I think he had foreseen a fatal illness soon after the unjustified move from Adelaide Road, and must have known what we did not suspect, how bad things would be for us should he die suddenly. After one serious attack of influenza, he was so exhausted, and so bitterly depressed, that for some days he lay down on the floor of the bedroom, and Mama could scarcely get him to move or answer her—not from rage, but gloom.

The smoking that was so bad for him, affecting his throat, and producing an incessant little cough which strained him, he made one great effort to give up. He cut it off entirely for six weeks, and his health improved; but during those weeks he couldn't write a chapter. So he went back to his Swiss cigars, and the clearing of his irritated throat.

Mama must have known how ill he was, and kept it from us while she turned to her friends. Of his illness in 1899 I have spoken, and of Uncle Ted Willard's concern and wish to help; Beatty-Kingston, writing to her at the same time, spoke of "the nervous shock from which Ben had found it difficult to rally," and speaks of his illness as a deplorable calamity. The shock was the carriage-accident in Monte Carlo, in which Aunt Rachel Willard had been nearly killed.

* * * *

Yet he still responded like magic to any hint of a big chance with a new book, a new play. When Alfred Harmsworth started the *Daily Mail*, he was commissioned to write the first serial. He wrote *Miriam Rozella*, a rather daring theme for him, of a pure girl flung by desperate circumstances into an equivocal position in a *roué's* household. It wouldn't seem daring now, but it created a stir in the paper, and brought in shoals of letters. As to his mode of writing, it was the mode of the time to write with a reticence we have almost forgotten about, and even Papa wasn't reticent enough for the *Daily Mail*. "Damn!" exclaimed Randolph in Papa's typescript. "Bother!" was what Papa found Randolph ejaculating in print. "Confound them!" cried Papa, in plain English.

He liked Alfred Harmsworth, but disliked the new style of journalism he was foisting on the public. Papa knew journalism in the days of Sala, Blanchard, and Russell, when it was not divorced from the dignity of letters But the *Daily Mail*, price two farthings a copy, was not even a department of letters in his eyes. Yet he never came back from seeing young Alfred in Fleet Street without saying, "I can't help liking that Ha'penny Cub, you know." And Alfred liked Papa, who never served his own turn with flattery, but jollied the "Ha'penny Cub" in his own office. Later on, Harmsworth took occasion to show real kindness to Joe and Bertie, in Papa's memory.

Of *Miriam Rozella* in book form Papa had again high hopes. It might have been a real seller, but his luck was out again; the firm that published it soon closed down. Then he set about turning it into a play, and there were nights when Uncle Ted Willard came to hear him read it in the study, and after Uncle Ted came Herbert

Waring. Each time Papa was buoyed up with hope, and Mama knew in her heart that there was too much talk in it. At the end of Act Two, Papa sat wiping the tears from his own eyes, as Miriam went upstairs with Randolph's little sister in her arms, and Randolph looked on, frustrated, from below. But Uncle Ted and Mr. Waring both said, "Yes, Ben, but where am *I*? The woman has it all!"

Other serials followed, in *Answers*—sensational ones, following the pattern of *M. Felix* and *Great Porter Square* of old. It was on the serials Papa mostly depended at last; the books sold respectably, but didn't meet the expenses of Lancaster Road.

* * * *

In 1900 *The Registry Office*, our comic opera, was done at St. George's Hall by the R.A.M Like *Trial by Jury*, it was without dialogue, Ernest Torrence played the Head of the Police Force in this one-act musical comment on the Servant Problem. It was better of its kind than *Floretta*—indeed, Miss Ewretta Lawrence, an actress who came to consult Papa at the time, said to me, "How dare you imitate Gilbert as well as that? If I were your Papa, I'd spank you!" A year later came *A Gentleman of the Road*, on the same lines, but with dialogue. This too was given production.

The librettos were sent to Gilbert (Papa was one of the few friends at the club with whom W. S. G. didn't quarrel), and no one would have imagined from the intermittent correspondence which Gilbert then began with me, that he was anything but the kindest-natured person. We never met; but I did not feel I should be afraid of him if we did. "I think your 'Registry Office' is quite as good as the 'Gentleman of the Road,' and you ought to have little difficulty in getting either piece produced if (as I have no doubt) the music is on a level With the libretto. But on this point, I regret to say, I am quite unqualified to express an opinion. With your permission I will take an early opportunity of bringing both books under the notice of Mrs. D'Oyley Carte." That kindness I think remained unperformed, as in his next letter he was aggrieved with the lady for having arranged some season or production without having thought it necessary to consult Gilbert first. His annoyance at this, expressed freely to a young girl he had never seen, was more on a par with what one had heard of him. It was a few years later that I returned from an absence abroad to learn that Gilbert had been knighted. I at once sent my congratulations, explaining the delay; back came his reply by return:

> "Dear Miss Farjeon,
>   Better congratulate than never!"

* * * *

In the new century, Papa received a letter in French from Egypt. It was from Abraham Fargeon, the Merchant of Tunis, at last! It began: "Mon cher parent!" expressed how deeply he wished to establish the ties of family with those of his blood in England, asked for full details of Papa's progeny, and gave them of his own; he included a family tree, that we pored over, delightedly discovering names like Schoua, Scialon, Halifa, David Bismuth. What names, rich in suggestion! Somewhere we touched them all, in a root planted too far off to be discoverable. Alas! the letter itself was never answered. We had to translate it to Papa, whose French was poor.

He was moved, and intended to write as fully as the old merchant desired. But perhaps because he thought he must write in French, which would have been a difficulty, he put it aside to attend to one of these days—one of those days which never came.

* * * *

I was still looking for some cataclysm to shake me out of myself, and force me to earnest attempts to use my powers, such as they might be. Instead of working the change from within, I began to depend on anything that seemed significant from without.

We were in the bus one night, on our way to the Alhambra. Suddenly the air was rent with the newsboys' cries. Papa said to Mama, "We must go home. There'll be no performance to-night." Queen Victoria was dead. I remember how this shook my universe, as we silently left the Light Green Atlas Bus going to Piccadilly Circus, and waited in a stream of murmuring people for one that went the other way to Swiss Cottage. Inside the bus, the "insulating" sound of hoofs and wheels enclosed me in my thoughts. I sat clasping my hands, saying some sort of vague prayer for the Queen, and thinking, "Now something has happened! something big has happened! after this I can't fritter any more." I felt quite sure, on the ride home, that the death of the Queen would bring about the birth of myself. But the exalted mood passed, and I was as I had been.

Then I was twenty-one. Perhaps *that* would do it! It was a glorious birthday. Papa had asked me, as once when I was small, whether I would rather have books or jewellery. I said "Books, please," and got both; and a host of other things from other people. There was

a specially gay home-party in the evening. Tom and
Nellie Gallon were at supper, and the Albery boys, and
others of our friends. Tom Gallon, the novelist, was the
last very intimate friend Papa made. He had come for
help and advice from "Mr. Farjeon," in various difficulties, and was soon devoted to "Ben." Tommy was
in the next generation of authors; he and his sister
Nellie lived close by, in Adelaide Road, and frequented
our house. I knew my health would be drunk at the
supper-table, and had prepared a ridiculous speech for
the occasion. Everything that night "looked successfully."
Surely, being twenty-one would do the trick!

What did the trick, if anything, was *Die Meistersinger*.
That summer I heard for the first time, and was swept
away by the glorious triumph of youth,—"Nun sang
er wie er *musst*, Und wie er *musst*, so *konnt* er's!" Oh
yes, let me only sing as I *must* sing, and I too, would
find that I *could* sing! The new "revelation."

I came home in a state of rapture, smelling the elder
in the summer night. Papa, always so quick and eager
to feed my transports, saw to it that I heard *Meistersinger* three times that season; and all that May I walked
by night in a glow. The exaltation died down; glow alone
isn't enough. The driving-force behind it had to gather,
and learn how to use the mood. Ecstasy cannot be constant, or it would kill. The glow comes and fades, comes
and fades as it has always done since I was a little girl.
Writing gets done in queer irregular ways at queer irregular
times. I still want everything so much, I don't know where
to choose. If I had had a regular, disciplined education,
should I have learned how and what to choose? Should
I have made more of the glow when it came, or would
it have stopped the glow from coming so often, and

dimmed it when it did come? I don't know. I have no rule to go by. It seems to me there are no rules, only instances; but perhaps that is because I learned no rules, and am only an instance myself.

* * * *

Sometimes the end of one's work out-shines the beginning.

In the first half of 1903, Papa was asked, through a member of the Club, to sign a copy of *Blade-o'-Grass* for an American lady. Her name was Mrs. Smith, and a story was attached to the request. Thirty years earlier, about the time when Margaret Jefferson in Hohokus was reading a Christmas Story by a certain unknown author, young Mrs. Smith was reading it in another State. She had lately lost a child, and her heart was moved by the tale of the waif who grew up in misery, without a chance, and the waif's twin-sister, who, adopted by gentle people, had her chance and grew up in happiness. If ever she was rich enough to do as she pleased, young Mrs. Smith determined to save from misery as many little Blades-o'-Grass as she could.

Her husband, Frank Smith, became the Borax King of America.

In Oakland, California, there is a lovely estate. On it are built ten homes for ten families of girls. The girls are discovered and adopted under all sorts of conditions; some are mere babies, some several years old. The families consist of children of varying age, each in the care of a "Mother." It is an even more important task to find the right Mothers than the right children, for any child in need is the right child to be given a chance to grow up in happiness. Those hundred girls had their chance.

They, many of whom had no homes, mothers, or families, became members of families in homes of their own. Their health, education and happiness were cared for, and their talents encouraged. Musicians and writers were to go out of those homes into the world—but if ever they needed to return, *their* home still stood open to these hundred Blades-o'-Grass.

I think Ben Farjeon's heart was bursting as he signed the book, for Mrs. Smith in America. He lived to receive her letter of thanks and tidings.

* * * *

A few months later he became ill again. Gravely ill. Then we began to realize something of the suffering that had intensified those outbursts which had nothing to do with his love of us.

It was the blazing July of 1903, in the height of the glamorous Edwardian Season. Things felt so dazzling and so brilliant then, perhaps they are as brilliant now, but then I was twenty-two. Mama had had her patriotic birthday on the Fourth. When we got up from the red-white-and-blue tea-table, Papa wanted her and me to stroll out with him. "Let's go to Zahringer's and buy Mama a present." She had a table full of presents already, but Papa was not content. Something more, always something more. Nothing was ever enough.

So, as the evening cooled the hot pavements a little, we strolled to the German Jeweller in College Crescent, and out of a tray Papa picked a tiny silver blue-enamelled ladybird to hang on the chain of "Charms" which Mama collected, and for me he picked a tiny silver spider-web, with a gilt spider on it. Then we strolled back again to Lancaster Road.

Everything that day was happy and tender, and radiant with the approach of a second, sudden visit from Willie and Christie, who—joy of joys!—were bringing Uncle Boll with them. He was to stay with us, in the little spare-room, and for Willie and Christie Mama had found rooms in Finchley Road.

Before they arrived, Papa went to bed. At first we children did not take his illness too seriously. Wasn't our infallible Doctor Gill in charge? So, in spite of the shadow of illness in the house, we went on laughing in the sunny garden, drinking iced drinks over absurd croquet championships, hearing from pretty Christie the latest tunes from the American "Musicals" (it was the time of "The Honeysuckle and the Bee"); and running all over London with Uncle Boll. Then, gradually, the tone of the house began to change.

Willie who, being a Jefferson, became an actor, but if he had not been a Jefferson would have been a surgeon, looked grave; he was at Mama's elbow in each decision. A night-nurse came; there were specialists and consultations; Mama's face grew more anxious from day to day; the words "catheter" and "operation" crept more and more into the whispered talk. Then, to our dismay, Doctor Gill, himself very ill, had to retire from the case, and a less familiar doctor took his place. The operation seemed inevitable.

Every day I went in to see Papa in bed, and relieve Mama for a little while. Every day as I sat with him I saw him more frequently contracted with spasms of pain. He groaned through his teeth, but afterwards smiled at me. One day, after stifling a sound, he said, "Give me your hand, Nell. I think if I hold it, it will help me through the next one." He did not moan through that next one; but I could have done so, he gripped my hand so hard.

Then he said abruptly, "You'd better go now, Nell." It is my last memory of him.

Next morning, after the doctor's visit, Willie came to me joyously in the garden. "Oh, Nellie, I could sing! dear Ben is so much better. There may not be an operation after all. The pain has gone entirely."

Why didn't I go in and see Papa that day? I meant, of course, to pay my usual visit, and if he had been in pain I wouldn't have missed it. But he was no longer in pain; it was going to be all right; and relief was in the air; Willie could sing for joy; Mama was smiling. It was golden summer, and perhaps we were engaged in some game or outing. It was quite accidental that I never saw Papa on that cheerful Twenty-second of July; it just happened that I did not go into his room, and nobody noticed. Did he? That night I slept better. There was not going to be an operation. That, at least, was true.

I was wakened by Mama coming into my room through the connecting cupboard; she was in her nightdress and dressing-gown, and she carried a candle. "Nellie!" she said softly, and I knew something was the matter.

"What is it, Mama?"

"Papa's very ill. We've sent fer the doctor. Tell Harry. Don't wake the boys."

I went upstairs, told Harry to come, and went back to my room, where Mama was sitting on the side of the bed. I sat beside her, holding her hand. Soon Harry came, and sat on her other side, holding her other hand. I think he had dressed, but Mama and I were in our nightdresses. She left us to go back to Papa's room, telling us not to come, and she returned and clutched our hands again, saying, "Oh children, he is very, very ill." I think he was dead then, and she knew it. The doctor came, and again Mama was in the bedroom with him and the nurse. Then we heard a cry, and she returned to us, choking out some words that told us Papa was dead. Once more we were sitting in a sort of icy silence, holding her hands tightly. Thirty years later, Harry and I were to sit again with Mother, from midnight till morning, holding her hands as fast—only then, she would not know it. *This* night-sitting till the dawn came, though it seemed to endure for hours, could not have lasted more than two, I think. My bedroom door was ajar, and we heard the doctor talking to the nurse in the passage. "Disappointing, nurse, isn't it?"

Mama looked at us rather wildly, cried with a queer smile, "He says it's *disappointing!*" and burst into dreadful tears. We held her hard; I don't now what we said, if we said anything.

Presently we were dressed, and she was lying on my bed. "Let Tommy know, ask him to come," she said. Tom and Nellie Gallon had had daily news of Papa. Someone took a message to Adelaide Road, then Harry went to tell Joe and Bertie, and I to tell Boll.

He sat up towsled and sleepy. "Oh Boll!" I whispered, "don't be too upset, but Papa is dead."

"What!" He looked shocked and scared.

"He died in the night. Will you tell willie and Christie?"

"I'll go right now, as soon as I can dress."

"Will you have breakfast first?'

"No, I guess I'll have it there."

Oh, the strange dream of death in the house. Boll had

gone, the boys were dressed, Mama was lying down, the nurse and maids were busy at their jobs, all so hushed and quiet. We children sat round the breakfast table. I don't think any of us cried, but we were all suffering from the queer constraint of not knowing what to say or do, or even how to feel. Perhaps we were surprised at feeling so little, that we could wonder how we ought to act.

The bell rang, and I ran to the door. "Tommy!"

He was white and shaking all over. He stared at me and said, "But he was my friend! he was my *friend!*" He trembled so hard that I had to put my arms round him to steady him.

"Tommy, Mama wants to see you."

"He was my friend," repeated Tommy, sobbingly.

"Tommy, listen, you *must* not cry like this when you see Mama. She wants you to help Harry. You will be calm, won't you?" I feared this shattering grief for Mama's sake, but for Tommy's too. He had heart-trouble.

"Yes, yes," he said, and got control of himself. I was not present at his talk with Mama. Willie and Christie arrived; they went straight to my room where she was lying down. I was thankful she had them with her, someone of her own other family. They said Frank would not come back again to sleep, but would have a room at their place in Finchley Road. Willie cried freely, Christie quietly; they were both comforting. Comings and going went on; letters, telegrams, doctors, strange men.—Aunt Esther, pitifully mourning for her brother— Nina and Dolly Corder, Nina hysterical, Dolly very controlled. "Irene, Irene!" cried Nina, "I can't understand you! I thought you'd be broken down." Dolly said, with the faintest touch of scorn, "I knew she wouldn't."

Then Aunty Fan, dear Aunt Mary Albery's kind, sensible sister. She too went straight to Mama, and afterwards came to find me. Her first words were "For God's sake, child, don't smile. Go and cry with your Mother."

I went upstairs obediently. If that was what my beloved Mama needed, I would make myself do it. She was lying on my bed, exhausted with tears. I put my arms round her and said, "Mama, I've come to cry with you." We clung to each other. I could not cry for Papa; but suddenly I was able to cry for her.

The dream went on. We four children, and Christie, were sitting round the table at lunch. There was fish. I felt it would make me sick. Harry looked round at us, and said quietly, "We've got to eat, you know," and we ate.

It was afternoon. I was told to go and rest. I went up to the boys' room, over Papa's, and lay down on one of the beds. A magazine lay close at hand. I opened it and began to ease the strain of things in some light wishy-washy story. The door opened, and Nellie Gallon came in. I shoved the magazine under the counterpane.

She sat down by the bed, and, like all other friends, was very kind. She asked how I was, and I asked how Tommy was. There was a brief pause, and then—for I suppose she wondered where consolation might lie for me—she said tentatively, "Do you believe in a future life?"

"I don't know," I answered. It seemed inadequate, but it was the truth. All I felt certain of was that "Since Nature's works be good, and Death doth serve as Nature's work"—I had no resentment against death.

When she left me, I pulled out the magazine again, and finished the story.

In the evening Mama said, "You need not go in and see Papa, and Joe and Bertie need not either." I don't know if Harry did. I was relieved that I need not; I did not want to. I do not know if the unspeakable beauty of death was on his face; but if it was, I dare say she feared its effect on my over-sensitive imagination. I had never seen a dead face in my life. But I do not remember fearing the presence of his dead body in the house.

Black clothes. Papa hated them, so did Mama, so did we all. Yet somebody thought I must have a black dress and hat. The funeral was coming; I wasn't going; but I suppose Aunty Fan thought it would not do for me to be in my flowered crêpe summer frock. I went to John Barnes in Finchley Road to buy something. I'd seldom had a ready-made before, and never a black dress. My skin was muddy, not good for black at all. I said to an assistant, "I want a black dress."

"What sort of dress?"

"I don't mind," I said.

She glanced at me and brought something in delaine. It went on me, an indifferent fit.

"Will that do?" she asked, standing me before a looking-glass. I scarcely looked, and answered "Yes." Then I bought some sort of a hat. When I got back Christie met me in the hall. She kissed me and said gently, "How sweet you look, Nellie." But I knew I looked horrid. It didn't matter anyhow.

The flowers began to come, the flowers and flowers. The drawing-room was full of them, wonderful wreaths from the Clubs, and the rich friends. Humble wreaths and bunches from poor ones. We liked them; they seemed to comfort mother. Then suddenly they became to me intolerable. The scent was overpowering. I could hardly bear to go into the drawing-room, where the wreaths had to lie on top of one another and the first were beginning to wilt. Yet they were comforting—there were so many many people who loved him. And oh, the letters!

"Answer these." Mama gave me them in handfuls. I thanked them for her, as well as I could. I wrote to Mr. Barrie, "I'd like you to know that after he read Sentimental Tommy, Father always said 'I take off my hat to J. M. Barrie,'" Henry Irving wrote again in reply to my letter, beginning not "My dear Nellie" but "My Dear Friend," and I wrote to him, "Thank you for calling me your friend." I suddenly realized I was no longer a child. Everything was about to change, for all of us.

The day of the funeral came. The blinds were drawn down. I stayed in my room with Mama, and Aunty Fan was there too. Mama was prostrate. The carriages stretched up the road, out of sight. The quiet bustle died away. The house was deadly still. Papa had gone; the three boys had gone with him.

Another bell. The maid said, "Mr. Willard." Uncle Ted! why he was to have been at the funeral! I ran downstairs. There he stood, immaculate as always, but his strong, dominant, intellectual face was twisted with pain. "Nellie, my dear! I have mistaken the time." "Yes, Uncle Ted, they've gone. Not long. You could——" He shook his head, kissed me, and turned to go. He appeared shocked with himself. Suddenly down the stairs ran Mama, her hair untidy, her eyes swollen. She threw herself into his arms. "Oh Ted! oh Ted! the children

are so good." "How can they help it, dear? They're
your children." He kissed her, the tears streaming down
his face, E. S. Willard, who was almost a great actor.
Papa said he would have been a great one, if he had had
a touch of heart.

* * * *

There was no money; none at all, except for the small
current bank-account. We had lived precariously on
Father's contracts, and the three hundred a year from
Grandfather. We could not afford the house in Lancaster
Road, but it was on a repairing lease, and some hundreds
of pounds were demanded if we left at once. Yet we must
leave it, and we hadn't hundreds of pounds. Our solicitor,
a man of infinite sympathy and help to my Mother
in this and later crises, put the state of things to the
lessors. They found a tenant, and agreed to let us leave
for half the stipulated sum, if we could do so in a fortnight.
This, and the moving expenses could just be managed;
the little balance in my father's bank was supplemented
by the ever-generous unseen Grandfather. Willie had
cabled to him immediately, not only the news of Father's
death, but for money. A hundred pounds was cabled
by return, and the funeral expenses were able to be met.
Then we must find a house. We hunted desperately
in the neighbourhood, and settled on the only one available
suited to a family of our size and occupations; it was a
little more than half the rent of the mansion in Lancaster
Road. A hectic fortnight followed, getting out and in.
The getting out was the difficulty. Of my Father's 8,000
books we sold 5,000, for almost nothing. A set of the
Annual Register from 1750 to 1850 or so, bound in the
original calf, fetched 12s. 6d. I had delved in it often,

for strange contemporary tales of the French Revolution, of the Chevalier d'Eon, of any curiosity that caught my eye. Farewell to that delight. Then the furniture, too much, and too big to go with us. I was to share a room with Mother; her big maple suite would overfill it; the fine American walnut bed, six foot by eight, must go. It went, with mattresses, and bolsters—for 12s. 6d.! Farewell to *that* delight. The other objects sold fetched similar prices.

And the attics! The clearing of the accumulations of years and years of sale-going! Those vast left-over stocks of wholesale stationers, milliners, and haberdashers! Those boxes by the gross of hat-ornaments, such frightful things! the manuscript paper, carbons of all colours, typewriting paper of all sizes, notebooks, pencils, india-rubbers—cases and cases, packets and packets of them! (Not exhausted yet.) The furniture, ornaments, pictures, the trunkfuls of rubbish that mustn't be discarded in case they were wanted; the decorations for the Christmas-tree, the toys, and books, and more books; and papers, letters——

We sold what we could out of hand, destroyed what was possible in the time, packed Father's drawers of uncompleted manuscripts, his teeming ideas, as wholesale as his purchases. We would sort them all later; and later clear out the hired room in Winchester Road, which accommodated the overflow of the attics.

The one thing that was not complicated was his will. It was the proverbial half-sheet of notepaper, leaving everything he had to Mother. It was properly worded, in three lines, and quickly settled.

At last we were clear; out of 11 Lancaster Road and into 137 Fellows Road, where my Mother was to live another thirty years; where the hopes and joys and agonies of our adult life were to be suffered, where the "Nursery" would not longer play a part. The same letter from Sir Alexander Mackenzie that expressed his sympathy for Mother, made Harry one of the youngest professors of Harmony ever appointed at the R.A.M. From the moment he became the head of the family, and its only modest wage-earner, he quietly took over its responsibilities, arranging with such thought and kindness all Mother's affairs, managing our expenses and our pleasures with so much care, that we felt less straitened than we actually were. His small makings as a teacher, and Grandfather's three hundred a year, were all we could depend on. Joe must find a theatrical job somewhere. Irving, who had given him his first engagement, had no opening, sweet Ellen Terry soon offered him a walk-on at the Imperial, and later Uncle Ted Willard would take him into his Repertory Company, and start him on small parts. Bertie at U.C.S., must abandon his passionate hopes of college. And I—now surely the turning-point had come, the time to accomplish something that really mattered. But first, there was an almost-finished book of my Father's to complete for Hutchinson: *The Amblers,* not a good book, and so badly completed! but the only one, among a score of Mss., half-done, part-done, just-begun, which could be turned to account.

So we came into Fellows Road, where I was to be let loose among the papers. And not till we were fairly in, ran down the garden to examine its possibilities, and looked over the wall at the bottom, did we realize that we were looking over into the garden of our childhood, the garden of 196 Adelaide Road, where we had walked in gold-paper crowns for the Queen's Jubilee, where the

Adelaide Poultry Farm had flourished and cackled, where Mama had stood in agony while Bertie waved to her from a top-floor window, where Papa had smoked the green-fly from his Gloire de Dijons, where the old green apple-tree had yielded apples of a taste no others have had for us before or since; where little Marie Barnes, and darling Gerrie Somerset, and Button, Bronnie and Bay, and Nina and Adrian, had shared our games; where Bertie had made a hundred not out, where the little Lutgens had climbed over the wall on one side, and the little Francs on the other, where we had played Greeks-and-Trojans, and TAR, and touchwood, where we had sat under the white-heart cherry-tree, and Papa had hung ear-rings on our ears. We weren't so far away from our Nursery, after all. It was just over the wall.

I went back to the papers; and among the manuscripts came upon three pencilled sheets. He must have written them under one of the shadows we knew nothing about. They were dated four years before his death, and were the words of a man who did not expect to live.

March 21st 1899

I desire that my body be cremated.

If any of my friends wish to send me flowers I beg them not to do so, but to give the money the flowers would cost to some deserving person or persons in poverty, so that my death may bring temporary happiness to a few poor people.

Let my dear Harry have my watch, chain, and greenstone. The rim of gold round the greenstone needs to be strengthened.

Let my dear Nellie have the silver inkstand that was presented to me in New Zealand. Also, the "Flora."

Let my dear Joe have the watch I bought in Geneva.

Let my dear Bertie have the box of old coins.

All the rest of the little property I possess, my Linotype shares, my cash, furniture, etc I leave to my dear wife, who will give our children any other memento of me they would like to have. She will give James Mortimer 100 of my cigars, and to Lily and Minnie Mortimer each a book out of my library. To my sister Esther £5.

I bid all my friends an affectionate farewell.

God bless my darling wife and children. It has been my strenuous endeavour to do my work to the best of my ability and to make a happy home. My dear wife and children have given me much happiness. I trust they have drawn happiness from me. Children, be good to your mother and to each other. Do your duty in life, and use your talents worthily.

NURSERY CALL

On the Last Day, when the Trump sounds for Judgment, and unorganised souls are rising in disorder from all parts of the earth and sea, tumbling over one another in their fear of extra penalties for being late: wherever I, or Joe, or Bertie may be lying, it will not be the Call of Gabriel that we shall hear.

Somewhere in space, a small right hand with fingers of iron will strike from a cottage piano the Nursery Call whose summons set us running. Wherever we might be, among the old trunks in the attic, bothering fat Mary in the kitchen, poring over curious dusty books in the Little Book-room, or piling up cricket centuries in the garden; let that Call ring on our ears, and we came to it. Harry wanted us for something important.

Even so will we come to it for the last time. We will shake off whatever earth we rest in: if we have the choice, mine will be Sussex chalk, Joe's Norfolk clay, and Bertie's Irish peat—but Harry's will be the stony soil of a South Hampstead garden: and we will forgather excitedly in some airy chamber that must be Harmony Gaol, where the fiats of the Law-giver go forth.

"Here I am, Harry!"

"Here I am, Harry!"

"Here I am, Cola! what do you want us for?"

"We're going out."

"Where to? Lord's?"

"Cromer Pier?"

"The Zoo?"

"You'll know when you get there. *Have you sponged?*"
Chalk, clay, and peat drop from us like magic.

"Yes, we have. Look!"

"Come on, then."

Harry goes forward, with his quick, light, stiff step;
I fall in, half a pace behind; Joe and Bertie follow, side
by side, lustily chanting "Chums are Going Up!"

In his ear I pant hopefully: "Cola! can we play Tar?"

"No, not yet. *We're Harry-Nellie-Joe-and-Bertie.*"

No more questions; this is to be another of Harry's
Surprises; something rather special. Up we go, a bit of a
climb; but there's the turnstile and the old man in the
ticket-office. The Zoo after all, then? What a crowd
there's going to be to-day! Some are pushing, some,
hanging back, are being pushed. But Harry keeps our
little phalanx steady; we take nobody's place, we've
been taught to play fair: and nobody is permitted to take
ours. Our turn comes at last.

The old man looks through his little window. Harry
produces four shillings. (He must have saved them for
this very purpose, the last time Papa played One-Two-
Three-Four.)

"We're all over twelve," says Harry, and lays them
down. But the old man pushes them back. "It's free
to-day."

The turnstile clicks four times, and we are standing
in the Grounds—standing a little dazed, a little at a loss,
wondering where to go, what to do next. And then,
by a common impulse, we turn and look at Harry, waiting
for him to tell us.

A POSTSCRIPT
Full Circle: 1959

A LITTLE WHILE BEFORE he died Harry said, "I have always known that the greatest thing in life is family."

He was not speaking only for ourselves, but I know that at that moment he was speaking especially of us. The sap at the roots of our nursery had so unified our lives that what happened to any of us happened to all of us. Father's death in 1903 closed the nursery door. Mother outlived him by thirty years. We had continued to live together in Fellows Road till Joe married in 1910 and Bertie in 1914. When they had their own homes and nurseries, what happened to any of us still happened to all of us to the end of our lives.

In 1934 I wrote *A Nursery in the Nineties** in order to preserve for myself and my brothers as full a record as possible of our childhood, from its beginnings in Father's exciting and Mother's enchanting backgrounds to the foreground in which we formed our characters. Without giving a thought to whom else it might appeal, I wrote the book for the public of four to whom it was dedicated in the slogan that dominated our nursery:

We're Harry-Nellie-Joe-and-Bertie

When it was published I was surprised by the number of letters it brought me from near relatives and distant connections in all parts of the world. Many of the letter-writers were old, some very old, people who had known our parents,

---

* It was published in America as *Portrait of a Family*.

or members of their families, long before I and my brothers
were born. Many were from friends and strangers of our
own generation, who had known in their childhood persons
and places I wrote about, and found them evocative. But
the book's dedication remained evocative only to us: the
words which, pronounced by Harry, restored us from a
world no one else inhabited back into the world of our
parents. Father and Mother never asked questions, but
perhaps they had inklings that in the nursery strange sea-
changes of personality took place, due to the rich air they
provided for us in our three South Hampstead homes.
I look back astonished at the seeming lack of discipline
with which, in that late-Victorian era, we were able to
exercise so freely our imaginations and our preferences.
Only a seeming lack because, while our parents laid down
no rules, we were submitted from birth to Harry's Socratic
sense of law and order. That we were *Harry-Nellie-Joe-
and-Bertie* was the most powerful of his edicts. Death did
not revoke it when in 1945, on Victory Day, Bertie was
cremated.

Three years later Harry, then almost paralysed, fell and
crushed his hip while groping for one of my books in
Father's bookcase. It occurred at the end of the July term
of the R.A.M., where, in the teeth of tremendous dis-
abilities, he was still teaching thirty students every week.
At New End Hospital I was told that Harry could not live
three days. His iron will kept him alive five months. I was
allowed to furnish his tiny private room according to the
painful needs of his eyes, to arrange his meals, and the
constant brief visits of his pupils, one of whom travelled
from the Midlands on the chance of a glimpse of him.
Every week-end Joe brought his typewriter from Ditchling
to sit with Harry, read him old letters and talk of old times.

The Matron gave Joe her private room to work and sleep in. Harry died on 29 December 1948, and his ashes were scattered in the New Year. After the funeral Joe said, "It's you and I holding the fort for them now, darling. Presently one of us will be holding it for the three others. It doesn't matter which."

In 1955, in a Sussex nursing-home, it was discovered that Joe had cancer of the liver. I stayed in Hove for the last two months of his life, was with him all day and, towards the end, at night. We talked of Harry and Bertie, and I read him the cricket-scores in the daily papers.* When he was too tired to talk or listen, I sat by his bed correcting the proofs of *The Little Bookroom*. He exclaimed joyfully when I showed him Edward Ardizzone's sketch of little Nellie squatting on the floor with her nose in a book. His *Oh!* was a wave of the hand to our nursery.

Joe changed the least of us. Harry seemed to me less to change than to grow, inevitably, from the "Being" he declared was "*not* a Boy", to an almost mystical conclusion. Bertie and I changed most, as I found my way out of fantasy into reality, and his brilliant wit disciplined his passionate nature. But something of the child he was in the nursery, the pure goodness, stayed in Joe all his life. It was felt by everybody in the Sussex nursing-home. Two days before he died the woman who cleaned his room took his hand and said, "It's an honour to have known you, sir." On the fourth of June, his seventy-second birthday, he was

---

* The paramount passion of Joe's and Bertie's boyhood never died in them. I take this chance to confess to an aberration in the Nursery book which has burdened my conscience for years. Somewhere, inexplicably and unpardonably, I state that G. L. Jessop played for Sussex. May Gloucestershire forgive me. It isn't as if I didn't *know*. My brothers were either too merciful or too shocked to mention it.

surrounded with flowers sent by friends in London and
Ditchling. He was too weak to do more than smile faintly as
the nurses ran in with fresh armfuls, and raked the other
rooms for bowls and vases; too weak to want to hear the
cricket-scores. He shook his head when I brought the
papers to him, but whispered, "What's Somerset doing?"

He died asleep in the early morning of the sixth of June,
our mother's wedding-day.

* * * *

When I began to write this postscript to our nursery story
in which I had got us born and almost launched on our
careers, I was not sure how much I would want to add. My
next book will pick up the story where I left it; it is not my
purpose to tell any of it now. But I find it comes natural to
take a leap over the half-century since 1903, and unite the
end of the tale to its beginning. I can write of my brothers'
deaths without sadness, and think of the past without
longing. I would not relive any of it if I could. It is enough
to have lived it once, and carry its ineffaceable memories
to my own end, looking forward, not backward.

There is, however, one thing more to be told, something
that does not belong to the years in between, but takes the
tale back to the first chapter of the book.

I received this year a letter from Dunedin, the great city
which was a little township when Ben Farjeon set foot in it
in 1861, and assisted in the birth of *The Otago Daily Times*.
The letter, dated February 1959, came from Mr. A. H.
Reed, who is the President of the Dunedin Library Associa-
tion. After recalling that we had written to one another in
1926 ("when we were both younger"), he went on:

"When I was in the Public Library yesterday I met an
American professor, here on holiday, who was doing some

research on your grandfather. You may be interested in the enclosed cutting which appeared in the O.D.T. this morning—your Father's old newspaper. I showed Professor Blanchard quite a little collection of Farjeon material, in which he was very interested. We have both Shadows on the Snow and Grif in the first editions—now very scarce, besides other Farjeon books, with inscriptions, and an autograph letter.

"I'm now gathering material for The Story of Early Dunedin, and for this I'm going through the old O.D.T. files, where your Father's name crops up frequently. This is a second volume. The first volume carried the story up to 1861, when your Father had just arrived here. I will send you a booklet containing many of those early pioneers, among them you will see Cutten, your father's old associate, and others whom he must have known well. For this next volume, I wonder if you could send me a portrait of your Father, and perhaps a photostat of the Charles Dickens letter. Perhaps you could remember something about him that you have not already given in the 'Nursery'. The centenary of the O.D.T. is drawing near, and anything concerning B.L.F. would be of interest. What became of the gold card case with brilliants given to B.L.F. on behalf of the O.D.T. when he left for London?
With all good wishes,
A. H. Reed."

Mr. Reed enclosed a typed page of the references to B.L.F. which he had culled from the earliest years of *The Daily Times*. They gave me tiny pin-points of light on Father's varied activities up to the time when Charles Dickens swept him back to England. One pregnant note is dated 11/1/1864:

"JOS JEFFERSON Began engagement at Princess Theatre today."

It was then that Ben first met his future father-in-law. I replied to this letter eagerly, and began to collect everything I could find in old desks and boxes of papers and photographs that might swell "the little collection of Farjeon material" in the Dunedin Public Library. The gold case, alas, which was still in our possession when Father died, had vanished; but I had a photostat made of the Dickens letter, and added to it some trifles of Dickensiana, including a letter from Charles Dickens Junior, written from the office of *All the Year Round*. I made a second collection of Jeffersoniana, and a packet of photographs; and because the name of B. L. Farjeon is in England that of an unread Victorian novelist, but belongs to Dunedin's early history, I parted with the pencilled sheets which were his last testament to his wife and children.

In the letters that passed to and fro, the idea of a collection swelled with, the material I sent. It appeared that although the Library possessed only a few of Father's books, it included quite a number of mine. I offered a complete set of our father's novels, further books and material of my own, and samples of the work of Harry, Joe and Bertie. The Library is to be enlarged through a civil grant, and in a few years' time all this material will be housed there as, I believe, the Farjeon Foundation.

Strangely it falls to the lot of the little girl who listened eagerly to Papa's tales, of adventure among the Bushmen and the Maoris—who browsed among Papa's books until her eyes smarted, who anxiously showed him her first tales and poems, and of whom sixty-four years ago his generous heart "had hopes"—strangely the child in the Nursery inherits the task of sending Papa on his second voyage round the world, to end his career in Dunedin, where it began. The story comes full circle.